Why Capitalism Works and Government Doesn't

Or, How Government Is Recycling the American Workforce to Pay Its Bills and How the Rich Profit from Big Government

EW Dedelow

authorHOUSE®

AuthorHouse™
1663 Liberty Drive
Bloomington, IN 47403
www.authorhouse.com
Phone: 1-800-839-8640

First published by AuthorHouse 5/20/2009

ISBN: 978-1-4389-7370-8 (sc)

Library of Congress Control Number: 2009903179

Printed in the United States of America
Bloomington, Indiana

This book is printed on acid-free paper.

scientificcapitalist.com

AUTHOR'S NOTE: THE 2008 ECONOMIC CRISIS

12/28/08

This book took years of reflection and even more years to write and does not mention the 2008 economic crisis, although it does foretell its possibility. Therefore, I felt that I should discuss that crisis.

To begin, I do not support current economic theories and am not a proponent of any political party. The book makes an emphatic statement that definitive economic solutions exist that are based on the economics of labor and not demand or supply side economics. Additionally, the old writers, Smith-Marx-Engels-Mandeville-Schumpeter-Keynes, were simply observers in an embryonic revolution. These brilliant men did not and possibly could not have known where capitalism would take society. They made meaningful observations, and they were thinkers, unlike modern economists, who, it seems, have limited themselves to a debate over old ideas.

Now to explain: In the book I suggest that a modern economy should be more stable, and indeed, we have had nearly twenty-five years of mostly uphill growth in the number employed and our stock market. The reckoning for stable economic growth was made based on the observation that the division of labor had been evolving in stages that I call Rural, Transitional, and Complex. Basically, labor has become so divided into professions, occupations, and work responsibilities that any individual catastrophic event would typically have only local consequences. Also, we have come to a point where private-sector businesses have the flexibility to adapt to market forces that are indicative of a Complex economy and needed to fulfill increasing government demands. Thus, given normal circumstances, our Complex economy would not suffer greatly from any event. The only ostensible cracks in this theory would be the recession related to the dot-com revolution and the 2008 debacle. The dot-coms did consume enormous amounts of capital and manpower, and that recession resolved itself quickly and with no meaningful disturbance in employment. Its occurrence is not an exception to the rule. There is one fly in the ointment, which brings us to the 2008 crisis.

The stability, as mentioned, did not lead to higher wages for many Americans because of the incredible overconsumption by our governments of the surpluses of growth. Wages for the lower 90 or so percent of workers in the private sector have actually declined. Not included in my definition of the private sector are government or pseudo-government entities such as the various authorities, corporations, schools, etc., that are regulated by a government agency, staff, or our elected politicians or the solicitors who are so well represented in our legislatures. Most of these have built-in guarantees, such as annual inflation and other wage increases, and their medical expenses, a major contributor to inflation, are also covered. Government unions are also major contributors to political campaigns and vigorously pursue wage and benefit enhancements.

Some existing income measurements prove that the wage decline has occurred, and some show a possible breakeven. Ironically, even supposedly conservative economists, rather than suggest wage decline, will point out how many iPods or TVs are owned by wage earners to prove the fruitfulness of our economy. What they don't do is separate out public- and private-sector wages. (Note: The majority of economists are government or pseudo-government employees.) In the book I'll say that wage decline is an unavoidable result of a growing government and not due to capitalist greed or anything to do with a free-market system. In an economy that is not overpowered by government excesses, an individual who loses his/her livelihood could typically anticipate an even better wage.

The key to a good economy is a private sector that outpaces growth in government demands. If this isn't occurring, then there are consequences. The way to look at this is to first divide productive workers from non-productive workers—non-productive workers again meaning government employees, those acting in response to regulation and labor restrictions in the private sector, many in our legal system, many pseudo-government agencies, etc. I don't have the financial capabilities to make an actual assessment of these two groups and no relevant study exists, so I used mathematical relevancies. The way to look at this is to determine how much more efficient productive workers need be to support an increase in the number of non-productive workers. Quite simply, on a graph you would put "needed efficiency increase" on one side and "ratio of productive to non-productive workers" at the bottom. As the ratio goes from, say, 51/49 to 50/50, the productive workers would need to be 2 percent more efficient just to break even. When you couple such changes with the guaranteed income increases in the governmentally controlled non-productive sector, it is obvious that the actual needed efficiency increase is growing significantly. And the increase would be more than would be indicated by the change in the ratio and the efficiency needed to offset would increase exponentially as the ratio increases. This major dynamic puts pressure on businesses to cut costs and has resulted in an increase in imports, an export of jobs, and a decline in private-sector wages. Suffice it to say that most foreign goods are so cheap that it would be impossible for U.S. workers to reproduce these imported goods, even assuming a declining wage structure.

One of the great hindrances to advancements in economic thought has been the lack of an accurate measurement of government and a belief, if you can believe it, that even government waste is good for the economy. I've found a major flaw in the way we compute the size of government. Economists will tell you that in 2007 taxes were only 32 percent of the U.S. economy (GDP) versus closer to 50 percent in some countries. Some economists believe we can therefore tax at a greater level. When preparing a financial statement for businesses great and small, an accountant must adhere to rules, laws, and the basic and indubitable equation that debits equal credits. Accountants do not, however, prepare the financials for the largest business in the world—USA, Inc. I checked with a local university, and their requirements for an economics major do not include a single accounting course. I've talked to economists about this measurement, and some simply said they weren't experts and some referred me to someone else. The so-called experts found it too far below their stature to even discuss. One suggested that I had a good question as to why burning dollars could be considered a contribution to the economy but that it had nothing to do with the measurement and he could disprove my idea in many ways. None of those ways was mentioned. In the context of putting money where my mouth is, I previously offered an award to the one who can prove me wrong.

By my measurement, taxes are nearer 45 percent of the economy and may be much higher, but that isn't all. That does not include the cost of regulation that government has imposed since the 1950s or the litigiousness imposed by the nearly 60 percent of our legislatures that are attorneys. Legal representation is one of the most important tenets of a free society; however, the cost to this society has gone way beyond reason and in all probability made attorneys the wealthiest of all professions. Nor does this measurement include responsibilities of the private sector that were once performed by government, such as building residential roads, limited access highways, and even interstate exit ramps. Suffice it to say that the 1950s size of government cannot be compared to the 2008 size of government.

It may seem confusing, but this growth in government has not impacted the rich and has in fact increased their numbers and/or their wealth. The rich actually benefit from government growth in three ways.

1. Government creates scarcity. For example, when laws were passed to regulate the pollution of cement producers, the old plants were grandfathered in. Any new

plant would have to comply with new law. Because existing prices didn't support the environmental cost of a new plant, the old plants became more valuable as demand and prices increased. Profits up, stock up, the rich get richer.

2. Government creates profit zones. Whether an enacted law is wasteful, good for the environment, or protective of people, someone will get rich providing the technology or the service to comply with the law. A best example is laws that generate the need for litigiousness.

3. The third and perhaps the greatest means by which government makes the rich richer is cost, simply the added cost of government. Whether it is regulation, taxes, or limitations on labor, these require an increase in investment and often an increase in net profit margins due to difficulties or the cost of compliance. So-called conservatives look at the increasing wealth of the rich as a good sign of the benefits of capitalism, while socialists and those in government see it as a need to increase taxes because the rich are unjustly rich.

Where does this bring us as to the 2008 crisis? Simply put, the increasing burden of government has placed too great a weight on private-sector workers. Unfortunately, we have no plausible means to measure that increase. But the logic to explain the potential for crisis goes like this: if you buy a home based on an income of $3,000 per month and your income declines to $2,500, you will have to make sacrifices. When you can no longer make sacrifices, your economy will collapse. When this happens to a large enough portion of the working population, the economy will falter. It is amazing to me, but even facing what could become a huge economic crisis, nearly every state and local government is looking for ways to raise revenues to increase spending, while the federal government is simply increasing its borrowing.

Obviously, much of the new money is used to make further increases in government wages, benefits, and pensions. If government continues on its dash to grow and if the economy is to rebound, private-sector wages will need to take another step downward. For years imports and a strong dollar have provided some relief to the pressures of out-of-control government spending and regulation. That ship has likely sailed, as the dollar is declining and cheaper imports may be harder to find.

In the years since about 1981, there have been several reasons that living standards have held up to any degree. Mortgage rates declined from about 17 percent to 5 percent, reducing housing costs; the prime rate went from about 21 percent to 5 percent (currently 3.25 percent), thus enhancing investment possibilities and lowering business costs; foreign countries provided cheap imports; businesses took advantage of foreign manufacturers with low wages to keep costs down; the dollar remained strong, keeping the price of imports low; there was a technological revolution that reduced business costs; and the unions lost many of the controls that forced inefficient business practices and slowed innovation. These were offsets to the ominous government growth. Most, such as the decline in interest rates, were technical adjustments that can not be duplicated in the ensuing years.

Contrast this with the prospects for growth in the cost of government. For example, there are built-in adjustments that demand tax increases, such as inflation increases to the wages of government employees, social security, employee pensions, and stated wage increases based on longevity or education; employee and retiree medical costs are rising as people age; baby boomers in the private sector and as government employees will soon be retiring en masse, and many government employees will be collecting three and four pensions even while they work; new programs may be enacted, such as universal health coverage; and the declining wages in the private sector will itself require increases in welfare, law enforcement, and government-sponsored medical benefits.

Rather than long periods of growth, we are likely to suffer ever-increasing economic crises. Without adjustments in the costs and method by which we govern, the U.S. economy will eventually collapse and possibly fall into a totalitarian state. If you Google "end of capitalism," you will find more references than you can imagine written by those who believe it is ending. Many people accept the idea that a democracy has a certain life and will end because people eventually discover that they can vote themselves benefits and accordingly place too many demands on the economy. The reality is that government is putting too many demands on the private sector. There is, however, a solution to the economic equation. We are at the beginning of an economic revolution/evolution that could reach far beyond all imagination, but only if we realize that a solution exists, and only if we devise an appropriate method for measuring the size of government, measuring the costs of regulation, exposing and eliminating government waste, and bringing parity to private- and public-sector wages and benefits.

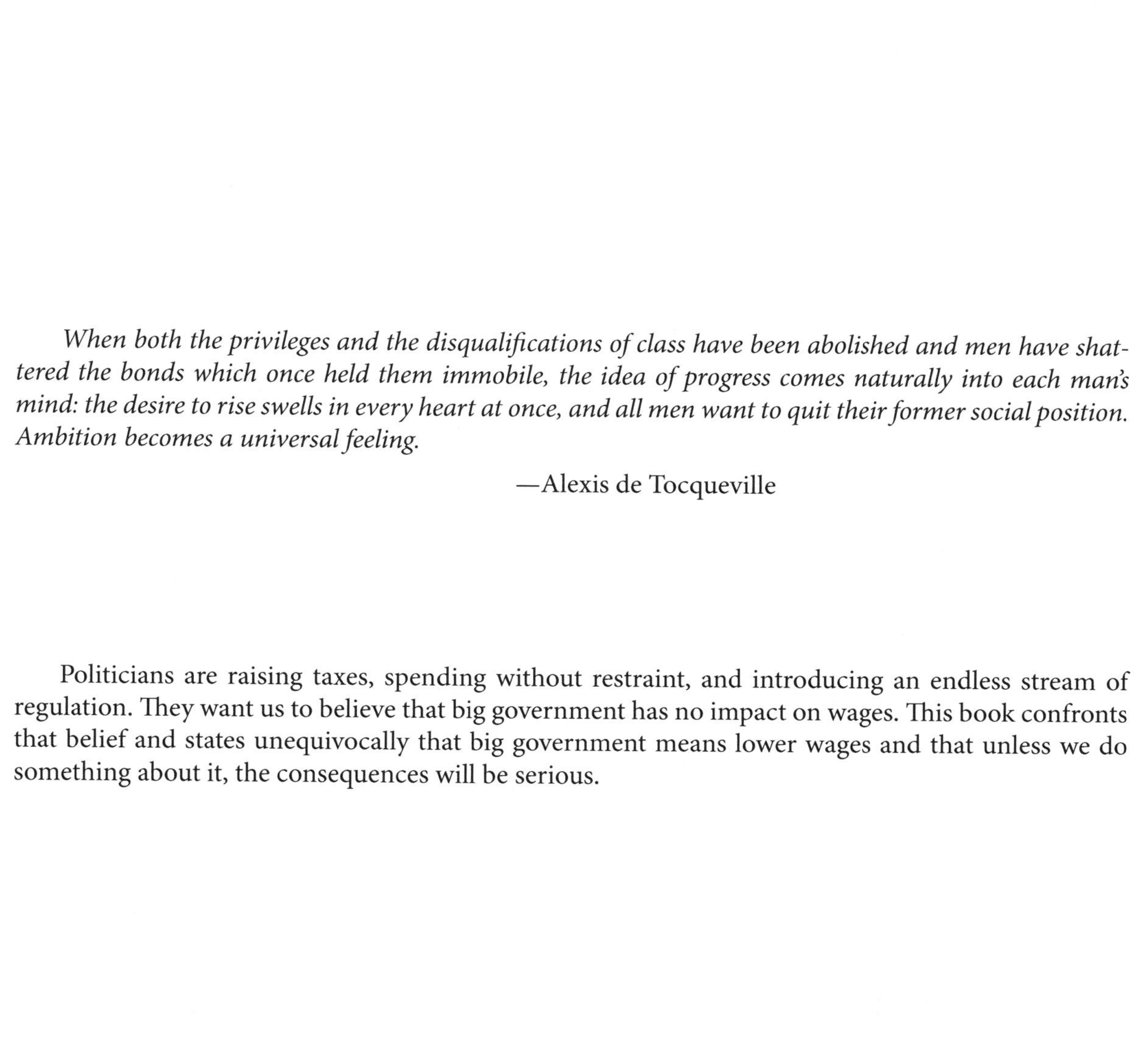

When both the privileges and the disqualifications of class have been abolished and men have shattered the bonds which once held them immobile, the idea of progress comes naturally into each man's mind: the desire to rise swells in every heart at once, and all men want to quit their former social position. Ambition becomes a universal feeling.

—Alexis de Tocqueville

Politicians are raising taxes, spending without restraint, and introducing an endless stream of regulation. They want us to believe that big government has no impact on wages. This book confronts that belief and states unequivocally that big government means lower wages and that unless we do something about it, the consequences will be serious.

This book is dedicated to William E. Dedelow, my father, who in my youth, when I asked how to spell a word, told me to look it up.

Contents

	PREFACE	xiii
	INTRODUCTION	xv
CHAPTER 1	ECONOMICS OF LABOR	1
CHAPTER 2	WHAT EVER HAPPENED TO THE "FREE"IN FREE ENTERPRISE	18
CHAPTER 3	HOW GOVERNMENT UNDERSTATES ITS SIZE WHY TAXES ARE REALLY PAID BY PRODUCTIVE PRIVATE-SECTOR WORKERS AND NOT THE RICH HOW TAX LAWS ENCOURAGE WASTED RESOURCES	23
CHAPTER 4	THE WHEEL-TURNERS	50
CHAPTER 5	EFFICIENCY AND PRODUCTIVITY-	53
CHAPTER 6	THE IMPORTANCE OF MONEY	60
CHAPTER 7	WEALTH	65
CHAPTER 8	RETURN ON INVESTMENT	82
CHAPTER 9	INFLATION	97
CHAPTER 10	THE SYMPTOMS OF EXCESSIVE GROWTH IN GOVERNMENT AND HOW LABOR IS AFFECTED	114
CHAPTER 11	THE GREAT DEPRESSION	124
CHAPTER 12	WHAT REALLY HAPPENED IN THE '70s AND '80s?	132

CHAPTER 13 RISK, ECONOMIC FORCES, AND THE WORKER 153

CHAPTER 14 GOVERNMENT AND THE FREE-ENTERPRISE SYSTEM 166

CHAPTER 15 WELFARE AND ITS EFFECT ON SOCIETY 175

CHAPTER 16 FREE ENTERPRISE AND THE BIG APPLE 183

CHAPTER 17 WHO GAINS AND WHO LOSES? 195

CHAPTER 18 THE NEWS MEDIA—AN IMPORTANT AND NECESSARY PART OF FREE ENTERPRISE 215

CHAPTER 19 THE COST OF WAR 223

CHAPTER 20 WHY UNIONS SHOULD BACK BUSINESS IN CONGRESS (WHY UNIONS HAVE THEIR MONEY RIDING ON THE WRONG HORSE) 227

CHAPTER 21 POLITICS (SO YOU THINK WHO SHOULD RUN THE COUNTRY) 232

PREFACE

Humankind has evolved over a recorded period of nearly seven thousand years. The essence of this evolution has been a struggle to provide sustenance and sanctuary from the powers of nature and the destruction brought by humankind itself. Fearing the unknown power of self-determination, the greater part of the earth's population choose to have their decisions made by an elite few, believing that the wisdom of absolute rulers guaranteed their welfare. Humankind has seldom trusted the unknown and has been compelled to place the power of decision in icons of flesh and stone. The story of Moses exemplifies the distrust of the unknown, wherein, despite having witnessed an unseen power part the water and destroy the forces that e nslaved them, the people turned their backs on the unseen power to worship a golden idol.

Throughout history, the power to make decisions has been yielded to monarchies, imagined emissaries of a deity, dictators, and individuals or organizations with totalitarian powers. For these rulers, humankind let their children bleed to death on sacrificial altars, protected the rulers with their own lives, and supported them with shares of their production. The people made these sacrifices as much to protect themselves from the rancor of these omnipotent rulers as from the unknown power of self. In 1776, a small share of the earth's people took the power from government and set out to learn how to live, while trusting the unseen power of self-determination. Whereas the faithful of Moses eventually were given freedom for their faith, the people of the United States provided themselves the highest standard of living in the world and won the admiration of nearly every human on earth. But the lesson of history is that history repeats itself. And, as the people of Moses turned back to idols, the people of the United States have turned back to government.

Today, the number who are losing faith in the power of self-determination is growing. As the number of faithless grow, socialists and advocates for government demand more of the workers' production and commandeer an increasing share of productive workers to fulfill the politician's demands while creating fear of the system that created a better way of life. Again, an unseen power is being scorned for an idyllic symbol: *government*.

The faithless don't seem to care that giving power to one omnipotent ruler is little different than giving it to several million bureaucrats. Ironically, workers are giving up a far larger share of production to support these bureaucrats and their beneficiaries than single rulers once required. The actual number of workers who produce our needs is declining, as government, in the appearance of creating jobs, is adding to the workers' burdens. Workers are not perceived as producing goods and services to fulfill our needs but as repositories of dollars to fulfill the needs of government and its idol worshipers. The dollar is seen as an all-powerful icon, rather than viewed as a simple tool of commerce. As humankind was once enslaved to omnipotent rulers, the demands of government, like the demands of any ruler, are first met before we may provide for our own lives. The worker is again enslaved to government, but this time the number to be served is growing, while the number of those serving declines.

As this book took shape, writing it became an enlightening experience. Beginning as a few letters to the editor, the notes took structure, the structure became chapters, and then chapters became a book. As I wrote it, I found answers to a thousand questions thought since childhood. And the answer to one question led to new questions and more answers. Every moment of my existence seems to have played a part in my writings. As the logic became stronger, and where at first, current economic theory was not intended to be questioned, I found logic contradicted common perceptions. There was a realization that most problems were not problems themselves but symptoms of a greater problem. The country that once put a man on the moon hasn't left the earth's gravitational pull in over thirty years and now pays people not to work. Those who feared what humankind did to the earth now close their eyes to what humankind has done for it. The Cold War is over, yet the leader of free enterprise doesn't see that omnipotent government was defeated; rather, government was the victor. The people have lost faith in freedom and free enterprise and lost trust in their fellow man.

Government should legislate a more efficient economy,
so as to enhance labor's value and availability.

INTRODUCTION

Your cup is half empty; your cup is half full. Perspective is obviously as important in life as it is to solving problems. When we think of our system, do we think of government and the economy as one? Our government could be democratic and not support a free-enterprise system. A government could support free enterprise without being democratic. Democracy and free enterprise, then, must be distinct and separate. Although the system and government do not operate independently of each other, they are not the same. We then must ask if free enterprise caused the problems that government must solve or vice versa—or both? Certainly, we have problems in free enterprise that we look to government to solve. But could government trust free enterprise to solve the problems of government?

In the newspapers, on the radio, in magazines, and on TV, there are reports on how well off we are and how beggared are the poor. We were once told the economy is growing, unemployment is down, incomes are up, and interest rates are down. But then the Federal Reserve raised rates in the hope that things would get worse, and the stock market goes up if they do. Are we better or worse off? Are the rich getting richer or poorer, or maybe we are all getting poor. Why do so many people feel as if they are working harder but getting less for their effort? Is something wrong with the statistics? Is something wrong with the explanation of how the economy works? As economists attempt to quantify and explain world economic activity and direction, they use monetary analysis, charts, cycles, graphs, paths, and questionnaires. Are they living in the past or projecting the future? Should basic premises be questioned? The depression-era ideology theorizes that money is static and needs to be placed into motion by an outside force—namely, government. Politicians tell us that government policies and spending produce benefits—but for whom? Is money like manure? Should government just spread it around and watch things grow. After all, spreading manure also grows healthy weeds and causes a bad odor. Is money just one of the tools? What makes an economy grow? Money? People? Government?

Perhaps the reason there are so many problems is that all the right questions haven't been asked. Perhaps economics has changed and is more complex than it was a hundred years ago. A hundred years ago, life and the economy were much simpler. Free enterprise then was only in its initial stages of development as a system. Perhaps economists don't realize that what they didn't know then, they don't understand now. There is a deep-rooted predisposition in our nation to simplify just about everything. In politics it is "Tippecanoe and Tyler too," "I like Ike," "Read my lips," or "Are you better off now than you were four years ago?" The same simplistic thinking reduces economic analyses to "It's good for the economy." Once, when requested to simplify a financial format and after several rejected revisions, I wrote total cash in, $$$; total cash out, $$$; net cash, $$$. Was this okay? The response: "I suppose so, but what does it mean?" I said, "Not a thing, but it is simple."

Is it sufficient for a politician to say, "The rich aren't taxed enough," "The poor need more benefits," and "I support the poor"? Do these aphorisms have meaning? After all, what they said was simple. There is no other economic system that allows a poor kid to get rich. So why is it unfair that some other kid didn't? Is it fair to be fair? Is the news media a part of the problem? Free enterprise brought us radio and TV and supports them with advertisements so the media can use thirty seconds to explain the event of the day. How truthful is a media that reports that government spending is being cut $5 billion, when spending is really going up? Is this all the truth or half the truth? Who decides which half we get? We rely upon the media to give us the truth, as we make decisions that affect the world. From the Bible to *Common Sense*, the written word affects lives and how they are lived. The free-enterprise system works; we should know that—just ask anyone who has lived without it.

How much do people know about free enterprise? Do they know all businesses combined need more money to support expansion than they earn? If government owned all the businesses, the government would be losing even more money? Year after year, government has expanded the workers' responsibilities. Can the workers do more for government and still enhance our lives? Wealth is created when production expands. Our ability to produce is directly related to our standard of living. Therefore, is wealth created when our standard of living grows?

Government, not the worker, is more and more deciding who will be blessed with the product of the private worker, as government provides for an increasing number of people who don't contribute. The heavy cost of government is found not only in the taxes we pay but also in the cost of what we consume. Government laws and rules that add jobs, both private and public, consume greater numbers of the productive workforce. Is government creating jobs or responsibilities? Does it matter? People are being paid not to work, as others work at unnecessary jobs so they can buy things in a presumed economically deprived community that needs unproductive workers to buy things. The idea of paying someone to make purchases, known as stimulating demand, is whimsical, but it is the explanation for not allowing inefficient and unnecessary workers to find useful tasks outside government's embrace.

The economic wisdom of today preaches that spending invigorates the economy. Fifty years ago, economists told us that to get more guns we had to give up butter. Do we give up something to get something else? Is this not a basic tenant of economics? Are we trading more production for more government and a lower standard of living? We must again have government explain the logic that it is more important to buy than to produce and that jobs, no matter how inefficient, ineffective, or burdensome, are somehow good for the community. As government taxes and burdens business, is it thus reducing real expansion or "stimulating" the economy? Why does government "stimulate" the economy when workers are in great demand? Our standard of living is measured by how much we consume, but isn't consumption dependant upon how much is produced? If jobs aren't plentiful, why do we import so much? Do we import because too few are actually productive?

According to some statistics, our fathers made more money and had a better life than we have. Are we going backwards, or are there trade-offs? To reflect upon how much government has grown, let's look at what government paid for in the 1950s. Then, there was little welfare, as most poor people didn't know they were poor. Any farmer who could record a plat for the land in the public records and sell the lots could plan housing subdivisions. When enough people lived on the subdivided land, government put in sewer, water, and street lights and paved the roads. Today, we have user fees, tap-in fees, engineering fees, police fees, road fees, and inspection fees for projects that are not near our subdivision. Moreover, today's building permits cost a hundred times what the last generation paid. Back then, our tax bills didn't show a special charge for a library, but every child got a book for each class, and we could have worked our way through college without government loans.

The free-enterprise system has two resources: money and labor—there are three if we count humankind's imagination. The specific characteristics of free enterprise are employment, unemployment, efficiency, wealth, deflation, inflation, and its singular most important mathematical tool, return on investment (ROI) computations. The tools of government are taxes, distribution of wealth, manipulation of investment, welfare, recessions, good intentions, guaranteed jobs, job creation, and a better credit rating. Government has first call on every dollar, yet free enterprise is efficient, and government causes inefficient uses of businesses resources.

There are a thousand questions with even more answers—not simple, not easily explained with a five word phrase. Things are complex now, so we must proceed past simple answers, or we may lose the freedom that gave us free enterprise. Supply side, demand side, the Federal Reserve—these are just parts of an equation. Also affecting us are tax laws, labor laws, spending laws, laws that reallocate resources, natural forces, efficiency, science, crime, redistribution, and on and on. Economics is like the atom—not just an atom and not just a proton, neutron, and nucleus, but many other parts and pieces. Just as science is discovering new atomic parts, there are, as yet, forces in the economy to be discovered.

We need to look at the forest and the trees. The world and free enterprise as we know it is not three thousand years old but barely three hundred. It took over 250 years of this 300 to establish a monetary system and even now, arguments continue over its explanation. Our government was founded to protect a way of life that was brought about by a natural force: humankind's freedom to choose. Free enterprise was the choice, and it endures not because government protects it but because free enterprise protects our government. It is the system wherein we provide for ourselves by providing for others. It is the system where human characteristics, even greed, can be a beneficent force. Free enterprise works because mankind is freed to ask and answer an infinite number of questions. It promotes competition to help our fellow humans. It is a system where the lack of organization encourages anyone to be involved and thus to create the greatest number of solutions. We are random-access minds that a computer can't duplicate. The lack of organization contradicts the effort by government to harmonize and regulate free enterprise, as government nets only *wasted spending and inefficient labor.* For now, free enterprise has overcome all the roadblocks, all the rules, the taxes, and the evil empires. Until just a few years ago, barely 15 percent of the world's population was involved in free enterprise. The potential of free enterprise with the whole world involved is beyond imagination. As we are now learning the very structure of DNA, we can only wonder what we will know three thousand years in the future.

CHAPTER 1

ECONOMICS OF LABOR

Rulers once decreed laws and ordained gods to guide and control people. The laws or gods didn't need to be fair or real; the intention was merely to bind people together. Individual thought by the masses was considered a threat rather than a potential advantage. Until the formation of the United States, freedoms were thus suppressed to favor the sovereignty of state. The people who colonized America left their old countries to seek the freedoms denied them, but once here, our forefathers enjoyed little commonality. The government that was established had to consider these differences, allowing each group to practice its own beliefs. The longing to be part of a group still exists within us. To satisfy this desire, there are multitudes of organizations, such as social, political, religious, business, educational, and labor. Applicants to these organizations go through a gauntlet of challenges to establish a kinship and to discourage outsiders. Roadblocks discourage members from crossing either out or in.

Our culture supports these lines in the sand, as they protect our rights and our customs. The protections come in the form of laws or rules but also as defensive comments or actions to avoid intermingling. These laws, rules, comments, and actions protect indefensible or fragile beliefs and even ignorance. Talk-show hosts may address health care, while refusing comments from doctors. Women proclaim that only women understand women, and sports aficionados will only tune into athletes or coaches. Politicians defeat opponents by calling them "mean-spirited."

The media proclaims that only professional politicians can govern and talk about the terrible "gridlock," to cast dispersions on a group that refuses to ascribe to another's views. As with the old civilizations, actualities or the facts are not pertinent. It isn't important that gridlock is a form of disagreement and an American birthright. Nor is it suggested that wise councils not bound to the group could come to a better conclusion. The line is drawn, but the many administrations that functioned without gridlock are thus vindicated. The many including Hitler, Mussolini, Genghis Khan, and that wonderful man who gave free speech and anyone who used it residence in Siberia, Stalin. After killing millions from his own country, Stalin never worried about gridlock.

Our congressional representatives are sent to present their thoughts and ideas, to discuss the issues, to reason. But as members of a group, they are encouraged to walk in lockstep formation with the president, their party chief, or their congressional leaders. Seniority rules dictate; where reason should govern. The dominant media discourages nonconformists who don't accept politically correct ideas, forgetting that many of today's conformists were once themselves politically incorrect.

Even that most respected and independent of all organizations, the Federal Reserve, builds its barriers. Its elitism showed in the 1980s, when Preston Martin, a businessman with strong financial experience, was installed as a governor on the Federal Reserve Board. He carried the tarnish of business experience and a less somber mood. Preston Martin once commented that central bankers "are expected to look and act as if they are moving from one funeral to the next." Despite Martin's close analysis of the economy, his comments were ignored. He was not one of them; he was an outsider.

A gregarious Westerner, he smiled and the greatest of all evils, he was a *businessman*. Women and children first; it's Freddy. God help us that a businessman should become a member of Congress or worse, the president. Many of the best minds in our society are thus considered nefarious or corrupt and are brutalized by the media because they carry the distinction of being partners in free enterprise. Achieving financial respect, while not on the public dole, is proof to the media that objectivity and independence is lost. Those who once fought corruption and whose own minds are now corrupt see outsiders as a threat. Disagreement and new ideas intimidate the group in control, and as it was three hundred years ago, the interspersion of ideas is a freedom that menaces the establishment.

In a conversation with a friend some time ago, the discussion of economics resulted in a short, heated dispute. The friend extolled the benefits of an economics degree over practical knowledge, and the discussion ended abruptly. As a first reaction, a letter to the friend was written denouncing the attitude, but nothing of substance had really been said. Whether by refusal to listen or the offensive manner of each, the exchange failed to give birth to a clear understanding. There was a generation gap, experience with different economies, and a difference in education and job experience. The education of the one had been the experience of the other. Most economists have not had the experience of operating a business, have not plied a trade, and learn only in academia. Without a professional independent status and a place to hang a shingle, economists look at schoolbook answers to field problems with the arrogance of learned philosophers. But the need for economists is growing. Each year, whether through war or peace, the world divides into new countries. Most people in the world, all but our own, strive for the wonders of free enterprise. As the leader of democracy and free enterprise, we confuse them, as our effort to divide the spoils takes precedence over creating the spoils. Because of our divergent paths, it is more important than ever for economists to consolidate their views of free enterprise. The day is here when independent economists need to be an active part of government as well as private enterprise. For now the economist is inconsequential, and businesses solicit politicians for laws to improve business without examining economic impacts. Though people may not realize it, economics is the next supreme belief after God. So powerful are economic beliefs that the concept of communism once suppressed over two-thirds of this planet's population. Freedom gave us divergent economics, but only free enterprise preserves freedom. Economists are the Merlins who, for good or evil, shape the rules to shepherd the politicians, who preside over the economy. Economists are the guides for the system called capitalism, private enterprise, and free enterprise. The terms have slightly different meanings, but each defines the freedom to act. The words free enterprise speaks best of what it is, but economists have yet to speak best for free enterprise; after three hundred years of evolution, the theories of economics have yet to be written.

Politicians who wonder if they have been redistributing the wealth find that answers are dependent upon who pays for the question. Economists tout the dogma the media will accept to correspond with the politicians' views of spending. Figures can support any view, and the media reports the view that seems kindest or sells best. Confused by their own editorials, the media believes itself expert. Politicians can thus justify spending to buy votes because the media-favored economic opinion encourages useless jobs that pay people to do little more than spend money. The inference is that if one king is good, a million are better, and an economic fantasyland swirls about us. Distribution advocated; creation castigated. Government policy is derived not with theoretical guidance but from politically correct evaluations. Prevailing views are opinions supported by studying depressions, recessions, consumer attitudes, business attitudes, unemployment, employment, inflation, and interest rates. But the periods of study don't compare to each other or to today. The goal is to find a magic index to explain economic directions, interest rates, and inflation. Like trying to predict the weather, unless we know why it happens, we will never know when it will happen. The real answers won't spring from opinions.

The media assures us that the economist and politician to be trusted learn their trade in the sterility of a classroom. Thus, they are without the taint of that practical but presumed biased: everyday knowledge. Business people don't attempt to apply their thoughts and ideas to school curriculum, so as not to cross a line they take for granted. In a system that was intended to guide and support alternatives, trust is not nearly the problem as is communication. We fail to listen or report, as all sides speak freely. The question of interrelationship through an objective definition of responsibilities is answered by attempts to advance knowledge only from within. Where civilizations once battled each other, groups now bring up the cannon, and the masses, as always, are trampled on the lines.

When all believed the world was flat, punishment could be the reward for thinking otherwise. Galileo was sequestered by the Christian Church for his study of the universe. Groups that now chastise Christians as fanatics use the same cultural precepts that restrained Galileo to bridle free thought on a pretense of liberation. The communications that fosters new ideas has been cut by rules and laws, written or not, and a media that only protects the free speech it favors. Freedom of speech, yes; freedom to believe incorrectly, no. The Dark Ages are again upon us, as the system that gave us freedoms evolves to destroy them.

And so we come to a discussion of economics, and having looked behind the line, we can see the difficulties that lie beyond it. Beyond the law, the rule, the gods, we move into the theoretical wonderland where humankind must go to solve problems. Most of the debate will involve one simple question: **to get more of one thing, do we have to give up something else?** Obviously the writer views the question as more important than it seems, because it is being asked herein. As is often true, the question cannot be answered totally until countless other questions are asked. The right question may be the last to be answered, but solutions stem from right questions. We now might ask, who is giving up what? What are they giving up? Who are they? Are workers giving up anything? Which workers do so, if any? And what kind of work ceases to fulfill another demand? The final question might be: does work contribute to the economy? We will ask and answer these questions many times but each time from a different viewpoint.

THE ECONOMICS OF LABOR

First, it is important to talk about money and labor. People think money is more important than labor, but what good is money unless someone will work for it? Here we find a question that might be answered. If money is important, then so is work. But which is more important? All should agree that there are only two ingredients in an economy: labor and incentive. Money is a common form of incentive, but the words money and labor are only parts of the definition:

Labor is a function of time,
efficiency, and the number who labor.

Incentives come in two forms:
reward and punishment.

The above definitions are implicit, not mandating further explanation. Money and labor each attract the other, but incentives are only the reason to labor, while labor produces products for limitless reasons. Economists have used considerable time and paper attempting to explain economics in monetary terms, giving money a greater precedence over the importance of labor. But money is only one kind of incentive and economics can't always be defined in terms of money. It is therefore important to pursue and define the **economics of labor**.

The economics of labor has to do mostly with the economic goals for which we struggle. There appear to be two:

- To improve and maintain our living standards
- To improve and maintain our environment

All of our labor, from morning wakeup until evening bed, fulfills one of these goals. Labor could cut a tree to provide shelter or save a tree to provide shade. These goals, at times, conflict with each other or cause us conflict between one another. The goals reflect in our living standards, in our clean river water, and our clean air to breathe. For us to measure the success at achieving these goals, we would need a happiness gauge. Most of any measurement would be of our consumption, and consumption is related to how much is produced. Simply adding money to an economy is usually a prelude to inflation. If labor, not money, is the impelling factor of production, then the number of people producing, not the number consuming, would be the key to consumption. The productivity and availability of labor then becomes of paramount importance. Living standards measured by consumption thus increase with the increase in production. We consequently derive the following formula:

COMPUTATION OF TOTAL PRODUCTION

Production per producer	x	number of workers	=	total production
a	x	b	=	c1

If productivity is a function of labor, then supporting nonproductive labor reduces the real output of a community. As long as this formula is valid, we can also measure wasted labor (z), or the cost of adding new demands on old labor. Lost production could be expressed as follows:

a	x	(b - z {z-waste, etc.})	=	total production
a	x	(b - z)	=	c2

AND

z	x	a	=	lp (lost production)

Presuming we would wish to maximize production, it would be important to minimize the waste or unnecessary allocations of labor to maximize our living standards. To examine labor more closely, we can divide labor into classifications. For simplicity, we can divide labor into two major work classifications: labor to produce consumer goods and services, and labor to satisfy government demands.

Workers are in one of two classifications: consumer-demanded production or government compliance.

Government supports the economic system and safeguards the currency that is needed to facilitate exchanges. Currency is the most common worker incentive and correspondingly, government has a first claim on that incentive. Government dictates the number who work, as well as the number who receive benefits from or at the behest of government, and the remainder of the citizens keep what is left over. Therefore, because government controls the major incentive, it controls a significant portion of the labor force. To find the greatest waste, we can concentrate our efforts on determining which of the two might be the most wasteful. By examining the controls of government and those of free enterprise, we can reveal which has the greatest potential for waste. The following arguments compare the two:

- Looking at the potential of employers to control waste, we find that voters can replace wasteful politicians. The politicians control the systems that inform us of whether government is wasteful. Consumer spending controls waste by eliminating the inefficient and costly producer.
- Because the politicians are concerned for their jobs, they fear bad economies and unemployment. The politicians' concern for efficient government can then be quieted by sympathy for employees, the position of government employees as voters, and the politicians' belief in economic stimulation. Businesspeople must be efficient to preserve their jobs and the jobs of those who work for them.
- Government spending has no consumer-related control to manage inefficient or unnecessary functions. Free enterprise creates its demand for labor in response to consumer spending. Because competition eventually dissolves waste, the jobs created are productive. An efficient pricing system will not support inefficient labor.
- Elected politicians serve terms of from two to four years, which gives voters only periodic chances to react to circumstances that reflect unfavorably upon candidates. Said circumstances often become vague or are covered over by the time an election occurs. The consumers can react immediately to adverse market publicity, economic difficulties, and bad or pricy products.
- In government, politicians can tax and spend to woo voters and win the elections that occur periodically. In free enterprise, businesses advertise to attract consumers to products with the intention of satisfying consumer demands. Consumers decide the future of those products and thus that of the private workers who produce them. Consumers vote daily to accept or reject products.
- Politicians are reluctant to eliminate jobs that are no longer efficient or necessary. Most economists counsel politicians to create jobs, for fear that free enterprise will

not. An economist who doesn't recommend job stimulation offers little to satisfy a politician's constituency. The market eliminates inefficient and unnecessary jobs.

- Politicians spend money to satisfy political forces and create jobs that are often intended to stimulate an economy. Free-enterprise jobs are consumer-created to fulfill real demands and desires.
- Government jobs are established by elected representatives who "think" they know what the consumer/voter wants. Businesses spend millions figuring out what the consumer wants, and bad products or services fade away.
- Government positions/operations don't compete on the basis of productivity and efficiency. Poor, inefficient production in free enterprise means lost jobs.
- Government functions are monopolistic. Government won't allow monopolies in free enterprise to avoid exploitation of the consumer.
- Politicians who run government are not generally administrators who are trained or seasoned by competition. A lack of experience can spell economic disaster for a private sector enterprise and its administrators.
- The politicians' concern for employment has little to do with efficiency or productivity and more to do with re-election. Businesses are less concerned with employment and more concerned with efficiency and profits.
- Politicians can raise tax revenue or borrow to pay higher wages and spend money. Politicians are criticized for laying people off. Politicians can benefit from being inefficient and can demand higher prices. In free enterprise, businesses can only ask for higher prices, which are subject to competition. Businesses can benefit from lower prices.
- In recessions, politicians can regulate spending to avoid raising taxes. In the private sector, businesses usually reduce prices, suffer profit losses, and possibly go out of business.
- Government can audit to provide *modest* assurances that funds have not been misappropriated, but audits can only verify that money has been spent; they are not intended to uncover fraud, waste, inefficiency, or unnecessary duplication of effort. In the private sector competition eventually weeds out businesses and components of businesses that are fraudulent, wasteful, inefficient, and duplications of effort. Audits in the private sector are intended to verify presentation of the financial statements that influence investors.
- Government raises taxes, legislates regulation, borrows, and sets up special assessments to increase spending or to set controls on the private sector. In the private sector when taxes are raised, competition is a means by which ways are found to absorb government taxes and regulation.

From the above comparison, we can theorize that government has the least number of controls on labor waste. Therefore, if productivity of society is a concern, the greatest problems likely lie with government. It can also be theorized that if government wastes labor, the burden to maintain productivity falls on the remaining fraction of the population, the group known as the private workers. Competition is the ultimate arbitrator in an efficient and productive market economy. For government, unless an employee has a sign on his/her back that reads "I don't work, but I sleep with the boss," such instances of waste and misappropriation will never be discovered and/or are likely covered up to avoid embarrassing public officials.

Competition is a natural law that dissolves waste, inefficiency, misappropriation and fraud.

To examine how and where government might waste labor, we note that government looks at the economy in monetary terms and attempts to influence it with money. There is a concept that a dollar spent passes through several hands and causes the economy to grow. The presumption is of static dollars and available labor, but if the labor force is at full employment, forced government expenditure must represent an alteration of free economic forces. Money is then used to create activity, without considering economic alternatives for productive workers. In other words, if we attempted to expand production and increase government's labor usage simultaneously at full employment, we would have difficulties controlling inflation. Whether at full employment or not, deploying money contracts the labor supply. We can demonstrate how government uses money. Most of the reasons government spends money are included in the following categories:

1. Welfare arrangements. As payments to labor for not working, welfare competes with useful employment. Welfare slows the workers' return to the workforce, as it inhibits the desire for work and worker mobility, and it competes with worker wages. Because of welfare, the reasons for returning to work are less critical and can even be detrimental.

2. Wheel turner subsidies. Pork-barrel spending, maintaining unnecessary military bases, and other unnecessary jobs intended to support a community represent wasted labor. Employees are, in essence, paid to buy things in a community.

3. Productive growth. This type of expenditure includes labor for basic needs, such as road construction, utilities, and even parks and playgrounds. Unfortunately, the success of many programs is not gauged by productivity but by the number of workers employed and the level of their compensation.

4. Sharing distributions. When government changes the share of the economy previously afforded an economic, political, or social division, it changes how the product of the economy is distributed. For example, if the productive members of the community receive a 2 percent increase, and the government-benefited recipients receive 4 percent, then the distribution of consumer goods has been reapportioned. Groups that benefit from government sharing have fewer reasons to work, reducing the availability of labor. Sharing arrangements also reduce the workers' ambition and mobility to seek their highest and best use.

5. Facilities maintenance. Government must maintain government assets, provide national and local protection, and provide crime prevention and prosecution. These are necessary functions and are responses to the needs of the community. However,

increasing welfare, for example, reduces the desire to work and can increase the necessity for police because of the welfare recipients' additional idle time.

6. Management. Government staff, audit, and revenue collection. Government expansion in staff is relative to the complexity of laws that can add significantly to the demands on the labor force.
7. Research and development. Government invests in leading edge research that is too large or speculative for free enterprise. Growth in other areas of government may cause declines in this beneficial aspect of government.

Traditionally, politicians have been concerned with constricting, not expanding, the labor supply. However, if it is valid to be concerned with contraction of the labor supply when unemployment is high, then expansion should be a concern when unemployment is low. We should, therefore, examine why politicians never voice an interest in expanding the labor force.

In the early history of the United States, creating jobs to help the economy or the concept of reallocating labor wasn't a concern. People worked to live and provided for their own needs in an economy that was almost 100 percent private enterprise. The use of government labor was minor and expended mostly for defense. Science and innovation only occasionally provided production efficiencies. The change from this tent culture to the efficient and evolving one of today has altered greatly how people function. Instead of each worker providing his own needs, labor specialized, and from specialization, businesses and factories grew as workers began performing distinct functions. Innovation resulted in a positive effect, yet there appeared to be problems. In what was thought would be a natural transition, people often went without work. This confounded economists, who attempted to find an acceptable explanation. The concept of government job creation was theorized to stimulate employment. The society that was governed by politicians who were elected on little more than a slogan was able to simplify everything. With job creation, politicians found a common economic method to solve problems in a free society.

Politicians needed the idea streamlined into an apparently innocent political phrase, and the concept of government job creation began to grow. The political proclamation that "It's good for the economy" reflected a desire of society to be knowledgeable and the gullibility to believe that politicians were knowledgeable. Anyone who had ever been without a job could relate to job creation. And, if it was good for the economy, productivity wasn't a concern. To put it another way, if a little is good, a lot is better. To supplement jobs created for economic stimulation, welfare became an avenue for cash input into the community. For politicians, there is never enough money. When given the opportunity to spend, politicians strive to be well thought of, so as to enhance election possibilities. Through this perceived redistribution—the arts, the environment, save the animals, and a million other ways—money is funneled through the community by government. So many points of redistribution exist that politicians complain of a shortage of money. This shortage is curious, as spending that was supposed to be so good for the economy should create lots of tax revenue.

The concept of spending money to improve the economy is generally attributed to John Maynard Keynes. Keynes wrote *The General Theory of Employment, Interest, and Money*, published in 1936. (Bernard Mandeville (1670–1733) wrote of the effects of money moving in an economy in *The Fable of the Bees.*) *The General Theory* was written with a view at the number of unemployed resulting from the Great Depression. The influence of the Depression led to the belief that free enterprise did not always function well and could not account for all economic activity. Keynesian economics supports money spending to create consumer demand. Politicians facilitate this theory by creating government jobs or encouraging enterprise to create them. Politicians side with this position because it implies that spending money helps the economy and thus, spending money helps them to get reelected. An alternate position by Adam Smith, an economist who wrote *Wealth of Nations* in 1776, defined work as a self-interest; he surmised that all would work to benefit themselves and, as a result, would serve others. Smith's economic solutions did not necessitate an active involvement for politicians and left them without a part to play. It is, of course, far more angelic and valuable for politicians to talk of job creation. The implication is that stimulating demand will bring about employment, rather than supporting a perceived opposite view of letting people create their own commerce. Because Smith spoke of "self-interest," his views are interpreted as being aligned with business. Voters, confused by the economic concepts, accept a "them or us" concept and usually vote for spending. At election time, politicians who create government jobs can brandish their own effectiveness and boast of how they helped the economy.

This precept of spending to improve the economy has fostered the belief that no matter how money is spent, money stokes the economic fires. Politicians not only exult spending but also emphasize that longevity in office puts them in a better position to obtain it. This point of view is supported *ad infinitum* by the success of re-election and the seniority systems in the legislatures of government. The economists, with their monetary-based view of economics, support this position; only occasionally is there a concern for wasted government spending. Only unnecessary projects that contradict correct political views are recounted, but wasted labor is never mentioned, with the focus being on money. The need for government stimuli is taken for granted. In this view, labor is unlimited and can be wasted because even with stimulus, there are always people out of work.

Keynes believed that demand was more important than "the level of employment," as in classical economics. He suggested burying bottles of money and allowing workers to dig them up to stimulate the economy. This sounds like a ridiculous idea, as even Keynes believed that economic stimulation should only occur when unemployment is high. High or low, politicians interpret the unemployment rate as always high and the economy as needing constant stimulation. To the contrary, if Keynes suggested using this strategy during high unemployment, he would have encouraged increasing the labor supply when unemployment was low.

A Keynesian interpretation extolled by a bureaucrat in 1994 was that the disastrous Mississippi floods would be good for the flooded area because of the terrific influx of money that rebuilding would necessitate. Such a nearsighted view is a sad portrayal of catastrophe and the role of government. The bureaucrat did not account for the loss of capital, structures, and personal goods, much less those that were irreplaceable. This callous remark displays vividly the lack of emotion, with an emphasis on money rather than people, in solving problems. When money is the answer, people are not important. Had the Mississippi Valley been a small country without a complex economy to support it, the effect of the disaster would have been clearer. Often, economists see the fiscal influence of government spending as necessary to reduce the cyclical effects of free enterprise. In any case, stimulation is accepted by politicians, influential members of the community, and a media that gives unenlightened support.

Keynes' speculation about burying bottles filled with bank notes included the idea that "the real income of the community would probably become a good deal larger than it is." The term "probably" suggests that Keynes was unsure of the idea he presented to desperate politicians in a time of depression. Perhaps Keynes may have reflected upon the activity that occurred during the great gold rush in the 1800s. This rare commodity is valued as a universally acceptable exchange for goods and services. Gold holds a strange fixation for most people. People can be sure of gold by its feel, its weight, and by the bite. New gold in the 1800s meant adding a trusted exchange to expedite exchanges in a time when shortages of currency existed. The gold-rush times are not valid comparisons to a depression, when cash money was readily available and acceptable. In other words, in a market that needed confidence and a method of exchange, the mining of gold and transition into gold-backed dollars guided the economy away from barter and into a dollar-based system. Gold made the economy work faster and improved productivity. Since gold was little more than a method to expedite business activity, rocks could be used as a mode of exchange if they held the trust of the people as a currency.

If we followed Keynes' thinking and used labor and money to dig gold, exchanged the gold for money, and buried the money, would things get better? Labor that could build a home or plant trees would just be wasted, and our society is long past the need for a trusted means of exchange. Comfort in life is not based on how many dollars we have but on how we spend them. Likewise, how we spend our labor is important if we are to improve our consumption. Our commitment should be to maximize production by utilizing labor efficiently. Increasing our money supply does not increase production, as it did a hundred years ago under an inefficient barter system. Production increases are directly related and facilitated by the efficient deployment of labor. The paranoia of government toward unemployment in an economy the size and complexity of the United States is absurd. Whether it's the politicians who sermonize, the media that publishes, or those who simply want to expand government, all espouse an economic theory that emphasizes spending as the motivating force of society. Rather than spending being the impetus for output, money merely directs labor to a useful or wasted purpose. As politicians are the sources from which economists derive notoriety, economic theory is too often based on the political atmosphere, rather than on absolute truth. Citizens echo this belief when they vote for big spenders.

We elect good talkers and merely ponder good thinkers;
rarely are they the same.

When we elect our congressional representatives, we also elect our economic theory. Shifting concern from the management of money to the management of labor is a must in solving the social, environmental, and economic difficulties of society. If government managed its own labor, rather than money and the economy, business cycles would be inconsequential, and consumption would fulfill our dreams.

If labor is important, then the success of an economy is a function of the efficiency, availability, and ability to match employee with employer. When labor is perceived as a limited supply, the theories of economics change. The beliefs of Adam Smith and John Maynard Keynes were based on their observations and their study of the history of business and economics. They could not have studied the functions of developed (i.e., *complex*) economies, wherein employee occupations are incredibly diverse, thus creating additional opportunities for work. Free enterprise has evolved to a point that bears resemblance to its past only in basic economic functions. In comparing one hundred years ago to today, one can only say that the economy was simple then, and today it is complex. It is so complex that it no longer functions as a single economy. Society functions as if there are economies within economies, wherein industries and communities are in differing stages of economic expansion or contraction.

The attempt to stimulate the economy has also spawned an effort to redistribute wealth. But wealth is merely a measurement of the capability to produce and cannot be distributed. Rather than a redistribution of wealth, redistribution is a reallocation of private-labor production. In other words, redistribution is a transfer of consumable goods and services to non-producers. The transfer of money from private worker to nonproducer affects only private workers, who must make good the non-producers' purchasing rights or suffer inflationary pressure and subsequent loss of income. Keynesian economic interpretations also supported the distribution of wealth. Keynesians believe that by increasing earning, pension, or other rewards of government-supported groups, the economy is stimulated to produce these items at the expense of the rich, who are taxed to pay for the increase. It should be obvious, however, that the rich, who may own a great deal of the wealth, still receive only a fraction of total production as profits and could not afford to support even a fraction of the pensioners and welfare recipients who are the government's beneficiaries. Likewise, if we study just the taxes paid by businesses, it is indubitably obvious that taxes increase business costs, and businesses must earn a profit on that cost, as they do other costs.

Attempted redistributions of wealth by government enhance the profits of the rich at the expense of the worker.

Wealth is enhanced at the expense of the worker, not distributed at the expense of the rich.

To examine this we can use the prior formula to determine wealth. Stock traded on the open market is generally valued by reflection on the earnings of a business, which in most economic situations reflects sales. As we relate value to sales, we can relate sales to production. The value of these businesses is therefore directly related to the production. Repeating the above formula, total production is determined thus:

Production per producer	x	number of workers	=	total production
a	x	b	=	c1

The value of a business is basically determined as follows:

Net income from production
----------------------------- = Value (Wealth)
Market capitalization rate

Net income reflects a gain on costs, and as taxes to redistribute wealth eventually reflect in the cost of production, wealth is enhanced when government taxes.

Society's goal is generally to improve individual livelihoods. Today, lives are less often gauged by wealth and more often by consumption. Consumption, however, is a function of production, and production is a function of the productivity, and productivity is based on the availability of labor. Stimulating demand by creating worthless jobs or restricting labor reflects a view that workers are unlimited and do not factor into production.

Unemployment is the excuse for most efforts to redistribute wealth. Some economists believe in a core level of unemployment, an understanding that should be implicit. Private workers, of course, have a multitude of explanations as to why they are unemployed. And unemployment levels change as the economy shifts, population moves, resources are allocated to new uses, the welfare-support level rises, and a miscellany of other causes. Because factors such as these change, the base level of unemployment changes. For many, the incentive to work is less than the government-paid incentives not to. Therefore, real unemployment figures don't include all that are of working age and condition. Instead of a system intended to provide temporary assistance, welfare raises the core level of unemployment. Complex societies with complex job structures need labor pools to support and facilitate productivity and the changing consumer demands. Restrictions on labor thus cause only higher levels of unemployment, as matching the worker to complex job requirements is already difficult. Welfare that results in permanent support also results in a permanent loss of production, due to an unnecessary shortage of labor. This lost production, combined with the government effort to redistribute consumption, causes a downward spiral of compensation for private workers, who must increase efficiency to enhance non-producer consumption because fewer are working.

We now come back to the question:

To get more of one thing, do we have to give up something else?

If the answer to question is yes, then consumer production must be lost when government allocates labor to its own causes or pays labor not to work.

**Because total production is a function of available labor,
all theories must be guided by the efficient use and the economics of labor.**

While we have attacked the concept of wasting labor to stimulate the economy, there still lingers the concern of Keynes and the politicians that free enterprise does not always function and cannot account for all economic activity, as was observed in the 1929 Depression. Perhaps what Keynes did not see in the Depression was a ***Transitional economy***. He may have been accurate in his observation that free enterprise, "supply-side economics," does not account for all economic activity. His observation may have been as those of a man standing in a flood and believing it to be a river. His observation was accurate, but his summation was not. Keynes wrote of "the economy." He said that "the economy is not like a moving seesaw, which will always right itself. Rather, it is like an elevator, which could be rising, lowering, or simply standing still at the bottom of a shaft."

What if "the economy" no longer functioned as a single economy? He could certainly be accurate about the elevator, but with several economies, like elevators, when one is going down, another is coming up. If the current economy represents several economies within a greater economy, then labor would always be in demand, and the greatest problem would be matching jobs to skills and location. Complexity also means diversity, and diversity means increasing the opportunity for ideas. Specifically, ideas come from individuals. As the opportunities for new businesses expand, so, too, do the jobs. If labor is restricted from entry into the workforce by the level of welfare payments or tied up in unnecessary jobs, the expansion of the workforce in useful endeavors is restricted. Since the population hasn't reached the maximum level of consumption, the opportunities for expansion still exist. Perhaps this may seem an absurd statement, but those who have had their businesses restrained by the lack of willing workers or by the cost of a worker find welfare an asinine answer to a country whose basket is not yet full.

Still, we have not explained why there was unemployment of such magnitude during the 1929 Depression. Adam Smith did not explain it, either. He spoke about individuals pursuing "their own self-interest" in commerce and trade. Self-interest is described as the "motivating force in a free market system." Societies that were 90 percent rural had limited transportation for marketing goods or for buying them, and most people, of necessity, could look forward to owning their own farmland. It was easy to imagine everyone with their own businesses. But in the economy of today, most individuals work for someone else. A broader view might show that the functioning rules of economics are the same for a thousand individuals with a thousand businesses, as with a thousand individuals with one business. However, it is inaccurate to suggest that economies are the same today as a hundred years ago or during the Depression. The Depression represents a period in between, a *Transitional* period, a period when workers went from a dominant single and *rural* occupation to one involving a limited mix of occupations. We can hypothesize that the transition from a rural to a complex economy caused difficulties, because the *Transitional* economy did not offer enough alternative occupations to circumvent the difficulties of an interdependent society. In the transition, production and investment could have been out of alignment with worker levels or consumer demands, thereby causing significant unemployment. In other words, the economy could have operated much like Keynes' single elevator. If this is an accurate assessment of the Depression, then the explanations that jobs created by government in our Complex economy are beneficial is built upon a false premise.

In other words, if the Depression resulted from the misunderstanding or mishandling due to ignorance, or if it was an unavoidable phase in the development of free enterprise, then the Keynesian-encouraged solutions of job creation are wrong—not only wrong but harmful to the advancement of living standards in a *Complex* society. With government expropriations of labor, total production would be less than the potential. The unneeded military bases, the construction of government buildings when others stand empty, the inefficient use of technology, and countless other superfluous expenditures will continue, as long as the politician interprets this spending as "good for the economy." Not even Keynes intended this. He said the State should function as a "catalyst" to repair the economy without actually dominating it.

As the transfer of workers to welfare and legislated jobs continues, inflation, followed by recession and lower wages for private workers, will be the result of government stimulus, not of private sector fluctuations.

Government stimulus doesn't allow for the labor needed for the production it encourages.

We also need to consider that the extent of government labor usage includes more than welfare and nonessential jobs. Government labor usage includes growth from bureaucratic expansion, federal mandates to state and local governments, law and rule changes that private enterprise must pay for, legal entanglements encouraged by laws, and on and on. It is implicit that government expenditures consume manpower and money but do not add product to the economy. As stimulus increases, demand for consumables increase. When demand exceeds the productivity of a dwindling workforce, the government's first right of assessing the economy forces the private workers to suffer the difference. The rich may lose dollars to taxes but will not likely reduce consumption. In other words, when production needs surpass the workers' efficiency, the private workers' earnings are adjusted down to facilitate lower consumption. The favored members in the community, those supported by government beneficence, will not suffer. Inflation results from this imbalance of labor with demand. The spending attitudes, so often blamed for inflation, are merely reflections of happy faces with an excess of government dollars.

In Complex economies, each micro-economy can suffer a recession without noticeable changes in indicators that represent mere averages. As private employees of one community suffer and lose earnings, others can have achieved a balance at new lower income levels. The lack of national recessions masks the loss of consumption for the private worker, who has been deprived of dollars by tax increases, inflation, and government regulation. For the government-benefited recipient, the maintenance of income is little more than a Ponzi scheme. The end of higher benefits will come when the efficiencies of private enterprise and imports cannot keep up or when too many workers find inflation-enhanced welfare more attractive than wages. A force acting on the economy as prominent as government is a serious threat to the forces of free enterprise. If government fails to become efficient, economic expansion could be shunted or cut off. Lost potential production can never be regained. The force and size of government is so significant that in an economy so diverse, economic failure will be the fault of government.

The natural function of free enterprise, coupled with the incredible diversity of a Complex economy, blends the economic forces that produce unemployment and employment. A government that may control more than 50 percent of the economy has a commanding presence. Its expansive reallocations of labor can be devastating. The redirecting of labor is in conflict with natural economic forces engendered in the desires of the populace. Even small additions to the benefits of the significant portion of the population supported by government can have devastating affects on the private worker's income.

The economy should be managed, based on the volume of labor in hourly and traditional monetary terms, with concerns for the resultant cost-benefit ratios. In other words, if welfare saves lives, how many lives in the private sector will be lost due to stress and anxiety? The popularity of today's decision leaves yesterdays casualties without a voice.

All things have a price that is often ignored
by those who balance the scale to enrich their own ego.

Those who support single issues will ignore
chaos to achieve their own goals.

The cost of government growth should be represented by the number of workers lost to more productive endeavors, not by the dollars paid by the rich.

In a community where the mobility of money is inefficient, as in the 1800s and where high unemployment or poor efficiency and/or utilization of labor existed, proper and useful stimulation can enable an economy. The *Complex* developed communities of today are too elaborate and active for government to provide any more than inane stimulus. As this type of funding outlasts any potential benefit, government stimulus supports the Ponzi scheme, while crippling production increases. Taking from those not supplemented by government and giving to those who are puts these beneficiaries in a continuum advantage. As in all such Ponzi schemes, it is not feasible for new entrants to achieve the same rewards. As for the United States and other Complex societies, this scheme, without incredible innovation, is nearing its natural end. With the presumption that labor is the primary factor that influences an economy, the rules that guide it should be based on the importance of the worker. The following observations are thus made:

A. Government taxes and regulation reduce productivity but enhance wealth for the rich because the workers' incomes are driven down to compensate for the increased burden that results in lower productivity. The incomes and wealth of the rich become greater when compared to those of the average worker, giving the appearance that the rich are getting richer and the worker getting poorer. Real wealth only increases when real productivity increases.

B. Economic production is dependent on the imagination, efficiency, and innovation of labor, and the direction or encouragement of incentives. The complexity of the economy increases the number of opportunities for jobs and wealth. Productivity advances resulting from innovation and efficiency are directly related to the population of the universe that practices free enterprise.

C. The incentive of wealth acts to fulfill the needs of the consumer in the most efficient manner and without a cost to consumers. The excess consumption earned by innovative and efficient producers is a fraction of the value of the overall production increase.

D. A Complex society is one in which products have differentiated in such a way that substitutes exist for nearly every product and from sufficient sources, so that no single supply controls the market. The expanse and diversity of employment is great enough that variances caused by efficiency and innovation do not materially affect unemployment rates. A Complex society operates as if there are several Complex economies functioning simultaneously.

E. In a Complex free-enterprise society, the creation of employment is spontaneous, but the diversity of job classifications causes a matching problem. The search for employment is a random walk. The search for employees is a random walk. The process is, therefore, a random walk in a random walk. Complex societies use labor to its maximum potential, subject to the difficulties of skill-matching.

F. Labor and revenue act to fulfill the needs of government first because of government's higher financial rating and absolute right of assessment. After the needs of the government are filled, private enterprise is allotted what remains.

G. In an efficient economy, all job classifications are important and are allocated a share of consumables, based on job complexity, demand, innovation, and supply of labor. Where labor is used efficiently, the failure to fill less-skilled positions reduces the efficiency above.

H. Welfare is an inefficient utilization of labor that impairs productivity and thus the potential of the community and the worker. There is a direct relationship between the maintenance level of welfare recipients to the incomes of workers and the number of recipients. Welfare reduces the desirability of work by penalizing earnings. Government does not compare the benefits of not working to the rewards for working in analyzing welfare support.

I. The lowest valued labor supports the basic structure of a community, and shortages can have a serious economic impact.

J. A foreign trade deficit in a Complex society is a reflection of inefficient labor allocation and/or a demand for the country's currency in a less complex world market. In a world composed mostly of Complex economies, where currencies are true reflections of the ability to produce, significant trade deficits reflect either inefficient labor allocations, the failure of the economy to stay abreast of competing economies, or investment that reflects the above conditions.

K. Money in a Complex society is sufficient to meet the demands for exchange as it is deployed to a near-maximum utilization. Therefore, government usage of money to redirect labor from the consumer's intended preference should be justified as to need and purpose.

L. The wealth of a nation is the value of its ability to produce. Because income reflects the growth in efficiency and innovation, wealth reflects normal profits plus the value of the potential to increase productivity. The greater the growth in wealth, the greater the expectation for an increase in the standard of living.

M. Wealth is enhanced by productive or nonproductive costs. Wealth of the rich is far greater in comparison to the average individual in an economy with inefficient labor allocations.

N. Only economies that understand the functions of free enterprise have markets that mirror the wealth of a nation.

O. Mature, Complex economies develop high levels of service industries, while manufacturing declines in importance. Because of the complexity of the economy, this transition does not have the same impact as in the transition from *Rural* to *Transitional.* An inefficient government will result in additional exploitation of the average worker by government.

P. The forces of supply and demand are less meaningful in a Complex society with multitudes of choices and competition. Competition and the availability of labor are greater forces. Any good or service is always more valuable to the buyer.

There is a utopian point in the economy where a comfortable subsistence can occur at low earning levels, when compared to the average consumption of the community. No economy has as yet reached this level, nor will it, as long as government disrupts the economy with wasted stimulus and exploits the benefits of efficiency that should flow to the worker. The interference is a constant disruption in the market system, as labor and benefits shift from producer to non-producer. Cost of living adjustments do not correlate with the average of private-sector earning changes. The reason is that government dips in the private workers' pockets to pay government beneficiaries for the costs that it created. This action effectively shifts the added government costs to workers in the private sector.

It is implausible that a single innovation could occur in a Complex economy that would allow private workers to outpace government expansionism. It is possible, however, that government could downsize significantly, while attaining the same or higher levels of service. If this were to happen, the living standards of the population would gain significantly. In the current circumstances, we are more likely to have an economy that stagnates from inflation. Each major or minor cycle reflects a worsening of the ratio of productive to nonproductive population. The release of labor into the market to enhance productivity has not been an option, due to the politician's propensity to seek solutions for societal problems with no regard for the economic consequences and their related costs to productive labor. This juggling of the economy puts private workers on a continuum to a lower economic scale while stagnating advances for non-producers. The intention for good, the desire to redistribute, and the politicians' ambition for office translate into more work and less pay for private workers. Fewer productive workers must satisfy the needs of an ever-growing number of government and government-mandated employees.

We can follow the logic that as the percentage of government workers inclines and as the welfare roles expand, people who actually produce food, transportation, shelter, clothing, and joy and happiness will be allowed to keep less and less of what they produce. Those whose earnings are not protected by government guarantees are guaranteed lower wages, unless market efficiency can keep pace with government expansion. This explains many of the phenomena that occur in the current economy, such as why only government unions have been effective, why imports have increased, why product quality became a problem, and, of course, why the standard of living has declined for many over the last few decades. The only positive result has been the forced input into production of more and more labor-saving devices. But these are only attempts to make up for losses of labor due to expropriations of labor by government. Fewer people sharing their product with a greater number does not create more wealth.

"Reallocation of economic resources by government creates a constant recycling of the private worker."

Reduce the size of government, increase labor for production, and living standards will increase.

In a period such as the late '80s, the computer, mobile telephone, and the fax machine helped magnify efficiencies that allowed for government growth and a drop in inflation and interest rates, something most economists didn't believe could happen. But it also followed a recession that was created by the problems and inflation of the '70s. The recycling of labor that began in the recession of the early '80s continues today. Private workers never saw the standard-of-living increases that the terrific efficiencies of the last decade and a half should have brought. Rather than increases, millions saw declines from lower wages and longer hours. For many, the change in living standards was abrupt and resulted in the loss of homes, transportation, savings, and incredible declines in people's lives.

CHAPTER 2

WHAT EVER HAPPENED TO THE "FREE" IN FREE ENTERPRISE

Capitalism is the more common term for free enterprise. But "free enterprise" suggests its origins—a system invented by free humankind. And as free enterprise cannot exist without free humankind, so humankind cannot be free without free enterprise. It is a simple system in which we benefit ourselves by benefiting others. Those who work will produce enough in their chosen occupation for other workers and for those who don't produce.

Free enterprise competed against and overcame a world of Communism while the news media bantered it, the politicians mocked it, and the educators called it unfair. People complain of the wealthy that free enterprise creates, but they want the wealthy to pay all the taxes and create all the jobs. The only ones who like the system are the ones who don't have it. Nurtured by the Pilgrims and cared for until the American Revolution, despite every effort to denounce it for causing the ills of the world, free enterprise is spreading. It is amazing free enterprise survives. The United States has always been a country from which all can freely leave, yet to which millions tempt death to be a part of it. In small and leaky boats, over barbed wire, through the hail of bullets, stowed away in the hulls of ships and the wheel wells of airplanes, immigrants have been a continuing testament to those of us who love the free-enterprise system and a confusion to those who don't. Obviously, free enterprise functions well; it is **governance** we can't get right!

In addition to the challenges from other systems, our politicians have manipulated government and caused difficulties by their constant propensity to change things. Prepare for star wars; prepare for no wars. Construction fuels the economy; it fuels inflation. Oil shale is the future; now, not even a thought. We are going to the stars; we can't leave earth. Feed the poor, starving world; no, feed our own poor. Regulate business; regulation is unfair. Save the earth; save the bureaucracy. We need to reduce the foreign trade deficit, but we expand welfare and pay workers not to work. Politicians play the economy, just as Nero played his fiddle. As the fiddle plays, we dance on the ashes. People are expendable because we have welfare, so when the owls have to be saved, the human's way of life doesn't need to be preserved. In politics, little has changed in three thousand years. The politicians create war to hold onto power, and the loyal subjects fight. But now the fight isn't with guns; we use our families, our friends, and our lifestyle. The battle is to maintain our living standard, the workers' way of life.

Americans have heard since birth that the American dream is real—that if we work hard, we can enjoy life, prosper, and look forward to a better future. It is not within us to be discouraged or to settle for the same old amenities year after year. We expect improvements in our life, and when they are threatened, we simply work harder. Hard work and time are supposed to make things easier. Today, however, private workers feel—and often comment—that they are working harder and getting less for their effort. In the past, workers have been maligned by cycles that make it hard to keep up. Many new job entrants, even under union-negotiated agreements, are accepting less for the same work that employees with job seniority are doing. New workers don't anticipate achieving earnings parity with older workers, and they wonder about receiving the same retirement benefits as older generations. Conversely, where once government workers struggled to keep up, they now receive the best pay, the most job protection, the most benefits, and the most vacation, and they enjoy an infinitesimal job turnover rate. Though unions have lost members, the strongest union ever includes only government employees. General liability insurance rates, employer payroll taxes, workers compensation, business taxes, and health insurance are high and growing at rates well in excess of inflation. While the politicians tell us these benefits are not costs that the employees pay, someone else's employees pay for them when they buy our employers' goods. And we are all someone else's employee.

Government supports directly about 20 percent of the workforce and indirectly as much as another 20 percent in the private sector to provide government orders for military hardware, office supplies, engineering, hammers, textbooks, and chairs. In addition, over the last forty years, private labor has been committed to clean air, clean water, integration, concern for the environment, the largest and the best-paid attorney-to-citizen ratio in the world, welfare payouts, Social Security, health care, many jobs once done by government, OSHA, and OH-sht, here they come again. Just about every thing we buy, sell, or do is now regulated by some local, state, or federal agency; or an industry association which association is subjected to regulation.

Despite the enormous size of government, most of the politicians who govern us have less work experience than grocery store stock boys. Private workers would find the lack of business sense in government too hopeless to manage. Politicians with political and law degrees learned as much or more about "playing" politics as about the governance of people. Experienced business managers hold few bureaucratic or political positions—a situation the news media ensures by haranguing political candidates who have private work experience. Politicians and the media degrade candidates from the private sector through humiliation and admonishment that politics should be left to the professional politician.

This idea that only "professional politicians" are desirable to represent us in government is an insult to the concept of freedom and a trifling of democracy. It is the media's intent to ridicule capitalism with the subtle warning that the interests of capitalism are not the interests of the people. As with all hard-working jackasses that pull the wagons or the plow, the media believes the worker should be corralled when the crop is divided, for fear they will engorge themselves on the harvest. It is not capitalism the politicians and media fear; it is workers they intend to control.

Our freedom has evolved to a system that provide for a government
And not a government that that manages a system.

In order to control advocates of free enterprise and the interest of the worker, colloquialism, not intelligence, is the weapon. Simple terms are employed, yet they are words that convey no real meaning or intellectual thought. Comments are used that question our mental aptitude or that of our candidate, implying that the candidate is "a joke," or "You don't believe that, do you?" or "The other guy is a crook," or "They are all crooks anyway." Our cynical friends will protect their own iniquitous politicians while standing ready to debase the opposition for a crooked smile. The remarks are intended to sound common, yet obvious and without need of evidence, as only a fool would question the thought. When they are questioned, the fools with whom we speak find explanations difficult and trite.

The legal profession has been the substitute for not electing working people, so instead of farmers and doctors, executives and laborers, mothers and maidens, builders and carpenters, union bosses and business kings, the legislatures are filled with lawyers. With so many lawyers in Congress, is it a wonder that we are the most litigious country in the world? Why shouldn't workers have a part in the decisions of this country? It is the workings of free enterprise that made this United States great and solved the problems of the world. It is not government that has been so successful.

The media suppresses politically incorrect deliberation and with it, intelligent and open debate of business and economic thought. The media-generated fever to support socialism puts freedom of expression on the level of a Dark Age taboo. Whereas engineering inventiveness has moved us to other planets, the inspiration in economic thought leaves us in the eighteenth century. Free enterprise has proved itself against all other economic systems—Fascism, Communism, feudalism, all of which free enterprise has defeated in peace and in war. Yet the media has given politicians the credit for the successes that our economic system should receive. Having shifted credence to the government, the politicians retain office by taking credit for things they didn't do and get elected making promises they can't keep. It is certain we are not in an era like the age of Aristotle or Socrates. Today, vitamins and cattle flatulence is given more media attention and prominence than the complexities of economics. Contemporary economists do little more than offer positive explanations for politically correct actions already taken. They profess, "It's good for the economy." Economics represents the only profession in which college graduates are experts—which to the politicians, they are. The greatest outrage caused by our dominant media is that jobs and reputations are too often dependent on correct political views and not on accurate and intelligent interpretations.

Socialism could be the last adversary of free humankind. But it is a far different opponent than Communism or Fascism. When an economic system controls an entire country, it is easier to count the bodies and the empty stores. Socialism is a cancer that grows from within. It is devious and devastates its opponents by blaming the economic host for the ill it creates. When programs fail, its bureaucrats decry the lack of funds or the failure of the economic system. Socialists no doubt believe what they say; their idealism is sincere. They also believe that the simple platitudes they use protect them from perceived contaminated logic. Their idealism protects them only from reason, and as true believers, they will never accept being wrong. It would be harder still for Socialists to understand that their effort encumbers the many that receive the benefits they advocate. But Socialist guidance must be subdued before those who receive their larder from socialism too far outnumber those who fill the storehouse. It is not the rich we need fear; we need protection from those whom we nurture.

Fifty years ago, the cost to play a round of golf was less than a dollar, not much more than minimum wage. A game of pocket pool only cost a dime, and novices paid by the rack, not the hour. Mill workers talked about four-day workweeks; we went to college so we wouldn't have to work in the mills, but we believed the mill job would always be there. Shoe shines were ten cents and worth fifty in pride. Kids could buy a car for a hundred bucks; insurance for a sixteen-year-old was another hundred, and "uninsured motorist coverage" wasn't on the policy. The rent for a small apartment was less than fifty dollars. The interest rates small businesses paid had something to do with inflation, and "strong as a dollar" was a common phrase. Subsidized building projects were "clean up, fix up, paint up" campaigns put on by the local Junior Chamber of Commerce (the Jaycees). Goods made by our "buyer beware" system were better quality than most products in our "Big Brother will protect you society." It was a time before Big Brother gave us the inflation that destroyed the quality that the white knight we voted for took credit for bringing back.

The old way wasn't better because the rich weren't taking advantage of us or because the government gave us welfare and subsidies. It was better because we less fortunate lived in a system that encouraged us and didn't tell us that we were deprived. Most of us didn't know what the rich had that we didn't. We made games out of tin cans, played basketball through a coat hanger on the door, and vacationed at Grandma's. Grandma was the only welfare worker anyone ever knew and most ever needed, and if we didn't have a grandma of our own, we could use someone else's. Paying people not to work was as shameless as accepting money for not working.

Today, despite inflation of less than 3 percent, government grows at the rate of 8 percent. The guaranteed wages and support paid by government outstrip wages of the private workers, who are getting less pay for more work. The statistics confuse us because all the indices that suggest we are better off are averages. But some workers are "averaging up," while others are "averaging down." More women have entered the workforce, and more men have left. Women supposedly are exercising their rights, but most are married mothers who now must help the family budget. And if women need work, what happened to the men? As parents separate to obtain welfare, people are perplexed, because jobs don't pay as well as they did for Dad. They blame each other, not the government, putting stress on the marriage. The role of husband and wife is no longer clear, as couples search for answers. Separated parents refuse or are unable to pay court-ordered child support. The young, aspiring rich obtain wealth, then lose it in the next recession. Middle-income groups diminish. Those in lower economic and skill levels find jobs, then lose them as growth in government brings the change that turns good jobs into threatened industries. The worker, cooked and chewed up, is spit out, recycled, discouraged, and credit-disabled. The lack of a self-employed tradition and banks that limit entrepreneurial lending make it difficult to cope in the New World. Our new social system saves Grandma from living with the kids or even from an early grave. But our brothers and sisters lay silent in the city morgue, live in a fantasy world high on drugs, languish in prison, or worse, prey on others, as a government-appointed paid attorney keep the criminals out of jail.

We live in a country with a strong belief that anyone can make it, and the actualities are that many do. Our arrogance perhaps has something to do with our failure to see the question. Is someone giving up something for more government? The real answer is that some are and some aren't, but it is not being given up; it is being taken.

The oldest and most basic concept of economics is that to get more of one thing, we must give up something else. There are challenges to this concept but inevitably, production is tied to labor. Therefore, if government requires more labor, fewer workers will provide for our consumption. We limit labor by granting special privileges to those who don't work, and because fewer of us work, production declines. Today, each U.S. worker is more efficient than ever, yet only the party in office professes that living standards are increasing, while statistics suggest that our incomes are shrinking. One economist commented, quite honestly but nescient, that at the rate efficiency is growing, we would be able to keep up with government growth. The statement relates acceptance of the taking from the private workers. Instead of all workers enjoying an increasing living standard, private workers suffer to keep even or are losing ground. Workers, to survive, must endeavor to be efficient. Government rules the biggest and best pasture, leaving the rest for the Indians. As the grazing gets sparse, the herd grows weaker, and those who prey upon them grow stronger—for a while, at least.

More equitable taxing and more inequitable sharing cannot overcome the failure of our living standards to grow. The basic of labor economics is that we need to add to the number producing and reduce the number not producing. Consequently, fewer would live off the work of others, and more would help free enterprise do what it does best.

The problems in the U.S. are the same problems that other developed countries are experiencing or will experience. It is not up to the U.S. to solve their problems, to feed the world population, or to build their roads. It is up to us, the U.S., as the leader of free enterprise, to lead the way and show other countries how to do for themselves what we should be doing for ourselves. Our greatness stems from freedom, not socialism. Free enterprise is the proven best solution for preserving the environment, solving the problems of overpopulation, starvation, health, energy, and prejudice, and for peace in the world, proven to all but the politicians and the media.

RULES OF FREE ENTERPRISE

- The only resources in society are labor and money.
- Money is a medium used to motivate labor and to facilitate the barter system.
- Efficiency and innovation increase the ability of a society to produce and, therefore, to consume. Consumption, adjusted for imports and exports, is in proportion to production,
- Total production varies directly with the ratio of the population that provides goods and services.
- Inflation is created by the increase in the proportion of the population dedicated to a non-productive function or production, either by the allocation of labor or re-allocation of production.
- Government is a cost to society and reduces productivity and, thus, consumption.
- Free enterprise is deflationary.
- Wealth is created when our ability to produce expands and is therefore unlimited.
- Our standard of living increases when our ability to produce increases (the absolute value of wealth equates to our standard of living).
- Solutions for saving the environment will best be found by free humankind practicing free enterprise.

CHAPTER 3

HOW GOVERNMENT UNDERSTATES ITS SIZE WHY TAXES ARE REALLY PAID BY PRODUCTIVE PRIVATE-SECTOR WORKERS AND NOT THE RICH HOW TAX LAWS ENCOURAGE WASTED RESOURCES

The most accepted and most important of all economic equations appears as one of the simplest: the calculation of gross domestic product (GDP). GDP is a summation intended by the economists to determine the total product of an economy. While the term GDP is not widely recognized, changes from period to period are recognized as guide posts by investors and politicians. For the these groups it signals a growing economy or perhaps one in recession, thus having the single greatest impact on the amount and direction of private as well as public spending, This formula is taught in high school and is considered much too rudimentary to be doubted. The economists have two methods used to determine GDP. Below is the first:

Personal Consumption Expenditures (PCE)

(This figure represents gross sales in the economy and includes state sales taxes and all taxes paid out directly or indirectly through businesses and the individual.)

Plus

Gross Private Domestic Investment (GPDI)

(This represents nonresidential and residential investments)

Plus

Government Purchases of Goods and Services (GPGS)

(Not including social payments (transfers) such as Social Security)

Plus/minus

An adjustment for imports/exports

Equals

Gross Domestic Product (GDP)

When total local, state, and federal tax collections are divided by GDP the result becomes the percentage of the economy taxes supposedly consume. In other words, this figure is supposed to represent how much of each dollar that we spend that goes to government. In 1993, that figure was about 34 percent or one in every three dollars. The Economist's method of computation is questionable in that it adds in the cost of government as a product, when the taxes used to pay these costs are already included in personal consumption expenditures (PCE). The effect is to add government costs as a product and to add those same costs into PCE. Not only is the size and growth in our economy overstated, but the amount of taxes per dollar taken out by government is understated. Instead of one of every three dollars, the figure is closer to one in every two dollars.

In addition to the potential understatement reflected above, when calculating the size of government, many costs are not included. These include costs once paid directly by government that have been transferred to the private sector, private-sector costs that have been added with the enactment of laws and regulations, costs for litigation that have been enacted upon the citizens by legislative and court decree, and assessments dumped into the private sector by way of special fees or lotteries, which often replace or supplement government spending.

In simple terms, government purchases of goods and services (GPGS) appears to be only a shadow of the cost to support the enormous government bureaucracy and the demands placed upon the private citizens by government. Besides results that don't consider costs the government has required of the private sector, this computation assumes that everything paid out by government is an addition to the product of the country. We may feel that maintaining a public park or education for our children is a service that should reflect in our personal consumption, but these costs as well as the national defense or our police force, no matter how necessary, are current expenses that maintain our system and which cost is realized through our purchases. These services are paid through businesses or out of the incomes we receive from those businesses. For example, through our purchases we pay real estate, intangible, excise, and gasoline taxes; corporate and other taxes that to a business is just a cost of operations. Out of the personal incomes reflected as a cost to business we likewise pay taxes. Thus, whether we make a purchase or pay taxes directly, we recognize GPGS as a personal consumption. Adding it again, by adding GPGS to GDP, results in including it twice.

There are other considerations as well; for example, purchases we make at the store are subjected to competitive forces, which force businesses tot be cost-conscious. Our jobs depend upon the profitability of our employer, but that is not so in government. Governments don't compete in that way and can raise taxes to supplement costs when not competitive. If too many people move out of our city because the city isn't competitive, not only may our taxes go up but our property may lose value or even become worthless, creating an invisible tax. In other words, the taxpayers suffer the consequences of government actions without our government suffering the risks found in the private sector. Therefore, true economic growth is reflected in our standard of living and not in the size of government.

Another way of looking at this, for those who are somewhat familiar with accounting, is that the computation of GDP should be a consolidation of a country's financial position to determine its total product. In the accepted method of determining sales, sales to consumers are totaled up to arrive at PCE. Such total reflects all costs, including the taxes that these businesses pay. In the computation of PCE, the value added by one business to the product when sold to another is eliminated to avoid duplication in the final figure for PCE. It is the ultimate sale to the consumer that is included in GDP. When we compute GDP, the taxes paid by the business and its employees are included in the cost of the product sold to a consumer, and just as in purchases from one business by another, this is value added.

The tax that businesses pay is costs for which the payee (the government) is just another business, presumably adding value to the product. We could look at government spending to see what the money was used for, but in a consolidation a cost is only added once. The U.S. government treats the computation of GDP like a consolidation, except when it comes to its own revenues/costs. In an apparent effort to show that government has a value, government's consumption is added to consumer purchases.

This same method appears to be applied elsewhere, in that business investment (GPDI) and the share of the sales price that represents capital cost (the amortization of business investment) are both included in the computation of GDP. This, too, is a double inclusion of business investment and distorts GDP and, likewise, leads to understating government's size. Only when the investments by businesses exceed the profits retained and the noncash deductions (cash flow) would a figure for GPDI show up in GDP. As profits are generally invested back into the business, the capital costs would be expected to exceed cash flow, and GPDI would generally be a positive figure.[1]

This fault may become clearer for some when the alternate method of computing GDP, called the Resource Cost-Income Approach, is examined.

The Resource Cost-Income Approach is summed up by adding the following:

The items below are gross before taxes and include expenditures on capital production. Don't forget that government wages (included in employee compensation below) are paid from tax revenue.

Employee compensation (wages)
(Includes capital production)
Proprietor's income
Rents
Corporate profits
Interest income
Indirect business taxes
Depreciation
(Represents capital consumption)
GNP-GDP adjustment
(Minus net income earned abroad)

Equal

Gross Domestic Product

This computation used by the economists also appears as a logical summation of product, except when we consider that all employee compensation and business profits are included, in addition to an amount called indirect business taxes. This gives us a clue to the realization that employee compensa-

1 Economists were questioned on the above revelations, even those who followed and used GDP results. None, however, had ever questioned, nor actually spent the time to analyze the seventy-plus-year-old computation. It is apparently too basic to be questioned.

tion, proprietor's income, rents, and corporate profits are pretax numbers. Since employee compensation and business income are before-tax figures, and employee compensation includes government wages, it is obvious that GDP includes both the revenue and expenditures of government and, therefore, duplicate the government input into the economy. Both depreciation for business capital and all wages including those wages creating an asset are also included.[2] Also, since profits and proprietor's income are often invested back into the business and those investments are composed of wages, adding both in results in the duplication of inputs. The computation is a confusion of cash and accrual basis accounting and is not one a skilled accountant would endorse. The economists produce numbers from each of these two methods that agree in order to prove their methods. The flaws in one merely offset the flaws in the other.

Another inconsistency is that wages and profits are added into GDP. Whereas profits and borrowed capital are usually spent on capital goods or capitalized research which cost reflects in the wage figure. The calculation becomes a hodgepodge of numbers.

These methods have been used with some variations for over seventy years.[3] The computation of GDP is something learned in basic economics and the results, which are actually an incredibly complicated summation of figures, are used without being questioned. But then not all fourteenth century Europeans questioned whether the world was flat, the Aztecs never developed the keystone and after a thousand years the Romans didn't have fireworks. Arguments (assumptions) such as this exist in even today's scientific world presenting barriers we must overcome.

WHY IS THIS IMPORTANT?

To begin with, if citizens really knew how much of their hard-earned dollars was controlled by government, they would likely revolt against further increases and demand that government cut spending and the regulations that inflict significant costs on their spending. Most politicians will claim that a shortage of government services is the fault of the rich and that we need to tax them ever more. But the rich don't earn or control over half of the annual cost of our consumption, and even though they control most of the wealth of the country, you can't spend wealth. Wealth is worthless when it can be taken without just compensation and where government has the right of confiscation; wealth is still worthless, just as it would be in Cuba or as it was in the USSR. ,

The next thought is, how are the GDP figures used?

1. To influence the ability of politicians to raise taxes (With spending appearing to be less a cost to the economy and with little apparent growth, politicians are encouraged to raise taxes.)
2. To gauge the size of the economy
3. To compare taxes in one country with another.
4. As a guide by the Federal Reserve to control short-term interest rates
5. To compare the size of government from one period to another

2 It is possible that this flaw has not been recognized, but both right- and left-wing political factions would have good cause for not disclosing the error. If liberal left-wing factions exposed the flaw, the massive size of government would be uncovered. On the conservative right-wing side, exposing the flaw would reduce the appearance of economic growth for a capitalist society. It is likely that neither side understands the impact that increasing government costs have on lowering wages, so neither would see any advantages in disclosure.

3 Simon Kuznet developed the method for computing GDP. The Bureau of Economic Affairs has figures for the U.S. going back to 1929.

6. To calculate changes in efficiency in the private sector
7. To measure whether government is being kept in check
8. To influence voters
9. To gauge the necessity of government spending

Unfortunately, government is currently expanding faster than inflation and our economy. If GDP is inflated, then so, too, is the growth in GDP and thus, our Federal Reserve may be stifling private capital growth because of an errant summation of total product.

A greater problem, however, is that the size of government is not only misstated, but the potential for growth and the actual growth in government is understated. And because of this false computation, the bigger government gets, the less it seems to grow. This means that if government took all income as taxes, using the current method, it would still only be about 50 percent of GDP. Therefore, government is not one-third (34 percent) of the economy; there is a hypothetical potential that it is two-thirds larger. With an accurate numerator (taxes) and denominator (GDP), the actual size of government tax collections could be nearer 45 percent, not counting the regulation and other costs forced upon the private sector. This method also distorts the change in tax revenue growth. Based on the current calculation and assuming that none of GPDS were included in GDP, taxes, instead of moving from 0 to 34 percent of GDP, would really go from 0 to 50 percent of our country's product, or fifty cents of every dollar we spend. Using the current method if taxes went from 34 to 50 percent of GDP, they would actually be going from 50 to 100 percent of product. In other words, a 34 percent change in the ratio of taxes to our product, as computed now, equates to only a 16 percent potential for change, not 66 percent. Therefore, changes in the perceived growth of government are seriously distorted as *the current computation defines a point that is impossible to reach*. Because of this anomaly, the current U.S. GDP figures cannot be used to make year-to-year comparisons, nor is our GDP comparable to any other country using the same or any other method.

The list below has been prepared to provide a visual argument to show which taxes are included in our purchases. As we review the list, let's keep in mind that federal income taxes on all levels supposedly amount to only 25 percent or 30 percent of all government revenue. The list breaks down production in terms that are not the same as those in normal accounting. It emphasizes the contribution of labor and the involvement of government. By examining this list, we can quickly deduce that an increase in taxes is a critical factor in the cost of production and, therefore, in our purchases. When viewed in this way, we can see government as a significant component of the goods we buy every day. Government, in essence, is adding to the cost of what we buy—a cost that must be recaptured in the price of a product to enable a business to survive. Whereas efforts by a worker add to the value of a product, taxes detract from the potential utility of product by raising costs.

Any consumable can be broken down as follows (Keep in mind that any one of these cost may included the others:

Corporate income net of capital expenditures

Capital expenditures above corporate income

Employee Compensation—net of taxes

Outside goods and services

Interest expense

Rent

Payroll taxes—employee and employer

Insurance and legal—payroll insurance, general liability, workers compensation, risk, product, fire, theft, etc, legal fees,

Taxes and licenses

- Federal corporation income taxes
- State, local income taxes
- Licensees
- Business fees
- Intangible, tangible, etc., taxes
- Sales and excise taxes
  - Paid by consumer
  - Paid by producer
- Gasoline and fuel taxes

Services performed to meet federal, state, and local laws, regulations and reporting

The above list is a demonstration and merely puts taxes in the perspective as a part of our purchases. Noting that each cost may included the others demonstrates that everything business buys is composed of the same costs listed here and each mostly consists of labor. This means that when a business buys paper or a desk, the business from which it was purchased paid all the expenses shown here.

Government taxes and assesses in an elaborate scheme. In 1991, for example, state and local government relied on corporate income taxes for 2 percent of tax revenues, while the federal government earned only 10 percent from this source. Simply put, the price of a candy bar varies little because of a change in the rate of corporate income taxes. Most taxes are assessed whether business or the consumers have earnings. To give this further perspective: we find that total corporate income before taxes amounted to only about 10 percent of consumer purchases, and only 20 percent of that translated into government revenue. Simply put, many taxes are hidden in our purchases.

The dollar that the worker gets is subject to a multitude of taxes, plus the workers will, in essence, reimburse business for the taxes paid by businesses with their purchases. The purpose of this discussion is to make it clear how taxes are paid and to put perspective on the impact of government.

For example, individual spending habits significantly alter the impact that government tax collection has on an individual. A wealthy taxpayer who pays large sums of income taxes but spends little may pay a small percentage of his or her income toward the cost of government. An individual in a low tax bracket, who spends all of his or her income, may pay a proportionally high share of his or her income in taxes.

The product of a country should be computed by either adding the sales price (or value as currently used) of products and adjusting for imports or by adding the costs of product consumed. After adjusting for business investment, we can manipulate one to equal the other. The current personal consumption expenditure (PCE) is close to this figure. It does not, however, include the consumer investments mentioned above. A possible way to breakdown PCE might be as follows:

PAYMENTS AND TAXES TO GOVERNMENT

Plus

PAYMENTS TO LABOR NET OF TAXES

Plus/minus

PAYMENTS TO/FROM INVESTORS

Plus/minus

PROFITS MINUS INVESTMENT

Equal

REVENUE FROM GOODS SOLD

In using this summation, we might make a more realistic assessment of the size of government, as taxes would now compare as a percentage of our consumption. The entire GDP computation, however, should be reviewed by accountants familiar with preparing consolidated financial statements. Once we determine the direct cost of government, relative to the size of the economy, we can also get a better visual picture of who actually pays the cost of government. All taxes assessed by government are included above and can be seen as reflecting in the cost of our purchases. Thus, government spending is not a separate cost that is added to the domestic product of a country. Payments by the employees and businesses are just payments to another entity (government), and government cost is thus consolidated into consumption expenditures. The cost of government computed as a percent of PCE also more easily defines its impact on inflation. We can now begin to envision how all taxes, even those paid from the earnings of a consumer, like sales taxes, reflect back into business costs. And we find that taxes reduce an employee's spendable income, which income is part of the cost of a purchase. This concept is at first difficult to grasp, it cannot be denied.

There is a second component of GDP that is included twice. Gross private domestic investment (GPDI) includes a business and a consumer figure (residential construction). The consumer figure is appropriately included in GDP as an end use product. Business investment should not be included as the price of the product would already reflect the cost of investments made by businesses. Having a figure for business investment is useful as an indicator of the prospects for growth in production after considering such things as population and government growth, but that doesn't justify its inclusion in GDP. Unfortunately because of the increasing amounts of government taxes, assessments, and mandated costs transferred to or inflicted upon the private sector and paid directly by businesses and individuals, it would be difficult to compare business investments of today to those of thirty years ago.

When a government taxes and builds a bridge, it is a government cost; if government stipulates that the private sector build and pay for the same bridge directly, it is not a cost of government.

It is interesting to note that according to the Economic Report of the President, that state and local expenditures totaled only $622 billion in 1991, and yet actual expenditures were $1,060 billion. The difference of $438 billion, 30 percent of the amount reported, is made up of borrowed funds, school tuition, liquor sales, utility sales, and other revenue. This $438 billion would translate into another 11 percent of PCE expenditures controlled directly by government. If we extrapolate from these figures, we must wonder how much spending government really controls and reinforces the need for a complete qualified review of the method for calculation GDP.

If there were no government, the reduced cost would eventually reflect in a lower cost to consumers. In a competitive marketplace, when government cuts its cost, the cost savings plus administrative costs and profits on that cost eventually pass to the consumer, not to the business in profits. Note: profits will decline when costs are lower; that is the advantage of a competitive economy. When *costs are increased by government, these are passed on,* and rather than reducing profits, business eventually earns a profit on them, as it does on all its costs. For example, if you purchase a piece of construction equipment and 60 percent of the cost stems from government taxes and regulation, the investor has to earn enough to cover repayment and make a profit on the entire investment, not just on the 40 percent.

An investor does not distinguish between costs created by government through taxation and regulation when calculating a return on investment.

Obviously, the true cost of government stretches far beyond the checks it writes. We are all well aware of government-impacted costs that employers and employees pay, such as workers compensation, general liability insurance, and waste disposal. Health insurance, as another example, bears a wide range of government-controlled costs for legal liability, the approval and use of medical instruments, and the approval of treatments and diagnosis. Real employee compensation is what the employee actually nets out of a paycheck, but the cost to business and the consumer are the totals of costs that the employee and employer pay. To put this in perspective, government may get thirty cents for every dollar the worker gets, but in Florida, for example, the added cost of workers compensation insurance can be more than 55 percent of the employees' wages. While taxes may be 30 percent of the workers earnings, workers compensation insurance might be 40 percent of the worker's paycheck. In this case, for a worker to get a dollar, the business pays $1.75. Only the naive would assume that the *employees' wages* are not impacted by these related costs, which the employer must consider before hiring an employee or making an investment.

An employee's wages are reduced by costs the employer pays.

To fully fund government edicts, all sources of receipts and expenditures must be considered as government costs. The budget deficit, borrowed funds on all levels of government, and *passed-on costs* **are** all government costs. Not only is the total expenditure a consideration, the change in the proportioning of productive vs. non-productive labor should be considered.

In an effort to spend without taxing, government passes regulations that force businesses and the consumer to pay regulated expenses (passed-on costs) directly.

These *passed-on costs* are seen in the form of regulation, mandates, tolls, park fees, lotteries, impact fees, and a multitude of other charges demanded of private businesses and individuals or made through government-controlled entities that once didn't exist.

Mandated costs required of local governments and regulated industries, such as requirements for the environment, social compliances, consumer disclosures, and many other expenses, become a part of the cost of government, and whether for good or not, these costs do not stem from free-market decisions. Also, many services that once were paid by government, such as drinking water, parks, street paving, and trash, are now paid for or supplemented by consumers or developers. Yet despite passing these many costs to the private sector, the president's report for "Purchases of Goods and Services" shows that government purchases as a percent of GDP have changed little since 1960. The comparison between the years is not an apple-to-apple comparison; it is so different that it would be like comparing apples to watermelons. When government mandates a cost, the cost must be paid before a product can be brought to market or used. Traditional views of the size of government do not take these costs into consideration. The change in the size of government is therefore further misrepresented.

There are no known studies of what passed-on costs add to consumer costs, so to give passed-on costs perspective, we will concoct them. The schedule below depicts the known growth in government expenditures from 1960 to 1993, and from this point we will attempt to estimate passed-on costs.[4]

4 If the number of productive workers (those fulfilling consumer demands and not those of government) were used, the increase in spending per productive worker would be much, much higher.

CHANGES IN FEDERAL, STATE, AND LOCAL EXPENDITURES 1960 - 1993

Figures are in billions

	Work Force	Government Outlays				Gross Domestic Product	Percent of GDP		Government as a Percent
	Change	Federal	State	Total		GDP	Federal	State	of GDP
1960	69.6	92.2	40.2	132.4	B	513.3	18.0%	7.8%	25.8%
1993	128.0	1408.2	784.5	2192.7	E	6374.0	22.1%	12.3%	34.4%
Increase	58.4	1316.0	744.3	2060.3					8.6%
Change as a Percent of 1960	184%	1527%	1951%	1656%	A				INCREASE
Percent Increase 1960 to 1993	84%	1427%	1851%	1556%					33.4%
Pre-inflation Increase Adjusted for the size of the Workforce		776%	1007%	846%					
Inflation Adjustment									
Inflation During the Period 1960–1993		388%							
1960 Spending Adjusted for Inflation		449.94	196.18	646.11	C				
Percent Increase in Outlays Adjusted for Inflation		213%	300%	239%					
SPENDING INCREASE BASED ON COMPARABLE WORKFORCE									
1960 Spending Adjusted for									
Workforce and Inflation	AxBxC	827.5	360.8	1188.3	D				
Spending 1993		1408.2	784.5	2192.7	E				
Inflation/Workforce Adjusted Increase		580.7	423.7	1004.4					
Percent Spending Increase from 1960 to 1993	E/D	70.2%	117.4%	84.5%					33.4%
SPENDING INCREASE PER WORKER									
Spending per Worker 1960 (inflation adjusted)	69.6	$6,465	$2,819	$9,283					
Spending per Worker 1993	128.0	$11,002	$6,129	$17,130					
Increase per Worker		$ 4,537	$3,310	$ 7,847					
Percent Increase		70.2%	117.4%	84.5%					

These figures represent government spending before passed-on costs. Thus, after adjusting for inflation and the workforce, government outlays increased by 84.5 percent. State and local government spending represented the largest share, with an enormous 117.4 percent increase. Spending for each member of the population increased by even more, with a 113.1 percent increase on the federal level and a 172.3 percent increase on the state and local level.

Passed-on costs can only be estimated, but because the federal government often acts in a monitoring function, we will look at state and local spending. Because a significant amount of mandated spending was passed on to state and local government, which passed them to the private sector, assume that the private sector was subjected to the same increase as state and local governments. Thus, the increase in private-sector spending would have been $3,310 per worker. That would bring total spending to $20,440 per worker, for a 120 percent increase in government-mandated spending from 1960 to 1993.

Figures with Assumed Increase for Passed-on Costs			Billions
1993 spending actual			$ 2,192.7
Allowance for Passed-on Costs	$ 3,310	128.0	$423.7
Total Adjusted Government-Mandated Spending			$ 2,616.4
Amount per Worker			$20,441

Undoubtedly, our estimate could be questioned, but any experienced manager who has worked in private enterprise these years might suggest that it is low, not high. The following chart looks at government cost as it relates to consumption.

CALCULATION OF GOVERNMENT COST AS A PERCENT OF CONSUMPTION (PCE)

Year	Government Outlays	Government Passed-on Cost	Total Government	PCE	Government **as a % of** PCE
1960	132.4	* NA	132.4	332.4	39.8%
1993	2192.7	423.7	2,616.42	4390.6	59.6%
Percent Increase with Estimated Passed-on Costs					49.7%
Excluding Passed-on Cost					
1993	2192.7		2,192.70	4390.6	49.9%
Percent Increase without Passed-on Costs					25.5%

* Having this figure would give a clearer picture of government costs, not having it is not an excuse to ignore it.

What this schedule attempts to do is describe the part of the cost of consumption that is created by government. In this case, rather than using the traditional GDP (gross domestic product), personnel consumption expenditures (PCE) are used as a basis for comparison. The reasons for not using GDP were described above. Obviously, the figure for PCE is much smaller than GDP. In this demonstration, the cost as a share of consumption attributable to government was 39.8 percent in 1960, and 60 percent in 1993. Even without the assumed passed-on cost, government spending amounts to half of our personal spending. The adjusted figure suggests that nearly two-thirds of the cost of any purchase was attributable to government. Our extrapolation is a logical comparison to the over 100 percent growth in government spending described in the preceding schedule. The traditional comparison with GDP fails to recognize that when government purchases something, it simply reaches in the seller's back pocket to pay for the goods. Describing government as 34.4 percent of GDP, rather than as a percent of the net personal consumption expenditures, conceals the true cost of government from the population and the workforce that supports the politicians.

To give another picture of government in using PCE, we adjust out government costs and funded purchases from transfer payments (social security, etc.), and derive an estimate of the well-being of the workforce. In other words, since government revenues are drawn from the sale of consumables, we can adjust them out to determine what the population is getting.

CALCULATION OF THE CHANGE IN EARNINGS ADJUSTED FOR GOVERNMENT GROWTH

	PCE	*LESS TOTAL GOVERNMENT AND BUSINESS INVESTMENT	NET WORKER CONSUMPTION	WORK FORCE	REMAINING CONSUMPTION CONSUMPTION PER WORKER	INFLATION ADJUSTED 388%
1960	332.4	179.8	152.6	69.6	2,193	10,524
1993	4390.6	3269.8	1120.8	128.0	8,756	8,756
DECLINE IN CONSUMPTION FOR THE WORKER						-1,768
PERCENTAGE DECLINE						16.80%

* Government spending and private investment, less residential spending, is subtracted from PCE to give a better picture of net current consumption. Residential spending is consumption, whereas business investment is recovered via future sales and generally paid for out of profits. If we had used only government outlays totaling $2192.7, incomes would have increased by only 14.6 percent over thirty-three years. The above schedule moves still further in the comparison of time periods. Transfer payments for Social Security, welfare, etc., are subtracted from total consumption, and additional factors are considered. The portion of income from purchases retained by business for investment is deducted from consumption. By subtracting this amount, the extra cost of government mandates and the profit needed to sustain the new cost structure is factored in.

The remaining 152.6 billion and 1120.8 billion is divided into the working population to determine workforce consumption. The workforce includes workers who should be excluded, such as government workers who receive guaranteed adjustments and those receiving passed-on cost income, but if we are looking at the productivity of all workers in relation to gross consumption, our inflation-adjusted consumption between 1960 and 1993 offers a valid comparison. We should not be surprised that this comparison demonstrates how over thirty-three years that the standard of living for many in the private workforce has indeed declined. We should also consider the following:

1. Some distortion occurs because inflation and efficiency do not impact all prices equally. As government costs increase, people may increase underground activities as well. Also, providing one's own needs improves living standards.

2. The actual investment (gross private domestic investment) for 1960 and 1993 was $78.7 billion and $892.0 billion, or 23.7 percent and 20.3 percent, respectively. The 1993 figure shows a decline in percent, when we would rather expect an increase, due to higher government cost. This may be because many mandated costs are expensed currently. Were PCE reduced by currently expendable government mandated costs, investment would likely show a significant percentage increase. Also, profits earned from currently expended mandated costs and taxes may be higher or lower than those typically earned because of their timing and demand. Producing an exacting answer is further complicated by the adjustment for those who earn passed-on income from passed-on cost. Real passed-on cost is an amount that may be impossible to estimate, as its recipients are part of the private workforce whose income is subject to the same forces as are the nongovernment-benefited employee.

Unfortunately, our computation reflects only average compensations, and as our government and economy have changed, so, too, has the distribution of purchasing power. Where recessions have the effect of adjusting incomes to the available goods and services, some workers are not affected. For example, government workers receive wage increases for inflation and often in the 1960–1993 periods received added compensation to allegedly equate their earnings with private-sector workers. Those receiving transfer benefits (welfare, Social Security, etc.) have had similar protections. Some private-sector industries get automatic adjustments as well. For example, the insurance industry increases rates when costs increase, and it is indubitably obvious that higher costs accrue higher profits for the insurance industry. The true wealthy benefit as well when higher taxes, welfare costs, and the expense of regulation translate into product costs that require increased profits to carry investments and provide working capital. It should be noted that the percent of the population that was working in 1993 is greater than in 1960, which implies the existence today of two-earner households. Having two wage earners causes an even greater distortion if incomes are measured on a per-family basis. Some workers increase living standards but they are not necessarily those for whom gain was intended. Workers, who at a point in time may benefit from government regulation, may be recycled into lower wages because of the ever-increasing government costs. Of course, it is probable that all but the truly wealthy and protected groups lost in some respect. When measured against the potential for gain, everybody loses. There is a very important corollary to be drawn from this hypothesis:

Added costs, including government taxes and passed-on costs, alter workers' consumption. The workers who lose the greatest share of consumption are those not protected by guarantees.

Extrapolating this corollary to its logical end, we might also say:

The general population eventually benefits from efficiency and the resultant lower costs. The rich benefit from higher costs including those created by government.

The fact that the rich *don't suffer* from government revenue augmentation, fairness doctrines, and redistribution should begin to take light. To often government spending is an inept translation of good intention resulting in a misuse of free enterprise. Eventually, the use, division, and productivity of the labor force determine living standards, not tax stimulation or redistribution. There is another step we can take to form a picture of what has happened to private worker compensation. If we translate both inflation and the imputed government cost into consumables, we find an additional negative effect on the income of workers.

Assume that inflation resulted in pay increases between 1960 and 1993 that mirror actual inflation for a worker. The question is how has the distribution of government costs effected purchasing power? And has purchasing power remained constant? Using the imputed government cost of a purchase determined above, adjusted spending power would be 60.2 percent of income in 1960 (100–39.8) and 32 percent of income in 1993 (100–68). Inflation for the period was approximately 400 percent.

1960 DOLLARS		1960 WAGES ADJUSTED		1993	LOSS IN	1993 GROSS @32%
RATE OF	1960 NET	FOR INFLATION IN 1993		NET	PURCHASING	THAT EQUATES
PAY 1960	60.2%	GROSS	1993 @ 60.2%	@ 32%	POWER	TO 1960 RATE
$ 2.00	$ 1.20	$ 7.76	$ 4.67	$ 2.48	46.8%	$ 14.60
$ 4.00	$ 2.41	$ 15.52	$ 9.34	$ 4.97	46.8%	$ 29.20
$ 8.00	$ 4.82	$ 31.04	$ 18.69	$ 9.93	46.8%	$ 58.39

The chart above adjusts for the loss in spending power due to the bigger bite taken out of spending. Thus, an individual needs to earn significantly more than 1960 earnings times four to allow for the added government charges. It should be noted that these figures are presented for demonstration only. Efficiencies were not taken into consideration, but if they had been, the worker would have to produce at about one-half the cost in 1993, as compared to 1960, in order to stay even. Any shortage would be reflected in lost wages. Inflation hides the effect of government expansion and private-sector production efficiencies. Because efficiencies, innovation, and government costs are not spread evenly, their impact is not evenly spread either. Much of government growth affected our daily needs (water, sewer, gasoline, automobiles, insurance, etc.). As a result, it is possible that lower income groups actually suffer greater losses of living standards because of the greater impact on basic needs. Government's attempt to transfer income to the poor likely has negative effects as the cost is transferred back into consumption costs. The schedule also suggests that were it not for the efficiency of free enterprise, the economy may have incurred an inflationary spiral or drop in consumption more severe than what actually occurred. The lack of information available to determine exactly how an inflated government has hurt the poor and the private worker precludes a detailed analysis.

As an example of how government affects workers differently, look at the impact of the workers compensation insurance laws, which are a state-controlled and manipulated business. In Florida, rates on a roofer are (were) 55 percent of the roofer's earnings, compared to less than 10 percent in some states. The charge is twice the combined federal taxes of employee and employer and only 13 percent below the 68 percent estimate that represents the average cost of government included in consumption. Because people can afford only so much for a roof (pricing being consumer, not seller, economics), there is a tradeoff between using cheaper shingles, charging more for the roof, ignoring a leaky roof, and lower worker wages. The implication of this cost is so great that a worker earning $24,000 per year, who saved 55 percent and earned 5 percent on the savings, could save $1,600,000 in forty years. Because of this high cost, many workers go without insurance coverage or attempt to take advantage of the laws and wrap their lives in convalescence. Because Florida incomes are not much different than those of homeowners in other states, roofers can be expected to earn less in Florida.

Next, we will examine how taxes become a part of cost and, as with all costs, how profits are maintained in the face of increased taxes. This can be illustrated using an imagined *increase* in taxes collected at the point of sale (sales tax). When the gap between consumer incomes and prices widens, as it would when sales taxes increase, costs in respect to the purchaser are essentially passed to business, because earnings reflect in purchases, and the purchaser must either reduce purchases or the seller must reduce prices. Obviously, sales taxes paid by consumers will initially reduce net purchases and thus, businesses net sales, as the income of a consumer doesn't suddenly increase because taxes increased.

Faced with lower sales, the economics of business dictate that profits must be regained for business to survive. Either costs must be reduced or sales volume must increase, if established businesses are to regain their viability. As changing a location can be costly and difficult for a business, reduced employee compensation through attrition and other means holds great potential. Or efficiencies that might have resulted in higher wages are mitigated. Of course, marginal businesses may go out of business and be replaced by businesses whose operation costs are less. The effect is a transfer of the tax to the seller because there are fewer dollars in the marketplace, necessitating lower operating costs to maintain economic viability. The reduction in consumer income results in a displacement of labor's wages to fund a government purpose. In other words, the business must continue to make a profit to survive, while workers are hit with lower wages.[5]

The most heinous lie perpetrated on the private workforce that supports the monolith known as our government is that someone else pays for the cost of government. Government collects most of its revenue through our purchases, hidden as a part of the goods and services we buy. To offset this cost and to resolve the economics of maintaining a business, worker earnings decay.

Preparing an individual tax return and paying taxes is only a portion of the complicated tax process that supports local, state, and federal expenditures and legislation. Personal income taxes are only about 28 percent of federal, state, and local revenue (excluding borrowing) and less than 20 percent of the total cost of government. Most taxes are paid by our daily trips to the store. For example, on a vacation to Florida, 10 percent of vacation resort purchases will go toward sales taxes. Below is a partial list of expenses and taxes that pay for or are controlled by government. As you read the list, take note that goods and services are composed of labor. When a tax is levied, the money doesn't add to production; the money draws workers out of production or is used to pay people who do not work. The promise that taxes are invested back into a community avoids the reality that government has a cost of handling and lacks competitive efficiency common to the private sector. And, with fewer productive workers, those workers carry a greater burden. Local and state government will also send significant amounts, 25 to 35 percent, as withholding taxes to the Federal Government in addition to significant amounts to insurance companies for liability and worker's compensation insurance and for pensions.

5 The additional revenue from the sales tax increase doesn't necessarily pass back into the market, as perhaps 30 percent or more of any wage will likely go to payroll taxes. There are additional costs, such as insurance and pensions, that aren't immediately returned to the market. Construction costs are often paid to outside contractors and manufacturers, and the wealthy, rather than the average worker, will benefit from profits earned on large construction projects. And an additional profit center may be created that funnels profits to the wealthy, which may actually increase tax revenues and eventually the government spending. The demand placed on the labor market might result in higher worker wages, as workers are pulled from the productive workforce to fulfill government's demands. This would likely result in the inflation that eventually readjusts the distribution of consumption toward protected workers, not the private sector. The added government workers become an added burden to workers in the private sector

Taxes paid directly by us

- Income tax
- Sales tax on consumer goods
- Real estate taxes
- Federal gasoline tax
- Utility tax on telephones, water, electric, gas, oil, etc.
- Drainage tax
- Estate tax
- Entertainment tax
- Impact fees and user fees
- Radon fees
- Intangible taxes
- Tangible taxes
- Social security taxes
- Luxury taxes
- State and local gasoline tax
- School tax
- Inheritance tax
- Tire tax
- Container tax
- Toll road fees

Government rules that add to cost (passed-on cost)

- Construction codes
- Environmental rules
- Street sizes
- Fire codes
- Security
- Labeling
- Insurance requirements
- Medical treatment approvals
- Drainage retention charges
- Environmental charges
- Arbor rules
- Professional licensing
- Business licensing
- Waste disposal
- Food and building inspection
- Safety rules
- Import and export restrictions
- Tax compliance reports
- Tariffs and import restrictions
- Farm controls and subsidies

Taxes that are paid by us through the goods and services we purchase.

- Sales taxes on business purchases
- Real estate taxes on rental
- Real estate taxes on businesses
- Federal corporation taxes
- State corporation taxes
- Federal employee taxes
- State unemployment taxes
- Lottery collections
- Impact fees
- Road taxes
- Business tangible taxes
- Business intangible taxes
- Federal Social Security taxes
- State business licenses
- Local business licenses
- Occupational licenses
- Vehicle taxes
- Gambling tax
- Property transfer taxes
- Transportation taxes and charges

Regulated industries (containing passed-on costs)

Direct

- Home owner's insurance
- General liability insurance
- Automobile insurance
- Uninsured motorist insurance
- Workers compensation insurance
- Trash
- Health insurance
- Title insurance
- Escrow insurance
- Commercial building insurance
- Uninsured motorist insurance
- Utility

Indirect

- Professional
- Legal
- Accounting
- Brokerages
- Real Estate
- Stock Market

Most of us are aware that environmental requirements are added to trash or utilities, but insurance is not as obvious. All insurance contains costs that are necessitated by government. There are required coverage, administration costs, legal representations, minimums, fees, and court interpretations, all of which government regulates. Both business and individuals pay insurance. General liability and workers compensation has been increased substantially in states where legal representation and large settlements drive up the cost. Insurance carriers may incur additional costs, but profits will always follow through higher premiums. Often, the high rates preclude many from buying the protection they should have. Far too often, government interference has a greater negative social impact than a positive one.

It was quite evident when the federal government deregulated telephone, trucking, and the airlines that the costs of these services came down. Subsequently, competition encouraged price reductions, whereas before deregulation, cost increases were causes for increased prices and profits, as government control results in added costs, not reduced costs. In many cases, to fulfill political demands and to keep the costs off government ledgers, government adds hidden burdens to business through regulations. Profits of the remaining regulated industries are still managed based on cost, which implies that price would decline if left unregulated and competitive.

As a typical example of how government has changed our costs, some costs added in the state of Florida to home construction and sales during the last thirty years are listed below. These are taxes, government costs, or cost that government controls that are paid when we purchase a home:

	COST	INCREASE[6]		COST	INCREASE
	Permitting fees	800%	*	Police impact fee	$ 200.00
	Sewer tap in fees	$3,000.00		School impact fee	$ 250.00
	Water tap in fees	$1,500.00		Road impact fee	$ 1,000.00
(1)	Title policy fees	0.33%		Workers compensation	10000%
(1)	Intangible taxes on mortgages	0.25%		General liability	500%
(1)	Documentary taxes on mortgages	0.50%		Radon gas fee	$ 35.00
	Fire impact fee	$150			
	(1) Amount of the sale price of a home				
	* Percent increase vs. dollar increase				

There are other ways that government adds to the burdens of free enterprise and the worker. Often government encourages inefficiency means or discourages efficient allocations of resources. For example, government encourages investments by legislating tax credits, quicker depreciation, depletion, and tax advantages that reduce the tax on income. These advantages are intended to provide a Keynesian push to the economy or to steer development of certain resources. People often believe that when the government encourages an investment, it is a good idea to be "in" that business and to take advantage of the government tax breaks and projections of demand. Promoters will often push the advantages off on investors, whether or not the market for the intended incentive is viable. A mystique of government, this belief has, in years past, pushed us into oil shale and, via predictions of food shortages, created a rush on farmland that resulted in greatest farm banking crisis since the 1920s.

When laws encourage "tax shelters," they discourage demand-originated investment. Capital is not allowed to flow freely to the area of the greatest need or demand, and the power of creation is put in the hands of an omnipotent governmental minority. Intruding on normal market forces interferes with and damages the free-market mechanism and the economic structure that allocates its own needs. The populace is thus robbed of their market-driven intentions, while government often wastes resources on overexpansion and unnecessary investments. The economy being the sum total of the produce of all labor, government payments for not working or reallocating labor to new areas often serves to reduce living standards. The operating term is "often." Government-induced research and production can contribute to the well-being of society, but often, government squanders opportunities.

There are exceptions to every rule. Government can set standards for, say, efficiency that, when universally applied, can result in savings in power costs, and future maintenance or standards will saves lives. For example, a mandate to eliminate lead from gasoline, practically eliminated the need for automobile tune ups and spark plug changes. Market forces generally have a significant impact on such standards, as consumers make demands for changes. Unfortunately, these standards are often unnecessary, restrictive, out of date, influenced by trade or business associations, and far more costly than is justified. For example, standards for punitive damages and legal responsibility in liability cases often place large judgments on the backs of the deep-pocketed business when their involvement is negligible.

Without tax shelters, the stock market and private investment operate to apportion investment. As an incredibly efficient avenue, the market is non-discriminating. Capital pulls labor to where re-

6 Since these figures were obtained, many of them, in some areas, have increased by another 300 to 1000 percent.

turns are the best. Consequently, the greatest needs of the citizens are met. It is important to distinguish between capital and labor. It is not money that does the work; it is humankind, as money simply provides the direction. The efficient use of money and labor is the strength of free enterprise. Tax incentives or disincentives should thus be avoided, so as not to void the democratic process embodied in free enterprise.

Consumer demand reflects an opinion of new ideas, a desire for goods and services, and the need to apportion labor.

Government taxation puts decisions into the hands of politicians who can only guess the apportionment of economic forces.

For example, a wasting of resources occurred from the passing of several tax laws encouraging the development of real estate from 1969 up to 1981. In the 1969 tax act, provisions allowed tax advantages to encourage construction of new residential rental real estate. The law had a significant impact on the investment computations (ROI) made to determine whether to invest in residential rentals. Reasoning behind the act was quite logical and seemed prudent. Baby boomers were entering the market, and there was a concern as to whether sufficient housing at reasonable prices would be available. Of course, the usual craving to stimulate the economy was also present, supposedly providing jobs for the baby boomers themselves. Other laws were intended solely to stimulate the economy. Laws to stimulate demand in areas where shortages are projected are typical of government. Such laws demonstrate the little faith that government has in free enterprise, despite the constant failure of government systems.

Free enterprise, even without the influence of laws, can actually respond very quickly to shortages and will not long create goods or services that are not affordable. Purveyors recognize that with multitudes of choices, it is purchaser economics (the ability to pay) that determines pricing, not seller economics or dictates. The general population has limited amounts of money to spend. To determine these economics, every industry, in thousands of locations, employs experienced people who analyze the economy and whose errors could cost them their jobs. Government, on the other hand, has few industry specific people and those that are involved have guaranteed jobs no matter the success of their projections. The question is, whom should we trust? These experienced people are well aware that constructing apartments that rent for $200 when the market can only support $100 is bad economics. Prices will drop, and apartments will remain vacant or the leasing market will be limited. If the market needs apartments that rent for $100, free enterprise will find a way. Growth of the population, the diversity of the market, excellent transportation, and competition has long ago made monopolies archaic in the U.S. When government interferes with the normal process by adding tax incentives, it alters the efficiency of the free-market system.

Residential real estate is not as inflexible as government computations and economic forecast portend. As an economy declines or rental rates raise, reflecting demand, households consolidate, rooms are rented, renters seek roommates, children move back home, older units get cleaned up, and suddenly, when shortages seem to be everywhere, vacancies begin to grow. This cushion helps in bad economies or high demand to bridge the gap to good economies and plentiful supply. There is no necessity to stimulate supply when, without government interference, rentals can be built in less than a year. If there are shortages, generally governmental bureaucracies are the likely cause.

Because tax laws aren't responded to as quickly as tax shortages, the surplus of real estate the '69 tax law created did not begin to show up until the mid-'70s. At a time when inflation was beginning to plague the United States, tax laws encouraged real estate overproduction. It was not long before failed real estate ventures returned property ownership to the banks and Savings & Loan ownership. Bankers who had made good loans based on sound banking practices in the early '70s not only lost jobs but also saw their institutions either taken over by the Federal Deposit Insurance Corporation or merged into other lenders. It was only a prelude to what would occur later in the '80s. Mostly individuals were blamed, not government, and charges were made that the banks were too small, regulation was too lax, and auditing standards were inadequate. The government witch hunt that follows these crises always fosters an abundance of legislation aimed at correcting the free-enterprise system of its failings. Never does it accept responsibility for or correct its own legislated and reprehensible behavior. In fact, very little mention of government interference in the market is ever mentioned.

To see how the 1969 tax law affected and encouraged rental housing construction, follow the computations below.

Rental housing investment returns under pre-1969 tax law change

ASSUMPTIONS

Project cost	$ 10,000,000	Cash flow	$ 2,000,000
Mortgage	$ 8,000,000		
Land cost	$ 2,000,000	Building cost	$ 8,000,000
Investment	$ 2,000,000	Years depreciated	45
		Depreciation	$ 177,778
		Taxable income	$ 22,222

Taxes with pre-1969 tax law using the highest tax bracket

Taxable	$ 22,222
Tax Rate	70%
Taxes	$ 15,556

Return on Investment (ROI) computation

Cash flow plus amortization		$ 200,000
Less taxes		15,556
Net cash flow		$ 184,444
Anticipated inflation	3%	$ 300,000
Total annual ROI		$ 484,444
Total ROI per year		24%

Although inflation is shown here, before 1969 it was not a significant consideration because building life and depreciation life were much the same. It is shown above for comparison purposes to the after-1969 tax-law computation, when inflation became a more significant factor.

ROI computations after 1969 tax act (The 1969 tax law affected new construction only)

Assuming the same circumstances

Cash flow plus amortization		$ 200,000
New 1969 depreciation rates		
Project cost	$ 10,000,000	
Depreciation years	40	
Accelerated Depreciation		$ 400,000
Tax loss		$(200,000)
Tax saving at highest rate (70%)	70%	$ 140,000
Total cash flow and tax savings		$ 340,000
Anticipated inflation 3%		$ 300,000
Total annual ROI		$ 640,000
ROI per year on investment	$ 2,000,000	32%
INCREASE IN CASH FLOW		
Return under old law		24%
Increase in return (1)		8%
Percent ROI increase		33%

(1) Investors who held onto real estate constructed for them received additional write-offs, such as interest during construction, points paid to lenders, and state mortgage. Other financing costs could be written off in time periods that were much less than building life.

As the above displays, with the tax change of 1969, apartments produced a good return, with the prospect for material increase in value in an inflationary economy. And of course, they were tremendous tax shelters. The opportunity to write off tax losses against other income was too good for taxpayers to pass up. The tax advantaged return, shown here as 33 percent, was enough to overcome investors' queasiness regarding real estate. This was a phenomenal return for investors who were able to take advantage of them and far greater than stock market returns. A significant amount of construction ensued, encouraged by lenders, insurance companies, and large financial institutions that not only provided capital but also took ownership positions. Thus, real estate investments were advantaged over-investments in industry and production where capital shortages kept stock prices and investment low. Wall Street took advantage of this situation by selling tax shelters, instead of stock, to taxpayers who were anxious to reduce taxes, and—not surprisingly—the stock market should only a 100 point increase in the years from the mid 60s to early 80s, and the shortage of capital to increase production in industry caused inflation.

When the law was first passed, prudent investors did market studies to determine the need for rental housing. With the anticipated growth in baby boomers projected by government agencies and politicians, investors came up with favorable projections. Problems occurred as this faddish trend had several investors doing the same market studies at the same time. With growing numbers of owners and their employees alike seeking to produce affirmative positions, rental projects popped up all at once.

All failed to consider the market system. When tax laws encouraged construction of apartments with tax-advantaged investment returns, the market drove up the cost and sales value of rental apartments. Because the opportunity to invest is what is usually important, the land on which to construct apartments increased in value first. Rather than establishing a lower rental rate, as was intended by the law, buildings went up in value, and cost increase necessitated higher rental rates. As the uncommon spread between actual cost and sales value enticed new projects into the market, values increased and construction continued. Eventually, low occupancy and declining rental rates adjusted to bring tax-advantaged investment returns down in equivalency to other forms of nontax-advantaged and comparable investment. Of course, when this happened and the economy slowed, government added new incentives for building.

Market mechanisms in a Complex society generally work when experienced capitalists are not deceived by laws skewed to create activity, as well as designed to attract inexperienced investors and investment advisors, who just might abuse the system to gain from their clients' enthusiasm. The experienced market plans and studies project demand with efficient results. What large businesses don't see, small ones do, as thousands and thousands of individuals observe market problems, conditions, opportunities, and, of course, tax advantages. Giving businesses tax benefits distorts procedures, thwarts the experienced, and encourages the inexperienced. Tax advantages justify higher values and growth, in spite of market conditions, but the needs of the market don't change because the government hands out incentives.

Unfortunately, this is not the end of the tale. As the market adjusted to the realities of the '69 tax act, occupancies declined, and values fell below replacement cost. Rental rates were kept low, and because of the poor occupancy, new apartments were not built in some areas for several years. The return on investment computations no longer worked, even with tax incentives. The decline wasn't interrupted until apartment rental rates allowed for investment returns on new construction. Fortunately for the lenders who had foreclosed and the fortunate investors who had managed to hold on, inflation in the last half of the '70s began to increase rental rates, along with apartment values. Apartments that were not as yet full began to show respectable cash flows, and the apartment business began to put itself on firmer ground.

Government at that time, however, was having other problems. The high inflation and increasing interest rates were restricting construction and the economy in a year before elections. In an effort to stimulate the economy and to aid the construction industry, which was begging for incentives, Congress conceived plans, and effective January 1, 1981, a new law was passed. Because of high interest rates and because the excesses of the '69 tax act was still on the books, the new act went even further to encourage construction.

Before passage of the 1981 act and using the same project cost as in the previous example—but with a 10 percent inflation rate—the investment return increased to 67 percent in 1980. This means that the same investment we studied under the 1969 law would yield a 67 percent return. But even with this already high return, investors were reluctant to invest and, in truth, cash flows and occupancies had not as yet recovered to the extent that justified new construction. With the 1984 act, returns came out as follows:

The 1981 act reduced the period allowed to depreciate real estate to fifteen years. This short deprecation period was extended to all real estate, new and old, commercial and residential. The ROI computations now showed irresistible returns of over 100 percent per year.

Assuming the same circumstances as above and before the 81 tax act, returns looked like this:

Cash flow			$ 200,000
Tax savings			140,000
Anticipated Inflation	$10,000,000	10%	1,000,000
Total ROI			$1,340,000
Investment			$2,000,000
Total annual ROI			67%

The below shows the effect of the 81 tax act with a cash flow and a 15-year write-off

Cash flow			$ 200,000
Depreciation	$ 8,000,000	/15x2	1,066,667
Tax loss			$ (866,667)
Tax savings at highest rate		70%	606,667
Total cash flow and net cash flow		40.3%	$ 806,667
Anticipated inflation	$10,000,000	12%	1,200,000
Total annual ROI			$2,006,667
ROI (Based on the $2 million investment)			100.3%

The term "anticipated cash flows" is used because few investors received returns, the cash flow or the inflation and never realized the 100 percent. Many who sold before prices fell received substantial gains that were later lost in real estate investments that they deemed more conservative. With the 1981 tax advantages, a new real estate boom ensued. As prices were bid up on rental real estate, the following was more likely to be anticipated:

Cost (inflation Adjusted)		$20,000,000	Cash flow and Amortization		$ -
Mortgage		$16,000,000	Depreciation	12.0%	$ 1,920,000
Investments		$ 4,000,000	Taxable		$(1,920,000)
Land Cost		$ 4,000,000			
Tax savings and cash flow	70%	$ 1,344,000			
Anticipated inflation	12%	2,400,000			
Total anticipated return per year		$ 3,744,000			
Anticipated ROI (1)		93.6%			

(1) Inflation in 1981 was much higher than in previous years.

The above chart is computed to show a 93.6 percent return, with the assumption that the investment had no cash flow from operations. But even if the cash flow from rental activity was a negative $1,000,000, the after-tax cash flow would still have been $1,050,000 and a 26 percent return. The consumer received some benefit from lower rental rates, and many investors received tax losses. However, what often occurred was that rental rates were pushed higher to support inflation-increased interest costs, despite vacancies. What consumers did gain because of lower rents, they lost in paying for the inflated cost of consumer goods because nonconstruction production was robbed of the manpower and capital to expand due to government's interference in the private sector.

The problem of oversupply was compounded by record-high inflation, a previous law passed to encourage public ownership through real estate investment trusts (REIT), and Wall Street's syndication of real estate tax shelters. Prices of existing offices or newly constructed hotels, motels, and any real estate with (and sometimes without) a cash flow or a good lead name were bid up. Higher prices were paid for name properties, with which other properties could be bundled in the REITs and sold by Wall Street. Fees and commissions of as much as 30 percent were added to the building cost, and the resultant package was sold to the public. Sellers, many of whom were not anxious to sell, received inflated "offers they couldn't refuse." With tax deductions, rental real estate was extremely attractive well into the early '80s. Occupancies as low as 70 to 80 percent were acceptable, when 95 percent had been the rule. Millions of square feet of property were developed. As rental agents attracted renters with below-market rates and incentives, older buildings in traditional locations, which would have lasted for many more years with care, became poorly maintained or were abandoned and/or became run-down.

Because inflation and write-offs were a major factor in the computations of anticipated returns, market-allowable returns declined to where cash flow was negative. Indeed, in the latter stages of this government-authored boom in real estate, brokerages reduced or eliminated real estate mortgage financing and sold interests to investors that were 100 percent equity to ensure that the investments would sustain themselves at low occupancies. As long as expenses were covered, along with *probable high management fees*, the investors needn't receive a cash flow. After all, this was a tax shelter.

Throughout the '70s and early '80s, many of the sellers were no less fools than the buyers, as sellers invested their proceeds into new offices, housing developments, golf course projects, apartments, and shopping centers. Mega-office projects and downtown reconstruction projects, needed as years of tax-sheltered investments in the suburbs had drained their tenants, began to take shape. Many office buildings constructed in this period remained vacant well into the 1990s.

Ironically, at a time when foreclosures and bank closing were going on, deal-makers, hotel operators, developers, and foreign investors were driving up prices and planning new projects. Far too many rental units were built, as construction continued past the point of profitability. Because real estate projects are easier to start than to stop and *because a large segment of the workforce relied on real estate construction, syndicating, and financing* for their daily bread, the system continued to develop new projects, eventually leaving many units only partially constructed or developed.

Real estate no longer functioned as a business. Businesses make money; rental real estate was a tax shelter. The only ones making money were the brokers who sold tax shelters. Resources of the economy had been misspent in the belief that the economy was stimulated to produce jobs and that government knew more than the market system. When the tax deductions and buyers disappeared, the oversupply was still there. Thus, resources were wasted, dissuaded from the economic sectors, where they were essential, to meet other demands of the consumer. Dissuaded from the good old democratic process that free enterprise engenders, away from investments that were not tax advantaged, and because labor was allocated to nonessential real estate, away from businesses starving for labor and capital.

The government intervention in the market encouraged hundreds of thousands of workers to build unneeded real estate projects. Thousands of people migrated to an enigmatic economy attracted by high wages, high profits, and our great savior, the federal government. The ride up was wonderful, but the fall came like a rock. Away went jobs, savings, investment, and hope for the future. Millions of apartments and square feet of offices sat idle, along with those who built them, its comrades often hanging on too long to keep any benefits and still oblivious to the knowledge that they had been had. Many today still believe it was the economy that did them in and that more tax advantages were needed to get real estate going again. The government, too, still believes in a theory that suggests money is more important than how it is used. Money isn't what does the work. People are the investment, and when the stimulation is gone, the people are still there. This is proof enough that political bureaucrats don't have the information, the skills or the needed contact with the private sector and thus should be extremely cautious about influencing the market.

In 1986 a tax act was passed that eliminated most of the tax advantages and ended the carnage. The extraordinary waste of resources that might have gone on still further was ended. The passive activity losses that these ventures were producing were restricted to deductions against only similar income. The tax rate was also reduced to a maximum of 28 percent, making shelters less attractive. A large public stock brokerage house put out a statement that the business of selling shelters was finished. Many blame the '86 act for ending the boom. They didn't seem to notice the empty apartments and offices. Market economics didn't matter.

Not only had there been incredible overbuilding, but also it occurred proceeding a decade when large and small businesses found new gadgets that would reduce the need for office space and out-of-town lodging.

The desktop computer and modems were making home offices usable. The fax machine made them expeditious, as car phones doubled individual work time. As decisions were accelerated and idleness eliminated, the numbers who needed space were reduced. Overnight mail and on-time delivery reduced inventory and downtime, along with the need for factory space. It was the dawn of a new world for the real estate business, none of which was included in the government projections.

As in all government-spawned crises, the politicians and bureaucrats took none of the blame. They said free enterprise had failed; it was the end of a cycle. As with all government failures, whether in real estate, oil shale, or food shortage projections, when it's over, it's *not* over. In the end, government intervention fostered the greatest financial crisis since the depression. In terms of dollar magnitude, it was a thousand times greater than the 1929 banking crisis, and many inside Washington wondered if the economy would overcome it.

To deal with the banking problems, a new government bureaucracy was formed to handle the squandered resources. The Resolution Trust Corporation (RTC) was set up to receive the empty buildings and the assets of thousands of Savings and Loan associations that went bankrupt or whose assets were insufficient to meet new government guidelines—guidelines that were established by officious government bureaucrats who prescribed real or forced write-downs of bank holdings. Along with the failed institutions, jobs were lost. The government had created all these jobs; now the government would take them away. New jobs were created, of course; the RTC would need people to engineer, then administer the multibillion-dollar task. Billions of dollars were borrowed from the economy with forty-year payoffs so that taxpayers would not see their taxes raised to pay for the damages.

The federal bureaucracy determined again that the banking laws were defective and that banks were too small. New laws were written. With losses too great to meet its obligations, the Federal Saving and Loan Insurance Corporation (FSLIC) that insured Saving and Loan depositors was abolished. The Federal Deposit Insurance Corporation (FDIC) was required to take over its function, and the insurance rates charged to banks—and thus to individuals—were raised to increase FDIC reserves against bank losses.

The only ones in private enterprise who might have held on to the money they made were the brokers who sold the partnerships, the real estate brokers who handled the sales, and those well off who purchased the orphaned ventures after the fall. An entire industry founded on tax laws disappeared. As cyclopean as the disaster was, it could have been much greater. The brokerages stood willing to continue the demand for property and the sales to investors, as long as the tax law would provide incentives.

The '86 tax act was probably the most important law ever to be approved, not because it created benefits for taxpayers but because it took them away. Most investors moved their emphasis to the stock market and other direct investments. Demand for capital—and subsequently, consumer demand—could now be satisfied. As well, in a time of tremendous government growth, the capital, manpower, and focus that was needed to modernize and expand production was finally available.

The disruption in the natural economic flow of resources could have bankrupted the country. A government that was attempting to transfer wealth to the poor now gave welfare to the tax-sheltered jobless. Investments not made to expand production showed up in the prices we paid. The money saved in taxes for many would-be taxpayers was twice spent for higher-priced goods and expanding government.

Over the years, the construction industry has been the subject of an incredible amount of legislation. This has had an impact on the lives of the people in it. Profits are great when construction is encouraged, and layoffs and bankruptcies are prevalent when overbuilding ensues. When interest rates go up because government spending raises inflation, the federal government is quick to develop construction projects that encourage employment. But new expressways in Miami won't help the carpenter in small-town Georgia. Government has too few minds to figure out where to put all the jobs believed to be needed, so the answer is to build a bridge that millions can see—and welfare that no one can.

The secret of free enterprise is the unlimited availability of minds that can create, answer, devise, duplicate, manage, invent, and innovate. After thousands of years of progress and evolution, kings, politicians, and economists still haven't figured out why man without government is better off than man with. It is ponderous to understand why we think one bureaucrat can reason better than a million minds.

It is surprising how few people recognized the problems caused by the '69 and '81 tax laws (And real estate tax laws passed in between). Many believe the '86 act was bad for them. They wanted legislation to bring back the tax shelters they associate with their own high income and high profits. Government did oblige them, somewhat. The 1994 tax act allowed anyone who is in the real estate or construction business to deduct rental losses against other income. Government also extended the years over which buildings could be depreciated to reduce the advantages of rental. Perhaps there are those in Congress who recognized the damage they did with the prior laws, or perhaps government just wanted to stimulate the economy again. Why plant corn, when all that is need is another apartment building? Our congressmen and congresswomen are far too caught up in impending elections to make anything but shortsighted decisions and should not indulge themselves in the free-market process.

This discussion isn't intended to analyze the fair distribution of taxes. Our tax structure, when added to mandated costs of an inefficient government, is so complex that new forms of tax collection will not alter fairness or investment. Improving collections only gives politicians and the media more reason to spend. Encouraging investment in an atmosphere that supports a clouded and government-laden cost structure that distorts incentives is not a solution to an even greater problem of government waste. The only solution to the possible decline in living standards is the efficient use of the labor force.

As taxes are an unfortunate necessity, government should use the tax system only in ways that cause the least interference in the natural market forces. Government need only involve itself in long-term, high-risk ventures, like space. It should allocate its labor force as if the worker paid the cost, because workers *do* pay the cost.

An economy functions to produce, then to distribute the worker's production in accordance with free market demands.

Taxes act as if paid by the productive worker.

Taxes act to redistribute consumption from the productive to the nonproductive.

(1) Economic Report of the President (1970 and 1994) from Economics, Private and Public Choice. James D. Gwartney, Richard L. Stroup. Seventh Edition, the Dryden Press.

CHAPTER 4

THE WHEEL-TURNERS

Let's suppose there were only a hundred people in the world, no children, and all were capable of performing the same amount of work. Let's say that things in this world were very simple, and all the people did or needed to do was to raise corn. They shared the corn equally and used the corn stalks for shelter. Then one day, one of them suggested that the old wheel that stood on the hill needed to be turned and if it were, they could all enjoy the wheel. Wheels, after all, needed to be cared for, and it would be a shame if their wheel was allowed to rust.

So, ten of the one hundred were selected, and they, who became *wheel-turners*, went to turn the wheel and left the ninety remaining to raise the corn. Before the ten left, they were promised that no matter what, they would work no more hours than they had worked previously and that they would get the same share of corn and corn stalks they had always received. This, of course, created a dilemma; the same amount of corn had to be raised to maintain the same consumption—no matter how bad the weather or hard the work, the ten would get their set share.

Let's consider the alternatives available to the ninety to fulfill their needs and those of the wheel-turners. The alternatives are:

A. Improvise to reduce the needed labor by 10 percent so the labor of ninety would provide a hundred shares of corn. This efficiency would allow the remaining ninety to work the same amount of time, which is how we determine the work standard in this world. We will call this standard the "standard of living," or ...

B. Simply by working a little more than 10 percent longer, the ninety can make up the time and produce the same amount of corn. Obviously, this is not the best choice, because an increase in the hours worked will mean a decrease in their "standard of living," or ...

C. The ninety could work no harder and simply take only eighty shares of corn in order to provide the wheel-turners the ten shares they had been promised. But this alternative would also result in a lower "standard of living."

In the above solutions, the ninety who remain were able to only maintain or lower but not to increase their standard of living. Neither innovation nor hard work created an increase in the standard of living, because before the standard could be increased, the workers would have to make up for the work of ten who no longer raised corn.

From a humorous point of view, consider that had the ten become government employees, they would have visited the corn growers, taken time to talk to the them (time needed to grow corn), asked them to fill out corn forms, taken samples, suggested ways to farm, told them where not to farm, inspected the corn, asked them to fill out more forms (to be sure wheel-turners got their share of corn), checked the trees for birds and the woods for animals, etc., etc. So had the wheel-turners been government employees, the growers would have had to work even harder. This, of course, is more fact than humor.

Coincidentally, despite the importance of producers, politicians increase government employment while believing they are improving the economy and reducing unemployment. In fact, government, except for the military, seems to have been exempt from any employment metamorphosis (changes in industries causing changes in employment) that free enterprise has found so necessary to survive and expand. Government has also been seemingly exempt from adjustments in income, should the corn growers not be efficient enough or work hard enough to grow the necessary corn. In fact, government has grown in bad times and good. Politicians, afraid to create layoffs, maintain employee payrolls when the economy does get bad. When government work slows or as new laws are passed to create new government work or welfare programs, government employees foster new bureaucracies with the requirements of new law—or the unenforced provisions of old law—to justify their existence. New programs or bureaucracies never go away, and new programs are heaped upon the old ones to show potent results to the media and to the voters. Even the money left over at year-end by these bureaucracies is purportedly spent to avoid a budget reduction for new fiscal years.

Most, if not all, of the politicians that have ever lived have talked about creating jobs to increase employment. Politicians worry about the rate of unemployment because their re-election is often dependent on a good economy. The Depression in 1929 has always been a reminder of how devastating not having a job can be. Creating wheel-turners may provide jobs, but wheel-turners bear no real burden for themselves or others. If we are to have more of one thing, we must give up something else. If labor is allocated for wheel turnings, those who remain must shoulder a greater burden. Americans never seem to be willing to give up anything, despite these additional government burdens, so people simply work harder or smarter. The struggle between performing extra work and achieving our desires causes us to be more creative and work more efficiently. This is the biggest reason why war brings a people out of a depression. Even when there is little to lose, people will fight to protect what is theirs, as long as it is theirs to protect.

The worth of a nation is determined by the total of the products it produces. Likewise, the number of producers affects the amount of product that is produced. Until we all have everything we want, only producers, not wheel-turners, are needed to produce products.

Total employment is not limited by the number of jobs available;
it is limited only by the number of people available to hold jobs.

Government actions should be geared toward encouraging efficiency, innovation, and elimination of restrictions on employment. Because of the seemingly infinite number of job classifications today, finding a job may be more difficult than one hundred years ago. Computers will someday simplify the task, as employer and employee are more easily matched. But today, if government wishes to improve our lives, it should aid in the matching of jobs with people, not creating jobs for those unmatched. When workers know their jobs are important, not created, the matching will be all the more easily achieved.

The effect that government has in reducing our living standards has been ignored. The employment of wheel-turners has become a permanent solution to a temporary problem. It has become the means by which the politician fulfills the media demand to show results at election time. The extra work of the workers who must meet these demands, with less help, is not considered because of the perception that jobs have been created. With some bewilderment, we find wheel-turner jobs are applauded for providing other workers with a need to work. The source of payment for these created jobs is an invisible tax that becomes a part of every loaf of bread, every shoe, every nail, and every breath we take. Simply paying someone to turn a wheel, no matter how hard the individual works, does not improve the livelihood of the community. Improvements in living standards come when our consumption comes closer to our desires.

The opening of the West two hundred years ago created opportunity and jobs for an influx of poor immigrants. Opening up Keynes' buried bottles is the end of an unnecessary labor that detracts from a labor of greater importance. We are taking from those who do and giving to those who *could* do. If the population were fixed, it would be obvious that only innovation could change our lives. The economy is a fluent, moving being that is difficult to analyze without draining its fluid and fixing its nature in time. If we drained it now, we would likely find it filled with well-oiled wheels.

This does not suggest that it is not important to aid in the maintenance of living standards for those who are laid off, fired, or for one reason or another are not producing and getting the resultant pay check. The rules of welfare, however, should not be structured to make it illegal to hold a job. Work should be a bonus for those on welfare; loss of benefits should not be a penalty for those who find work. Everyone should be taught that at any level, productive work is important.

CHAPTER 5

EFFICIENCY AND PRODUCTIVITY-

Six factors encompass the economic elements of a better living standard:

1. Invention and innovation. New components of the market basket or production methods
2. Methods of production or delivery of presentation. Efficiency of labor to produce, prepare or sell
3. Distribution of informative data. Advertising and media presentations
4. Speed of delivery of products and information
5. The laws of mathematics. Investment and math functions that control the outcome of actions taken by both public and private organizations
6. Method, speed and location for the exchange of goods and services; compensation

Some of these will be discussed directly and others indirectly in this and other chapters. The second component, methods of production or delivery of presentation, has to do with production and the marketplace, where goods and services are supplied to and presented for selection by the consumer. The efficiency and ingenuity with which goods and services are produced and sold are major factors in determining how much we will consume. Let's first take an overview of the progress of efficiency and the attitude toward efficiency.

Before industrialization, most job classifications were described as farming, herding, medical, transportation to market, and tool- and clothes-making . Farming had once required over 90 percent of the workforce and demanded contributions from the spouse and children. In fewer than one hundred years, the proportion of the population that farmed decreased from 70 percent to less than 3 percent. The United States changed from a simple agricultural society to one that was complex and developed.

In the early stages of industrialization, mass movements of labor resulting from efficiency on the farm meant cheap labor and huge profits to industry. Again and again, much of the money was returned to labor to expand the industrial structure. For the worker, jobs and pay were steady, compared to the farm. Work was also hard and the pay low, but employees found themselves able to buy many of the new inventions, as the growth of industry created higher standards of living. To early industrialists, wealth meant the accumulation of cash hordes, deemed necessary to withstand economic crises. The economic variances also gave the wealthy leverage that was used against employees to procure longer workdays at lower pay. Eventually, unions sprang up, and the pendulum of power began swinging to favor employees.

The beginnings of the twentieth century had a great impact on economic thought. This was the Transitional period, when the economy was moving from a Rural to a Complex economy. The full force of complex advancement impacted the elementary economic characteristics, causing the Great Depression, and that left an indelible stain on our memories. History had never before recorded such a transition, and its participants were not prepared. The lack of experience with the free-enterprise mechanism allowed its disadvantages to dominate its progressive influences. Workers and leaders developed a fear of unemployment. (Fear of unemployment and capitalism enhanced government's ability to tax and to regulate the economy.)

Some adapted to efficiency and progress. Farmers were so often affected by invention that for them, innovation became a way of life. A more productive seed could quickly reduce the number of farmers needed to grow grains, so farmers turned adversity into opportunity. To take advantage of the demand for meat and the difficulty for city dwellers to hunt, farmers used excess grains to raise cattle, chickens, and hogs. Research developed other uses for grains, such as sugar for beer, table syrup, and automobile fuel. Farmers became fiercely independent and adaptive workers, knowing that failure to change could cost them the farm.

The Complex period brought other problems, most workers were not so independent and the threat of efficiency was beyond their control. The Complex economy makes looking for a job a difficult task, and finding a job that matches one's ability is not always easy. The newspapers are full of advertisements for employees, but as the number of job specialties increases, aligning skills with available jobs becomes more difficult. It seems a wonder to many that in times of high unemployment, the number of employment ads is also high. Obviously unemployment is greatly affected by the difficulty of matching skills and wages to willing workers and finding an appropriate job is a hit-or-miss effort, not much different than finding a mate. As with farmers, workers are learning to adapt, acquiring different skills and when necessary reeducating themselves.

There are advantages to this job diversity that outweigh any difficulties. Complex societies respond differently than economies that depend on a few occupations for survival. As job types increase, the percentage of the workforce that can be affected by product or workplace change becomes proportionately less. Specialization enhances job security, as workers become more difficult to replace. The diversity in the market also compounds the opportunity for product development and with new products, new jobs are created. The constant changes contribute to a constant job demand. Furthermore, the chances of recessions and depressions decline, as the factors that cause them impact smaller proportions of the economy.

The varying stages of growth and development and the diversity of jobs form a complex environment that strengthens employment. Job change complements growth, and growth is more dependent upon the available work pool than on money. Today, efficiency occurs with regularity and is anticipated rather than rejected by private workers. Its constant acceptance and installation allows for a gradual change that is less likely to cause unemployment or disturbances in the workplace.

In passing through the Rural and Transitional industrial stages, the United States has become a senior member of a world filled with an assemblage of simple (Rural), Transitional, and Complex societies. The world community has responded as one capable of absorbing the changes caused by growth. The fear of efficiency, however, is a major hindrance to the advancement of our living standards. With the number of Transitional-phase countries increasing each year, understanding the phases of free enterprise is ever more important.

Unfortunately, we live in a world that, as yet, does not fully understand the free-enterprise system. Most economists have failed to interpret correctly how the change from agrarian society to Complex society affects economic assumptions. Accordingly, the ground rules for economic management have changed, while current management still relies on Depression-era philosophies. The future should be built on the opportunities of the present, rather than managed by reflecting on the ghosts of the past. Economic and human failure would not be as possible now, if the effort to protect society with government growth, unemployment, and welfare were less and the effort to enhance basic skills, a good education, and the promise of free enterprise were greater.

Government has not always played such an active role in the economy. Its involvement escalated after World War II, when the unions gained strength and a government that had supported management became the union's new partner. As the power of government was brought to bear upon business, labor's cause was advanced by slowing the installation of efficient and innovative methods. Protectionism was viewed as an aid to this cause, as favored industries were protected from both domestic and foreign competition. Protectionism was reinforced by fear of another depression and a lament that the "Japanese bought our scrap and sent it back as bombs." In the 50s, 60s and 70s when steel production was threatened by national strikes, the cry went up; government intervened, negotiated, mediated, haggled with customers, or set import limits, duties, and other restraints to discourage competition. Labor unions controlled the major industries and extracted high wages, high benefits, and long vacations. Efficiency was discouraged, as production cost savings became reason for union members with clear memories of the Great Depression to threaten strikes. The strikes and wage demands created their own bad memories for consumers, who paid the cost but resented the union role. Eventually, competition and the fear of business collapse broke union power and a calamitous fixing engulfed the steel and other industries. The consequences of not adapting gradually to efficiency and change forced a sudden and massive metamorphosis that began in the 1980s. Several large corporations went into bankruptcy or reorganization and the effect on the workforce was devastating. Workers felt the loss or reduction of compensation, medical benefits, pensions, and other business-derived benefits. Mankind was yet to take long-term advantage of the benefits to living standards that free enterprise built.

Even governments in countries with low employment and strong trade balances encourage inefficiencies that restrain economic advances. In Japan, for example, which is perceived as efficient and productive, many consumers pay inflated prices. Intended to protect business and workers, Japan's policies retarded living standards. Japan supported an ancient multilevel distribution system, farm subsidies, land restrictions, and the protection of traditional labor practices. Exporting much of a country's production, coupled with excessive savings and import restrictions in the face of labor restraints, is a formula for lower, not higher, living standards. By not encouraging foreign competition, Japan failed to exercise the same rules of efficiency at home that made it a world economic power, with results that are no different than those that affected the U.S. industries. As penance, Japanese profits turned to losses, domestic assets crumbled in value, and foreign investments of trade-surplus gains declined in value against an appreciating yen. At home, the inflated real estate and stock prices that were encouraged by excessive savings and foreign-trade restrictions dropped significantly. Despite this, the Japanese continue to pursue a foreign-trade surplus. As wealth reflects production, so, too, does production reflect living standards. But, as with the Japanese, when a society has a significant and continuing positive trade balance, someone else benefits from its production. Many Japanese may die wealthy, while failing to achieve a living standard that balanced trade will bring.

The protectionist policies that hinder domestic efficiency are a cost to the Japanese family. The restrictions that protect business and workers create wealth, but the resultant inflated wealth is an added cost to the consumer. And, values and jobs that form around protectionism are jobs and values that are subject to the whims of the politicians. It is inevitable that a protected business would be subjected to competition. Besides questionable job security of protected industries, production ensues at rates that are inefficient in comparison to potential domestic and/or world rates. Meanwhile, the resultant inefficient allocation of labor limits economic growth. Complex economies are ill-informed to be protectionist.

Protective trade practices are not the only cause of inflated wealth. Government waste, growth in wages and benefits that are not in line with the private sector, unnecessary restrictions on labor, and other pumped up government costs also inflate wealth, but only so long as the private sector can carry the weight. Sustaining such costs results in a loss of private sector living standards and if continued can put everyone's economic future in a precarious position. Freeing all labor of inefficient restrictions is necessary to maintain strong economic growth and an equitable distribution of domestic consumption. A trade deficit in a Complex economy will often reflect a shortage of productive workers whose ranks have been depleted by excessive government burdens. In a less-developed country that has a high ratio of population compared to productivity, importing might be expected as these countries grow their infrastructure. A country that already has advanced stages of capital and the ability to form endless additions should not support a large welfare system or fund unnecessary jobs. Free trade and unrestricted labor in a country with ample capital fosters efficiency and innovation. In this positive economic environment, living standards strengthen throughout the economy.

Unrestricted labor forces workers to attain their highest and best use, while providing the maximum amount and greatest valued good or service. Ideal results, foreign and domestic, require competitive trade practices. Government's good intentions only decrease competition, resulting in a loss of production and a loss of consumption. Supporting inefficient government and a supposedly benevolent welfare system results in the exploitation of private workers. A nation that needs a foreign-trade deficit to fill its own breadbasket exploits the workers of other nations.

In the United States, the unemployment level has, for years, hovered around a probable minimum that echoes limitations on the expansion of production which in turn fosters a trade deficit. While many look at a trade deficit as a failure to match foreign wage competition, we must be reminded that money doesn't build factories; people build them. An effort to enhance investment opportunities with tax incentives is often coupled with government restrictions on labor, make-work government jobs, raises in the welfare support levels that compete with employment demands, and added burdens on business as well as government through inefficient mandates and obligations. Unfortunately, periods of rapid private sector growth also enhance government revenues, which politicians see as an opportunity to spend with a resultant expanded demand on the private work force.

Government simultaneously encourages productive job expansion via investment, while adding burdens that absorb the productive labor that would enhance productivity and reduce a trade deficit. Politicians then take credit for keeping employment high, while business and the private worker struggle to accelerate efficiencies to offset the government costs rather than to expand production. The paradox is antecedent to an even larger trade deficit and a lower living standard for many in the private sector. From the perspective of politicians, a growing difference in incomes of the wealthy and the poor demonstrates to the politicians that it is not the time for government to become efficient but rather to seek means of wealth distribution. Because politicians are inexperienced in business, they are oblivious to the attractive benefits that nurture government jobs and welfare roles and to the burden that expanding government wages and benefits add to the private worker. Politicians look out the window, see the herd rushing to them, and assume that what they are doing is right. The politicians don't realize that the herd is rushing from the high cost of government.

Today, most businesses operate in harmony with their employees. But government interferes in all aspects of employment. Production has been shunted because businesses must adapt to excessive payroll burdens, implied racial quotas, safety requirements, legal constraints, regulation, environmental wandering, and bureaucratic laggardness. The goals intended by legislation are not herein condemned, but they should be accomplished using the same rules of enterprise that render our living standard. Accepting the advantage of efficient labor utilization is perhaps the final challenge to the promise of a better way of life. The accord reached between industry and private workers in the 1980s and 1990s allowed innovative and efficient methods to be established. However, because government has failed to institute its laws efficiently, the compounding growth in local, state, and federal spending is a serious threat to economic stability.

Most people found it surprising that in the fifteen years following 1981 that inflation moderated and interest rates fell. In the face of tremendous government growth in spending and the imposition of regulations, significant costs were absorbed into the expense of a product. It was also a surprise to politicians that huge layoffs at major manufacturers, like IBM, GM, Ford, and John Deere, were followed by lower unemployment rates, rather then higher. The reason for the seemingly curious result was the underlying demand for labor that existed because innovations and invention lacked the labor to be accomplished or were held back by labor customs that limited the input of efficiencies for fear of job losses. In our Complex economy and with a serious recession at their backs, workers were willing to accept innovation, work-rules changes, and pay adjustments. A Complex economy requires worker flexibility.

Because many consumers have lost incomes, businesses have been forced to find ways to maintain pricing and absorb additional costs thrust upon them by government. Government, to accommodate the consumer and while neglecting its own inefficiency, has endeavored to reduce costs in the private sector by eliminating the regulation that once guaranteed high wages for workers in regulated industries. Regulated industries have been deregulated, imports have been encouraged, and a hands-off position has been practiced in labor negotiations to encourage competitiveness in the private sector. The old policies that were condemned as benefits to business protected employee incomes for a select few, while burdening others. Rather than leveling the playing field for workers and encouraging productivity, government actions were limited to the private sector, as government payrolls were enhanced with higher benefits and more job security. The elimination of regulation was ostensibly undertaken to protect the consumer, but the likely intent was to control the inflation resulting from the escalation of government costs. Thus, simultaneous with the deregulation of government-controlled industries, government is imposing costly rules and regulations and imposing additional assessments on the production of nearly every product in the private sector, while ignoring its own inefficiency and deficit cash flows.

While price maintenance is the primary focus of business today, efficiency in the time of Henry Ford's production line afforded a higher living standard. Ford's assembly line may have caused layoffs at other shops, but at Ford's factory, the effect was higher wages, more jobs, and lower-priced automobiles. As lower prices expanded demand for Ford's cars and afforded the consumer access to a speedier method of transportation, the consumers' surplus spending shifted to consumption, like vacations and radios. Still, for the individual, efficiency is a "damned if you do, damned if you don't" decision. When inefficiency necessitates the closure of a business, either a few individuals will make small sacrifices, or many will make large sacrifices to support the inefficiencies. Whether one is a Michael Eisner or a cleaning lady, more than ever, jobs depend on increasing productivity. Failure to adopt efficient methods eventually leads to lost jobs, as high prices stifle sales. Labor-saving devices are too often seen as job-stealers, rather than job-savers. When a job is lost because of efficiency, the pain is noticed, but not noticed are the jobs added or saved. The only time efficiency seems important is when businesses are shut down for its lack. Efficiency and the productivity increases allow for marked changes in living standards. As profits mirror how well business satisfies society's demands, job security reflects efficiency and innovation, as one secures the worker's present and the other, the worker's future. Efficiency leads to lower prices, expansion of the consumer market basket, and job creation. The net effect is an increase in the standard of living or—worst case, as in today's economy when government is taking an increasing share of every dollar spent by the consumer—help in maintaining standards.

In a free and complex society, there is no shortage of options for the consumer. If a product is too costly, of poor quality, or if the consumer just doesn't like the way the company does business, the consumers can alter their spending in a moment and influence the decisions of a business. Options, however, are not always available to taxpayers when it is inefficient, costly, or bad government. Most individuals and small businesses are tied to their home and country, and it is nearly impossible to break this tie and move to more equitable ground.

Politicians, therefore, should be dedicated to minimizing costs while achieving their goals, so as to reduce the impact on the consumer. In other words, if business needs to be efficient to maintain its pricing, government, as a part of cost, should also be efficient. This situation is exacerbated by the community of government workers who see free enterprise as in need of the government's monitoring of its products and employees. Government workers can vote at the ballot box to increases their welfare; their special status guarantees their jobs, and they have closeness to the politicians who can provide for their desires (or demands) by forcing others to pay the bill. And because of the special status afforded government employees, they are not likely to venture out or be thrust into the private sector, where they may suffer a lower living standard and no job guarantees. The failure of government to guide both the public and private sector towards worker productivity increases could very likely result in material losses in these promises and guarantees when and if the private sector collapses under the burden government has thrust upon it.

The fear of unemployment is exacerbated by a lack of understanding of advantages of a free market in labor. The unemployed are the source of economic expansion. The free-enterprise system, which fosters the efficiencies that increase living standards, releases the employees that new businesses draw upon for the production or development of new products. The failure to understand this encourages the belief that free enterprise can't create enough jobs or economic stability to provide the same job guarantees found in government. The politicians rely on this failure when campaigning for votes. The misconception is astounding—or perhaps suspicious, in view of the government's steps to eliminate price regulation, which doubtlessly result in layoffs. While demanding price efficiency in the private sector, government encourages inefficiency and misappropriation of funds in the public sector. This attitude has fostered a political process that creates many more problems than it solves. Politicians have taken advantage of the concern for jobs to enhance their political careers, as they author pork-barrel legislation and support spending to infer action at time of election. Government schemes to subsidize non-workers and unnecessary employment to maintain purchasing reduce employee availability and interrupt individual progress. As a result, business is forced to adjust to the growth in government, rather than government's adjusting to the growth in business.

If government compiled detailed records of labor efficiency, the cost of a product imputed by government inefficiency could be recognized and dealt with. Failure to measure efficiency ignores government's effect on product cost, with the result being potential inflation and/or deflating wages. As the real cost of government is not computed, the real effect that greater efficiency has on consumption is not assimilated. Without its due credit, free enterprise gets blamed for the problems, whether not producing enough, being too efficient, laying off workers, importing too much, exporting too little, or not paying enough taxes. Business must pay the cost of a product imputed by government, in addition to its own taxes. Government, on some level, through laws and regulation, controls everything we consume.

Jobs in government are exempt from and do not stand up to the same test of competition as jobs in private businesses. Consequently, government suffers from low productivity and an overblown cost-to-benefit ratio. The real ratio of private, productive nongovernment jobs (jobs not including government employees and jobs created by laws and regulation) to the total population is declining. Government has become a force colossal enough to cause excessive unemployment, to destabilize a Complex economy, and to threaten our living standards. Government has in the past inflated the economy, then shackled it with lofty interest rates to reduce the inflation that will inevitably result in lower private-sector wages. Cycles in a Complex economy are a result of a private sector that is unable to keep up with government expansionism. This government-induced situation causes the economic distortions we blame on free enterprise.

The cost of a government job is more than the wage alone. To wages and benefits must be added the tools at work and any alternative product this labor could produce. Government employees are an extra mouth to feed at the table, and just like at home, these *dependants* get theirs first. Today, for every two employed federal, state, or local government employees (directly and indirectly), there are approximately four private-sector employees. Of that four, at least one is satisfying government laws or mandates. The numbers suggest that when government expands employment by one, business must also add an employee, and private workers must support both. Government does not make the food, shelter, entertainment, transportation, and health care, and the wealth it creates goes mostly to benefit the rich. Product is the result of labor and no matter how efficient or justifiable, labor is a burden to society when it encumbers those who make products. More simply, it is efficient to add product producers and inefficient to add government employees.

If business asks too much for its product, we simply buy something else. When government demands a higher price, there is no choice but to comply. Even when we had kings and aristocracy to rule us, what they took either was limited or the kingdom forced the rulers from power. Under feudalism, what government demanded was in exchange for protection and order. The commoners, whose loyalty was given to royalty, outnumbered the servants who protected the king. It was possible, then, to bring about a settlement of unjust government. Today, the king and queen to be served are Congress, and those blessed with its generosity are its servants. The generosity is that of government, yet the private worker fills the cup and builds the castles. Today, the king's court and beneficiaries outnumber those who provide for the kingdom. Unlike governance under feudalism, where taxes could be limited by the product of the land, our government has the unlimited ability to tax because of the unlimited advantages of capitalism and the potential for imports.

The potential of the people to vote themselves benefits was a concern of our founding fathers. In the name of unemployment and with efficiency to be damned, government employees and dependents have been given income increases and benefit protection. It may not be exactly what was foretold, but the results are the same. Those who live for today and do not prepare for tomorrow will "reap what they sow." As business has transformed to efficient producers, government must succumb to an equitable distribution of economic benefits. Said distribution can be based only on a free, efficient labor force and an ethical spirit of work. The spirit is one in which we provide benefits to our fellow citizens, thus receiving our own. It is the efficient who prosper.

Our problems are best solved by the entrepreneurial ideas that free enterprise encourages, not the bureaucracy that government protects. The millions of a society can solve the problems of employment, but a few thousand government bureaucrats will never solve the problems of free enterprise. The choice is an efficient system where one works to satisfy his desires by serving others or a system where one votes himself benefits to be carried on the backs of private workers.

CHAPTER 6

THE IMPORTANCE OF MONEY

In this chapter we discuss number six: Method, speed, and location for the exchange of goods and services. The six factors are repeated below for reference.

1. Invention and innovation. New components of the market basket or production methods
2. Methods of production or delivery of presentation. Efficiency of labor to produce, prepare or sell
3. Distribution of informative data. Advertising and media presentations
4. Speed of delivery of products and information
5. The laws of mathematics. Investment and math functions that control the outcome of actions taken by both public and private organizations
6. Method, speed and location for the exchange of goods and services; compensation

Currency is a tool that eliminates the difficulty of bartering.

Money manages labor;
labor builds product;
product is allocated through the distribution of money.

Legislated/regulated reallocations of money alter the free-market determination of living standards.

Using currency is a method to exchange goods and services for a promise, with the promise being acceptable by society in general.

The subject of method, speed, and location for exchanges includes such topics as bartering, market location, banking, banking methods, currency transfers methods, currency types, and other related topics.

To fully understand the association of money with free enterprise, we look at methods, speed, and location. Methods relate to currency (the medium), bank checks, credit cards, and other forms of payments made to settle purchases. The acceptance of a medium is important because universal acceptability encourages trade. Gold has been an accepted medium, but it is costly to transport and not always available in quantities sufficient to support a large economy. Paper currency is popular because it is light, can be tied to gold, and can be conveyed by instruments such as checks, credit cards, and bank transfers. Important, too, paper currency lacks the allure of gold. People are less likely to hold on to paper and thus, the number of transactions increases.

Speed has most to do with the ease of conveyance. The acceptance of paper put trade into definable terms and once that was done, other methods of transfer were accomplished. Credit cards and loans meant that one could transact in anticipation of income. Faxes convey acceptance of transactions and methods of conveyance. Money orders provide security, and electronic transfers make the movement of money nearly instantaneous.

Location may seem to hold an odd relationship with money, but having a monetary system that allows national or world banking to occur in even the smallest of cities increases the opportunity for trade. All these factors help to increase the number of transactions, which allows an economy to operate in the optimum and, again, to improve living standards.[6]

Whether as cash or gold ingots, money has no practical use, unless one likes looking at gold or keeps warm burning cash. No doubt there are many who would much rather look at cash than anything else, but in an economic sense, cash facilitates the delivery of goods, services, or wealth and is, therefore, mostly important as a conduit. The more acceptable a medium and the quicker its delivery, the quicker and more often transactions are made. The speed of that delivery increases the economic events that occur and therefore, the efficiency of trade and our resulting living standard.

If Henry Ford had started his production line when everything was bartered, it wouldn't have mattered how fast Ford's Model T was built. If the farmer had to raise and transfer four thousand chickens to the factory in exchange for a new car, and Ford had to keep the chickens until he exchanged them or paid them as wages to his employees, we would still be riding horses. Or, if Ford didn't want to trade his car for chickens, the farmer would have to negotiate trades until something acceptable to Ford was found. The point is that bartering is slow, difficult, and inefficient.

Our "medium of exchange" has evolved greatly. Because gold was too burdensome to carry, cash became the medium of choice; now cash is hardly used and is a problem to carry, and checks and credit cards are used. The market is now evolving past checking accounts and credit cards to again speed the economic process and, again, enhance our standard of living. People will choose the least troublesome method to make exchanges. A complicated world, however, now has specialists who define monetary aggregates to meet specialized needs that only the specialists understand. Today, except for that small amount we have in our pockets and the required reserves placed with the Federal Reserve by the banks, most money is in use, invested, or loaned out. Each day, banks need the currency coming in to replace what goes out. A medium of exchange is therefore a factor in the evolution of free

---

6 Throughout civilization an acceptable exchange and its availability has been a vital force in the economy. Paper backed by government, for most of us, is the only means of exchange we accept. However, for much of the history of civilization, paper was the least acceptable means of exchange. The earliest method to exchange goods and services was the barter system, the exchange of one good or service directly for another. With barter, people knew exactly what they were getting and giving. To expedite and facilitate trade, mediums were developed; even rocks and seashells have been used. Having a medium was important because cities that traded the most prospered most. When we think of money we often think of wealth. Adam Smith defined wealth as the value of goods and services. Except to measure wealth, he did not include money in the definition. The important question is what were traders really attempting to accomplish once they ventured beyond barter to the use of currency? The simple answer is that money is a means to expedite and maximize the exchange of goods and services. Money is a storehouse for our desire to make exchanges. Money is just a handy way to exchange our labor, goods, services, and wealth for something we may not as yet have selected. We would all readily accept cash as wealth, anytime and anywhere. However, money is merely a conduit.

enterprise. As the egg is to the chicken, the means of exchange is to free enterprise. Each is necessary for the other to occur.

Because money can be printed and is controlled, there are problems that occur when the supplies of money change. If there is too much currency, its value declines in relation to the value of goods and services, and the inclination to make exchanges for currency can diminish. When there is too little currency, money becomes too valuable and the propensity to make exchanges is again diminished. To facilitate commerce, a proper balance between currency and production of goods and services is important.

As an example of how an excess of money can affect commerce, assume the community needs a restaurant, and land prices at the best location are high—price inflation caused by an excess of money is factored into the asking price. In such a case, an inefficient location may have to suffice. Settling for a less than desirable location can result in lower sales, an extra effort for customers to get to the restaurant, and a potentially failed business. And failed business represents an inefficient utilization of resources. A dependable currency is therefore important because it affects the method, speed, and location at which transactions occur.

Many economists have blamed the inflation in the 1970s on the 1971 abandonment of the Bretton Woods agreement, wherein a gold standard existed. In the last several decades, there has been some discussion about the need to return to a gold standard and the potential problems caused by the abandonment of Bretton Woods. Under Bretton Woods, the value of currency was fixed to gold. But today, countries like Peru and Venezuela are using dollars to steady their currency. Others countries, like Cuba and Russia, find dollars are used for trade on their streets. The use of the dollar flourishes because it isn't the value of a paper or the like that determines the acceptance of a medium; it is the confidence in and the need for a currency. Tomorrow, a hole in the earth may be drilled for steam, and liquid gold may flow out, and the value of gold could be destroyed. Alternately, fixing the price of gold limits its production, while unleashing the price increases production. Gold is a commodity that can be the subject of a great deal of speculation, and it is valuable as a hedge against the possibility of a currency losing acceptability; as a hedge, it has a use. However, with a full understanding of the relationship of currency to the utilization of labor and maximizing of production, the collapse in the value of a currency need never occur. We must consider the factors that affected the 1970s, specifically the growth in government. What happened then had more to do with the competition for labor caused by the growth of government programs. The cause for inflation was the restriction and allocation of labor to new functions, not the availability of money.

Money cannot simply be printed without potential inflationary pressures. Money supplies should respond to demands, based on the expansion of production and the changes in the speed of transactions. If cost and price inflation or deflation is a factor in the economy, monetary growth should be based on an accurate measure of change, yet money should always be adequate to meet demands and allow for growth. Deflation or inflation reflects the effects of invention, innovation, and the efficient utilization of the workforce, which in turn determine living standards. The failure to see labor as a resource that must be efficiently managed, as is money, causes most inflation.

The strength of a paper currency is dependent on the ability of society to make good on an implied promise to produce goods and services sufficiently to avoid inflation and to allow the economy to expand.

Tying the value of a currency to a rare metal can limit economic expansion, both domestic and foreign. Confidence in paper money, however, is not a given; like respect, it is earned. The U.S. currency earned respect because of the country's economic prowess. Currently, however, confidence in the dollar is largely due to the demand for a strong currency in an evolving world economy, as demonstrated by our constantly increasing trade deficit. The world of the 1990s needed a strong currency, a host currency, that was well respected by all countries and a currency that would thus encourage trade. The dollar helped developing countries to nurture their own workforce by providing a respected medium. This is not an everlasting confidence. Countries with strong currencies can enjoy a trade deficit as countries with a weaker currency compete to develop their economies through exportation. The country hosting the strong currency benefits from this situation, as the host obtains goods at more favorable prices. The United States currency has enjoyed the status as a "host currency," but the advantage in personal consumption that should result in an exceptionally high living standard is being offset by the incredible demand for labor directly by government and the labor demanded of the increasing government regulation in the private sector.

Money manages labor.

The net effect of trade is to determine production. The essence, then, of money is to manage production and therefore labor. Today, however, money has been given a status that emphasizes money movement while de-emphasizing the importance of production and trade. In other words, money has become more important than the trade it is to foster. As government pays many not to work, and other jobs are funded so these unnecessary workers can buy things, politicians are encouraged to believe that they are putting static money into circulation. They are advocating logic that spending money stimulates transactions and encourages a chain reaction. There was a time in the early years of our country's existence when the movement of money was restricted. A fractionated banking system, indeterminate currency values, a lack of sufficient gold to back currency, and the nature of people to hold, rather than bank or spend gold put limits on transactions. When a flexible currency was put into circulation, trade increased and the economy benefited. But money now fulfills its obligation to the economy and no longer needs to have its pot stirred. Money is no longer static; it is in constant motion. Loaned out here, invested there, hardly a nickel is unaccounted for, as banks look for overnight investments and send out prearranged credit applications. Money is now continuously mobile. Money not used for one purpose will be used for another, and the need to stimulate an economy is a dubious consideration.

Today, when politicians spend money, they take it from one pocket and put it in another. As money has a direct relationship to the allocations of labor, when money is extracted from the economy by taxation, a consumer usage is preempted for another usage controlled by government. Activities in the whole of society do not increase. An investment or a consumer-planned production is taken for government consumption. Trade is limited, not enhanced, as government places a first right on labor allocations on the pretense of creating jobs. The speed of a currency is often slowed, rather than enhanced, by government, as special assessments or allocations may be piled up in banks until sufficient funds are available for large government projects. Money is the force that guides labor—putting money into circulation a hundred years ago elicited totally different results than it does now. After all, spending money is no more than voting production.

Being a host country and being partially supported by less-developed countries while failing to sufficiently increase the capital structure, the U.S. has become the world's money printer. As world trade grows, other currencies will strengthen—the demand for a host currency will fade, and the price of foreign goods will rise. The result will be high inflation unless labor becomes more productive or losses sufficient value to compensate for fewer imports. If this occurs, it will be the private labor force that will endure the added pressure to provide for an ever-growing unproductive population. Efficient labor allocations must replace money as the driving force to resolve domestic as well as foreign deficits and to avoid a world and domestic crisis.

As demonstrated by the strength of the U.S. dollar, the world demand for a currency to facilitate trade has a great influence on the exchange of goods and services. The trade deficit, which is a problem for the U.S., is the solution for many countries that need a strong currency. Despite the inability of the U.S. to fulfill consumer demands domestically, the dollar maintains a relatively strong value because other countries need an acceptable currency to promote their own trade. Our foreign trade deficit has inadvertently provided a medium to assist world trade, in a world with evolving free enterprise. With some countries now using dollar-backed currencies and many others using it for street trade, dollars hold the same position that was previously held only by gold. The world use of U.S. currency as its standard demonstrates the importance of a world currency that may someday be based on expatriated dollars. The establishment of a universally acceptable world currency will facilitate the continued expansion of the world economy. Before this happens, there must be universally acceptable understanding of the science of economics.

The demand for dollars has created an interesting push/pull in U.S. economic trade. As the world pushes goods to get dollars, the United States pulls in goods to meet demand. As foreign, less-developed (Transitional and Rural) economies provide more and more of our production needs, our technology and production is transferred to them. Just as in the U.S., when our technology outpaced that of more developed European countries and they suffered inflation, we may suffer inflation while foreign currencies become stronger. The excessive trade deficits will continue until the world either loses its need for dollars or until the U.S. satisfies its own needs to produce enough to satisfy consumer demands. It should be noted that despite devaluation of the dollar against stronger currencies, like the yen or mark, the dollar, in relation to lesser currencies, has remained strong. Since the early '80s, there have been predications that the trade deficit would be resolved by devaluation of the dollar. The continued deficit demonstrates more the strength of dollar demand than the strength of the dollar.

Free trade between Complex countries should be balanced so that neither takes advantage of another's workforce without just reward, such as obtaining technology. If currencies are properly matched, then less-expensive foreign labor will substitute for comparable domestic labor, pushing the domestic labor into more efficient, productive, and valuable functions. Should foreign labor be less expensive, it is likely that the exchange rate would not represent a true relationship between the two countries, and an adjustment would be in order. If the monetary relationship is equitable, then free trade would benefit both countries, as each becomes more productive.

In the face of the demand for dollars in developing countries and a failure of domestic production to meet demand, the Federal Reserve acts by raising interest rates. The effort by the U.S. to resolve its foreign deficit is exacerbated by this action. As the Federal Reserve holds up interest rates, it contributes to reducing investment and the reduced enhancement in the utilization of the labor force needed to increase production. The result is a cacophonous interjection into an already entangled situation. The strength of a currency is not dependent upon its quantities, gold, or other relations; it is ultimately dependent on the productivity of labor that results in from production of the civilization that creates the money.

CHAPTER 7

WEALTH

Of all elements of free enterprise, wealth is the most contentious. Socialists invariably talk of wealth's inequitable distribution. Economists who side with them speak of an effort to redistribute wealth and the happenstance of birth or life that allowed one to have it and another not. Politicians seek out contributions from the wealthy and boast of taxing the rich. Workers want jobs with rich or wealthy corporations, but when disgruntled, attack the corporations for the corporation's success and the workers' problems. Many talk of the unfairness of wealth, while brandishing their own to demonstrate how their circumstances are different. Few turn down wealth. Wealth, it seems, is mostly unfair for those who don't have it.

Wealth is the dream of success. The dream isn't always a desire for wealth or money; it's something each of us wants to do, like act, play basketball, build buildings, or be powerful. It's not just for the money, but unless success is purely personal, the measure of success is what others pay us for what we do. After all, isn't freedom's greatest promise the right to choose how best to serve mankind? And isn't the key to wealth in knowing how best to serve others and thus, to earn our dream? Freedom is the key to wealth, as wealth is the key to free enterprise, and free enterprise is the key to prosperous and happy lives. Not everyone has a dream, but because of dreams, we all live better and healthier lives.

Does someone else's dream make our lives brighter? Of course, the idea is not so fantastic when we think of the entertainment that we get from watching Michael Jordon, the Beatles, or John Wayne. After all, they are idols. But what about Bill Gates, Henry Ford, George Washington Carver, or Thomas Edison, and the hundreds of millions who followed as the captains of industries or the privates in arms? They all gave us something—whether through the desire to inspire or to conspire, to scheme or to serve, to strive or to survive, through their philanthropy or their greed. Before these notables got what they wanted, someone else got something first. Free enterprise is a plan in which everyone is offered something, but to get our something as capitalists, we must serve someone else.

The usual viewpoint on capitalism, especially the one exploited by the politician, is to describe the worker in a struggle with management. Management, however, in an effort with labor, plays a role in maintaining our living standards. It becomes easier to punish the wealthy for being rich if the consequence to the wage earners is ignored. With the consequences of their actions overlooked, politicians and the media can rationalize their blissful goal of distributing wealth to the needy. Even though the system was designed by "the people" to enhance wealth and provide for the individual by providing for others, wealth is berated and, along with it, the advantages of enhanced productivity.

This distrust of wealth and the wealthy is implicit in our ancestry, when rulers, kings, and dictators plundered to obtain their riches, and all others lived or died at their liking. Accumulation of wealth occurred at the expense of others, and the rich were not wholly deserving of what they had. Then, wealth and riches were defined only in terms such as gold, silver, jewels, kingdoms, and power. From the king to the serf, rights and positions were transferred by inheritance or war. A stock market to value wealth was nonexistent or limited. But the kind of wealth that exists now existed then. In fact, then as now, wealth had more meaning to the population than the monarchy.

Wars and pillaging were a daily concern, five hundred or six hundred years ago, so people banded together around their rulers. The people pledged their lives and works to the rulers and in return, the rulers offered protection. Warriors could boast an exalted skill. To become rich, one needed to be a highly skilled trader or an enduring fighter. Most skills, the ones that provided daily needs, were deemed replaceable. Wealth represented material objects like gold, and when the village or castle was overtaken, gold seized the invaders' interest. Knowledge held such little esteem that whole civilizations were erased, along with their written works and traditions. Yet valuing the wealth of the commoner freed mankind from omnipotent rulers—and could eventually free us from war.

Skills, knowledge, tools made by hand, and services were the riches of the masses. These skills were held by the masses and passed from generation to generation, with little value and even less hope for improvement. What changed this was free enterprise. As free enterprise evolved, so, too, did the value of knowledge. With the establishment of a market system and the stock market, the two factors that produce advances in technology—knowledge and capital—were finally brought together. Knowledge attracted capital, and capital built factories. Kings and queens had few skills beyond waging wars and providing government, but royalty did have riches. With the promise of a share of the profits to the wealthy, the skillful and knowledgeable transformed gold into a new wealth—not a physical wealth but a paper wealth called stocks and bonds. The rich no longer needed to rule; they became capitalists who looked among the masses for entrepreneurs, who needed money to build their dreams so as to make both rich.

Wealth made the masses important and valuable.

In the late 1800s and early 1900s, invention or knowledge was accorded the same honor as athletic skills are today. Basketball contracts can make the poor rich and popular now, as invention did then. Wealth was applauded, and the newly rich were the heroes that our athletes are today. The people were closer to the foundation of free enterprise. They understood the choices, the opportunity, and new goods that freedom gave them, and with the little they had, their gains from invention were mountainous. People got rich by improving lives, making simple things like electric toasters. They were happy and were sure it could never get better.

The world was an evolving one, and over the last two hundred years, wars (cold or hot) haven't been fought for plunder but for a way of life. War determines which system prevails, as it is the old way against the new system, and a newer system against a still newer system. The fight is to determine which system is to create what manner of life for all, and which system and people can provide the most protection. These systems were voted on or fought for by the people and were designed with the intention of improving life. But only one system included freedom and the right to be wealthy, and that is the system that prevailed. The battles that were won did not occur just on the battlefield; they transpired in homes and factories, not just as a war of arms but a war of living standards.

As a way of life had a value, so now do people. Today, the capitalists look at foreign countries not as a king's treasures to plunder but as customers. And armed with Cokes and dishwashers, they step to the front. Germany, Japan, Brazil, the U.S., and England all march, armed to the teeth, in China, but no one is wounded; no one is killed. As value is placed on capital, knowledge, and skills, an even greater value is placed on something more important: the *customer*. Governance be damned; capitalists need people who can buy. As wealth is begotten from knowledge and knowledge from mankind, the desire to create wealth affords life a greater value. Wars destroy wealth as well as lives. The new slogan could be "create wealth, not war, and we will all have time to make love." When wealth has no value, war is just a way to create jobs.

Wealth values human skill.

There are economists who look at acquiring wealth as a matter of luck. This belief is probably encouraged by the rich or their wives, who, to avoid displays of arrogance or ignorance in explaining how they got rich, simply profess luck rather than hard work. But if it is luck, it is hard work that increases our chances. Free enterprise even guarantees this luck, as the lucky and their heirs become the capitalists who finance the next generation. It is the community, however, that decides who will be rich. In the Complex society in which we live, there are enough options that consumers can choose the skills and products most desired and the price they are willing to pay. In this way, we choose who the wealthy will be. And if we no longer want the one we choose, we simply choose another.

Adam Smith defined wealth as the value of goods and services. Today, with expansive stock markets that allow quick capitalization and the exchange of business interests, a different wealth exists. Wealth today is not only as Adam Smith defined; it is now the value of goods and services and the value of this ability to provide goods and services. Wealth is created from knowledge and skills, as stock values are based on an illusory belief that stock certificates can be bought and sold with the prospect of gain. Lead has finally been turned to gold, as where once wealth did not exist, now it does.

As an example of how wealth is created, suppose we made a product, and every one of 200 million in the U.S. population each bought one of that product every year. On each sale of this product, a penny was made. The income, not the wealth, of the product would be $2 million per year. Because the stock market values the ability to earn, this company now has worth, and we have created wealth. If the market values a business at ten times its income, the value of this business would be $20,000,000. No one had to give up anything for this wealth; the purchasers of the product benefited by what they bought, the workers earned a living, and the company only earned a penny. Since new companies don't typically pay dividends, the entire $2 million will likely be reinvested in more sales and jobs. Wealth grows and grows as income goes back into more jobs, improving sales, skills, and products. The stockholders may never get a nickel. Of course, not only would our company pay taxes, if we sold the company, we, as owners, are likely to pay in taxes several times what the company earned.

Let's look at wealth another way. Assume that government decided to confiscate the wealth of the richest people in the country so as to distribute that wealth to the people. We would all be rich, right?

Say we get three trillion	$3,000,000,000,000
Number in U.S. population	300,000,000
Amount each	$10,000

If we actually got cash, which we wouldn't, it won't make anyone rich, for most it may not last a month. But wait, we don't get this in cash. Because government had confiscated the wealth, no one would dare buy the assets, paper wealth would be worthless. We could distribute the assets, couldn't we? If we did, there would be some cash. Mostly there would be factories, cars, trucks, desks, computers, parking lots, vacant land, file cabinets, office buildings, patents (no longer valuable), customer lists (no longer valuable), and other such things. And unless we fired everyone, the cash in the businesses is needed for working capital and is probably borrowed and, by agreement with the lender, cannot be distributed. There will be one other asset; the business has good will. What's good will worth? If we check out the New York Stock Exchange, we would find that most businesses sell for about twice net book value or one-times sales. This is the portion of the value that exists only because the free market imagines it, this is the paper profit. As a matter of fact, nearly all wealth exists because the free market imagines it. Instead of calling it good will maybe we could call it "the value of freedom," a fantastic value that only exists with the freedom to be wealthy. If wealth is distributed, both freedom and good will disappear.[7]

A rich man's wealth is seldom in cash. It is represented primarily by the value of the stock in the businesses he created, acquired, or inherited. Of course, also valued are the "valuables"—the jewelry, antique cars, vacation homes, etc. But without the rich to buy them, luxury items are worthless, and how many would spend their lives finding or making something that had no value? As to the home in Acapulco, even if we took turns, we couldn't all get in. A central government that confiscates wealth could never decide who gets the diamonds (history shows that those who govern with absolute authority keep for themselves whatever they desire). A central government can't distribute wealth or diamonds fairly. Instead of distributing large diamonds, to be equitable, they would be broken into small ones. It should be no mystery as to why most Communist governments were corrupt. Since being fair was impossible, the next best thing was to be fair to those in power. If we destroy the rich, wealth disappears for everyone but those who rule. Isn't that how we started? Isn't that the system we thought was unfair?

Let's look at wealth in yet another way. The value of the Standard & Poor's 500 in August 1995 was $3.5 trillion or only $13,500 for each of the 260 million citizens of the United States. With dividends at less than 3 percent, an equal division of income derived from these stocks would be about $400 per citizen per year. Obviously, a distribution of this wealth would provide for very little, and if most of this capital were not reinvested, businesses and jobs would stop growing. A more significant value than all the wealth in the stock market is the value of our jobs, our homes, our parks, and our schools.

Wealth is embodied in the places we work. From work we draw our economic shares, which allow us to make the decisions for families and ourselves and to determine what others will produce for us. If the incentive to create jobs is taken away, jobs disappear along with our dreams. As our right to choose is depleted, our freedom to choose is destroyed. Taking wealth, rather than creating our own, is destroying something we already have.

Wealth is a principle embodied only in the rights of free civilizations.

Wealth reflects a belief that freedom should exist.

Thousands of corporations listed on the New York Stock Exchange., which represent billions of dollars in value, have never paid a dividend. Even the corporations that do pay dividends pay less than 5 percent. Ironically, the American dream of success is founded on a piece of paper called a stock certificate that is often taxed by government, whether it pays its owner an income or not.

In fact, all businesses put together actually require more investment every year than they earn. In other words, if the U.S. economy, or any properly functioning economy, were a cash business, it would

7 The media often report the incredible amounts of compensation paid to some corporate executives and suggest that employees should get this instead. What the media never report is that unlike actors and athletes, who get paid in cash, as much as 97 percent of an executive's compensation may be in the form of stock options. Stock options are the right to purchase company stock and cost the stockholders, not the company. Options also mean additional capital for the company when they are exercised. (Note: as per Forbes 110695, p. 300)

be losing money. To meet the needs of investment, not only the annual earning of business but individual savings and borrowed funds are needed to meet the needed investment obligations. Investment is how we meet the increasing demand for goods and services found calling to us from the maternity wards, or that, if we are lucky, result in an improved standard of living. In essence, a portion of our labor must be put back to provide additional goods and services. A society supports investment when the system allows businesses to earn an income and this income creates paper wealth. Paper wealth is now desired more than money or gold. Because wealth is a function of income, growth in income is a function of investment, and unless wealth is increasing, production is not growing.

From the inception of our country, government sought to expand wealth by encouraging innovation, hard work, and exploitation of its many gifts. But starting mostly in the early 1960s, redistribution manifested itself. Politicians attempted to spread wealth by feeding on the existing framework, rather than by creating new wealth, as has been our history and our heritage. Even the term "worker" is redefined by politicians and heralded by the news media to exclude working people who own or manage businesses in order to encourage and popularize the concept of spreading wealth. The insinuation is that those who manage a business don't work as hard or deserve their wealth, whereas many "bosses," owners, managers, and self-employed work fifty to one hundred hours a week. For many hardworking owners and managers, their only advantage is working all the hours they want and not having to pay themselves overtime.

The insensitive media definition of "worker" fosters contemptuousness in the workplace. Leaders and followers are degraded, as the importance of one reflects on the other. All workers can thus be viewed as having little consequence, as politicians imply a position of loftiness for themselves. The result in the workplace is a loss of individual respect and of pride in workmanship. College students who believe the only ways to serve humanity is through government jobs are relating an impression acquired as a result of the lost esteem for private workers. Many young adults don't believe they serve their fellow citizens by working in private jobs. Private employers and employees are seen as insidious and dastardly or ignorant and helpless. It is little wonder that today's TV programs often depict anyone who is not a government employee as corrupt, lame brained, or both. The politicians, many of whom have only insignificant visitations with work, find excuses for their failure to contribute in the workplace. They are "experienced politicians," and work experience becomes a barrier to entrance in their private club.

The effort to separate business leaders from the general population is intended to form a political and class distinction and is a cause for casting votes. Politicians, interested mostly in a paycheck and power, rather than devising real solutions to economic problems, use class distinction as a subterfuge and a stratagem to attain office. It is then easier for them to say one thing and do another. To satisfy their constituents, they vote for excessive government spending and the loading of business with restrictions and costs that reduce economic production and living standards. The socialization of free enterprise, on the pretense of benefiting the masses, reduces individual value and depletes the country's assets.

Free enterprise can operate under monarchies or dictatorships because neither defines an economic system under which commerce is to occur. However, socialism and communism define economic functions that lack the incentives offered by free enterprise. They assume that a redistribution of wealth and a concentration of power will improve living standards. For these systems to function, however, it is necessary that another workable system be in place to create the wealth they attempt to distribute. As the prior demonstration showed, there are not sufficient amounts of wealth existent to make material differences in our lives. Attempting to distribute wealth is like trying to hand out our own workplace. Our hopes lie with work and productivity, not redistribution.

Socialist and communist advocates don't comprehend the investment businesses indubitably required to meet growing demands. Even successful businesses can need many times their earnings for expansion. It is possible that should a business not expand, it can fail. The cure for such situations exists with free enterprise and is the reason for capitalism's success.

The belief that possessions of the wealthy have values that can be distributed like free beer ignores how worthless possessions would be if government confiscated all wealth. Values of material property reflect the same kind of wealth we see in stocks. A two-hundred-year-old painting that may be worth $30–40 million costs relatively little in labor to construct and maintain. The wealth it represents is based on the desire to possess it. When the painting is sold, wealth is not consumed; it's merely passed on. And for government, such values represent taxing opportunities. Without value, there would be no tax. When sold, wealth is merely exchanged for wealth. Like listed businesses that lose money and pay no dividends, possessions have values because of their potential. Such opportunities only happen in free civilizations.

It is only in free civilizations, too, that artifacts of all values are likely to be preserved. Both Russia and China have demonstrated their desire to sell such items of ethnic heritage to people of free nations. When a communist or socialist economy fails, treasures of the past are likely the first to lose the funding needed for maintenance and in both the USSR and China, clean air and water were unimportant because without freedom, there was no one to speak for their benefits, there was not wealth in their creation.

Money is what motivates most people, whether for the purpose of survival, as an incentive to produce, or just so they can give it away. Not all people desire money in unlimited amounts or are desirous to become entrepreneurs. But it is the entrepreneurs who look for efficient ways to satisfy consumers, environmentalists, or the ever-expanding demands of government. Leaders and followers can't exist without the other, and both are important. Years ago, a somewhat arrogant college graduate was put in place by a friend who cared little about investment. "A good job, fishing boat, dogs, wife, and kids are all that I need," he avowed. People like this are easy to respect because they know what they want and are willing to work for it, recognizing they want little more. They are not jealous of the wealthy; not everyone wants to be an entrepreneur. Most followers realize that it takes extra effort to become a leader. There is a respect between leaders and followers, as both have something the other wants, though neither will give up what they are to obtain it.

The only equality is a right to pursue happiness.

In the example with the corn growers written in chapter 4, corn was shared equally with the wheel-turners. But in the real world, sharing isn't equal. Unless we are prisoners, it is impossible for things to be equal. People are different; needs, desires, abilities, and goals are different. In fact, there are no two people exactly alike. Suppose we attempted to make things equal. We would place a larger burden, a tax, on those who work harder and earn a greater share. We would burden those who consume the most, those who sell things, buy things, or those who sell certain things. Maybe we would tax those who consume gas or electricity. Are we being fair or just finding ways to tax? The way we tax impacts all groups, even the poor.

What if all goods that exist were divided equally? Of course, each individual would end up with a lot of unnecessary things. People who didn't need their share of a heart surgery or two cars would trade them, and there would have to be places to trade. Since some traders are better than others, things would end up unequal again. Then, of course, to be fair, we could set up a government agency, and someone else would decide what we should have and what we could trade. Eventually it would be like having to ask to go to the bathroom when we were in first grade, remember the teacher wanted to know what you were doing so you signaled one finger or two. The Russians tried that; does anyone believe it worked?

In the purest form of the free enterprise system, the individual decides how spending and time will be allocated and, therefore, whether to consume or to accumulate wealth. That is the basic difference between free enterprise and all other systems.

Capitalism is about individual choice.

Free enterprise gives people the freedom to select the goods and services they wish and creates the most opportunities for other individuals to respond to those wishes. With creativity comes new ideas and products to the marketplace. When government interferes and attempts to make these decisions government is doomed to failure and the free market will be wasteful and distorted as it was when tax laws were passed to encourage real estate development in the 1960s, 70s and 80s. Bureaucrats would need to have society vote on product which is exactly what the free market does. Even specialized businesses find it difficult to determine consumer wants. Communist countries, like the USSR, couldn't satisfy their own needs for bread, meat, and shoes. Can we imagine our congressmen voting on what we would eat next year or telling our daughters what some obtuse Congressman said she would have to wear? Even with the tremendous marketing efforts businesses make, half of all new product introductions are failures and, it takes a massive amount of capital to finance each endeavor. Because government does not accept failure, would government ever make new products? Being fair is the excuse for the politician's inability to understand or explain how freedom and free enterprise work. This leads us to a Fairness Doctrine.

Fairness, when used to determine how resources are to be allocated, reduces competition, usurps market choice and formulates solutions at the lowest levels of comprehension and the highest level of incompetence.

The opposite of competition is monopoly.

Government operates under the Fairness Doctrine.

Fairness encourages solutions that discourage competition and are the least complicated. Thus, the government spawns the least number of solutions and reduces economic growth by discouraging new ideas and invention. The Fairness Doctrine frustrates individuals and leads to the degeneration of the economic and moral fabric in a society.

The only fairness is the right of individual choice.

By now, it should be conspicuously obvious that wealth can't be distributed. Distribution advocates attempt to reduce the consumption of the wealthy, but unless it can be demonstrated that the wealthy eat significantly more than other people, any attempt to tax, reduce, or distribute consumption of the wealthy would make no material difference in overall consumption. The wealthy are more likely to reduce investment to maintain consumption, which limits the growth in production. Redistribution programs only affect the non-rich, as they operate to reduce investment, reduce the workforce, and place a greater burden on those in private employment.

In transferring free-market decisions to government from individuals, government reallocates a limited labor force to non-market–driven causes and acts to reduce the accumulation of wealth by the masses.

Money enables a market exchange of one's own labor for another's and shepherds production. Except for certain public-works projects and research, government produces little for consumption and is itself a consumer. In attempting to redistribute wealth, government makes a market decision. When government makes decisions for the consumer, the consumer's desired investments are preempted and the accumulation of wealth declines. That additional piece of the pie we were going to get from that extra investment to produce a good or service is gone. Instead of being used to create wealth, tax money allocates labor on behalf of government programs. Private workers are conscripted to perform a government service or, in the case of welfare, rewarded not to work. This is an allocation of labor from a useful and productive function into a government-directed, non-productive function. The impact to the economy is to reduce the available labor resource that provided (or would have provided) a usable product. Additional demands are then placed on those who continue in private employment.

Government creates burdens for productive workers, not jobs.

No matter how altruistic or charitable an attempt to bless the needy with someone else's wealth, overall living standards decline when workers stop providing useful products. If we were actually taking from the rich to give to the poor, the rich would have to perform actual labor, which is exactly what the communist demanded of their rich. Short of success, the communists simply killed off as many consumers as possible. Again, when wealth is destroyed, freedoms are lost.

The attention given the distribution of wealth is to invent for the less fortunate a vision that incredible amounts of wealth exist to be distributed. This misconception is the focus of a significant effort by politicians and economists, who have little experience and even less understanding of the free-enterprise system. This belief, and the notion that unemployment is a fault of the system to provide jobs, becomes an excuse to expand both government jobs and the welfare roles. Although unemployment in a population may fluctuate, in the long run its level has much to do with the support given the unemployed through government itself. Social dictums, employment education, job complexity, and economic maturity are more likely to impact unemployment on complex economic levels.

Labor is not unlimited.
Increasing populations are dependent on a proportional division of labor in order for a community to function properly.
Only efficiencies of production change these proportions.

The total production of a community is directly related to the number producing. If a population grows, aside from efficiencies, production will only grow if the number producing increases. Government actions to redistribute wealth through employment and welfare reduce the productive labor force and alter worker proportions. This may be offset with efficiency, but efficiency in production requires investment. As government taxes to pay the cost of redistribution, government simultaneously acts to reduce investment, as well as the productive labor force. Meanwhile production demands can be counted on to be ever increasing. Capital and labor shortages eventually translate into unfulfilled consumer demand and potential inflation. Absent efficiencies, the balancing of demand with supply is resolved through wage reductions, longer hours, and imports. In practice, the acceleration of cost-effective measures, private worker concessions, and foreign trade deficits are the only way to resolve supply deficits. A sampling of incomes for intended recipients of government redistribution may give the appearance of redistribution. This perception implies that wealth has been distributed, but the rich are not the ones whose incomes have been reduced. The assumption neglects realities.

Imbalances in private workforce responsibilities, caused through the effort to redistribute wealth, can reduce overall living standards but not necessarily wealth.

The business effort to respond to redistribution is one of maintaining costs and limiting production.

Redistribution causes upheavals in businesses. Small businesses may divide into single-employee units to avoid taxes, assessments, and regulation, giving the appearance of business formations. Damaged businesses disappear, are bought up, or are taken from the public market through sale to private investors, leveraged buyouts, takeovers, and management buyouts. Businesses may go through bankruptcies to rid themselves of expenses, including labor contracts. Large businesses might use this opportunity to reduce, rather than to expand employment or to raise prices and reduce employee costs. With less competition, profits increase. The result of attempted redistribution is that the names of the wealthy may change, but the wealth remains and often in more limited hands. The hardest hit are the middle class, whose limited capital or potential to be rich is lost, and the workers, who feel the pain of lost pay and lost jobs in a government orchestrated alterations.

When higher business taxes, mandated costs, and capital redistribution cause inflation, private businesses will be seriously disrupted. A choice between going out of business, raising prices, or cutting back on growth often results in reduced investment that would increase production. When inflation increases the cost to expand production beyond the price that inflation brings for products, businesses will be unable to expand to meet demand, causing more inflation. As interest rates and inflation increase, underling assets lose value. Recession is not a solution to this scenario, as while interest rates decline, the wealthy buy up the assets (wealth) at garage-sale prices and reap tremendous returns. Large businesses solidify their market position and have the opportunity to increase or consolidate their holdings. Government costs simply act as costs that earn a profit. Again, the rich get rich, the poor get more welfare, and those in the middle are sandwich spread.

Wealth redistribution may cause the rich to suffer temporary losses of incomes and corresponding reductions in investment opportunities. Earnings, however, will eventually be regained and improved as increased taxes and regulation make it difficult for new competition to enter a market, as the increased costs and knowledge add to capital requirements. The shortages caused by reductions in investment produce higher prices that have the effect of enhancing, not diminishing, wealth.

Government is more likely to create more rich than to distribute wealth. Besides out right theft, fraud, or collusion, there are three ways government actually creates wealth and makes the rich, richer.

- Government creates scarcity. For example, pollution laws often made new investments in existing products unprofitable at existing prices while it was necessary to Grandfather in existing plants. As demand grows for a product, say concrete, the price inflates to the point where new production is affordable. As this occurs the profit margins of existing production facilities increase significantly and stock values grow. The rich get richer and with no competition wealth is transferred from consumer to owners.
- Government creates profit centers. For example, a new pollution laws and class action laws created profit centers for those who provided the product or service. Wealth created, the rich got richer.
- Government cost creates wealth. The compounding of money through the "miracle of compounding interest" is a much talked about phenomenon. Basically it is the increasing in the value of your money with each period's addition of interest. Adding cost creates the same miracle. If you have ever seen eight electric utility workers standing around watching one dig, you may wonder how the company can afford this apparent inefficiency. They can afford it because the cost becomes part of the basis for profits for these government regulated businesses. The cost has the same effect in unregulated businesses that aren't destroyed by tax increases or the addition of a mandated cost.

The economic policies that attempt to fairly distribute wealth cause a roller coaster, boom-to-bust economy, leaving casualties in the wake. In the bust, government will, of course, over stimulate the economy and compound the problem. The result is not greater division of wealth but consolidation. Large businesses buy up the smaller and weaker ones in serious government-sponsored recessions, reducing competition, while growing businesses regress to individual or closely held corporations. Unseasoned businesses disappear and the beginnings of new family wealth evaporate. Cyclical businesses, whose consumption is discretionary, such as construction or furniture, are particularly affected by recession. These businesses suffer when consumers affected by government growth reduce spending to allow for their loss of purchasing power. In many countries, businesses and their capital are taken over by government in order to preserve them, in which case wealth gets destroyed and the desire to create wealth is diminished. Ironically, rich politicians living on other people's money (OPM), inheritance, and the like seem to be the ones who wish most to give wealth away. In the end, government is supported by the labor of the private workers, who share greater portions of their production with the non-private sector through the government-augmented wage programs and by providing staples for a bureaucracy.

The poor, by definition, can't accumulate large sums of capital but accumulated capital does finance jobs and businesses for the poor. An unknown philosopher once said, "I've never been hired by a poor man." The government's attempt to distribute wealth actually expands the ranks of the poor and diminishes the middle class. The only accomplishments are to degrade entry-level jobs, create competition between welfare and wages, discourage investment, reduce middle-class incomes, raise taxes, and expand the government's inefficient labor force.

It is impossible for the truly rich to spend all they earn on consumption. Most of their earnings are put back into the economy, either through savings that are loaned out to consumers and businesses or through direct investments in production.

The successful become wealthy, the wealthy become capital bearers, capital bearers vote on future investments and success creates the wealthy.

Should investments be planned by a centralized bureaucratic government system that has an endless source of capital and little knowledge of the consumer? Or should individuals, such as the greedy rich, who fear losing money producing something the consumer won't like, make decisions? The wealthy and the businesses they foster are the capital bearers, responding to the shuffling in the free-market system and the stimuli given by government, as they constantly prod the system to identify opportunities, problems, disturbances, weaknesses, trends, inefficiencies, and efficiencies. The capitalist's quest to find investments and profit from them improves the system, and makes the economy more efficient, modern, cleaner, and with a resultant increase in the standard of living for all. This job is not performed by one bureaucrat in Washington but by millions of greedy souls who unwittingly improve things for all of us.

It is better to have a thousand greedy citizens make your communities investments than one powerful politician.

Because the role of the wealthy is attacked and ridiculed and certainly is not taught, the creation of wealth is degraded, rather then emphasized. If the standard of living for the community is to improve, we need more rich poor, not more poor rich. Wealth cannot be spread, but it can be consumed or destroyed along with future productivity. If there were no accumulation of wealth, capital would not be available to finance growth or, eventually, to pay government welfare. Taxing wealth is a ruse that doesn't reduce wealth. Government spending simply funds the reallocations of labor to fulfill the politician's deep-pocketed goals and desires for power. Rather than satisfying individual desires, taxing takes labor from productive to nonproductive endeavors.

The wealth of a nation is determined by its ability to produce goods and services. A nation's living standard mirrors its ability to produce.

Increases in consumption (living standards) are directly related to increases in wealth.

Taxes and government regulation enhance the wealth of the wealthy without enhancing consumer production, as the cost becomes a cost of production on which an income must be earned.

Private workers lose income when government expands. Businesses, on the other hand, must profit to survive. And it doesn't matter whether a business writes 70 percent of its expenses to labor and 30 percent for taxes, or 30 percent to labor and 70 percent for taxes. Wealth is a function of production cost, whether bloated by taxes and regulation or an efficient reflection of free enterprise. Of course, there are other factors that are used by the market to determine the value of a business. Values (i.e., wealth) reflect the following factors:

1) The cost of production
2) Industry margins that are established by historical relationships such as:
    a) Initial capital requirements
    b) Historical capitalization rates
    c) Standard industrial policies and practices
    d) Historical research and development expenditures
    e) Knowledge
    f) Risk
    g) Government imposed restrictions on entry
3) Future profit potential
4) Market capitalization rate adjusted for the following factors:
    a) Anticipated long-term interest rates
    b) Risk
    c) Anticipated rate of sales growth
    d) Competitive capitalization rates

$$\frac{\textbf{TOTAL PRODUCTION VALUE}}{\textbf{MARKET CAPITALIZATION RATE}} = \textbf{WEALTH}$$

Entire books could be written justifying the above relationship. The value of individual industries could correspondingly take volumes to compute. Suffice it to say herein that production cost is a major factor in determining the value of a business. If or when production cost is overshadowed by demand, competition in the market will eventually resolve price to a base of costs. Therefore, when mandates, rules, laws, taxes, and other causes from any source increase the cost of a product, other costs must adjust to compensate in order to maintain market share.

When price adjusts for cost increases, the change is temporary and/or the market-basket share of the product will change.

Several forces act on price and prices change when costs rise. Our assumption is that new costs become a part of total product cost and inflate the price. To a degree, costs do inflate price, as inflation makes adjustments in the overall market basket. In the long run, inflation is the ultimate reconciler. "In the long run" defines a period that may be several years. The question now is why are we discussing the aspect of price? The point to make here is that when taxes increase, overall wealth doesn't decline, although costs must reconcile with price. Taxes and government mandates are an absolute in the cost of a product because government has a first right on all receipts. If we add up all factors comprising cost, they will absolutely include taxes.

COST OF LABOR	XXX
COST OF LAND	XXX
COST OF GOVERNMENT MANDATES	XXX
COST OF TAXES	XXX
TOTAL COST	YYYY

"In the long run" residual costs, such as labor and land, are the only costs that can change, and the cost and availability of land is often limited by government regulation. The profits of a business don't change because each business operates with those unique margins that sustain its production and expand its capital. Because profits thus remain the same, "in the long run" the wealthy suffer no loss. Only the names may change because active businesses, operating at the time when new costs are mandated, may not be able to correctly manage the cost. In Complex societies, wealth may appear to grow, but fluctuations occur only with the changing market interest rates, inflation, population, and changes in the absolute volume of production.

In the long run, the cost or the production of a product adjusts to the consumer's ability to pay through adjustments to variable costs (residual costs).

Residual costs, or leftover costs, are the costs that can change. Only land and labor are leftover costs. The phrase "leftover" is used because the money that is **left over** after all the required/mandated costs are paid is what will be paid out for these costs. The value of land is subjected to an incredible maze of alternative uses, inflationary pressure, its own governmental restrictions, and mandates and emotional circumstances. The variance in the price of land would reflect local incentives, transference of location to foreign markets, and taxes. Labor can vary greater than the cost than land, as labor is a recurring cost, impacts existing businesses, has no residual value, is a greater share of a product, and has a carrying cost if not in use that is much less than that of land. Land may be a minor factor in the computation of cost and in any case cannot be depended upon to provide a sufficient balance to offset added costs; once in use, its cost doesn't change. Labor and its efficient utilization are the only constant left "over" costs.

Land and labor are residual costs (left over).

This relationship is not an obvious one. Adjustments for an industry may take years, even generations to be effected. Sales volume, alternate products, second-hand markets, efficiency, innovation, invention, a plethora of other factors, and of course private sector unions will affect the time frame in which changes to the cost of labor occur. But changes will occur, and the income of the worker will decline if production efficiencies do not offset additional governmental costs. Aside from labor and efficiency, the only other offset to added product cost is for the productive labor market to expand in relation to the total population. Ironically, government expansionism simultaneously adds to the welfare roles and exacerbates the dilemma for the worker, as the labor supply is effectively being reduced. The logical end to this is that when government adds to the cost of a product, in real terms, the value of a business will remain the same, and its workers will eventually receive lower compensation. This is no fault of the wealthy but rather a consequence of government expansionism and a function of viable commerce that isn't subsidized. More precisely, it is the result of the laws of mathematics, one of the six factors previously written herein, that influences our living standards.

Government expansion widens the gap between the rich and the private working class.

In recent years businesses have attempted to maintain income growth for their employees, while satisfying the mathematical requirements to hold down costs. As a substitute for real wages, these businesses have "shared the wealth" with the employees through various stock option and stock-matching plans. This creates the appearance of transferring wealth to the employees, but as government expansionism continues pressure on the private worker, the question will be whether or not employees will hold onto this company stock or the wealth it represents. Employees may be forced to liquidate these holdings when their companies lay off workers or transfer operations in order to facilitate further government expansionism. Obviously, the turbulence caused by government expansion has a lot to do with employee turnover. As companies seek to reduce costs, employees are laid off and recycled to other employers going through the same crisis. Rates of pay, however, for the employee will likely be lower in the new companies. The employee's savings, including the old employer's stock, are likely to be spent finding a new job. Because the new job may come at lower pay rate, savings might also be used after finding a job to maintain spending. Since maintaining lifestyle and paying the mortgage can be important, a likely scenario is cause for a spouse to seek employment.

We have discussed why government expansionism doesn't change wealth and causes wages to fall. We will now look at what happens when a business reduces its cost and its capital structure. This basically is the relationship of wealth, efficiency, and the expansion of enterprise, given that investments equate to the expansion of production and thus of wealth. This is the relationship that would most interest the socialist. It is that of the formation of capital and job creation. To begin with, we will discuss how businesses attract capital to expand their production.

If a company increases its profits, its capital increases in different ways. Borrowing capability increases as earnings grow because lending institutions endorse a relationship of income to debt. The greater the income, the greater the ability to borrow, and the ability to borrow translates into the potential for investments. Although lenders do not have a set formula for all industries, they do recognize certain traditional borrowing ratios for different industries. Lenders may base the amount they will lend on factors such as capital assets, cash flows, receivables, and the collateral of the owners, but the income of the business is always on the lender's mind as a major consideration. Income is also the basis for value.

Additional earnings x borrowing ratio = additional ability to expand capital

Besides borrowing, the sale of corporation stock is a means of financing expansion. When earnings increase, typically stock values increase and the ability of a company to fund growth by selling company stock is enhanced. A price earnings (PE) ratio is the ratio of stock price to income per share and conversely, the number by which earnings can be multiplied to get the value of a stock. Stocks of different business types usually trade in traditional PE ranges. PE ratios are discounted to an interest rate that reflects an anticipated long-term yield, plus the discounted value of the growth in earnings that are anticipated, capitalized at a rate for a standard PE of all businesses. If earnings are increasing, the PE of a business is likely to be high in relation to other stocks.

Earnings x PE ratio = value of business
(and value for stock sales)

Since most businesses are in constant need of capital to fund expansion, it is important to be in a strong position with lenders and investors in order to obtain the best rates or values for the business. The value of a stock, the wealth of the stockholder and the expansion of the economy are therefore closely related. Stockholder wealth is computed in much the same way a company determines its ability to fund expansion.

Wealth = Earnings x Price Earnings Ratio (PE)

Now, let's suppose a job is eliminated through efficiency. The potential for growth is the amount saved, capitalized at the companies respective rate of capitalization. If a job that paid $80,000 was eliminated that, after taxes, saved $50,000 per year, the value of the savings for a company that had a PE ratio of 16 would be $800,000. Assuming this translated into higher earnings and the PE ratio increased because of it, price would increase even more. Even if management compensated itself with a share of the additional profits, the remaining balance would still finance more jobs than the one lost. And, the incentive to expand a business is far greater than immediate gratification of additional compensation.

The company would have options. It could sell stock and because the market anticipates that it is a healthy company, market acceptance may translate into a high PE ratio. Obviously, a company can realize an amount in stock sales that significantly exceeds extra earnings.

If a company borrowed money, it would have additional capital based on the following formula:

Total new capital = $50,000 + [$50,000 x borrow ratio]

Translating new capital into jobs created with the money from stock sales or from borrowing, the potential jobs created would be greater than any jobs lost, and the economy would be more efficient. In a normal market, this savings would eventually be transferred to the consumer, with the effect that the consumers would have more to spend and the cause for job expansion would come from the new demand. Thus, there are three different possibilities for jobs to expand beyond the number of jobs lost.

- New jobs created from new capital
- New jobs created from new demand
- New jobs created because of the availability of knowledgeable personal

Companies that recognize the value of trained employees are more apt to retrain them for other work. Rather than a net loss of jobs, there is a net gain.

If we were to look at job losses in relation to the whole economy, job efficiency results in making employees available for other duties and enhances overall productivity. Assuming that each employee produces five times his own consumption, overall productivity of the economy would increase by five times the jobs lost to efficiency.

If instead of the additional profits inurning to the benefit of the business, this money is spent on a government mandate or paid in taxes, a job is lost, the additional productivity is offset by government's expansion, living standards would not improve, government might create a job that becomes both a current and future burden, or government may simply expand compensation to existing employees. Unfortunately a business is merely offsetting costs due to government expansionism and the potential for a company to expand through stock sales, borrowing, or increased sales would be gone. In the case when efficiency merely offsets a government mandate, the company is, in essence, investing in a government-dictated activity and not a consumer desire.

Government expansion substitutes for consumer expansion.

The offset through efficiency to government expansionism may be a better option than a loss of living standards, but rather than jobs expanding within a business, efficiency may call for job reshuffling. This leads us back to the potential for private workers to lose incomes in the imbalance of income distributions fostered by government actions. This is why the Great Society failed to increase living standards and was one of the reasons that incomes declined. The attempt to distribute wealth resulted in a loss of productivity, loss in productive investments, and a reallocation of labor to nonproductive, sometimes inefficient, and wasted causes.

Politicians have failed to comprehend that the wealth of business is a perception stemming from the investors' imagination and based solely on the income that flows from production. Wealth does not represent actual goods themselves. Unlike physical assets, stock wealth is an interpretation of the value of the flow or potential flow of goods, not the goods. Therefore, the wealth that is represented by the value of a business cannot be redistributed.

Without government interference, wealth would spread in the natural evolution in which families grow and in the effort of the wealthy to expand their wealth. Aside from the economic alterations caused by government, production changes when populations grow or efficiencies occur. Therefore, real wealth doesn't change unless the volume of production grows. This is a relationship to which we invariably return.

For the wealthy, it is important to optimize growth. In Complex societies, the relationship of growth to efficiencies is recognizable, as investors realize that wealth is created investing with entrepreneurs. Entrepreneurs are motivated, require less supervision, are more likely to take risks, and are inclined to have ideas that are profitable. Entrepreneurs recognize that ownership motivates, which is why stock incentives are offered to employees. As the economy becomes more complex and efficient, and when workers are recognized as the limited resource that they are, wealth will be distributed in a natural process that will allow all workers to be recognized for their value. Therefore, in an endless evolution of wealth, wealth will beget wealth as it distributes itself.

In a triangulating process, wealth spreads itself to all workers as humankind's living standards are increased.

CHAPTER 8

RETURN ON INVESTMENT

Of all the laws that affect our lives, the laws of math have the greatest command. Affecting investment computations is the relationship between the cost of an investment, the consumers' ability to pay, the government's incentives, the market's ability to alter cost, and the availability and mass of product. For example, the size and price of labor to build the home change with the consumer's income. Although we may not notice product and compensation changes, the economy cannot operate outside mathematical possibilities over extended periods of time. Eventually, the economy acts to correct anomalies.

Mathematics is the most important of all factors that encompass the economic elements of a better living standard; investment and math functions control the outcome of actions taken by both public and private organizations

Knowledgeable business people make their decisions to invest based on computations to estimate the financial return. These calculations are called return on investment computations (ROI).

Consumer initiated investments are made in response to consumer demand and are composed of time and money.

Outside forces tend to reduce the productivity of labor.

Government is an outside force that interferes with the natural laws of mathematics.

Two of the principles of money are repeated here:

Money manages labor.
Labor builds product.

Politicians appear to legislate as if math had no relationship to the economy. They are professional politicians, not administrators, and seem to lack business acumen or mathematical skills—or more likely, the system in which they operate requires verbal not mathematical skills. This reflects in their management of the economy because they are incorrigible in their efforts to defy mathematical laws with tax incentives and other economic manipulations. Politicians constantly pass legislation to turn what would be a *bad investment* into a good one. When they successfully alter investment computations that affect particular business, the stimulus often causes wasteful investments after which politicians are forced to act to remedy the problem that they themselves created. Rather than calculations manipulated by Congress to satisfy media hype, investments should be the reflections of the consumers' desires and a realistic assessment of societies needs. Economic disasters are usually attributed to enterprise, never to Congress. Unfortunately, Congress lacks not only the process to examine its own failings, a congressperson's first goal is reelection and disclosing bad, weak or poor decisions can make that goal difficult to achieve. If Congress provides a tax incentive or other incentive to encourage investment, thousands, even millions may attempt to take advantage of the generosity. Good business sense and past history will guide many wise heads to prophesy the decline in the value of such investments, so as to buy in after the market influenced market falls apart.

Good investments accomplish their purpose without incentives. If not, money and time are a waste, and a lesson is learned and applied for future benefit. We will begin by probing investment logic and listing the important rules of investment that all investors should follow and of which politicians should be aware.

Rule #1: There are no *good* bad investments.

This is the one rule everyone needs to follow. The idea that write-offs are good investments probably comes from the wonderland of Hollywood, where the scripts suggests a fanciful gain so as to demonize the rich. Apparently the movie stars believe that such a thing exists or perhaps Hollywood's investment advisers save their jobs by convincing the actors that their bad investment is a good tax deduction. There are realities in life, two of which are that there is no good ways to lose money in a bad investment, and there is no such thing as a little bit pregnant. ROI computations are made to aid in answering the only wise investment inquiry: will the investment satisfy a consumer demand and produce a profit? Those who make good investments, like actors, will continue to benefit society with their skills.

There is no assurance that any investment will produce a profit, but in the assemblage of labor required to generate a profit, if all the employed are knowledgeable of their trades and the risks, then all are more likely to succeed. From the top to the bottom, the more people who believe their job is important, the greater the chance of success.

Risk is an inherent trait of free enterprise.

Limiting risk in a society limits mankind's imagination. Sophisticated societies with the fewest guarantees, wherein all members realize their individual importance and skills, will have the highest consumption.

When society embraces risk, the future holds less doubt.

Today, in a mystique of logic, we debate why a business is allowed to grow or shrink while demanding more from that business, then debating who is to pay the tab. Anti-business sentiment created by small numbers at all levels of government uses legal and emotional means to restrict, eliminate, and primarily raise the cost and control over businesses and investments. Instead of allowing free enterprise to provide for the world as it has, impatient government bureaucrats scorn what they don't understand. Defying the rules of math will only make worse what the ignorant believe they made better. Rather than creating a better life for tomorrow, they are taxing us and our children. The future is not so far away that we will not bear its burden. If the future is bankrupt, our children may want to clean up more than our rivers. Even those who have "worked hard all their lives" should be reminded that never in history has anyone been owed a living. What is owed, we owe to ourselves. The beggars should not own the streets, nor should the needy be the greedy.

The media and many politicians have built a dislike for progress and the innovation that replaces jobs. Their concern is an echo of Nikolai Lenin, who taught that the "capital, created by labor … would create an army of the unemployed." Like Lenin, the politicians or media that create the fear don't understand the evolution of efficiencies and production. This ignorance encourages politicians to create jobs that are useless, despite a system that creates endless jobs of value. When workers are displaced by innovation, so, too, is the money that paid the worker. And both worker and money will find new ventures. Investment nets a more efficient community and higher productivity, not fewer jobs. Those Leninists who criticize machines and efficiency should try building their communities with shovels and handcarts. The others of us will build with tractors and trucks, and we will see who feeds more, lives better, and works hardest. There is a balance between labor and machine, with one pushing the other to greater importance. Machines replace labor or perform where workers cannot, as we work less for the same—or the same for more.

Despite the advantages that investment has brought us, our lives have not improved to a degree we should expect because of the outrageous demands of government. Investment has therefore been more important today than ever. We have all seen the advantages of efficiency when the price of products we like decline. But if investment is good for us, why are many working harder and getting less? Is efficiency reducing the value of jobs, or are the burdens placed on us by government greater than the advantages of efficiency that investment has made? Politicians constantly exploit voters by promising to correct the contrived damage done to the worker by business, while simultaneously interfering with the ability of businesses to control costs. For the sake of a growing government, politicians have sacrificed unions, workers, businesses, and living standards. Politicians protest business profits, but the costs added by them to our products far exceed those profits. Government-controlled costs, such as workers compensation, health insurance, trash, and utilities have all been heavily burdened with government regulation, taxes, litigation, and price control. While regulated businesses raise prices, the deregulated businesses reduce them. Rather than fighting corrupt, overgenerous welfare and inefficient government, politicians on all levels raise the costs they control, then act as heroes when, in "fairness to the consumer," they deregulate.

Federal and state mandates to local governments have necessitated higher building fees, sales tax, gas tax, income tax, intangible tax, real estate tax, tangible tax, and lottery tax—and of course, there is a tax on the tax. "Don't tax me; don't tax thee; tax that fellow under the tree." Much like country singers, the politicians stay at the top of the charts by talking of love, the poor, and the worker. Could it be that the government is the foe and investment and efficiency is the friend? Could it be that without investments, the burden of the worker would be impossible to carry?

Investment is often associated with the rich, and the rich do make a lot of investments. The rich long ago ascertained that stacking gold in the corner doesn't make them richer, and trinkets delight them for only so long. Getting rich and staying rich is no longer a matter of ravaging the neighbors to steal their gold. Most of the "rich" learn that being rich brings with it responsibility. Only the neophyte believes wealth is an end of responsibility, rather than a beginning. Riches are now gained and held by investment, but without the consumer to buy, there are no profits. One invests to provide for others, as all should work to provide for themselves. The citizenry of the land consume what is produced, and all depend upon that production. Those we call the rich guide the decisions, based on their judgment of popular demands. Whether for greed, power, or to just make a living, investors get ahead, just like workers, by putting in time making something for someone else.

If we are working harder and getting less, could it be that the rich aren't to blame? The established media blames the rich for the poor, knowing that the cost of government has gone up significantly and the burden of workers who owe their wages to taxes and regulation has grown. There are more who live on welfare, and welfare payments and government wages and benefits keep going up. Are we working harder because there are too few good jobs, or are too few producing consumable goods and services? For many the belief in free enterprise is so strong that even they don't see why it's happening. Believers say that government is too big, and the way we tax is unfair. The dream that free enterprise offers is good if only we work harder, and work harder we do. The price for a good life has increased, while the politician takes credit or casts blame, depending on where he stands and who is in power.

Is money the only investment, or do people count? If people count, then how we "invest people" matters, and who is investing the most "people" is what matters most. Government requires a lot of people to meet its demands, but not all government workers work directly for government. Those employed in the private sector to satisfy or exploit governmental guidelines and mandates are no less employed by government. These "mandated government employees" represent a tax that is hidden from view. Could it be that the reason practically every business in the United States is downsizing or exporting jobs is to create an indirect means to provide the labor to fill "government jobs" and fulfill government demands?

Investment is how the economy keeps up with demand. Simple logic implies that shortages will not occur, and inflation is not a problem when production equals demand. *Investment is the production we do today to provide for tomorrow.* Investors spend and lose fortunes, guessing our tomorrows. The people making these guesses aren't neophytes in their trades; they are experts in oil, autos, toilet paper, and ice cream. Their decisions are made from information that is mathematical, mental, and material to the product. And others of even greater experience usually check their decisions. There are millions of products and services in the world. The people who understand them and make the investment decisions regarding them know a billion bits of information. In general, government doesn't have the people who understand even one product enough to run a business and make a product. The principal reason for the failure of Communism was the reliance on centralized planning. This is an important detail in the functioning of free enterprise, but it is not one that the majority of economists, politicians, or the population has accepted carte blanche. We may want absolute control in our own work but would prefer one authority that would guide all the others. The constant economic tinkering by the politicians is evidence that centralized planning is less than divine knowledge. Economic books have little or no discussion on decentralized thinking (investment) and only briefly mention or fail to define Adam Smith's invisible hand.

Whether politicians realize it or not, their world protects them from questioning the license for power voted them by the electorate. Those within who question the omnipotence of government are ostracized or girdled until they agree. In other words, anyone who knows too much about enterprise and questions the importance of government involvement isn't allowed in government. The result is an attempt by politicians to guide the economy while ignoring those billion bits of information.

Government is capable of making only big decisions. Selling cheap hamburgers through a window with arches over it would have been construed as a waste of the citizen's money. Government makes decisions such as whether to land on the Moon or Mars and even them is often to willing to abandon the billions spent with a simple "never mind." The little decisions are made, one by one, by people who determine each need or desire and the means by which it will be satisfied. Why did communism fail? It failed because centralized planners are unimaginative, inarticulate, incapable of delegating responsibilities, and not one would dare to dream of building a Disneyland. If they had, communism would have failed because government cannot legislate all the little decisions, and workers would have no incentive to follow.

The most accurate decisions are made at the lowest relevant economic level. (The invisible hand)

Investment decisions are the formulation of our imagination.

The real question is whether we can have faith in the imagination of our fellow humans to solve problems. But then, after all, if we have no faith in ourselves, don't our fellow humans run government? Government often generates its crisis to stress its importance. For example, reporters seemed sure of a pending disaster when computers throughout the world would fail because they weren't programmed past the year 2000 (Known as the Y2K problem or millennium bug,). Estimates to resolve the problem were as much as $300 billion and, of course, it was government that needed to do something. Oh, how stupid they must think we are; what mindless imbeciles we are! The mind that powers ships with an atom, sends humans into space, and talks through satellites from the jungles cannot change a clock without government. Programs to cure the problem, had Y2K been a problem, were as little as twenty-five dollars.

Some economists actually believe that good ideas are a matter of luck. Because good ideas are only luck and because everyone's luck is different, the situation mandates government involvement to resolve inequities. These are the same kind of people who belittle McDonald's because the simplicity of such a concept is presumed below that of a centralized intelligence. But centralized intelligence didn't choose McDonald's; people chose McDonald's—people, just like the ones who work there. The process through which McDonald's was selected for success was the only true democratic process of selection that exists or ever will, and it parallels the same democratic process that has chosen free enterprise every day for the last three hundred years. If luck alone makes us rich, then by chance, free people are lucky and the Communist Chinese, Russians, and Cubans are not. Investment is the key to the progress of mankind. If we understand how investment works, who makes decisions, who provides the investment, and how government alters costs, we will understand how free enterprise improves life.

As the discussion moves into monetary terms, think of money in terms of people, and a tax and mandated costs as paying government workers. An investment represents the force that directs labor to an area where demand is created. Assuming a good free-market investment, both consumer and risk-taker receive benefits. The definition of investment seems obvious, but we should think how money best moves labor and what makes investments successful.

An investment is made to benefit society and profit is made when society is benefited.

If something is produced that the consumer does not want or already has enough of, then neither the investor nor the consumer will benefit. What is good for one is good for the other. Therefore, we first decide if we have a reason to invest. There are good reasons and there are bad reasons.

Good reasons for making investments in productivity:

- Meet or get ahead of competition
- Reduce cost
- Meet environmental standards
- Manufacture new products
- Take advantage of new technology
- Expand or establish sales
- Update the appearance or usefulness of facilities
- Increase supply
- Meet new safety standards
- Better serve the community
- Increase investment returns
- Replace existing equipment
- Establish new businesses
- Update good or service

Bad reasons to invest:

- Because everyone else is doing it
- Because it is a government-subsidized industry
- Shelter income

All the good investment decisions are made with the anticipation of providing a benefit to the community. "Because government subsidizes a business" and "to create a tax shelter" are reasons that lack business direction and are good indicators of future losses. Only the neophytes and charlatans see the advantages of tax shelters, and one preys upon the other. A tax shelter is just a way of burning money. Ironically, investments made with the express purpose of making money usually fail because the investors ignore consumers. If an investment doesn't make money without tax benefits, it won't make money with it, unless, of course, we are in the business of selling tax shelters.

Once proper reasons are established for making an investment, the next step is to determine if the proposed investment makes economic sense and has the potential to return the investment and show a profit. The three factors of cost are money, availability of labor, and risk. If the type of business is cyclical, investors may, for example, fear the inevitability of recession, which increases risk. The greater the risk, the greater the return needed to justify the risk. To reduce risk, businesses do a preliminary investigation to eliminate as much risk as possible. First, investors look at general factors that affect the need for a product, and then they compute the sales and costs that are needed to support an investment.

Investigations that precede an investment decision:

* Market research
* Market atmosphere/ stability
* Government stability and attitude
* Labor atmosphere
* Competition

Factors that affect sales and cost:

* Interest rates
* Income tax rates
* Real and personal taxes
* Building, equipment, labor
* Payroll insurance
* Liability insurance
* Cost of financing
* Anticipated pricing
* Payroll tax and benefit cost
* Environmental and safety cost

*** Factors that are significantly impacted by government**

By far one the most important consideration regarding an investment is the income tax rate. A combination of risk, interest rates, market, leverage, and industry standards determine/demand a certain profit margin for each specific business. Income taxes on the net profits will therefore have an incredible impact on the final decision to invest. What this means is that if the market demands a 10 percent profit on sales, a 50 percent tax would require a 20 percent net profit. A 13 percent tax would require only an 11.5 percent net profit on sales or an 8.5 percent difference in price. If pricing won't support the higher price, the investment can't be made. Tax rates affect when, where, and whether an investment will be made. As such, high corporate income taxes can be the primary reason that jobs are exported to another country or that investments are not justified. High taxes on business will slow economic growth considerably.

The factors that precede investment decisions are research-oriented and based on judgment, opinions, and economic conditions. Once a decision to invest is made, feasibility comes down to a profit analysis. Because free enterprise acts to reduce rather than inflate cost, and unless cost is affected by outside forces such as government mandates, new investments often contemplate production at a lower cost. There are two categories of expenses: operating—the day-to-day or periodic expenses; and capital expenditures—what we usually call plant and equipment or fixed costs. Any of the factors listed can be interchangeable—labor for machinery, for example. If labor is cheap relative to an automatic hamburger machine, the machine may not be economical. Higher capital cost may result in lower operating costs. The decision to use man or machine is often based on how best to satisfy the consumer, but a direct relationship between the cost of capital and the cost of labor does exist.

The more costly the labor, the more valuable the machine.
The less costly the labor, the less valuable the machine.

One of the differences between labor and machine is that labor usually has very little upfront cost, as compared to machines, while machines are paid for upfront and have a predictable maintenance cost. A major factor in the cost of a machine, as with the entire investment, is the cost of money. Money, in relation to interest, functions much the same as the cost of labor.

The higher the interest rate, the more costly the capital.
The lower the interest rate, the cheaper the capital.

The cost of money changes when interest rates change. Interest rates are controlled greatly by the Federal Reserve, an agency of the government, and often mirror government rather than business actions. Financing costs must also be considered and are often the subject of intangible taxes, bank-required insurance, capital requirements, and regulation. Businesses leverage their investments, and high gross margins aren't necessary in order to net high profits. Restaurant operators, for example, typically finance real estate costs at market rates that are below the returns anticipated on the investor's investment. In other words, an investment doesn't have to earn 10 percent to net the investor 10 percent when portions of the investment are borrowed. If funds can be borrowed at 5 percent, and the investment only earns 6 percent, you can still net 20 percent when you borrow 95 percent. Leveraging is basic to investment returns, but the general and often fatal belief of the novice is that investors make outlandish profits. The point is that changing interest rates affects vast numbers of investments at even low levels, where a quarter percent or a half percent can be the difference between success, failure, or not investing.

Leverage financing acts to reduce profit margins and increase investor returns.

Leveraging benefits the consumer and the investor. To demonstrate how leverage financing works, let's suppose an investor borrows $12,000,000 for twenty-five years to purchase a new plant; it costs $14 million and will pay back 10 percent on the total investment. Of course, as interest rates increase, the desirability decreases.

INTEREST RATE	MONTHLY PAYMENT	PAYMENT INCREASE	RETURN ON $2,000,000 INVESTMENT	TIMES LENDERS RATE
6	$77,320	NA	23.60%	4
7	$84,820	9.7%	19.10%	2.7
8	$92,620	19.8%	14.40%	1.8
9	$100,710	30.0%	9.60%	1

When price is too low or costs are too high, investment returns can be too low to cover payments, and investments are delayed. When this happens, prices must go higher before plants can be built, or the cost of labor must go down. This situation usually occurs when inflation is a problem and the cost of labor is rising. Since the failure to invest results in inflation, inflation begets higher interest rates, which beget higher cost, which beget higher prices, which beget high inflation, which begets higher interest rates. Other than increasing interest rates to force a recession and reduce labor rates, increased efficiency and additions to the supply of labor are the only cures for inflation.

Investment returns can be further illustrated if we look at what it takes to get rich. We hear about the rich on Wall Street, but what is not obvious is the small return it takes to compound a fortune. If we had a mere $10,000 and doubled it every five years for only twenty-five years, we would end up with $320,000. Twenty-five years is hardly a lifetime. If that were $1,000,000, it would become $32,000,000. Below is a schedule showing what a $10,000 and $1,000,000 investment would become after twenty-five years, at various compounded rates of return.

COMPOUNDED INVESTMENT AFTER 25 YEARS

COMPOUNDED	INVESTED		COMPOUNDED	INVESTED	
RETURN	$10,000	$1,000,000	RETURN	$10,000	$1,000,000
3%	$21,000	$2,100,000	10%	$108,000	$10,800,000
4%	$27,000	$2,700,000	11%	$135,000	$13,500,000
5%	$34,000	$3,400,000	12%	$170,000	$17,000,000
6%	$43,000	$4,300,000	13%	$212,000	$21,120,000
7%	$54,000	$5,400,000	14%	$265,000	$26,500,000
8%	$68,000	$6,800,000	15%	$329,000	$32,900,000
9%	$86,000	$8,600,000	16%	$409,000	$40,900,000

Sustained returns above 10 percent are not common. Pure investors are happy to earn after tax returns of 5–6 percent. Corporations that earn after tax returns of 10–15 percent on a consistent basis are considered successful. But businesses net a higher yield because of the risk and the need to invest in expansion. Businesses that earn high returns generally offer the best values or products to consumers, or efficiency and innovation to producers, and they often reinvest much more than they earn. When all businesses are considered, most invest more than they earn to maintain productivity. True cash returns are often negative. Fortunately, the market values both income and investment.

The number of opportunities is affected by returns, as investments that return 3 percent are more numerous and have less risk than those that pay 10 percent.

Interest rates have an inverse relationship to the number of investment opportunities.

Because of this relationship, when interest rates are high, investments with lower yields are held up. In other words, as the interest rates of the early 1980s declined from 20 percent and more, the opportunity to invest was greater because many investments made economic sense only at lower rates. Because investment increases productivity and reduces inflation, lower rates accelerate opportunities and deflation, just as higher rates decelerated them. Therefore:

Rising interest rates delay investments, reducing productivity and causing inflation, thereby further reducing investment opportunities at an accelerating rate.

Tax-law changes generally have an impact on investors, but the 1993 tax act that raised taxes appeared to result in only an economic ripple. It was only a ripple because of the unique number of opportunities that occur when interest rates decline. Regardless, the cost to businesses did increase and investments were delayed. Ironically, because all tax changes have an impact on economic growth, this phenomenon will result in lower tax revenues over the longer term. Businesses reduce investments to compensate for the lower returns that increased tax engenders, and the economy slows to capitalize profits at higher levels, thereby reducing tax revenues. Taxes eventually grow when the adjustment to cost or price occurs, but not to the same extent if they had remained lower. Tax-revenue increases occur through the indirect transfer of income from the consumer and the worker, without a commensurate growth in the value of wages that investment assures. In addition, the idled labor and the potential for growth can never be regained.

The flip side is that when taxes are reduced, investment flourishes and can result in an economy that expands too fast. Tax reductions should be coupled with reduced restrictions on labor, such as fixing or lowering welfare payments. Also, workers can be added to allow for a compounding-inflation free economy by removing restrictions on labor, reducing the government demand for workers and more investments. As a side note, this view would support the increase in minimum wages to force more efficiency upon business.

Part of the excuse for raising taxes is more spending to redistribute wealth. But interest and other costs, including taxes, eventually increase the value of assets owned by the rich, thus damning those who thought they were distributing wealth. This effect is hidden because in the short term, existing assets become less valuable when higher taxes reduce income. However, calculations done to determine the feasibility of an investment consider all costs, including taxes. When cost or price changes enough to yield the desired net return, the increased taxes, in essence, transfer to the worker or the consumer. In a sophisticated investment environment, net profit reflects income taxes that increase the needed working capital, and earnings increase sufficiently to yield income on the increased taxes. This recapitalization of corporate profits does not operate in the full spectrum of escalating taxes and costs. When government assessments become confiscatory, recapitalization is limited, and expansion can become impossible. At the point price or cost can't be adjusted sufficiently, new investments are stunted. The inflation that ensues will only yield to lower taxes, imports, technological advances, and/or real wage reduction.

A multitude of outside forces affect the financial structure of investment returns. Income taxes, local taxes, real estate taxes, financing cost, mandated costs, and sometimes incentives for investment are just a few. If acceptable investment returns are 10 percent, then higher taxes may raise acceptance to 10½ percent or higher. The response occurs on all levels of investment, as those seeking 14 percent might now want 15 percent. To understand this, consider that capital is not currently deductible against taxable income, thus only a portion of the profits become available to repay debt or to capitalize growth. A difference of half a percent in an investment does not seem material, but as demonstrated above, over long periods of time, a small amount can translate into a big difference. A half-point difference over twenty-five years translates to a 12 percent difference in capital accumulation and 1 percent to a 25 percent difference in profits. If tax rates change by 5 percent, the effect is not immediate, but any change eventually triggers a response. Half-point differences are nearly inconspicuous in the near term, but their effect magnifies over time, and if we can think of these differences as losses in our living standards, the effect becomes apparent.

The entire idea of taxing business works at cross purposes with the good of the community and its citizens. Taxing businesses increase costs, which inflates wealth, which increase prices, profits or reduces wages, which reduces the feasibility of new investments, which limits increases in labor's productivity, which reduces labor's value (wealth), which reduces labor's compensation, which increases the need for humanitarian aid, police protection, and reduces individual tax revenue, that reduces government tax receipts, and increases the need for raising taxes. If politicians want to help its citizens, they should focus on increasing the productivity of labor so as to fund needed projects while reducing wasted Keynesian type spending and welfare. Hypothetically, if a local community wanted to fund a new stadium for the local NBA team,, would it be better to reduce taxes and thus increase both local investment and incomes to a point where admissions would support the private funding of such a project?

Effectively, all costs are passed to consumers, as delays in investments cause shortages that eventually translate into price and, consequently, the rearrangement of the consumer's market basket. In this Complex society, with alternatives to choose from, a cost increase can result in lower wages and the loss or downsizing of industries that can't adjust. Higher costs often destine an investment to the trash bin as the market basket is reshaped to exclude a product, reduce the size and quality of products, reduce the volume of consumption of a product, push production to a foreign country, or cause a switch to lower cost alternatives. In this world, something that isn't done isn't counted. However, the result of reducing investments is a reduction in the potential, if not the actual economy and individual living standards. If, for example, a half percent in extra cost to the economy is not offset by efficiency, over twenty-five years the economy will be 12 percent smaller. As demonstrated in the following chart, even minor changes that affect growth of the economy have major impacts.

	Economic Growth/Decline after 25 years At respective rate	
Rate of Growth/ Decline	Growth	Decline
½%	13	12
1%	28	22
1½ %	45	31
2%	64	39
2½ %	85	47
3%	109	53

Politicians ignore the long-term effects of cost increases because they deal so much in current affairs, rather than long-term economic planning. The significant differences in opinions and ignorance regarding the mechanism of an economy are, of course, a huge factor, and economic planning is not often even a consideration. Many politicians think they can simply tax the rich to pay the bill for government intrusions in the economy. The investors' response, on the other hand, is one of experience built over years. Obviously, the investors who survive are those who have made the proper decisions, whereas a politician's failures can be swept away. Even short-term cost changes can have long-term effects. A vivid picture of how taxes are imputed into cost can be obtained by computing the pretax yields needed to achieve a desired net yield and then computing the increase in pretax earnings resulting from adding the higher taxes to expenses and overlaying the two computations. An accurate computation will disclose that taxes are not only passed to the consumer, but that businesses also earn income on the higher tax because added costs mean greater risks. There are an infinite number of computations that can be made based on changes, such as inflation, interest rates, business cycles, capacities, and other factors.

Traditional industry margins are a special interest. These are gross profit margins and net after tax yields that industries customarily use to determine pricing. Each industry has a traditional margin of profit to achieve the necessary gross profit that compensates for risk, knowledge, investment, typical cash flows, typical borrowing practices, research, and a multitude of other factors. In the old days, business people might say, "You gotta double your cost to get price," or some other standard that time had shown to ensure profits. Today's market-changers, such as Sam Walton, understood these traditions in every detail. He understood them enough so as to use modern technology and purchasing power to change them and to change the industry.

Bankers look at investments the same way. Their traditional margin was 3 percent over their cost of funds. That margin was a historic measure developed by time. It represented the edge at which enough is recovered to pay costs, cover losses, earn profits, and avoid undue competition. Business people are usually quite knowledgeable about their special margins for profit. In today's environment, however, government has increased business risks, which translates into higher investment returns, bigger margins, and new avenues of income that are needed to survive economic trials.

In general, business acts not much differently than utilities managed by government. The exception is that government-regulated industries are rewarded for cost increases and free enterprise is rewarded for cost reductions. Obviously, this means that unregulated businesses are more efficient. Unlike unregulated industries, regulated utilities are guaranteed a return on their investments by the regulation agencies. Business must also make a certain return, or the market economy will become unstable. The attempt by government to mimic free enterprise in its treatment of utilities and other controlled businesses is a failure because it has also eliminated risk and, therefore, the efficiency of the market system. The sacrifice that a few make as a result of risk is offset a thousand times by the gains made by millions who thwart it. The keen sense of responsibility and value in a society at risk augment its potential. In a complex and risk-oriented world, the resultant higher living standard would support the few indigents who remained in a loftier fashion than even those on welfare today. A society that endures risk also finds education a greater advantage, whether in the schools or on the streets.

Government has such a great impact on the economy that any discussion without mention of the impact would be lacking. In a prior list, factors were noted with asterisks to emphasize how government controls many factors involved in making investment decisions. Only two are not directly affected, one of which is price. Many salient government officials have said, "Just raise the price." To a government employee whose wages are constantly adjusted for inflation, it may seem a solution. But with today's governmental control, unless we are its beneficiary, we may not get raises to compensate for higher prices. Since government guarantees more than half of all incomes, significantly less than half must make the adjustment to price increases and are harmed by them. For example, people buying a house find out which loan they qualify for and look for a house within their means. They don't suddenly qualify for more money because the cost goes up. The same thing happens with everything we buy and the way we buy it. For many, when "there is too much month at the end of the money," they go without. When government adds cost to a house, new houses get smaller. If the price of a product does go up, the consumer sacrifices it or something else. Those at the high end of the income scale are advantaged by this formula. Their consumption is relatively miniscule as compared to the masses, and prices are set at optimum levels of production. The masses may use credit or savings to make up differences, but over the long run, there must be an allowance for higher cost through changes in spending patterns.

As the consumer makes changes, so, too, must investors.

Consumer prices and the availability of products are a function of the consumer's spendable resources, not of cost.

Price is determined by dividing the consumer's ability to spend by future production.

Spending is a function of total production.

To demonstrate how products are affected by added government costs, the illustration below enunciates the impact of changes in the cost of a home over twenty years in the state of Florida. For new-home construction in Florida, the cost of the building (exclusive of land, financing, sales costs, and profits) is typically from 50 to 55 percent of the total cost. Using a $100,000 home as an example, we come up with the following:

	YEAR	
	1975	1995
ENVIRONMENTAL RULES AFFECTING (trash, materials, material price)	200	5,600
BUILDING CODE CHANGES AFFECTING (hurricane anchoring, termite spray, wind loads)	200	2500
ENGINEERING FEES	-	200
SOCIAL SECURITY AND UNEMPLOYMENT TAXES	3,000	4,000
SALES TAX	1,500	2,100
OTHER TAXES (intangible, tangible, documentary, gas, utility)	200	500
OTHER COSTS (license, fees, permits)	200	900
WORKERS COMPENSATION	1,100	6,600
GENERAL LIABILITY INSURANCE	100	1,000
BUILDING INSURANCE	50	200
IMPACT FEES INCLUDING- (roads, school, fire, police, other)		3,200
TAP-IN FEES	300	3,000
MISCELLANEOUS FEES- (radon, arbor, driveway, public works)		100
TOTAL OF THE ABOVE COSTS	6,900	29,900
Less COSTS PRIOR		(6,900)
ADDITIONAL COST OF A $100,000 HOME		23,000
THE CONSTRUCTION COST OF A HOME SELLING FOR $100,000		55,000
REMAINING TO BUILD THE HOME		32,000
DECREASE IN SPENDING ON OUR NEW HOME CONSTRUCTION		(42%)

The above illustration is based on experience; actual changes would vary with each jurisdiction. Therefore, the costs are estimates, where changes are known to have occurred. These added costs don't all reflect added protection. For example, soil treatment, although regulated to be more expensive, is significantly less effective because of controls on sprays. Workers who were once covered with workers compensation insurance are no longer protected because of the high cost. Radon fees are required in areas where radon is well established as being a nonexistent problem. Hurricane anchoring, before changes, was possibly a problem of local enforcement of existing codes, and many fees simply replaced funding once derived from other sources with a resultant increase in government revenue.

In addition to the changes in cost that affected building costs, the lot cost would have been affected by the following cost to be incurred in 1995 (they were not incurred in 1975).

COSTS THAT HAVE AFFECTED DEVELOPMENT COSTS:

Drainage	Intangible and real taxes
Sewer and water	Esthetics
Legal	Street sizes
Fire codes	School cost
Land set asides	

Environmental costs have been significant, such as the cost of lumber impacted when millions of acres of forest were restricted from harvest to preserve an owl. Taxes and costs of regulated industries, like workers compensation, are the next most significant cost. No adjustment has been made for inflation, but many workers wages are often little more than in 1975. No adjustment is made for efficiency, innovation, or the loss of skilled labor because of low wage rates. Interest rates in 1975 were about 7 percent. In 1995, rates were 8.5 or 9 percent—not a 1–2 percent difference but a 21–28 percent difference.

Land cost, which was a traditional 30 percent of the sales price, would not change appreciably. Lots would get smaller and would not resemble the dream hoped for, as constraints in cost and restrictive government rules would actually result in additional tree removal. Based on this illustration, the home bought in 1995 would be 40 percent smaller. Because construction methods improved and because workers earned less money, the home might have retained some of its size, but workers probably would not be as skilled due to turnover. Some costs would be less because business units, carpenters, etc., broke down into simpler business forms to save taxes and insurance. Many workers, therefore, would no longer be protected by workers compensation or unemployment insurance. This presentation leaves little doubt that government has a major impact on cost and the supply of goods. Government also has a negative impact on the worker's protection and job stability.

But there is something the illustration does not show. If we want to build a bigger home, we can reduce costs by buying cheaper land. Land is a **leftover cost.** After we total up the other costs, we decide what is left over for land. If the price of what we want is too high, we find it cheaper or offer less. When we can't find land cheap enough, we don't build. Unfortunately, labor is like land: if other costs go up, we look for cheaper labor. If we can't find cheaper labor, we can't hire until we do. This is how the consumer adjusts the cost of labor to spending ability. The biggest cost of government spending is hidden in the wages that workers never get. **The worker is a leftover cost.** Government, however, is not subjected to competition and so assures itself of not being a leftover cost. All taxes, fees, and permits adjust to inflation, and government beneficiaries usually get annual raises.

The '70s and '80s are a prime example of what happens when government expands too quickly for businesses to respond with offsetting efficiencies. Not only do real wages decline, but also incredible investment opportunities result in the aftermath of recession. The combined effects of the growing government-mandated costs, high interest, and inflation in the '70s and early '80s put business in a position where it could not respond quickly enough with lower costs or increased prices. The discounted investment values were not sufficient to afford the improvements needed to increase production, which compounded inflation. When recession followed inflation, these businesses were ripe for "breakups," "leverage buyouts," and other forms of asset reorganization. The pent-up opportunities for improvements and lower interest rates that always follow recessions were coupled with a high unemployment rate that put pressure on wages and was the undoing of many restrictive work rules. The potential returns for risk-takers willing to acquire these industries were compounded. Inflation had hidden inefficiencies, and the free market acted to correct them. As J.P. Morgan said, "Buy low, sell high." Low was when industries were discounted well below their intrinsic value and potential.

The result of the '80s scenario was a revolution in business that continued for years. Sam Walton at Wal-Mart—and thousands like him—used his imagination and lower interest rates to break down traditions and reorganize industry. With each tick down of the interest rate, opportunities were added, as they moved like a wave through the economy. As interest rates reach lower and lower and pent-up opportunities for efficiency have been exploited, the wave will hit the beach and either inflation will resume or wages will further decline. The way to avoid this is for government to reorganize, reduce labor restrictions, and cut costs. If not, any inflationary spiral could be compounded by cost-of-living adjustments for welfare and pensions that would raise government assessments. In the face of already low private-worker wages, a post-recession, '80s-style adjustment could be impossible. The high stock market reflected these corporate reorganizations, plus the influx of money left over by the elimination of most tax shelters in 1986. With the proliferation of the desktop computer, car phone, etc., free enterprise has shown itself to be resilient, so no one can be sure when the wave will hit—or even if it has.

Return on investment computations reveal how costs are absorbed in society and how consumption expands. As much as our well-meaning politicians and the media have wished to distribute the wealth of the country, the revaluation of assets means that nothing has changed. The rich are getting richer, businesses that are marginal are failing, the poor on welfare get inflation adjustments, but the workers—the ones who actually make the product—are recycled to a lower wage. Many who fail are added to the welfare rolls, and fewer graduate from middle class to rich, while the riches of the rich grow. Business or the rich should not be blamed for what is happening to the worker. The response is to the laws of math. Indeed, if adjustments were not made, the economy would be in still further trouble as it attempted to keep up with nonproductive government spending.

Great investments are the result of knowledge, skill, experience, and planning—mostly planning. Investment decisions are often seen as quick thinking at an opportune moment in time. But the mind works at it own pace. Quick thinking is merely the result of prior planning.

CHAPTER 9

INFLATION

Consumer attitudes and excesses in monetary aggregates are the customary explanation for inflation, but shortages in supply shortages hint at shortages in labor. Yet in the Complex economic community of today, concepts like on-time delivery, alternative sources, computer-aided projections, and world competition act as serious threats to the problems of unanticipated or excessive labor demands. These factors and the emphasis on efficiency have reduced unit costs as well, while the labor released to the market has been absorbed and the unemployment rate has declined. Labor, thus, does not appear as seemingly unlimited as politicians often imply. In spite of the tremendous changes in business operations and the ability of retailers to procure unlimited goods for sale, inflation fears continue as a problem. With the tremendous layoffs and reduction in unit manpower and labor-rate costs, traditional economic theory would suggest that unemployment should increase and inflation should be nearly zero.

However, inflation fears have led the Federal Reserve to maintain a prime rate well above the rate of inflation. Whereas the prime rate usually follows market fluctuations, it is now a defensive measure used to thwart inflation or to stimulate the economy. High interest is presumably a cure to inflation, but is this idea valid? Is the government-manipulated high interest rates resolving or exacerbating inflation problems? Efforts to control demand with high rates of interest presume to lower demand, but with interest being a factor of cost, it also adds to inflation. High rates definitely add to the cost of investment, slowing expansion and adding to the cost of product and growth. High rates also raise the cost of federal borrowing, expanding the deficit that is also presumed to provoke inflation. Continual high interest rates are intended to cause "soft landings," rather than recession, but isn't supply augmentation the solution to inflation and the way to improve living standards? Is slow growth or no growth the government goal? If the computation of gross domestic product overstates economic growth, is the Federal Reserve following a faulty economic measure?

This dichotomy of economic manipulations and goals reveals a system in the winds of a hurricane in the hands of cabin boys. We should find it curious that in the most exciting period of change in products and production since the 1920s, an aggressive approach toward economic growth cannot be taken. On the other hand, if the Federal Reserve displays a dislike for the actions of Congress, it speaks loud and clear, though perhaps no one is listening. Because of the abundance of mixed messages besieging us, we can infer a need to understand inflation fully. As an enigma whose current cure is to reduce growth, inflation must be first on our list in resolving this dilemma and improving living standards. Let us start by asking how the inflation/deflation mechanism functions in an economy.

Inflation is the mechanism by which a limited production and excessive demand are reconciled with monetary aggregates.

Inflation is the response to forces that alter the distribution of labor or change the distribution of the market basket.

Deflation is the mechanism by which competition spreads the benefits of lower costs or currency shortages.

Analysis of inflation is a dissection. When we cut it open, we find different parts with different functions. Each part performs separately, but movement in one area causes movement in others. To start, inflation will be divided into *price inflation* and *cost inflation.*

Price inflation has more to do with excess money supplies, but it is construed as an acceptable element of free enterprise, because price deflation is often equated to a sick economy. Deflation in the nineteenth century resulted in a lower living standard. However, in the 1800s, the money supply failed to keep up with production, and exchanges were therefore limited. When money supplies are limited, inefficient bartering is the primary means to facilitate exchanges. Despite the concerns for deflation, our traditional expectation is for prices to go down, not up, as *free enterprise is a deflationary, not an inflationary system.* Price deflation, caused by efficiency, actually occurs constantly and must occur to enhance our living standards. When goods drop in price, consumers add purchases or increase quality. In the transition from farm to factory, we saw a great deal of deflation. As we industrialized, the dollar was strong because a massive supply of labor came from the farm to the factory, and that expanded production and deflated costs. Currently, our money supplies more closely align with production, and there has been no lack in the availability of a medium to facilitate exchanges. With a money supply that matches production, deflation leads to higher living standards.

Price inflation (having to do with monetary supplies): Real inflation occurs when money supplies or other currency-related tools, like bank checks and credit cards, are expanded and push the power to purchase beyond the ability of labor to produce.

MONEY >(Greater Than) PRODUCTION

In some situations, as when money is not sufficient to make exchanges, adding monetary aggregates can help an economy. Inflation is the result, however, when monetary expansion puts too much pressure on labor to expand production. Despite strict controls on the money supply, government cannot control the volume of all forms of credit, and money supplies are difficult to forecast. Money can be created by simple entries in an accountant's ledger and is dependent upon the habits and demographic makeup of the population. Government, too, expands monetary aggregates when it increases revenues to fund its operations or changes the distribution of incomes by increasing pensions or welfare. Changing purchasing distributions affects monetary aggregates because those who lose in the redistribution involuntarily relinquish spending power. The losers then will undoubtedly attempt to maintain living standards by other means. Redistribution, therefore, causes monetary expansion that can result in inflation. Expansion of monetary aggregates can have serious results and as long as we have printing presses, currency is unlimited.

To summarize, either a shortage or surplus of currency can be bad for the economy. If there is a shortage, exchanges are limited and consequently, economic growth is restricted. Should surpluses occur the result would be *price inflation.* These conclusions do not imply that expansion of the money supply is better than contraction. When monetary expansion is intended to redistribute incomes or when it results in recessions, investments are discouraged, and productive workers may lose work and living standards.

Cost inflation (involving labor allocations): Cost inflation occurs when demands are added to the labor force.

DEMAND FOR LABOR >(Greater than) SUPPLY of LABOR

The simple act of raising or lowering taxes doesn't add to inflation—at least, not in the sense that it raises costs, although tax changes may raise or lower the money supply. When government spends the money, the labor pool is affected and inflation can occur. New products, economic restrictions, new laws, or anything that places demands on the labor supply is inflationary.

It is implicit that whether the forces of *cost inflation* or *price inflation* act on an economy, their presence yields an imbalance between demand and production that can be solved with an increase in production. Increasing production requires more labor. If labor can be viewed as a solution to inflation, labor can also be ascribed as a cause. We can thus further the explanations of inflation by grouping the population into functions, so we can visualize how inflation is affected by changes in the way labor is grouped .

The population is made up of groups of workers and nonworkers. A broad division representing the entire population would be as follows:

- A) Government workforce
  - 1) Direct
  - 2) Indirect: providing goods and services to government
  - 3) Pseudo-government: government-controlled agencies funded directly by fees and charges (Example: toll-road authority)
  - 4) Mandated: fulfilling government requirements (regulation-law)
- B) Private workforce
  - 1) Current production
  - 2) Future production
- C) Welfare supported
  - 1) Nonworking
  - 2) Working
- D) Pension, retired
  - 1) Nonworking
  - 2) Working
- E) Other supported persons

If the population total is the only element of the economic equation that changes, with no changes in percentages in each category or in the categories within each category, we should expect an inflation-free economy. But the private workforce provides for all groups, and if it is reduced or reallocated for mandated or legal services, we would logically expect inflation. Demand might stay constant relative to the population, but demand on a private workforce that is declining as a percentage of the population would be inflationary.

If the percentage allocations in work classifications change in relation to the population, the imbalance affects price stability.

Direct government employment is only 20 percent of the workforce, but considering indirect government employment—such as making paper clips and rockets, lobbying, mandated private programs and projects, litigation, and government-required paper work—government-related employment likely commands half of the workforce. With the working population representing about 40 percent of the population, only 20 percent remain to provide food, shelter, entertainment, and transportation for the entire population. In other words, each nongovernment-sponsored worker produces for five citizens. And if government increases its share of the workforce by one, production is reduced by five, plus the support necessary to carry a new government worker. With the assumption that production is dependant upon labor, adding to the share of government workers may not change consumer demand, but we can identify this as a cause for inflationary pressures.

Evidence that changes have occurred in the relative size of the population groups is inherent in record-high ratio of workforce to the population over age sixteen (Civilian Labor Force Participation Rate)[8] and the low unemployment in the 1990s and into the 2000s. With this high employment we should expect historically high living standards and low inflation. Not coincidentally, the import/export deficit is high and most assuredly the result of an attempt to supplement the lost production caused by labor shortages resulting from a reallocation of labor to fulfill government mandates. Over the last forty-five years, official government employment has grown little, but the share of the workforce mandated by government has grown significantly. Not only can it be assumed that the impact is inflationary but also that business efficiency has been offset by the expanded role of government in the economy. Conversely, if government operated with fewer employees relative to the population, an increase in production could be expected to reduce inflationary forces. *Because increasing demand is inflationary and increasing production is deflationary, an economy can grow without inflation, if labor is shifted into the private work sector.* Therefore, the economy can grow without inflation if the workforce is monitored to limit growth in government-related employment and welfare. It can also be observed that published government payrolls have little meaning in relation to the actual impact of government on the labor force and inflation.

When monetary aggregates are sufficient, growth in production is dependent upon labor supplies, not upon investment.

Complex communities can determine and provide necessary currencies, which leaves only the shortage of labor to restrict economic growth.

Even when the ratio of population in each of the above categories remains stable, inflationary pressures can occur when the income is reapportioned. For example, inflationary pressure can occur when higher taxes or an increased cost of liability insurance reduces the income of one group and increases that of another, or when income is reapportioned within a group. When individuals whose income declines struggle to maintain living standards (economic rebalancing), that result heightens

8 J. D. Gwartney and Richard L. Stroup. *Economics: Private and Public Choice*, Harcourt Brace & Company: 1976. Summary of population and labor force and statistics on the consumer price index from the economic report of the president.a

spending. Researching monetary and labor-shifting in detail would provide a basis for determining the effect of government and other economic actions within population groups.

Because reapportioning causes the group whose income is reduced to struggle to maintain living standards, reapportioning income is inflationary.

As reapportioning income can cause inflation, so can changing spending patterns. If we break down spending allocations in categories, we can examine how inflation and possible deflation (the type that causes economic contraction) can occur.

Let us look at how spending can impact inflation. All spending can be broken down into the following categories:

A) Investment, expansion of production
B) Consumption
  1) Individual
  2) Government
    i) Direct (as government)
    ii) Indirect (through laws and mandates to business or individuals)
C) Infrastructure (roads, forest, waterways, etc.)
  1) Direct (as government)
  2) Indirect (through laws and mandates to business or individuals)
D) Social order (military, law and order)

Investment is good for an economy, but it is too high if the capacity produced exceeds the ability to consume. Over-investment operates to commit a disproportionate share of the workforce to build for the future. An excessive allocation of labor to one group detracts from labor needed in others and is inflationary. When a group expands production beyond the needs of the future, the structure of the group that over-invests will eventually break down, causing unemployment, or if jobs are guaranteed, workers will be wasted. If the over-investment impacts a large segment of the economy, the result can be economic collapse. The effect of over-investment on Complex societies is different and can change from a yawn to calamity when the incentives to invest are impacted by government legislation or mandates. Over-investment was evidenced in the period of the Great Depression and had a significant impact in that Transitional and unstable economy. In Complex societies, adverse effects are more likely to be felt in industries or communities by not throughout all communities or industries. Government on the other hand, can alter tax or regulatory incentives that distort normal investment calculations in such a manner that communities in an entire country can be affected.

Under-investment is also inflationary. A share of the workforce is always needed to provide for future production to keep up with population growth. When this normal expansion does not occur, shortages can occur that provoke inflation. Expansion is difficult to achieve in an atmosphere that is short of labor.

Spending for individual consumption in a Complex society can be assumed as a constant when the economy functions without outside interference. Without outside interference, free enterprise can act to enhance living standards without inflation. When the government increases its consumption, the labor available for consumer production declines. Businesses that get shorted may attempt to augment payrolls with higher wages or reduce demand with higher prices. In either case the effects are inflationary. Inflation acts to reapportion the limited production while labor is reallocated to a stable grouping.

Government consumption, infrastructure, and social order expenditures all have to do with decisions by government. Because the results of these expenditures are different and may affect living standards, they deserve separate notice but not long explanations. What we must grasp is that government expenditures are not always made by government. The highways built by a developer or the air purifier at the bread factory are still government mandated. Simply transferring the responsibility for writing a check to the private sector doesn't change historical implications. They must be accounted for as government expenditure, because they are the result of a change created by government that affects production costs. This hidden government spending growth is inflationary.

If we were to categorize spending over a period of years, according to our aforementioned analysis, we would recognize the effect that spending patterns have on inflation, deflation, and living standards. From this point we could project inflation and our progress on augmenting living standards. Such projections would also speak to the importance of efficient labor allocations and the way in which labor allocations are impacted by spending.

The above patterns of spending and population groupings appear to be ignored as inflation indicators. Too often, the rationale for inflation fighting and high interest rates, absent any major crisis, is consumer confidence. There are too many other forces acting on the economy to suspect that consumer enthusiasm could be more than just a minor force. The speculation that the inability of the consumer to control spending creates inflation brings with it economic solutions that affect how we live and how we perceive free enterprise.

Here, the concern is the confidence of the consumer. If we ask the question, "How is the inflationary impact of consumer confidence overcome?" our answer will be, "Raise interest rates on consumers and producers until spending is reduced and inflation subsides, and hope that a severe recession doesn't follow." Hope for the soft landing. In other words, the government solution is a predictable one that seeks to punish the population for positive results, rather than provide rewards. From experience, we know that inflation is reduced when the economy goes into a recession, but if the goal of government is improving our living standards and growth in employment, why is consumption punished? By implying that consumer confidence is the driving force behind the economy, we indict consumers and businesses for failure to control themselves. Consumers who have lost spending power due to high taxes can easily be pictured as spending beyond their means. Those whose wages or incomes are increased could be as likely to save as to spend and higher earnings is more likely a reflection of the higher productivity that preceded the gain in wages. Ensuing government-forced recessions are perceived as the necessary end to a consumer problem. The logic behind consumer confidence ignores the possibilities for increasing production to reduce inflation. And invariably after recessions, government stimulates the economy, and the consumer is again blamed for overreacting and for failing to save, rather than spend. Focusing on reducing rather than increasing production results in unwarranted cycles, punishment of the consumer, burdening the private workers with the cost of the recession, and abrogation of the potential for improving the standard of living.

When excessive demand leads to inflation, production inadequacies are likely the result of labor shortages caused by added stress on the labor force. Government's good intentions place the greatest demand on labor, while government policies that create inflation are resolved with unemployment. Government stimulus to bolster the economy strains private workers by adding to their responsibilities. If we took the position that consumer spending habits do not change appreciably and that spending is reflective of consumer income, we would look elsewhere for solutions to inflation. It is noteworthy that people with jobs have less time to shop.

Government increases earnings of select groups, raises welfare levels, reduces incentives of workers to take jobs, creates unnecessary jobs, and mandates private work functions. These measures all impact the labor supply and are inflationary solutions to unemployment. With government expenditures at nearly one-half of consumer spending, government is the largest spender and the single greatest cause of inflation.[9] Alternately, individuals who don't contribute to the market basket would represent the single greatest potential for enhancing production. Were they to contribute food, transportation, shelter, or entertainment, production would be enhanced.

To continue with the discussion, we require additional definitions. As *price inflation* and *cost inflation* have been explained and groups have been defined, we must next examine definitions for the workings of changes in these groups. The terms below relate to the monetary actions and labor-force changes that have inflationary effects.

Reallocation is the action of a force that is the result of a choice the consumer did not make.

Allocation is an action of a force that is the result of a choice made by consumers.

Reallocation of the market basket is the reapportionment of the market basket by changing the distribution of purchasing power as a result of actions by government organizations.

Allocation of the market basket is how the market basket is apportioned as a result of freely conceived buyer and business selections.

Reallocation of labor is the effect that government has on the distribution and functions of the workforce into active or inactive pursuits (employed or not).

Allocation of labor is the effect that freely conceived buyer and business decisions have on the distribution of the workforce.

Advocates of reallocating labor and the market basket (those espousing government growth) will say that additional expenditures provide jobs, put government employees on a pay scale equivalent to private employment, and supplement incomes of the needy. Advocates proclaim these expenditures enrich us all at a cost to the rich or at no cost at all. To them, spending increases demand, jobs, and the utilization of existing facilities. These activities are looked upon as simulative but not inflationary. Their response seems predicated on the assumption that the money came from thin air, and that those in private employment don't have enough to do. In fact, government expenditures already far exceed the income of the rich and all corporations combined. Demand, encouraged by demand-side economic beliefs, makes the assertion that the expansion of the money supply equates to product expansion. In other words, demand-side economics ignores the logic that it takes a given amount of labor to provide a given amount of goods; thus, the use and value of labor to production is not a consideration. Advocates of demand-side economics are unwittingly asserting a position that money, not labor, builds products.

Demand-side economics (or "good for the economy" economics) offers baffling conclusions, because to subscribe to the theory, we must believe that providing unproductive and meaningless jobs increases living standards, and that production is unlimited and not affected by the availability of labor. If this were true, inflation could not occur. The demand that causes inflation would also increase production from an ongoing surplus labor supply. On the other hand, if labor is ever limited, then

9 This measure uses government figures. It does not allow for government-mandated and controlled expenditures and because the calculation of GDP is questionable, government-influenced control is more likely over 60 percent of all spending.

labor allocated to an unnecessary job, an inefficient job, or a job that was restricted from inclusion in the productive sector of the economy is acting to reduce overall production and, consequently, the living standards of society. Likewise, if labor were an unlimited production additive, then the action taken by the Federal Reserve to slow consumption and to push the economy into recession or a soft landing would not be necessary.

Reallocations of labor reduce consumer production.

Reallocations of labor are inflationary.

To the Keynesian and the socialist, unemployment, welfare, and government spending are self-certifications of their necessity. However, if government jobs are necessary to reduce unemployment, then with government employment at the 20 percent actual or 50 percent imputed, and with unemployment at only 5 percent, we would have to assume that without government employment, unemployment would be an astronomical 25–55 percent. Logically, even with unemployment that high, the unemployed could receive checks equivalent to the government payrolls, and we could at least save on the natural resources consumed in their jobs. The perplexing circumstance, wherein Congress stimulates the economy while the Federal Reserve restrains it, is certified evidence that our government is not capable of managing the economy. It also provides evidence of the injudicious Ponzi scheme that inflates government.

Although some people are aware that government reallocations have an effect on the cost of the living, many of them don't pay taxes directly and they believe that taxing the rich to pay the cost of government doesn't have an effect. This is understandable, as the taxes we pay directly are obvious; the tax we pay included in our purchases is not. But businesses expand with the income they retain or through investments from those who can afford to invest. To facilitate expansion, businesses must raise prices or cut costs when taxes increase, because only income attracts sensible investors. And investors are needed to provide the added product demanded by a growing population. The logic here is almost too simple to relate. No matter what politicians tell us about how government costs are paid, costs are all paid through the products bought by consumers, rich or poor, and through the reduced wages of private workers. The imbalance that the growing cost of government creates is settled in a chain of events in which inflationary pressures readjust individual market baskets (living standards) for various affected groups in the economy.

The traditional rationale for government spending is almost too simple not to be embraced. We are all cognizant of the media's negative referrals to supply-side economics as "trickle-down economics." The alternative demand-side economics suggests stimulation, and who would not want "their" economy stimulated? The fixation on the need for stimulus is drawn from logic derived from emotion, philanthropies, and job preservation. There is a large group, called lobbyists, whose daily bread is earned by asking government to stimulate the economy of those they represent. A lobbyist's job is dependent upon performance, any performance. Often, their goals defy understanding, as many lobbyists spend their time in Washington trying to get laws passed to encourage competition among the businesses they represent. But in their defense, when people in a free system are told something needs to be done, an army will come with ideas. Everyone complains about government, and those in government complain about special-interest groups. It is some consolation to know that because of lobbyists, politicians have their own devils to deal with.

To finalize the dissection of inflation, we must consider two other elements. Inflation can be permanent or temporary. If it is necessary for government to act because of inflation, it is important to know to which type government is responding. When permanent inflation occurs, only events such as recession, depression, political change, or change in law or agreements can reduce the inflation. Nothing is absolute, as any conditions of change can occur, but a great deal of inflation has turned out to be permanent. The consumer price index has been readjusted to different base years several times, but the official record manifest inflation from the 1950s to the 1990s of about 500 percent.

Permanent inflation is usually the result of changes in the way labor is allocated or reallocated in the general workforce or from a reallocation of the market basket. For example, if government's demand for labor changes from 45 to 50 percent of the available workforce, the percentage of the productive workforce would decline from 55 to 50 percent. Dollars have shifted labor to increase purchasing power in one category, and unless offsetting efficiencies occur elsewhere, prices will increase to ration available supplies and rebalance the economy.

Temporary inflation is usually the result of an allocation of the market basket that causes supply shortages or demand increases that we expect to be reversed. Often, there are permanent factors affecting what may be temporary inflation, and consequently, many inflationary adjustments are a combination of the two. For example, increases in prices that may be caused by temporary heavy demand may result in permanent inflation when COLAs (cost of living adjustments) are introduced for large sectors of the population. In such an instance, the alternative cause, the permanent COLA adjustments, are the real cause of inflation. Temporary inflation is normally the result of monetary allocations. Simple price increases due to temporary high demand may affect the distribution of purchasing, but it is not likely to have material consequences in the long run. For example, heavy demand for autos may prompt dealers to be less flexible on price, and manufacturers may be less apt to give rebates. The auto industry may also pay more for labor, but most of the labor cost will be in overtime, and the rise and fall of production is more or less factored into the pricing-and-profit structure of the industry. In other words, these changes are expected in both market labor allocations and financial markets. A sustained noncyclical order of business, in any industry, is not the norm. Therefore, although dollars are shifted from one group to another, those dollars are apt to shift back or occasion only slight ripples in the economy. Following are examples of causes of inflation and deflation, broken down into permanent and temporary categories:

PERMANENT:

CAUSED BY ALLOCATIONS OF LABOR AND THE REAPPORTIONMENT OF PURCHASING POWER

CAUSED BY REALLOCATIONS OF LABOR AND THE REAPPORTIONMENT OF PURCHASING POWER

TEMPORARY:

CAUSED BY ALLOCATIONS OF LABOR AND THE REAPPORTIONMENT OF PURCHASING POWER

CAUSED BY REALLOCATIONS OF LABOR AND THE REAPPORTIONMENT OF PURCHASING POWER

EXAMPLES OF PERMANENT INFLATION CAUSED BY ALLOCATIONS OF LABOR AND THE REAPPORTIONMENT OF PURCHASING POWER:

A. INNOVATION AND EFFICIENCY

Obviously, the greatest factor affecting inflation is innovations and efficiencies. They reduce the labor to produce goods and services to allow for more or improved products. When the number of hours to form a product changes, production inputs are realigned, machinery is modified, or a new factory is built, labor usage is affected.

B. INVENTION

Invention alters or adds products and production. The introduction of new products is inflationary because of the extra labor allocated to produce them. These products may, however, allow producers or consumers to be efficient, reduce other purchases, or create additional time for earnings. The impact can be temporary or permanent. Looking at an economy in balance with only fundamental unemployment, the labor necessary to produce and sell new products engenders inflationary pressures in the new competition for labor. Had TVs, cars, telephones, and electricity become available to consumers all in one year, a massive influx of labor and capital would be needed to build them.

Even inventions that will reduce production costs initially have an inflationary impact, as the cost to manufacture them ads to the demand for labor. But without innovation, efficiency, and invention to reduce production labor, progress would be nonexistent. We are so accustomed to declining costs that we may not recognize the inflationary pressure that invention produces. However, like the allocations of labor to investment, each invention may simply take place of another.

C. SPEED OF DELIVERY

Transportation changes are little more than innovation, but transportation warrants a separate consideration because of its effect on costs. Simply getting materials from manufacture or mine to retailers or processors represents anywhere from a few percent to the most significant cost of a product, and increased delivery speed fosters added transactions.

D.OVERHEAD SALES AND MARKETING

These areas are greatly affected by organizational methods, and they require tremendous allocations of labor. Overhead was once defined as a fixed cost, but it is not fixed in relation to manufacturing units. If overhead is X dollars per unit and the number of units built are doubled with the same overhead, overhead becomes X/2. Overhead is therefore the variable, and production is the fixed component in respect to unit cost. It follows that if production costs are higher, unit production is faster, and overhead remains unchanged, unit costs are reduced. Alterations in the flow and structure of management affect unit costs.

E. RAW-MATERIAL COSTS

Raw-material prices change when materials become scarce, abundant, or when replacements are discovered. Price changes can become permanent, but price increases attract investment and conservation that decrease long-term effects. Permanent price changes are unlikely unless supplies are dwindling or limited in relation to growing demand. Typically, new sources are more costly.

F. LABOR SHORTAGES

Labor shortages produce permanent inflation in the absence of other forces, as competition for labor drives up wages. High wages relative to the community attract efficiency, invention, and innovation that, in turn, provide a balancing of inflationary pressures. Labor restrictions are inflationary and can cause price increases and constrain productivity. Labor surpluses, however, are likely to fuel increasing productivity with deflationary effects.

G. CHANCE

Throughout most of the three thousand years of recorded history, mankind achieved few notable advances. Totalitarian governments, superstition, religious doctrine, and the harshness of life curbed advancements. Individuals were deemed insignificant unless otherwise decreed by an authoritarian voice. It is not by chance that progress began when democratic governments afforded humanity the freedom to improve self. Though progress did not begin by chance, the chances for progress are enhanced by freedom. When freedom came, the potential number who had the ability and opportunity to invent and change the world for the remainder suddenly increased in exponential fashion. As the free population increases, so, too, do the possibilities for progress. Where once only thousands had this opportunity, the day is fast approaching when billions will be able to procure wealth for themselves and benefits for all. It is the sheer number of opportunities to improve mankind that improve living standards and overcome inflationary repression. The influence of chance does not mean that the wealthy were lucky; rather, individual freedom simply increased the possibilities for hard work and a good imagination to be meaningful.

Most of the allocations discussed above were opportunities to improve living standards and deflate prices. Real growth comes from the private sector, whereas real inflation will usually come from government. Price deflation relative to the hours of work is the key to advancing living standards. Consequently, as long as productivity equates to the expansion of dollars, real inflation will not occur. The private sector allocates the labor force to either provide new products or to act as a deflationary force upon the economy. If at full employment there were no new efficient forces, new products could not be added without causing inflation. In this chicken-or-egg scenario, efficiency precedes production of new goods and services to avoid inflation. Often in this new product impasse, necessity will be the mother of invention, as extra work time, technological innovation, or human imagination create the means to do the double task in order to allocate the labor to bring about new products.

Before heading farther into the reallocations of labor, we need to briefly refine the aforementioned term. Reallocation has to do with the mandated labor that is not a matter of free consumer selections. Reallocated labor includes environmental, regulatory, and work rules. These change the utilization of labor, rather than enhancing the basic qualities or attractiveness of a product, impacting usage, work environments, safety, etc. They occur by agreement, legislation, court decisions, or societal tradition. Reallocations are a required aspect of cost. For example, government-controlled insurance for health, liability, unemployment, workers compensation, social security, and automobile are part of the cost of what we buy. Workers compensation for some trades in some states is as high as 50 percent. Other government-mandated costs are not obvious, like environmental, safety, legal, construction codes, engineering, etc. These government-controlled costs reflect both direct and mandated government expenditures.

EXAMPLES OF PERMANENT INFLATION CAUSED BY REALLOCATION OF LABOR AND REAPPORTIONMENT OF PURCHASING POWER:

A. LEGISLATION

Legislation is the obvious force that affects inflation, but the list of areas affected is nearly endless. Legislation reallocates labor and simultaneously reapportions the market basket to new groups. Some programs are beneficial, or deflationary, such as research and development, but the majority is inflationary. Examples of legislation that reallocates labor are as follows:

Social programs
Tax preferences
Environmental regulation
Work rules: OSHA

Military
Highway spending
Consumer protection
Bureaucratic management of
reapportionment
Civil protection
Education
Construction codes
Bureaucratic road blocks

Reapportionment of spending power from one group to another has two effects. First, as funds are initially transferred, those who lost spending power will attempt to maintain living standards through savings or credit. Second, the recipients may be recategorized from working to nonworking or for support of the nonworking, thus impacting the size of the working population. Government often spends more to administer a program than it pays out in benefits. Reallocating spending power can have some deflationary effects. As living standards of the private workers decline, they work harder to find cures for their income loss. Examples of legislation that reallocates spending are as follows:

Retirement benefits
Welfare benefits
Worker protection programs
Wage increases
Paid holidays
Social programs
Unemployment benefits
Cost of living adjustments
Fringe benefits

B. AGREEMENTS

Agreements, rulings, and bureaucratic regulation have a great effect on allocations of labor and innovation, but they are usually low cost to administer. Agreements that benefit consumers can be deflationary, while those that benefit labor or business are usually inflationary. Agreements often benefit special-interest groups, but the general population suffers the consequences. They include:

Union agreements
Utility commission rulings
Cooperatives
Mutual protection packs
Industry codes and standards
Foreign trade agreements
and banking arrangements
Brokerage and banking margin
Association standards cartels

C. JUDICIAL DOCTRINE

The judiciary continues to have an overwhelming impact on the allocations of labor. Rulings designed to protect criminals, protect plants and animals, foster integration, and punish producers have added employment in judiciary and criminal-justice programs, raised product costs, and limited the availability of goods and services. Settlements in civil cases have reached astronomic proportions, turning the judiciary into a lottery. Producers pay out a large part of product costs for liability, legal, and safety expenditures. Examples of rulings and involvement that have caused inflationary pressures include:

Penitentiary crowding	Evidence rulings
Increasing liability settlements	Integration enforcement
Punitive damages	Malpractice
Class-action suits	School busing, districting
Death-row pleas	Product liability suits
Workers compensation	Environmental interpretation
Social issues	Electrical energy production

D. COST OF LIVING ADJUSTMENTS

COLAs are a part of legislation, judicial doctrine, and agreements. COLAs result in the reapportionment of the market basket. Rather than a response to inflation, COLA payments probably account for half of all inflation; they themselves are inflationary. Government and pseudo-government employees, private workers, and pensioners are apportioned purchasing power, while others are losing. When inflation is the result of cost inflation, those with COLAs benefit, and those without suffer the consequences. If everyone received COLAs, then without efficiencies and someone to carry the cost, COLA adjustments would compound until money became worthless or the economy collapsed. This is the single greatest reason that the private worker is losing his living standards. Using COLAs to stabilize income is like dipping sand in the tide, the more sand we dip out, the more sand washes in. Those dipping get bigger sand piles, while those in the tide get drowned.

TEMPORARY inflation (deflation) is caused by price changes that will return to prior levels.

EXAMPLES OF TEMPORARY INFLATION

A. INVENTION, INNOVATION, AND EFFICIENCY

Although these are the lifeblood of progress, the additional labor that must be allocated to new pursuits is inflationary. The impacts may be only temporary, as the labor to bring about new products is offset by efficiencies. An economy that is well balanced has a built-in allocation of labor that is constantly applied to new invention and innovations while the realization of other efficiencies is taking place. If the proportion of the labor force that produces efficiencies equates to the efficiencies produced, there will be little noticeable trace of inflation.

B. MONEY COSTS

The Federal Reserve now encourages interest rates that are above traditional spreads between inflation and interest. Intended to control spending, the additional cost can permanently reduce living standards for lower income groups. The resultant added interest paid to wealthier depositors and investors acts to raise their standards. High rates retard expansion, short and long term, with a long-term inflationary impact and reduced living standards. Rates that are significantly above the inflation rate act as a recession inducement and expedite inflationary rebalancing. In addition, when spending is restricted, industry expansion and consumer demand can be delayed. When this pent-up demand is released, the result is temporary inflation.

C. DEMAND CHANGES

Purchasers' buying enthusiasm is more likely the result of the decline or increase of income and the introduction of new products. Consumer attitudes, which are said to affect decisions measurably, are probably overrated, as the size and diversity of the population and sources for information vary greatly. Fluctuating demand in a Complex marketplace is not likely to have a material impact on inflation. Individual products are more apt to be affected by buyer attitudes, when prices ebb as desire falls. Looking at the overall economy, we find that spiked demands are built in for new products. Hot items emerge, one after another, with ascending and then descending prices. When studied as to total impact, hot items doubtless have little effect on inflation.

D. SUPPLY CHANGES

When excess or shortages in supplies occur, prices will either attract or deter investment until prices stabilize. This is usually a temporary pricing situation.

The size of the economy, the multitude of sources and alternatives, and the computerized ability to forecast demand make inflation caused by a failure to produce implausible. Unless labor restrictions reduce the workforce or increase the workload, supply changes are more prone to be influenced by other forces. For example, environmental laws may not require alterations in existing production facilities but will be mandated in future facilities. In this circumstance, price structures may not change as long as existing facilities can match demand. However, unless innovation and efficiency can offset the cost of providing for environmental mandates, price increases will be necessary before facilities are expanded. Although supply shortages may indicate a failure of industry to keep up with demand, there may be mitigating circumstances.

Economic cycles (Inflationary cycles) are caused by restrictions on the labor force, excessive growth in government, and pseudo-government controls.

The Federal Reserve, stock market analysts, and business commentators believe in economic cycles. In a complex economy the cycle they describe that begins after one recession and continues into the next, is more likely caused by government intrusions in the private sector. The cycle generally starts with low interest rates and economic encouragement from government and continues until interest rates are forced up by the Federal Reserve to slow activity and initiate the next downturn. The intent of the Federal Reserve is to tinker with the discount rate and the money supply to control inflation. Adjustments are made in response to indicators, such as inflation, monetary indicators, consumer reports, interest-rate fluctuations, and recently, economic growth. There is no mention of adjustments for production efficiency, production expansion, or labor market supply changes. The Federal Reserve board members have commented on government expansionism but have made no effort to quantify expansionism in terms of inflation. The federal budget deficit has been a concern, but the long period over which it has existed has quieted a great deal of anxiety.

Using the growth in gross domestic product figures (GDP), as discussed in chapter 3, the Federal Reserve widened the typical spread between interest rates and inflation in the 1990s.[10] The intention of the Federal Reserve is to slow the economy and reduce inflation by quieting business and consumer consumption. In the long term, high interest rates cause inflationary pressure when stalled business expansion and pent-up demand come head to head with the opportunity for consumers to indulge

10 It is notable that because of the distortion in the computation of GDP, that GDP is inflated by increased government spending. This distortion is mentioned here because economic growth is indicated when in actuality, the economy might be getting smaller.

themselves. If higher rates have the effect intended by the Federal Reserve board, interest-sensitive industries reduce employment. The "soft landing" recession that is intended is not intended to produce *significant* unemployment.

Whether a recession or soft landing, the consequences are never shared by the population equally. The greatest damage is felt by small, new, and cyclical businesses. We can anticipate that new and minority populations, which have not established business footholds or who lack the experience of family generations, will suffer the hardest landing. Minorities and unskilled employees have, by tradition, entered the workforce through cyclical businesses, such as construction. Here, jobs losses after business downturns encourage older, more skilled employees to seek stable employment. The result of this economic roller coaster is to do double-damage to the aspiring groups on which billions are spent to assist. Many in these groups are slow or unable to adapt to new skills, and they become discouraged when hopeful, well-paying jobs become financial traps. The widened interest spread exacerbates the difficulty of lower income groups to sustain incomes and add to savings. A lack of savings can also mean adding credit payments with high rates for business and personal purchases.

The unemployment that occurs during recessions is the excuse for new government programs for welfare, unemployment, and related spending. Every recession propagates its own government programs that supposedly are the cure for the problems of the poor and the economy. COLAs and other welfare enhancements make productive work less competitive, as working wages without COLA augmentation become relatively nearer to the government-designed poverty level. The result is bigger government and a large, unproductive workforce. Welfare programs and private enterprise then compete for labor in a recovering economy. By intruding upon the available workforce and government's failure to release workers from its recession-enacted programs, government enhances the prospects for inflation, as a recovery ensues and pent-up investment and consumer demand reestablish their claim on labor. With the possibility of government intervention in the financial markets increasing as unemployment drops, private enterprise is depicted as entering a phase in the cycle. COLAs further exacerbate the economic cycles by limiting mobility of covered workers who might find more productive work.

These cycles, rather than being a natural economic occurrence of free enterprise, bear all indications of being caused by the largest controlling segment of the economy: government. This seems even more obvious when we consider that as the economy recovers and tax revenues increase, government begins programs that place additional demands on the labor force. Thus, government begins programs and deficit spends to soak up labor in a recessionary economy and begins programs when the economy grows to reflect increased revenue. It seems inflation-induced recession in a Complex economy is more a reflection of government mismanagement of the labor force than of private-sector growth.

It is hard to judge how the effects of a soft landing differ from distinct recessions. The primary concern should be whether welfare is too competitive with working labor. Drawing labor from the workforce is inflationary. Should these reallocations of labor in the market be greater than the effects of innovation and efficiency, severe inflation and hard landings (recession) will appear to be the fault of the private sector. Most assuredly, formulating a soft landing merely holds down growth in the economy, as living standards are adjusted down. Thus, recessional outcomes are spread over a longer period of time. To state it another way, instead of a gunshot to the heart, a soft landing, for many, is a slow-bleeding gut wound.

Inflation is the failure of production to meet demand and is corrected by adding labor to the market. In the great inflation cycle of the late 1970s and early 1980s, the U.S. was confronted with an industry that was old, inefficient, and intolerant of efficiency while growth in government availed itself of any possible labor source and used tax laws to encourage expansion in a real estate sector that had already over produced. In that time, union members, who were not so old they couldn't remember the Depression, were reluctant to allow innovation, and they took advantage of the labor shortage. Strikes for higher wages inhibited production, and wages in manufacturing were high relative to the general population. The opportunity for cutting the cost of producing was greatly inhibited. If the current government continues to reallocate resources and its workers attempt to control productivity or reapportion a greater share of goods and services, inflation might rise to the point at which innovation and efficiency can no longer keep up, just as it did in the '70s. The approach we take to inflation makes a difference. When the consumer is controlled, we can rightly predict the recession cycle, with the private worker bearing the brunt of the impact. Rather, growth should be fueled with labor additions, not additional demands.

The Federal Reserve is not significantly to blame for this scenario, as the Fed is primarily attempting to offset the economic mismanagement by the combined governing bodies. In this situation, one body of government is constricting the labor market and stimulating consumer purchasing, while the other is increasing the money supply to facilitate exchanges and attempting to discourage consumption with higher interest rates. The influences that monetary controls have on the market hold both permanent and temporary consequences. Meanwhile, enterprise must attempt to navigate the maze of obstacles, roadblocks, and diverse signals given off by government that often lead to dead ends, wasted efforts, poor timing, failed enterprises, and lost jobs. Eliminating welfare restrictions and providing incentives to government workers to improve productivity could accomplish growth with less disruption, improve living standards, and eliminate inflation.

The use of monetary controls does not represent the success of the Federal Reserve to control the economy; rather, it represents the failure of the federal government to fulfill its obligation to manage a safe and stable environment in which free humankind will flourish. It represents the failure of government to bring about desired changes in an orderly manner with an efficient and righteous use of the workforce. And it represents the failure of government to recognize that although investors and businesses (read: **the rich**) may benefit from the profits that free enterprise leaves, the greater gain in goods and services is harvested by the masses. As the profits of the rich are much too small to pay the cost of government, the share of consumption by the rich would hardly improve the lives of even a small fraction of humanity. The truly rich lose only money and give up little of their beans and rice when taxed. The competition for goods and services will always be won by those with the most money. If government must reallocate labor to impart the least amount of sacrifice in living standards, it should do so on a miserly basis. Government must remove restrictions on the labor force, rather than commission labor with new limitations and additional assignments.

Inflation could be eliminated if it were clearly and concisely understood. A hundred years ago, we had a system with few guarantees. Then, if money was tightened by reducing supply, the effect on the population was distributed somewhat equally. Most employment was on individually owned farms. In today's Complex society, interest rate changes and recessions affect different employment groups in different ways, as a significant portion of the population has guaranteed jobs, adjustments for inflation, and built-in raises. With 20 percent of the employed population working directly for the government, with an additional large number receiving welfare and pensions, and with the many who have guaranteed jobs in private enterprise, a great number of individuals are not affected by interest-rate increases and, indeed, may benefit. When it is necessary to slow the economy, the burden befalls the small, unprotected portion of the working population. While one group of workers is given wage increases to compensate for inflation caused by added costs to the society, the group not so protected pays the check.

As a group unprotected from the economic swings caused by government's manipulations, construction employees have been put through the wringer so many times that lenders have placed them in a special category and limit or totally refuse to extend credit to them. With skilled construction workers looking for other work after each cycle, construction businesses suffer extensive costs caused by the constant education of new workers. The shortage of experience in construction employees exacerbates quality problems.

These government-initiated cycles assail the lower income group, the newly employed, the job seekers, the less skilled, and those on the fringe of welfare whose wages are smaller in comparison to older workers. The very process of government growth and the reallocation of resources grows the number of poor, not only from the attraction of free benefits but due to the recycling of labor caused by the pressure on the workforce from government growth. Economic growth does not cause inflation, and growth without inflation is only limited by the size, mobility, and education of the workforce. The free-enterprise system, as a complex structure, is a resonant system that is affected only by mass hysteria and poor government.

This analysis of inflation should adequately reveal that the number of forces acting on the economy are numerous but definable. The simplest assertions drawn from consumer confidence, leading indicators, and the many other attempts to forecast inflation and economic activity are too elemental to focus on even the rudimentary changes in the productive workforce that affect inflation. These economic indicators fail to focus on the basis for economic change (i.e., the workforce). The indicators often emphasize employment growth in certain industries as potentials for exciting job opportunities, rather then detractions from productive endeavors. The foundation of an economy is its workforce and the belief in paying people to make purchases, rather than to produce, defies the natural laws of economics. The belief that monetary documentation provides all the evidence of economic change hides the evolution of free enterprise.

Symptoms, interpreted as causes, mask solutions.

CHAPTER 10

THE SYMPTOMS OF EXCESSIVE GROWTH IN GOVERNMENT AND HOW LABOR IS AFFECTED

To continue the discussion on government growth, it is important to define the term in the way it is used herein. Ordinarily, government growth is defined in terms of dollars, perhaps dollar spending in excess of inflation. To a politician, government growth is defined as money that someone in the other party spent. However, the effect on labor is what is important; money is merely a tool that directs labor. Like a hammer moves a nail, money moves labor. Whether for useful purposes or not, it is money that determines how labor is to be allocated, and whoever uses the money does the allocation. Government controls an amount that is more than half of what is spent on consumer consumption and exercises an absolute right to levy for its needs. Because government has this control and is generally not disciplined by competition,[11] the actions of government are a concern.

Government growth is the reallocation of labor from free-market choices to government control.

Government actions modify living standards through the reallocation of the market basket and reduce the potential growth in the economy by reallocating labor away from free-market choices.

Because money is merely a tool whose value changes, labor is more easily measured on a consistent basis than is money. For example, if the units of production increase and hours of labor decline, then we are more efficient. If the share of the workforce plying a trade changes, then forces have acted to change the allocation of labor to that purpose. In a review of the labor in an economy, there is no need to make inflation adjustments. In the analysis of labor, the success of our economy is measured simply in the labor needed to provide a service or a good.

11 Politicians may compete for votes and governments may compete for business with tax breaks or special laws, but the day-to-day operations are not subjected to the daily market, and politicians can only be fired every two to six years. Employees don't bid for their jobs and have guarantees that limit their need to perform; departments aren't subject to competitive bidding to provide services; operations aren't limited by sales and can simply increase budgets; taxpayers can't pick their services—they must buy the whole package or nothing and when competitive bidding is used, the arduous process may limit bidders, while economics of a project may not be considered. And the biggest problem is that decisions may be politically motivated and influenced by special-interest groups whose goal is to limit competition.

It is important to make measurements of an economy on the basis of unit labor allocations in order to focus on allocations, reallocations, and efficiency. For example, economic forces affect groups differently. In order to measure these effects, we could measure the changes in income per unit of labor from period to period for all the groups in the economy. In analyzing 100 percent of workforce, we could identify changes caused by outside forces and in their respective shares of gross income. With adjustments for growth of the population and consumption, we could also determine productivity. If the market is free and no group has an unwarranted advantage over another, then the arduousness, complexity, imagination, invention, popularity, and work ethic of a group will reflect in its compensation. Most importantly, we can visualize the importance of labor as a limited, rather than unlimited, resource. Doing so will make it clear why at any instant in time, it takes a specific amount of labor to build a car, grow vegetables, police a city, etc. And we will be able to note how changes in free enterprise or government alter living standards or the natural balance of free enterprise.

The business definition for "inputs to production" is labor, material, equipment, and overhead, all of which are composed of labor at some point. Machines, for example, provide help to the labor force but are themselves the direct result of labor, whose cost is a factor determined by that input. Utilities are likewise the results of labor, whose input, even in the case of hydroelectric power is still dependent upon the labor required to construct and manage the facility. Even imports or exports represent an exchange of labor, as the dollars we earned with our labor are exchanged for the fruit of another's labor, and vice versa. Cash is simply a temporary medium used to avoid the inefficiency and inconvenience of bartering. Obviously, a one-way exchange of goods for money would eventually render a currency worthless. Even the value of commodities or jewels is dependent upon the ease of access, as more will be spent on labor to access rarer gems. In the end, investment decisions are based upon the amount of labor to be bought.

By identifying labor as the resource for input, we can limit our discussion to labor and money. Money is used to prod the labor supply. There are other incentives, but money commands the greatest control. Money can make labor work, sit down, or stand around. The concern is how labor has been utilized. *Most important is how proportions are allocated, how these allocations impact living standards, and how they might be allocated to improve lives.* How many are growing corn or turning wheels? Knowing answers to this question would allow government to price its actions in human terms.

Whether in small or large communities, when labor is transferred to new responsibilities, the status quo is changed. Unless we reduce labor demands in another area, work harder, make innovative advances, or adjust living standards, our economy will be unbalanced.

As an economy becomes more complex,
imbalances become less noticeable.

If there were no outside forces, the percentage of the population assigned to each task would not change. Labor balances itself to provide the goods demanded by consumers and provides the labor for future growth. Because of a concern for unemployment, imbalances are ignored when creating jobs is considered "good for the economy." However, unemployment varies over time by less than three percentage points, changing mostly due to or during a recession. Large labor allocations can, of course, occur spontaneously—if the percentage of nonworking retired people were to change; if there were a war, a baby boom, or a time of invention. However, in the last fifty years, recessions have typically been initiated by government, following periods of excessive government growth—this relationship between recessions and government growth is not coincidental.

Government growth is generally defined as changes in the budget of a government, but there is another aspect of government growth. If government passes a law that necessitates more labor to make cars, that law changes the allocation of labor between market and government-imposed allocations of labor. The share of direct consumer labor will decline and the amount of indirect government labor will grow. If the percent of the workforce allocated to government grows as the population grows, and if no other changes take place, such as efficiency, then there would not be sufficient labor to increase production for a larger population. We could presume that inflation would follow, and some would lose their living standard in order to match new demand with existing supply. We must keep in mind that it takes an increasing number of workers in all areas to maintain production equilibrium with a growing population. If government requires business to perform a new task, the cost bears little difference to a tax, except that taxes are often contingent on income, and new government mandates can be so costly that they destroy businesses and jobs.

Government growth includes all new reallocations of labor for direct or indirect government-mandated work.

The general population believes that when the government announces that living standards have increased that everyone's share increases. This supposition is never true. Groups are affected differently. Some benefit, some lose, but all are affected. When government manipulates the money that controls labor and transfers purchasing power, economic sharing changes. Most people desire clean air, clean water, and equal rights, but these changes add to the costs in the economy. When change inflates prices, government compensates its workers with inflation adjustments and the new costs are transferred to those who don't get increases. Government's use of money impacts labor, which impacts production, which impacts consumption, which reapportions living standards.

Government manipulates market-basket sharing.

Government growth shifts purchasing power from one group to another.

Growth in government can occur as a consequence of laws, mandates, rules, new taxes, union contracts, pay raises, court judgments, or by government's inefficiency. Most government growth is evidenced by changes in labor use. But any shift in purchasing power requires some members of society to work harder or suffer a loss of living standard. An example is the lottery. State lotteries establish a new group of government employees, impact the need and use of employees in private enterprise, shift purchasing power within a major group, establish a new group of "winners" that may reduce the labor supply, and shift purchasing power from a private-sector group to a public-sector group. Some might say that the winner puts the winning back into the community, but isn't that the community where the money came from? All taxes are "returned to the community," but in the case of the lottery at least 35 percent will go to the federal government. Because taxes had been paid on lottery money, and there is no federal or state tax deduction for gambling, wouldn't it be better if government never took the money? Laws change workloads.

When government grows, a shift in purchasing power places a greater burden on those who are not government beneficiaries.

Government growth has the following effects on the labor supply:

Reduces the available labor supply and establishes working and nonworking groups

Impacts the need and use of employees in private enterprise

Shifts purchasing power from private to public sector

Shifts purchasing power within or outside a group

The following are specific examples of how increases in government affect the productive labor supply and the allocations of individual purchasing power:

A. Increases in welfare payments reduce labor supply. As the value of being employed is reduced, purchasing power shifts.

B. Failure to increase what Social Security recipients can earn without losing benefits decreases the supply of labor.

C. Setting up new government programs increases the use of labor and shifts purchasing power.

D. Increasing the purchase of supplies for a new government program increases government allocations of labor.

E. Government pay raises that are not matched in the private sector shift purchasing power.

F. Mandating the use of higher cost labor for government projects shifts purchasing power.

G. Increasing safety requirements on a construction site or in a factory establishes a new group of both private and public employees in order to fulfill new requirements and shift purchasing power.

H. Increasing the standards of materials used in the construction of a home affects the supply and/or increases the use of materials, thereby shifting purchasing power and increasing the demand for labor, both on the job and in factories.

I. Establishing laws that increase the ability to file lawsuits or court-approved judgments that exceed established norms attracts additional labor to prosecute and defend, increasing insurance costs. The labor supply is reduced and purchasing power is shifted. Involvement of third-party private sector labor reduces labor supply and alters purchasing power.

J. Limiting access to resources with animal protection laws creates new demands for government and private-sector labor and shifts markets to alternate resources that might have larger labor demands. The result reduces labor supplies.

K. Adding tariffs to imports shifts purchasing power into potentially less-efficient labor, reducing labor supply and shifting labor from potentially higher returns. Purchasing power is reduced.

L. All government actions that require increased domestic labor potentially shift purchasing power to foreign goods, increasing the supply of domestic labor and reducing domestic competitiveness.

Logic leads our discussion to the private-sector response to government growth. How would people and businesses adjust? In general, as government grows, the private sector would attempt to satisfy the demands of the community, make up for the loss of productive labor, and regain its purchasing power. Government demands, however, have the force of law and must be met first. The private sector would compete with government for labor on an unlevel playing field, with government able to pay whatever needed to be paid to attract labor. As consumers attempt to maintain their standard of living, they would look for ways to respond, such as borrowing or dipping into savings. The economy would expand but would no longer be balanced as it once was. New products might be delayed for lack of labor, and as demand increased due to the shift in purchasing power, labor price would increase, causing inflation with the potential for a loss of both purchasing power and productivity within the private sector. The result is the inflation that follows to rebalance the market basket and purchasing power.

Not only is the economy not in balance, but there also are imbalances within sectors or occupations. Inside and outside government, job classifications that have COLAs, guaranteed promotions, negotiated pay increases, or favored reallocations receive an increase in their purchasing power. Environmental engineers, for example, may be put in a preferential position to receive added shares of the economy if laws affecting the environment are passed. In other words, there are winners and losers. The net effect is for spending to expand an economy that is no longer capable of expanding, with productive activities getting a smaller share of labor. Due to this imbalance and the potential inflation, many will no longer be able to maintain their living standards. If enough people can no longer sustain their credit and they can no longer pay the rent, the mortgage, or make needed purchases and the numbers are large enough, a recession may ensue.

Below are listed several recognizable symptoms of government growth. These symptoms can occur even when reported inflation is low. Most of these will be intuitively obvious.

A. Borrowed funds

The loss of purchasing power can occur when inflation, a higher discount rate intended to control economic growth, or high real estate taxes push up mortgage payments and escrow funding on existing mortgages. Inflation or new government programs resulting in higher tax collections can strain family budgets, forcing families who must still meet existing credit payments to seek new sources of funds. Not realizing the loss of purchasing power, consumers find that they are suddenly forced to make large cuts in spending and to expand credit to pay on existing credit. Obtaining credit does not mean consumers are increasing real spending because of a growing economy; rather, it is a natural attempt to maintain the standard of living at existing levels. Those benefited by government will likely be able to increase spending commensurate with increased and inflation-adjusted income.

Businesses suffering from higher taxes or new government-mandated requirements may expand credit in order to pay for legislated obligations and may sacrifice expanding credit to enhance production.

B. Cheaper goods

Consumers try less expensive goods in order to make ends meet. Name brands are no longer as important. Lower quality is accepted in the hope that the inferior substitute will not have to be replaced too soon. Store sales become more important; cheaper but equal replacements are sought out and coupon use increases. In an inflationary economy whose labor shortages are caused by government expansion, consumers are not as likely to make sacrifices until they begin to feel the stress caused by higher prices and lower income relative to inflation and when credit cards are no longer an option.

Businesses with high-quality products lose sales and find it difficult to maintain quality against low-priced competition. Quality businesses strive to cheapen products to match competition and lose sales. The old business interests believe sales will return when people tire of the low-quality goods. After years of struggle, these businesses will be bought up by cheaper brands seeking quality names. Established businesses reduce costs or go out of business. Those who are bought out will have quality stripped for quick sales. Consumers complain of the low quality of domestic goods.

C. Imports

Consumers and businesses, under pressure to cut spending, are less likely to check for the country of origin when purchasing. When quality and country are less important than living standards or survival, consumers and businesses will take chances on foreign-made goods to save money.

Foreign manufactures will expand to new modern plants and will increase quality. With domestic labor costs increasing, foreign competition will put pressure on pricing. As the foreign manufacturers are enjoying the advantages of economies of scale, domestic producers will feel the reverse and be pressured to cut quality, reduce production, and scale down operations.

Imports will reduce some of the stress on the economy as excess demand is supplied with foreign goods, but the balance of trade will begin to run deficits.

D. Innovation and efficiency

Consumers innovate to keep costs down, such as buying goods like day-old bread, cooking at home, shopping at garage sales, or finding ways to reduce consumption without affecting living standards (e.g., turning off the air conditioning when not at home). However, the biggest savings that consumers recognize is taking advantage of business innovation, such as shopping at Wal-Mart. But innovation is slow, due to labor's reluctance to accept new methods. Workers are more concerned with losing jobs to efficiency than protecting jobs by efficiency.

E. Living standards

Some simply adjust living standards down to match reduced income. Small businesses may eliminate employee benefits or adjust owner's compensation.

F. Illegal aliens

Illegal aliens crossing into the country represent a push/pull situation—the alien's desire to come into the country, and the employers desire to hire cheap labor. Where once only ranchers routinely hired illegal immigrants, they now are found in many jobs. Individuals and businesses feel the pressure to hire "illegals" as cheap labor in an inflationary market. With government growth exceeding the ability to innovate, low-cost labor from any source is in demand.

G. Two-earner families

The quickest way to increase or maintain living standards is for both husband and wife to have jobs, as the situation reflects a need to increase family income. As standards increase for two-earner families, one-earner families lose ground.

H. Welfare recipients

Welfare programs are perennial recipients of government growth. Intended to raise living standards, federal assistance raises the floor level at which entry into the workforce is preferable to welfare. This is the welfare trap. Because of the "trap," there is a drain on the workforce, as those who want to enter the workforce are discouraged because work produces minimal, nonexistent, and even negative benefits. Welfare is also used simply to avoid work. Levels at which individuals can receive welfare are such that if all eligible participants took advantage of benefits, the system could not support the loss of labor.

I. Families and fraud

Welfare payments structured to help single-parent families also discourage two-parent families and encourage fraud. Families break up initially for appearances, so as to get welfare, but the strain is too much and the break becomes permanent as marriage loses importance. Prospective welfare applicants and recipients who are having a rough time may lie when putting food on the table becomes a problem. Once the line of honesty has been crossed, fraud is taken for granted. Welfare becomes an attraction, pulling harder on the work ethic.

J. Crime

A system that protects the rights of privacy also restricts the comparison of welfare information within government agencies, thus encouraging fraudulent claims and fraudulent welfare spending. When government encourages one illegal activity, everyone in a welfare community has something to hide; thus, other illegal activities are encouraged. Lawbreakers aware of who is committing welfare fraud can use the information to suppress crime reporting. When welfare recipients are forced to live in crime-prone areas and cannot report income without fear of losing welfare, they develop disdain, distrust, and dislike for government. Idle time becomes an opportunity to commit acts of crime and violence. The old saying "An idle hand is the devil's workshop" bears truth.

K. Inflation

Buying pressure from government growth and labor restrictions in the private sector causes inflation. Congressmen complain that consumers are "consuming too much," while consumers are just trying to maintain the living standard they had and to keep up with inflation. Businesses cannot afford to expand.

L. Interest rates

Concern over the foreign trade deficit and inflation causes banking authorities to push up rates to reduce spending. Businesses find expansion to meet demands even harder to justify, because returns must be higher to pay the extra interest. Borrowing for expansion in anticipation of higher prices occurs with disastrous results, as interest rates go higher along with costs. When recession occurs, forced and voluntary belt-tightening makes previous expansion decisions look ill-timed.

M. Salaries

Labor enjoys higher salaries, but prices rise as well. Unions become more restrictive and demand higher wages that exceed inflation and restrict growth in manufacturing. Eventually, the only way to match demand with supply is to reduce demand or to decrease labor cost with efficiency and lower wages. Incomes not protected by government go down, as do living standards.

N. Exports

Most of the interest in exports is the export of manufacturing to foreign countries in the face of domestic labor shortages and high costs. Although large companies continue to export, the primary interest is in meeting domestic demand in the face of labor shortages. Small companies are more than satisfied with domestic demand and have no interest in foreign sales.

O. Bankruptcies

The squeeze between higher labor costs and price competition leaves many manufacturers susceptible to bankruptcy. Aspiring entrepreneurs lose their fortunes to recessions. As high interest rates and government-inspired labor competition make business extremely unprofitable, bankruptcies increase.

P. Competition.

Politicians, seeing the need to reduce consumer cost to allow for bigger government deregulate businesses like trucking and airlines. Consequently, both the business and employees lose income protection as these businesses must now reorganize. Protection against imports and a favorable attitude toward unions is no longer affordable. Businesses must get efficient or go out of business. Labor is the real loser, as lockouts become prevalent, and increased competition forces replacement of high-paid employees with low-paid workers. Labor blames business when government is the cause.

Q. Major consumer purchases

People begin to hold on to automobiles longer. Laws passed to improve the environment and high manufacturing wage demands put pressure on quality and eventually, sales suffer. Manufacturers misread the demand for smaller, less costly, and more efficient cars. They also realize that small cars mean small profits and are caught in a catch-22 situation that is only resolved by a major reorganization. Similar occurrences with other large manufacturers put pressure on worker wages. Efficiency and innovation are a must for survival. Businesses that didn't adjust will fail or will be bought up, sold off, and/or reorganized.*

* Starting in the early '70s, laws were passed in most states that prohibited the changing of odometers, a practice that had been a given when cars were traded. Mileage on the car was always important. A car with 100,000 miles on the odometer was considered junk, but a car with an actual 80,000 miles on it was still in good enough condition to be rolled back to 30,000 miles. Cars on the road that were ten years old were common. Vehicles that averaged 15,000 to 20,000 miles a year easily got 200,000 miles before they headed to the junkyard. Since the odometer didn't show hundreds of thousands until recently, people learned slowly that repairs were cheaper than new cars, and old favorites could be held well into the 100,000-mile range. Besides, dealers wouldn't give much for cars they couldn't roll back. Unleaded gas helped to reduce maintenance and extend auto life.

R. Government stimulus

Government responds to an inflationary economy heading into a recession with stimulus. Congress passes laws to encourage construction in the face of high interest rates and vacancies. Investment needed in manufacturing is wasted on the overproduction of developed real estate.

S. Housing

Homes get smaller as interest rates escalate. Builders who fail to adjust to the higher costs with smaller homes go out of business or file bankruptcy.

T. Student loans

The share of college graduates who work themselves through school without assistance declines. With government-sponsored teaching facilities and their employees getting a bigger share of the economy, the cost of schooling goes up. Concurrently, the students' ability to obtain jobs is limited by the added cost of owning, maintaining, and especially insuring automobiles. Cars are no longer bought for a hundred bucks, insured for another hundred, and repaired by the student. Old cars now cost three thousand, the insurance for young drivers is ten to thirty times what their fathers paid, and today's cars are too complicated for a novice to repair. Without automobiles, it becomes as difficult for a student to drive to a job as it is to live at home and drive to school. The number of student loans escalates significantly. Student and parent believe that the student will earn enough to repay the loans and that wages equate to the parents' earnings, but the new workers' earnings are less than their fathers.

U. Younger workers find it harder to earn a living. The new entrants to the workforce find employment in jobs that do not have job or income protection. They also find that wages aren't as high as they anticipated and won't pay their expenses. Much of the added cost of living is spent on basic expenses. Automobiles, utilities, insurance, traffic fines, interest rates, and housing costs all increase beyond the inflation rate. The older generation looks down on the young as misfits, thinking the younger ones should be able to make it, just like they did.

The list could go on, as even flea markets proliferate in the struggle to maintain living standards. Consumers on one side turn their "trash into treasures" and on the other find used goods at a fraction of the cost of new. In the 1950s, only the poor bought or sold castoffs, most being too proud to take what they felt was charity. Treasures were abundant in any Salvation Army store. As necessity is the mother of invention and lifestyle the mother of necessity, what was once unpopular has become fun, popular, and necessary. Not only is such recycling an efficient method of exchange but also politically correct and environmentally sound. Garage sales and flea markets allow most traded goods to be used as originally intended.

The referenced symptoms are not hypothetical but represent a reflection on the occurrences in the '70s and '80s, whose economic characteristics will be discussed later in more detail. Not only did government growth put pressure on businesses in the '70s; the unions had their own growth in mind. Unions were making it more difficult to innovate and be more efficient. Eventually, because government demanded power and growth, unions and private workers alike made the sacrifice so that government could sustain itself. Because government has the power and a first demand on all resources, a labor shortage in government and the private sector was resolved in the favor of government. Since incomes could not be adjusted to meet lifestyle, lifestyles were adjusted to incomes

If spending programs of government are permanent—and they always are—the only way for most people to maintain their living standard is for innovation and efficiency in the economy to reduce their cost of goods and services. Everyone is affected by government growth in some manner. The truly rich may gain in the imbalance, while the poor, many pensioners, and the government workers are protected with inflation adjustments. Private working-class citizens are all that is left to absorb the added costs. Those most severely affected are the middle class, small businesses, and individuals who attempt to improve or leverage themselves too deeply to be able to withstand additional strains.

With living-standard indices showing increases, it isn't obvious that many are feeling declines. Because the affected group is the employed, government does not see them as a concern. As government requisitions a greater share of production and the labor force to meet its requirements, the workers affected look to government for solutions. But labor that may have produced consumer goods to solve the problem now is paid to be idle, to work for the government or to satisfy new laws. Overall, even if innovation is sufficient to increase consumer goods, there will still be winners and losers. Some will need to adjust to a lower standard of living, while others may increase theirs.

Unfortunately, the symptoms can be interpreted in different ways. People need help because government has burdened productive labor far too much, but it appears the rich are at fault. The growing numbers on welfare is evidence that welfare is needed, not that welfare competes against work. And we have a trade deficit because the high cost of government is far in excess of what foreign manufactures pay, not simply because workers are cheaper. Unfortunately, economists don't emphasize the importance productive labor and place all the emphasis on money. What people do isn't important. If, for a moment, money disappeared, maybe worker would become important again in the eyes of the political and economic leadership.

Income taxes are contingent on income.

Government mandates to private businesses are taxes that are contingent only on staying in business.

CHAPTER 11

THE GREAT DEPRESSION

In 1936, John Maynard Keynes published his *General Theory of Employment, Interest, and Money*. Keynes defined reasons for and solutions to the occurrence of the Great Depression of 1929 to the satisfaction of nearly every economist in the world. The timing of his writings had much to do with the popularity of his theories, as politicians and economists were desperate for explanations and solutions to the Great Depression. According to accounts of economic academe, prior theory failed to explain the period of prolonged unemployment that occurred from 1929 and into the '30s, and Keynes had the explanation. Keynes reasoned that the market adjustments to the cost of labor and price of goods that were to occur to correct for unemployment did not always occur and that the price of labor and goods was not as flexible as previously thought. The basis of his theory was that spending induced business to supply goods and services; thus, stimulating demand is good for the economy. Keynes also implied that "regulation of expenditures is the crux of sound macroeconomic policy." Keynes suggested that for a stimulated economy to remain stable, some regulation was necessary. Regulation would provide a hypothetical balance against stimulation. "If we could assure aggregate expenditures large enough to achieve capacity output, but not so large as to result in inflation," the Keynesian view implies "that maximum output, full employment, and price stability could be attained." His statements thus provided the foundation for what has become a gas-pedal-and-brakes economic management. It was not Keynes' intention, but he encouraged constant tampering by government to stimulate growth. In the view of J.D. Gwartney and R.L. Stroup in *Economics: Private and Public Choice* (1995 edition), "The theory … has exerted enormous influence on modern macroeconomics," and "[m] odern macroeconomics is built on the foundation of Keynesian analysis." The modern interpretation of Keynesian economic theories by the politicians with the power and the wherewithal to tax is that spending money is "good for the economy." And thus, we "tax and spend." The power and influence of Keynesian economics having been asserted, the question here is: What if Keynes was wrong in his explanation for the prolonged unemployment?

The 1929 crash and subsequent depression obviously had a considerable influence on economic thought. The spending habits of politicians and their attitude toward unemployment and economic stimuli are based on a "good for the economy" approach. Keynes thus has advanced a credulous and often misused concept of useless job creation, "equable earnings awards," and welfare. Evaluating the Great Depression therefore, becomes so important that the ability of government to manage the economy is dependent on that evaluation. The depression is doubly important because the "crash" is often interpreted as a forewarning of future occurrences. Could it have been just a phase, a transition from agricultural to a complex economy? There are other explanations for the '29 crash that seem to vary, depending upon the political orientation or discipleship of the writer, but explanations generally include the following:

1. Keynesian explanation that government needed to stimulate demand
2. Smoot-Hawley Tariff that restricted imports and triggered similar responses from other nations
3. Monetary explanation that the Federal Reserve overreacted to the market decline and restricted cash more than was necessary
4. Lenin's belief that "capital, created by labor of the worker" would oppress "the worker by undermining the small proprietor and creating an army of the unemployed" (in essence, over investment)

Lenin's belief certainly has not been expressed often in the free world. However, Lenin's Communist ideology should not be reason to ignore his thoughts. His ideas were devised with the intent of improving mankind and perhaps the failure of Communism was just one step toward the eventual perfection of an economic system. Could he have been closer to the truth than any other? All of the explanations would have borne some truth. If overinvestment is a possible cause of the Great Depression, it should be examined.

To begin our discussion, let's set the stage leading up to the 1929 crash. In the 1920s, there was an exuberant investors' attitude that encouraged everyone in the country to invest. Starting in the early 1900s, ordinary citizens had, for the first time ever, broad access to business ownership through local stock market brokerages and banks. The banks had few restrictions on their operations in that time, as banks also sold stock. The economy was immature, and nothing in the recorded history of the time would have explained what was happening. Free enterprise was operating at an astounding level. There was a plentiful unrestricted supply of labor, astounding progress in production methods, and new products that piqued the desires of every human on earth. There was nothing people of that era couldn't do. Despite the relatively low cost of labor, living standards in the "Roaring Twenties" were improving practically on a daily basis. More efficient production methods and an abundance of inventions gave us radios, airplanes, indoor plumbing, recorded music, fast cars (for the time), toasters, farm tractors, and more. Along with all this exuberance came the interest and desire for the formation of capital.

The Great War had created or improved machines and fostered new methods of manufacturing. Great gadgets sparked the imagination of an already imaginative people. The Roaring Twenties, the feel of the times, probably engendered more emotion than any other period in history. Radios, telephones, automobiles, phonographs, and Coca-Cola proliferated. The highways got paved and buildings touched the sky. Many things existed that only decades earlier had seemed impossible or improbable. With the tractor, the farm grew bigger, and farmers grew fewer. The ample supply of labor to the factories gave people all they could imagine. And, so that everyone access to the stock market, the telephone companies ran wires from coast to coast and continent to continent.

The U.S. was in the process of moving from an agrarian society to a manufacturing community. Accumulating wealth was beginning to mean stocks and bonds instead of money or gold. Never before had stocks and bonds been so available. Anyone in the U.S.—or the world—could buy. The value of a business's assets and earnings could not only provide collateral for the business, but its stock became collateral as well. Stocks were treated like money, and prices went up, as if they would not stop. But how high is up? When did it occur to everyone that there was a limit? When did investors realize they weren't buying chickens and eggs, that what they bought was paper and the profits were paper too? In the 1800s, people would have preferred gold, but in the Roaring Twenties, they wanted stock, as stocks and bonds were achieving the respect and negotiability of gold and paper money. And then, as often in our latter history, which would we rather have—gold or stocks? The world loved gold, but the U.S. citizen was infatuated with stocks—we could never own enough. Stocks were the hula hoops of the '20s.

Hypothetical the investment community of the '20s was, for the most part, located in a single room. The floor of the Wall Street Exchange held the potential for faddish beliefs to take root, even in that presumed modern, educated atmosphere. It was the most significant growth period in the history of mankind, as peers reinforced these excesses in investment. In the 1990s, the existence of fads involving business behavior—like consolidations, divestiture, methods of management, downsizing, overseas production, and other movements—was seen in cycles, as business people were attracted by enthusiasm or by government laws and actions. Business fads occur now and did in the 1920s.

Advancements occurred in every area of consumption and commerce. In travel, shipping, machinery, vehicles, plant mechanization, and farming, changes were widespread. Despite the large influx of labor from the farm and displacement of the old labor-intensive methods, the surplus labor was quickly absorbed. In addition, this cheap and unrestricted labor meant large profits that were plowed back into production. In fact, the enthusiasm of the investment community was so strong that investment in production outstripped demand in an environment where future demand couldn't be judged.

From 1890 to 1920, rising productivity in agriculture, forestry, and fishing reduced the workforce in those areas from 43 percent to 27 percent, and from 1920 to 1950, from 27 percent to 12 percent. Conversely industry was devoting significant amounts of production to farming equipment. Farming labor fed industry, and industry fed farming. Productivity gains that reduced the number of farm employees were simultaneously reducing the need for farm industrialization. As a farmer might put it, manufacturing was digging its own hole.

It took a significant allocation of labor to build this new farm equipment. In fact, a large allocation of labor was building plants to produce all kinds of equipment. Along with the financial commitments to investment, a major portion of the labor force came to build more buildings and more manufacturing. That meant more jobs. A significant share of the labor force was involved in the construction for future production. When the Depression came, this share of the labor force was no longer needed, or perhaps, the Depression came because the production was not needed. It wasn't only workers building new plants, plant equipment, and commercial real estate who were laid off but those in the production of the goods and services that supplied these workers' needs. This was a very significant cause for unemployment.

The economy had over invested. The massive unemployment that resulted in the Great Depression occurred because too large a percentage of the labor force was allocated to the expansion of the economy. It was a phase of economic growth, brought about by the success of free enterprise, not by its failure. This economic failure was foretold not by a capitalist but rather by a Communist. Nikolai Lenin's concern was that "capital created by labor of the worker" would create "an army of unemployed." But the freedom that allowed Lenin and Karl Marx to express their own idealistic approach to economics and to foretell this aspect of the future did not give them even a glimpse of what was to occur afterwards. Their insight was limited to only a phase of free enterprise. No one had imagined that the modern world of the 1920s was merely a prelude of what was to come. The Great Depression was a transitional response to an economic imbalance. The economy was transforming from a simple rural society, in which 90 percent of the active employment was in farming, to the complex society of today, in which less than 3 percent of the working population works in farming.

If there was fault, it was the failure of government to understand the balance that needed to be maintained in the allocations of labor. In other words, this was a failure to understand the economics of labor. In this transitional phase of economic development, the diversification of goods and services meant a diversification in job descriptions. Along with this change came a division of the productive workforce into current and future production. An imbalance in this allocation of labor between future and current production would mean the potential to produce would eventually exceed the potential to consume. Compounding the situation, prospective products were limited in comparison to today's' complex array of goods and services. This meant that manufactures could easily be committed to excessive production of similar products especially when fads developed. Unfortunately, government or the economists haven't thought of the Great Depression as a phase, and the current behavior in economic management is quite possibly based on erroneous conclusions made as to the Depression's causes. The result is mismanagement of the economy by modern politicians, based on the fear that government must provide jobs in the event of recessions and to avoid a depression.

Other factors may have contributed to the depth of the Great Depression. The United States, in the years prior to 1929, was not unaccustomed to recessions and depressions. The people of the depression, having had some experience, had an idea of how to reduce consumption to deal with economic downturns. Living standards were still simplistic enough that many needs could be resolved at home. The factory worker and spouse had not left the farm so long ago that practical knowledge had been forgotten. They could satisfy their own needs for food canning, repair, sewing, and such. After all, there was a time when farmers needed little more than what they produced. The households of the Depression certainly had a substantial increase in the time and the necessity to satisfy their own needs. In a comparison to today, if the time a family spends watching TV were used to provide for household needs, we can only imagine the savings in family income and the greater economic efficiency and productivity. We can also imagine how the need for new manufacturing facilities could suddenly disappear. Simply speaking, prior to the Depression, production and efficiency overtook demand, and when the economy contracted, people went back to the old ways of taking care of their needs, which further contracted demand.

The Depression quite possibly happened not just as a failure of business to plan but because of the number making the same plans in an atmosphere of enthusiasm and due to the people's ability to resolve financial difficulties at home. Today in our complex society with the millions of professions and diverse products it is doubtful an exacerbated allocation of labor to future production could occur. Fads are always present, but the decision-making process in Complex societies is incredibly diversified and people are much more dependent on shopping for their daily needs. Whereas economic downturns were once predictable by the rise and fall of women's hemlines, today we find styles in a miscellany of shapes, exposures, fabrics, and, of course, skirt lengths. This fashion analogy reflects today's complexity and diversity in ideas, modes, and methods.

The overinvestment that occurred prior to the Depression had precedent. Overinvestment was credited for recessions and depressions that affected the country in the latter half of the 1800s, when railroad expansion fluctuated greatly. More recently, it happened in the 1970s and '80s, but unlike in 1929, this latest economic disaster impacted mostly a single economic activity. In the '70s and '80s, the construction of housing and commercial rental real estate was invited by the passage of tax laws in the years from 1969 through 1981. These laws provided increased tax write offs and spirited an oversupply of developed real estate. In the Depression and in the '80s, the potential supply exceeded demand by several years. Both periods left high construction unemployment, not to mention a banking crisis. The enormity of the real estate problem of the '80s was near equal in size to the problem of the entire economy in the '20s and '30s. And like the Depression, the problem of overproduced real estate was apparent several years thereafter. In the latter period this surplus of commercially developed properties was attested by 1994 vacancy figures, showing that most major cities were still suffering vacancies above 12 percent. In Dallas and Los Angeles, where real estate and oil production were popular government-sponsored tax shelters and stimuli, the rates of vacancy were 34 percent and 24 percent, respectively (Forbes November 21, 1994). Ten years after the annulment of lucrative tax deductions in 1986, the cost of new construction in many areas still wasn't justified by rental rates.

These are important contrasts between the two times. The fear of the '80s crisis growing into a depression was there, silently held by government officials. The most important contrast, however, is that despite these fears, it didn't. Likely, government applauds itself for the handling of the situation, but the circumstances were quite different. The economy in the '80s was not an evolving "Transitional" one; it was "Complex," diversified, and no longer controlled from a single room. Each industry was nearly large enough to be its own economy, in an atmosphere where financiers looked for opportunities to take control of suffering businesses. No industry or community was dependent upon any other to sustain itself. Indeed, the excesses in real estate had drawn needed capital and labor away from other industries. The return of capital and labor was welcomed and quickly absorbed. There is one other mentionable difference: in the Depression free enterprise had over stimulated itself; the real estate crisis in the '70s and '80s occurred because government overstimulated free enterprise. In a fair analysis of these occurrences, the Keynesian interpretation of the Great Depression was very much the cause of the real estate recession of the '70s and '80s.

The most commonly explained causes for the Great Depression surely contributed to the problem. Free trade would have allowed the exchange of the excess goods we produced for other goods we did not. Quick action to absorb excess manufacturing and construction labor would have limited the impact of layoffs. Easier consumer credit might have encouraged additional consumption. But the actions that needed to be taken should have occurred before the crash, not after. Higher margin requirements on the purchase of listed stock would have reduced capital formation and the construction of plant and equipment. Credit restrictions on business and higher taxes to reduce the attraction of investments would have slowed investment until demand caught up. But then as now, allocations of labor should have had the attention of economic advisories.

In the years that followed the crash of 1929, cash actually grew plentiful, but cash is not enough to generate a growing economy. Faith in the dollar was strong but faith in the new median of exchange—stocks—had to be restored. To spark the imagination, restore faith in the stock market, and consume the surplus capital, new gadgets to spark demand and utilize production space were needed. It is unfortunate that war was the spark, but WWI, WWII brought new gadgets and with the gadgets came the faith. This time around, there were enough who were less anxious to get involved in investment. There was a more realistic assessment of the values and control on financing, financial reporting, and trading. Government also restricted the margins available to stockholders. It did this to protect banks, but the effect was also to restrict investment, which, based on the experience of the Great Depression, was a needed control.

War was a solution for the Depression because it created a need for the excess capacity, dollars to spend, and a shortages of goods on which to spend the money. For government to solve the problem, it would have necessitated the viable use of vacant plant space, vacancies that could have fostered new demands for goods that were not yet household items. TVs, still-faster cars, dishwashers, or the like would have helped. The important lesson of the 1929 crash is not that spending money is "good for the economy" but that how labor is allocated is important, if the needs of society are to be fulfilled. Government doesn't need to create jobs to encourage free enterprise; free enterprise does it all on its own. Given an open labor market, society's greatest problem might be finding workers.

After WW II and the Korean War, the economy again began to soar, but now there was fear—fear of war, fear of a depression, and *fear of unemployment*. And to take advantage of this fear, the devil created politicians to scare the hell out of us when he can't. Politicians take credit for employment and boast of creating jobs. Citizens, of course, are more than willing to give the politician the credit for having a job or the blame for the lack of a job. In either case, electing a politician is always the answer. If the citizens of this country were asked the question, "Which do you have more faith in, government or free enterprise?" would it be any surprise if the response were government? But based on the most protracted competition ever to be held in the history of the earth, in the competition between government control and individual management, individuals won. The experiment of Communism represented not only the failure of Communism but also an astounding example of the failure of government. Communism gave government the power to solve problems and afforded government with every opportunity to succeed. Free humankind through a system of free enterprise solved most problems, improved living standards, and won the competition. There is no greater evidence that government is an inefficient problem-solver. Government is not contrived to succeed, whether managed by dictators in a totalitarian environment or led by freely elected officials in a democratic process. Unlike government, free enterprise doesn't simply assign someone to prepare a report when there is a problem. Free enterprise uses the imagination of every man, woman, and child to advance humankind when problems or opportunities wouldn't even be apparent to a government bureaucrat. Humankind is not bound by specifications, quotas, forms to file, or the limitations of a politician's pork barrel. It is imagination and an ever-increasing population that creates jobs.

The most important lesson is that our economy is no longer comparable to the one that preceded the Great Depression; the transition from farm to factory has been made. Because the intricacy and complexity of today's economy constitutes an abundance of separate economies, significant innovation causing lost employment in one economy will be absorbed by another looking for labor. This complexity is further enhanced by the world economy. Where one country might be stagnant or losing employment, others are likely to be growing; where investment is needed to spur an economy, it will be attracted by available, unrestricted, and willing labor.

A Complex society displays diversity in the allocations of labor and freedom of the rights of employee and employer.

Efforts to protect employment invariably suppress investment, reduce profits, and stall expansion. Entrepreneurs are discouraged from entering the market, and government interference eventually leads to the concentration, not distribution, of wealth. The potential dream that free enterprise represents has been lost for millions by the efforts of an incompetent government seeking to protect those same millions.

Government is a growing assembly of unproductive labor. It is an inefficient monolith, rather than a source of guidance to a society whose greatest problem is a surplus of inspiration.

One more conclusion can be drawn from the catastrophe of the Great Depression. As the transition from a Rural to a Complex society proceeded, the power of the economy shifted from a primitive concentration of government to a decentralized free-enterprise system. However, the power of this free system was still limited to only a few entrepreneurs and was, therefore, still concentrated. This concentration of power had much to do with the overzealous and corresponding similar decisions that lead to overinvestment and an infatuation with the stock market. One of the greatest strengths of free enterprise is the decentralization of power and, therefore, of decision making. With diversity comes the ability to specialize and to improve the quality of decisions, as well as the potential to offset good against bad decisions when they do occur. However, in the world of the 1990s, power was again concentrated by government. Government created the laws that resulted in the oversupply of real estate and a crisis in the 1970s and '80s, and its overconcentration efforts in any direction will have negative results. Government is not suited to making decisions without causing major and serious movements in the allocations of labor. The increasing size of governments may be the cause of economic catastrophe. The current efforts of government are to reduce the federal deficit by finding a more and better way to tax. The reality is that even in balance, government on all levels continues to grow in size and power. Our rights and freedom are diminishing with our living standard.

Communists who saw the Great Depression as fulfilling one of Lenin's predictions may have delayed the ending of the Cold War because his belief was reinforced. They may have awaited another prediction. The workers, they were taught, would rise against the capitalist. According to Marx, wealth would become concentrated in the hands of a diminishing number of capitalists and under the "iron law of wages," wage earners would become impoverished. Indeed, it is ironic that the spread between the rich and the private worker is widening. But it is not the wealthy or free enterprise that is to blame. Government is demanding that the private worker complete an ever-increasing number of tasks, and all facets of the economy must rebate increasing amounts of taxes. As businesses must survive, the added cost must earn a profit or the business will fail, thus adding capital and profits to the owners of business. Government, often in an effort to distribute the wealth, has widened the gap between leader and follower, the capitalist and the capitalist worker.

Business cost can be divided into flexible and inflexible costs:
Free and productive labor is a flexible cost;
Government mandated costs and taxes are inflexible.

An increase in the legally binding costs of government requires that a business, in order to stay in business, must reduce flexible costs to maintain pricing and competitiveness.

When the cost of government increases, free market wages will decline.

Unless the private workers realize that government could be taking well over 60 percent of what they produce (earn), Lenin's prediction might yet come true. However, it will not be the rich, freedom, or free enterprise that will be responsible for economic problems; it will be an expansionist government. An evolving world needs guidance to forestall it from the problems Lenin predicted. Government needs to discover its proper role, or freedom and free enterprise might become a short chapter in the long history of the world.

Countries that are presently evolving through the agricultural stage of capitalism would be stifled by the imposition of Keynesian standards. A lack of absolute knowledge about free enterprise would allow the ill advised benevolent to impose welfare standards on unwary developing countries. If this occurs, those private workers will suffer the same or worse stagnation and declining living standards as is seen in the U.S. today. As long as government does not restrict or interfere seriously in domestic or foreign investment, excess labor will be the attraction that shortens the difficulties of developing countries. As part of a Complex world, emerging nations do not need to suffer the extreme problems of overcapitalization seen in the Great Depression or the great real-estate crisis in the '80s. Monitoring labor allocations would provide the information to balance free enterprise, welfare needs, government growth, and the production of current and future needs. A full comprehension of free enterprise can hasten the advancement of the world's social, environmental, and economic goals.

CHAPTER 12

WHAT REALLY HAPPENED IN THE '70s AND '80s?

In 1981, President Reagan came into office and assumed responsibility for a blotted, super-heated economy created by the excesses of government expansion and wage increases that no longer equated to productivity. Inflation had just begun to peak as the discount rate, established by the Federal Reserve, pushed the prime rate over 20 percent. Businesses were losing to foreign competition, and major industries were facing disaster as the unions demanded and got big raises, in addition to cost-of-living adjustments (COLAs). Production was losing ground to the growth of dollars, and the Federal Reserve used high interest rates to coerce the economy into recession. Large portions of the populace would now be forced to adjust their living standards down to align consumption with production. Those with guaranteed incomes and COLAs would not be affected; the burden that had to be borne would fall on the unprotected.

Private workers lost jobs in the recession that followed, but new jobs also meant lower pay and declining living standards. Unions that had clauses covering job protection and inflation found their contracts meaningless in industries that could no longer compete in a market facing recession and stiff competition. Layoffs spread, and plant closures were imminent. The scene was set for major union difficulties and business closures. When the air traffic controllers went on strike, it was assumed that government would respond as usual, meeting their demands and continuing the spiral. Instead, the controllers were told to go back to work or be replaced. Thus, a signal was given to business that the Reagan administration would take a hands-off position in the reorganizations of businesses that was to come. The cost of the Great Society in taxes and numerous regulations that forced the private sector to spend on compliance was to be swallowed whole by business and the workers. To do this, industry had to become efficient, but what it couldn't make up in efficiency, workers had to make up in a smaller share of society's redistributed purchasing power.

In the '80s and into the '90s, large businesses begged, borrowed, sold, laid off, and did whatever was necessary to reorganize U.S. industry. It was time to utilize the efficient production methods that the United States had pioneered. Despite the immense layoffs made to make business more efficient, post-recession unemployment declined. The decline surprised the anti-business media that anticipated business-orchestrated unemployment. But labor-starved businesses were simply putting workers to more efficient uses, as the continued growth in government increased demands on the workforce, while limiting gains in productivity. The need to reduce production costs was a necessity for business to survive, and the employment deck was merely reshuffled. Opportunities for employment increased for private workers who were qualified and willing to work, but wages did not increase. As large corporations reorganized, prices were held down, despite government-inspired cost inflation. Production was being rejuvenated. This odd circumstance gave us a booming economy with concurrent declining interest and inflation rates. In essence, productivity was outpacing monumental government growth, offsetting some of the '70s cost inflation and exhibiting the forces of free enterprise.

However, the government's absolute power to tax and to demand compliance with its law and regulation places its rights to the gains in economic production ahead of the rights of the consumer and the private-sector workforce. Therefore, those not protected by guaranteed income augmentations had difficulties enhancing their living standards. Being only averages, the typical measurements used to describe household incomes failed to show the plight of the private worker. Instead of a lock-step movement, in which everyone was taking one step forward to a better life, the movement was a teeter-totter with a heavy end. Those blessed by government were on the up side, and those not were weighted down with the load. Only private workers with the imagination to take advantage of the situation rose above or stayed even with the rising government costs.

It was unfortunate, but the traditional views of economics ignored labor as a productive element. Keynesian economic stimulus was seen as a necessary tool to ensure full employment and acted as an excuse for inflating government payrolls and passing added costs to business. The demands placed on the labor force were perceived as reducing unemployment in a society believed to be filled with infinitely available workers. In the early part of the '80s supply side stimulus was no less wasteful. The enactment of the 1986s tax law to cut or eliminate many real estate tax shelters eliminated much of that waste. The misallocation of productive workers to an economic activity to produce product the consumer didn't need during a period when over production was already existence, put significant strains on labor demands. This, plus the increased government demands, caused one of the greatest cycles of inflation ever suffered in the United States, and resulted in a near collapse in the banking system.

How did all this begin in a country that considered a better life through self-determination a birthright? Things began to change in the 1960s when the Great Society legislation was passed. And in the '70s, government began using its power to manage every facet of life, as it passed legislation to improve the environment and assist the poor. Professional politicians (who championed the poor) and peace and love took the place of many with work experience. Using textbook economics and progressive tax rates in an inflationary economy, the righteous politicians cried spend, spend, spend! As the labor force began fulfilling the politicians' dreams, prices rose along with wages. A new work ethic was formed to suggest that spending was more important than working, and welfare was good for the poor and good for the economy. Tax laws that encouraged real estate ownership helped to inflate real estate prices and encouraged wasted investments. Later, these investments became traps for those not quick enough to sell out. Price inflation was greater than wage inflation, and those with insufficient earnings sought other ways to finance their consumption. Many consumers used credit cards, savings, and household equity and often ended up in the welfare ranks. Welfare recipients, whose income was adjusted for inflation, gained by comparison, because the amount of additional welfare exceeded inflated costs. The middle class was the big loser, as inflation rebalanced their life styles to new government-imposed costs.

Much of what happened in the '70s, with the exception of the growth in government, was nearly the exact opposite of what happened in the '80s. Both periods saw a tremendous change in how labor was used, but to understand the differences, we need to look at the forces acting on each period. The best and simplest way to do this is the same way that Jimmy the Greek, a famous gambler, figured a football game. He added up all the strengths and weaknesses on both sides and weighted one against the other. (Ben Franklin is credited with the method.)

With inflation/deflation we list the factors that cause each. The way Jimmy the Greek did it, we only need a brief look at the list to find more reasons for inflation in the '70s and more reasons for deflation in the '80s. To give a greater perspective of their impact, we will discuss many of the reasons.

The '70s

Factors causing inflation

Vietnam War
Baby boomers' education and upbringing
Oil cartel
Union and government COLAs
Social Security COLAs
Union work rules
Welfare increases plus cost-of-living increases
Electric utility cleanup
The 1969 tax reform act
Equal Rights Amendment
New environmental rules
Higher rates of return to justify investment
Increases in health care and pension reform
Declining saving and stock market prices
Proliferation of credit cards
Increase in the size of legal settlements (class-action suits)
Redistribution of wealth
Loss of efficiencies of scale
Fewer opportunities at higher rates of return

Factors creating deflation

Free enterprise
Higher ROI attracts capital
Normal efficiencies of production
Conservation
Increased imports
Lower quality consumer goods
Two-earner families

Contrast the above with the '80s

Factors causing inflation

New factors

Overall government growth in excess of inflation
Military buildup
Bigger spread between the rates banks pay and charge
The 1981 Tax Reform Act

Old factors whose growth rates

Factors creating deflation

New factors

Baby boomers in the workforce
Strong dollar
Added labor from integration and immigration
The '86 tax act eliminated wasteful tax shelters
Deregulation of several industries

Reduced ROI requirements

were still compounded

Legal settlements

Environmental concerns

Welfare and COLAs

Government wage increases

increased opportunities

The stock market became attractive

Unions became more flexible

End of the Cold War

Lower inflation begets lower inflation

Computers, cellular phones, and fax machines

Improved business atmosphere

Excess supply of rental buildings

Lower oil prices

Pent-up desire for innovation

Initial impact of large government increases had been absorbed

Factors still applying from the '70s

Free enterprise

Imports

Two-earner families

The sheer magnitude of factors impacting inflation from both government and nongovernment causes in the '70s was obvious. Expenditures in "growth businesses" like the environment, however, were considered as job providers, not causes for inflation. Taking the factors one by one, and starting with the 1970s, the picture of inflation becomes clear.

A. The Vietnam War required manpower, added production, tremendous amounts of armaments, and monetary support for the Vietnam government. In addition, Vietnam was a more conventional war, and the innovation that normally occurs with war did not happen to the same extent. The cost had to be borne without offsets from later consumer improvements. Postwar expenses included care for the disabled, the wounded, and payments for pensions.

B. Baby boomers came on the scene and consumed goods far beyond their ability to produce them. Housing, for example, is one of the largest purchases a consumer makes, but people must be housed. Unlike food or clothing that can be purchased with one's current labor, housing is bought with future labor. The price of housing was bid up. The boomers were also new additions to the workforce who, as neophytes, required training and education, were not as efficient as older workers, and lacked the skills to handle computers that could have reduced inflation.

C. Oil price increases from foreign cartels had to be absorbed, creating obvious inflation and a capital and labor rush to develop new resources. Oil prices increased 1000 percent, going from $3 to $33 per barrel. Tremendous amounts of manpower got involved in every facet of oil production, from venture forming to the development of new deep-water techniques. Available supplies increased significantly, but these sources cost far more than traditional supplies.

D. Union cost-of-living adjustment (COLA) clauses and an activist position caused a disproportionate portion of gross consumer income to be allocated to union members, as prices were increased to compensate for high labor costs. Non-union labor in competing industries was affected, as manufacturers raised wages to keep unions from forming. Government, from local to federal, made COLA adjustments to employee wages as well. Workers not able to make up for higher prices with earnings adjustments lost economic status. Eventually, wage increases worked to the disadvantage of union members, when producers with more efficient labor brought down cost and prices, causing shutdowns or significant layoffs in union shops.

As for government, with the power to accomplish its supposed evenhanded goals, it, too, added burdensome and inflationary wage hikes that, once granted, are never recanted. Government wages, reputed at the time to be low in comparison to those of private enterprise, were increased at rates above inflation. With wage increases greater than those of many private workers, government workers did not share in the new cost of government. Government pay and benefits went above what free enterprise could support because of government disruptions. Unfortunately, government provides no incentives for efficiency. A low employee turnover is testimony of the job security achieved in government.

E. Similar COLA adjustments to Social Security added income for retirees and by a quirk in the law, the increase exceeded inflation.

F. Union work rules were already too restrictive to allow innovation in many industries, as the bloated economy of the '70s put unions in an even stronger position to inflate wages and add restrictions to job duties. Normal offsets to high labor costs by way of innovation were hindered and even aided by local laws that restricted innovative materials, thus adding to the demand for labor. Export growth was restrained by the high cost and limited supply of labor, forcing U.S. firms to invest in foreign countries. Unlike the two hundred years prior, the U.S. workforce was now a highly skilled but overcompensated and less flexible labor market, which refused installation of innovative and efficient methods. In the incredible effort to increase union control and compensation, the golden goose was being fleeced.

A tremendous opportunity for the U.S. economy to grow was being lost. Most shortsightedly, the worker's desire for current benefits sacrificed the incredible future growth and living-standard increases that would have otherwise occurred. Current benefits took precedence over future job security that efficiency would foster. Unions promoted inefficient job growth to increase membership roles and enhance the power of labor leadership.

G. Additional welfare programs, plus the COLA adjustments to the existing programs, were making welfare as attractive as some working wages. The increased attraction of welfare thus multiplied the welfare ranks and reduced the workforce. Since recipients of welfare perform unskilled tasks, those functions still needing to be accomplished by more adroit labor, reducing productivity. The welfare system expanded beyond intention, as welfare payments encroached on business wage levels. With price inflation for private workers being unbalanced with wage appreciation, the real income and economic status of private workers declined. People on welfare became discouraged, as those within the ranks looking out found safety in their current status.

H. Utility companies were required to clean up air and water emissions. At the same time cleaner, more efficient nuclear power plants were either priced out of reality by new safety requirements or banned completely. Cost increases caused by the cleanup went unnoticed by the consumer, because fuel-price increases were a much greater concern.

I. In 1969, the tax law was changed to allow faster write-offs for residential rental housing. This altered the economically sensible investment computations and attracted a disproportionate share of investment to obtain tax write-offs that eventually proved to be very real losses. Congress, at the time, considered the law necessary to provide housing for the baby boomers and to hype up the economy. The result was to waste capital on construction not justified by demand and to deter investors from less financially attractive but more socially useful endeavors. The new housing also helped to precipitate the decline of the inner cities, as those who could afford it moved to new quarters in the suburbs. Left behind were the less economically advantaged, house and apartment vacancies, and a declining inner-city environment that should have been one spurred by baby-boomer demand.

J. Failure to accept the African-American and other maligned society members reduced their potential contribution of goods and services to the community. Their capabilities, enthusiasm, and potential for success had not yet been realized, due to preconceived attitudes. Eventually, integration would aid in the fight against inflation, like the influx of immigrants had fostered growth in prior years. The elimination of prejudice brings a new, hungry worker to the market. But before that could happen, changes had to be made. The courts filled with lawsuits; government and business attempted to make up for injustice by hiring many that were not best prepared for specific jobs; schools were required to bus; welfare was expanded; and bureaucracies, at a cost of billions, were formed to support the effort.

K. Environmental rules and laws were enacted that raised the cost of industry, added to the required investment, and changed investment calculations. Many businesses that could not afford changes simply went out of business. Changes that were not made retroactive delayed normal expansion until inflation-adjusted prices warranted the cost. At a time when money costs and investment-return rates were rising, added costs made investments unattractive. Only highly profitable investments and those subsidized by tax laws, like real estate, were justified. Investment in actual plant expansion was limited, as capital had to be spent on environmental concerns.

L. As the demand for labor increased, pension plans, health insurance, and other employee benefits became necessary to attract new employees. These industries also required an additional share of workforce. Insured medical treatment turned health care into a growth industry, increasing the demand for care and capital assets. As an expanding industry, health care produced higher rates of return and readily attracted capital, as payment for treatment was now often guaranteed. Although beneficial, new health treatments were expensive experiments to future advances. Over the long term, keeping experienced workers in the workforce was beneficial, but the cost to establish the system for treatment was significant.

M. Higher interest rates, increased the needed return and limited investments to high-risk or high-return ventures. Tax shelters, the housing demands of baby boomers, and inflation-enhanced, leveraged augmented gains in real estate focused capital in inflation-favored investments. Anticipated real estate returns were high, compared to the stock market and other business investments. Thus, higher prices were necessary for non-real–estate consumer industries to attract the capital needed to increase the supply that would control pricing. Inflation was feeding on itself, as the physical cost of expansion and the rising cost of investment capital actually deflated potential investment recoveries to below acceptable rates of return.

N. At a time when businesses needed extra capital, savings rates were declining. Some investments were attractive, but higher prices required more of the consumer's surplus dollars to pay for everyday goods. The desire to own goods, rather than to own deflating dollars, engenders some blame for pushing up prices, but higher investment returns augmented by increased profits should have attracted more savings. The extra money was just not there. The many people who were losers in the reallocation of resources and redistribution of earnings attempted to keep up with their normal living standard using savings, credit cards, or credit. Much of the money that was saved flowed into tax shelters, rather than investment-starved businesses. Businesses with depressed stock prices borrowed at inflated rates to fund environmental mandates, limiting their own possibilities of expansion.

O. Credit cards began to proliferate, as for many individuals, plastic became the way to maintain their eroding living standard. This was the beginning of the age when everybody had the opportunity to "charge it."

   For the baby boomers, credit cards were especially useful in satisfying capital needs for appliances, furniture, and even automobiles. Lenders received higher returns than could be obtained by conventional small or business loans, which carried the risk but not the high interest rates. The high returns meant that lenders were less selective in disbursing credit cards, because the profits would cover extra losses. Small businesses were simultaneously shorted bank loans needed to provide for the expanding credit card market. As credit worthiness declined, unreal credit expectations, bad debts, and other related losses became an ever-increasing cost of business. The usual high moral fiber of U.S. citizens was being tarnished.

P. With a growing anti-business sentiment on the part of jurors, and the notion that only business and insurance companies paid legal costs, lawyers used jury trials to bolster legal court settlements. Laws that hold the "deep-pocketed" large businesses liable for 100 percent of court-directed settlements (even when fault was negligible) attracted multitudes of lawsuits. Punitive damage awards, intended to punish wrongdoers in a society bent on punishing business, multiplied actual damages by thousands, millions, and billions. New laws allowing class-action suits, originally intended to reduce court loads, resulted in massive suits and created a legal witch hunt. Law firms, working off a traditional percentage of the settlement, fronted costs that resulted in billions of dollars in legal benefits. At first bankrupting many insurance companies, legal decisions eventually resulted in higher rates and a boom to the insurance industry. The legal costs were paid directly through rate hikes to the consumer or indirectly through businesses, as product price increases. Businesses went out of business, sold out, or began to take extraordinary precautions to reduce or eliminate the possibilities of a lawsuit, adding further to product costs.

State insurance commissioners, who controlled insurance rates in the same way they control utilities rates, in effect guaranteed profits for insurance companies by approving rate increases based on cost. Such practices encouraged losses, as higher losses also guaranteed higher rates and higher profits. With the hike in insurance rates and the difficulty in maintaining living standards because of government growth, many went without insurance spawning exploding growth in uninsured motorist coverage. Government responded with penalties for those who didn't carry insurance or who broke traffic laws. Because the cost of insurance is a matter of liability, not income, those with lower incomes who could afford insurance paid a greater share of their income than did the rich. Many of the young found they could no longer meet societal requirements because of an empire whose doctrine is to create crimes of punishment and to reward litigants with lifetime vacations. Doubtless, the dollar cost can be calculated, but the cost in principles cannot.

With each new program, government passed new crimes to punish and new reasons to sue. Businesses benefiting from the growing litigation expanded employment and earned for themselves a greater share of the economy. Government—intent upon protecting consumers, cleansing the environment, and increasing safety—produced suspiciously large benefits for a profession in which large numbers of politicians had like degrees.

Q. During the 1970s, the attempt to redistribute wealth was accelerated. This effort was well under way in many large cities, where sympathy for the poor was already taxing working citizens. As welfare recipients grew in numbers, so, too, did government employees with altruistic intentions. As a result, large nonworking populations came to exist in areas where the economy was destroyed because potential workers were penalized for having jobs. Tax-sheltered real estate construction not only pulled jobs away from the inner city to the suburbs but encouraged more prosperous members to leave older apartments. With apartments left empty, buildings deteriorated for lack of the rental income to pay repairs. Crime was encouraged in this impossible quest to improve living standards, as the poor who were paid not to work now had added time to exploit. The welfare trap was destroying people and their communities. Programs to redistribute wealth simply meant increased personal, wages and pensions for employees in these new government programs.

R. The loss of efficiencies of scale was a critical factor in a newly evolving world. As sales of quality products were lost to low-quality foreign competition, unit cost of domestic products escalated. The efficiencies of scale were being reversed. Costs and quality had to be reduced to meet competition and regain sales. Foreign manufacturers conversely expanded production and filled the void for high quality products. Thus, while foreign manufacturers increased their efficiencies of scale, improved their products, and captured large segments of the market, domestic manufacturers were struggling to break even, as many reduced quality to match foreign pricing.

The disaster of the '70s occurred because government made a preposterous effort to exact the greatest social experiment in history, while imposing laws to clean and protect the environment and to stimulate investment with wasteful tax shelters. Government was simultaneously demanding more production of its workers, while passing laws to reduce their numbers. Goals conflicted with each other, as charitable actions of bumbling politicians, backed by a media living in a fantasyland, extracted billions from a system that was seen by them as a big cookie jar. The goals were supported by an economic formula that stressed monetary performance over the relevance of a worker. A government that placed money on the altar of worship was raping the capitalist system that gives emphasis to the importance of the individual. Beneficial or not, just or not, government pillaged the economy and raped the private worker of livelihood.

The factors offsetting inflation were mostly mechanical responses of a free productive system. Some offsets resulted in higher future costs. In the '70s, the price deflators were not nearly as plentiful or effective. However, without these offsets, inflation would have been worse.

A. The free-enterprise system adapts and adjusts to absorb the effects of cost increases and make proper allocations of resources. As demand increases and shortages of skilled labor appear, workers work longer, harder, and more intelligently. Often, the incentives of unfettered free enterprise are sufficient to overcome enormous obstacles. But the magnitude of opposing forces and the constraints on the '70s workforce was far too efficacious.

B. As prices rose, investment returns increased to compensate for high demand. The free-enterprise solution to an increase in demand is higher prices, and its result is expanded production, often resulting in lower cost methods and lower prices. However, as the Federal Reserve increased the costs of funds in the '70s, the cost of financing rose, as still-higher pricing was needed to warrant investment. The solutions to inflation compounded the difficulty of increasing production. Little of the inflation was overcome by free enterprise, as the prerequisites to expansion were burdened with overcoming environmental problems and other problems from the past. New businesses, not so encumbered by the past or restrictive unions, began to form and to grow during this time.

C. As the units of production increased, so, too, did the efficiencies of scale. Up to certain limits, factories increased production with little increase in equipment costs. As second and third shifts were added, overhead expanded only slightly. Sales forces did not need to be expanded, as customer orders were simply increased. Shipping became more efficient, as large orders proved less costly to ship. Problems occurred in the '70s when limits to the efficiencies of scale were reached, and the solution was expansion in an atmosphere of rising costs and downward pressure on pricing.

D. Conservation of a different sort began, as the garage sale and flea market became popular. Cars were driven longer and any source of discounting or quantity purchasing was investigated. Conservation became a common term to a country that once felt its resources were unlimited. Consumers began to look for ways to save on electricity and gasoline, while vehicles lost miles per gallon to environmental equipment.

E. Expanding imports helped fight inflation with lower prices and competition. Importing also ushered in new technology, resolved temporary shortages, and eliminated the need for business to expand. Even when prices for foreign goods were higher, they augmented domestic labor. Imports were an attraction simply because they satisfied consumer demand. With an overvalued dollar, imports became even cheaper, as the representative exchange in labor put the importing country ahead. Importing was and is a major factor in controlling inflation and filling the labor void brought about by government expansionism.

F. Lower-quality goods became acceptable. In the search to maintain living standards with available incomes, price became important. Buyers were less discriminating, accepting goods of unknown quality and manufacture. Eventually, lower quality also meant quicker replacement, but in the short run, producing goods that required fewer resources helped stretch dollars. Name-brand businesses responded to pressures by lowering quality in hopes of maintaining market share. Quality problems abounded in the '70s as manufacturers with well-known brand names became unprofitable and either went out of business or were sold to other manufacturers. As a result of the '70s quality crisis, U.S. businesses later required incredible amounts of labor and money to improve quality and overcome the negative attitudes of the customers, whose trust they had lost.

G. Wives added their labor to the workforce and got jobs to supplement the husbands' income and to keep up with rising costs. Many relationships were strained, however, as couples lacked the ritual customs needed to deal with this dual financial responsibility, and prior generations scorned husbands for "making" wives work. Divorces increased, and the single-parent households became common. Fathers having the responsibility for child support found it difficult to manage financially and often refused to pay child support, putting the load over onto welfare agencies to supplement the mothers' income and to go after delinquent fathers.

Along with the loss of quality products, inner-city stores declined in number. Privately owned stores with quality service and products lost market share to national stores with "blue-light specials," less personal service, and the same products at lower prices. Shopping centers and discount locations were built away from downtown, at cheaper, more accessible locations. Complaints of lower quality abounded, but businesses that were reliant on high quality for their livelihoods fell by the wayside, as cheaper foreign goods captured sales.

The potential offsets to inflation were no match for its causes, and inflation rose to over 13 percent, annually. In 1981, interest rates were forced up by the Federal Reserve. As always, the final result of the inept management of the economy followed: a recession. Individuals and businesses adjusted to lower living standards to reconcile demand with production. Some went over the edge to welfare and bankruptcy. "Downsizing" became a new term on Wall Street. The crisis could have been more severe, but free enterprise managed some adjustments. There was a cost: the standard of living for most private workers declined, and two working family members would often be needed to purchase a home. Wage earners did not benefit by the redistribution of wealth, because production, not wealth, was redistributed. The wealthy may have been slowed from gaining, but they didn't lose. Only private workers in middle in lower income groups lost.

By the end of the '70s, the dollar was no longer the rock it had been, and the phrase "sound as a dollar" became a memory for the elders. A greater share of product cost now comprised costs that had once caused inflation. While government legislated thousands of accountants, environmentalists, sociologists, and government providers, and while the welfare role increased, government expenditures compounded. The share of the population that produced traditional consumer goods had declined. Not only were the people on welfare nonproductive, but those who attended to them were nonproducers.

Contrast this with the '80s and early '90s.

As inflation-enhanced tax revenues, so, too, did the 1986 tax act that eliminated tax shelters and lowered tax rates but netted additional collections. Government on all levels found new ways to spend the large increases, and when those ran out, every dollar that moved was taxed at least twice. New terms for taxes were coined: "state mandates," "riverboat gambling," "revenue enhancement," and so as not to forget the poor, state lotteries were voter-approved to tax peoples dreams and purportedly enhance favored programs such as schools. Tax collections spiraled up but not enough to cover new federal spending. The federal budget deficit expanded with the expectation that the deficit would fuel inflation. As inflation declined, media reported that economists were befuddled, having equated deficits with inflation. But the deficits were simply a "not tax" tax. Borrowing is the fairest of all taxes, as only those willing to pay will do so. Taxes were raised on state and local levels to pay federally forced and mandated expenses and costs once paid from federal funds. The term "user fees" became common, as free services disappeared.

Fortunately, the private labor market became less restrictive, allowing efficiencies and innovation to occur. To everyone's surprise, interest rates declined. Expansion was sufficient to offset government-benefit increases and growth, as well as to renew much of the U.S. manufacturing base. Those blessed with job guarantees, inflation adjustments, and seniority raises (such as government employees) began to net additional spending power, as prices dropped in the early 1980s recession. However, potential real growths in income from efficiencies in the producing sectors of free enterprise were lost to government programs. Interest rates declined but were well above inflation, leaving the spread between inflation and market rates in excess of historical standards. This was the reverse of the '70s, when interest rates were often below inflation. The economy of the '80s was prevented from growing as it could have, but after the early recession, no notable downturn occurred throughout the '80s and into the '90s. The factors that might have caused inflation outweighed those that would deflate it. Some of the old forces still existed, but new forces were present:

A. Although there were no major new government programs introduced, expansion of the existing programs proceeded at a brisk rate. COLAs, incentives, and job protection have a cost. Local governments and businesses found they needed to comply with federal regulation and mandates that were underfunded or simply unfunded. Schools, trash, and environmental rules created new responsibilities, added paper handlers, and increased salaries. The efficiencies that were realized in the free-enterprise sector provided government with the manpower and the room to grow and the excuse not to lay off workers. The economy absorbed tremendous amounts of government growth and inefficiencies. Resistance to innovation was low, as private workers put in more hours and thought of little more than keeping their jobs and their homes. The news media saw solutions to problems in dollars, in a world filled with people. The competition that welfare offered to jobs was not important to the media. To the media, welfare recipients were a group the system had failed. But welfare merely imprisoned recipients in an irremediable trap. Those politicians who promised the poor were anglicized. Many laws that were passed in the 1970s were still without teeth when implementation began in the 1980s. Adding unnecessary government employees continued to be looked upon by politicians as job creation. Serious thought was rarely given and seldom implemented to eliminate unneeded government jobs. Politicians looked for voids in the job market to fill with government programs.

B. A military buildup in the '80s began in response to the loss in military prowess in the '70s. An idea named "Star Wars"—to defend U.S. soil from missile attack with missile defenses—was researched as an ultimate deterrent to war. A strengthening in the need for this program came as the USSR appeared to be flexing its muscles in an attempt to expand its boundaries with the occupation of Afghanistan. The additional pressure, following previous Cold War tension, strained a Communist system that lacked the incentives of free enterprise, and it collapsed.

C. The nontraditional high spread between interest rates and inflation created a disincentive for potential business expansion. Thus expansion of production was delayed pending further price increases that were associated with declines in living standards for the private-sector worker.

D. In 1980, the economy was on the brink of disaster, as soaring inflation and high interest rates began to strangle construction and other activity. Consumer production could not match the demands of the '70s, and the "recession solution" loomed on the horizon. With an election coming up, Congress readied a pure Keynesian economic solution: more **stimulation of construction.** Effective on January 1, 1981, the tax rules were changed to allow incredibly fast write-offs of both residential and commercial buildings. As much as 12.5 percent of the cost of a building could be deducted in one year, against a high tax rate of 70 percent. The investment returns for rental buildings were enhanced by the tax change, thus sparking a boom in activity. The resultant high vacancies and surplus developments existed in many areas fifteen years hence. Available capital was wasted in an industry where the computer, home offices, and cellular phones reduced the need for office space. Later in the '80s, the largest banking crisis since the Depression began: resulting from the inflation that forced a reapportionment of consumption and the economic stimulus programs that encouraged wasted spending on real estate construction.

With the government-sired '80s recession, the need for free enterprise to revive itself was one of desperation. Government officials and the media touted this recession as a failure of free enterprise and of the consumers to restrict spending; the empire took no responsibility. Indeed, many saw the necessity for more, rather than less, government interference. To reinvigorate the economy, removal of restrictions on labor in the private sector and the advancement of labor-saving innovation were needed.

The following factors offset inflation in the '80s:

A. At the start of the '80s, much of the growth in government that had happened in the '70s had been assimilated into the economy. In other words, as the initial impact of government growth became a part of the normal allocations, further growth did not have as inflationary an impact. For example, if government constituted one-third of the economy and grew to where it was one-half, government grew by 50 percent. From that point, if the growth pattern repeated itself, the increase would represent only a 33 percent growth, even though the physical number was the same. Time and numbers have different effects. Many environmental costs were now factored in, along with employee benefits, welfare costs, and utility costs. The effect of an increase did not have the impact that starting from zero did. Technology to clean the air or to dispose of trash was well underway, and implementation was achieving major results. Much of the cost of the Vietnam War had been paid.

B. Baby boomers, having fulfilled their desire for housing and other big-ticket items, were inclined to invest. As with a biological clock, the retirement clock impacted the household with the investment sensation. The market began its move after the air traffic controller's strike as businesses began their reorganization and moved up quickly after enactment of the 1986 tax act.

C. With the breakup of the USSR, the U.S. and its economic system were ostensibly asserted the winner. The world needed a universally acceptable currency that would expedite the reformation of free enterprise. The demand for the dollar encouraged the exchange of foreign goods for our overvalued currency. Many governments, whether with strong currencies, like Japan, or weak ones, like emerging countries, were willing to take dollars because dollars are acceptable throughout the world. The Japanese used them to invest in Third World countries at lucrative exchange rates, to purchase raw material, or to expand their production. Talk of setting up gold-based currencies became talk of dollar-based currencies. Dollars were easier to transfer, available, and not subject to the fluctuations of gold.

D. In 1986, new real estate was still constructed and planned to satisfy the demands for the tax-shelter industry. At the same time the Savings and Loan industry was suffering a crisis resulting from real estate foreclosures that the government-encouraged excesses in construction had fostered. This non-coincidental occurrence exemplified the astounding incompetence of government and politicians in their tinkering with the economy. Taxes in reverse, tax law had put return-on-investment computations out of whack with tax incentives, as the typical motivation to earn cash returns was not a consideration. Investment firms, which made large fees selling these tax shelters, had bid up the price of real estate to levels that only made sense if one could realize the savings the write offs would generate. The passage of the 1986 Tax Reform Act ended the gluttonous allocation of resources into rental real estate as the cleanup of the largest banking crisis in world history began. By passage of the 1986 act, wasteful government-sponsored tax shelters were eliminated, thousands of investment-firm employees would need to find new jobs, and millions of investors would again need to start saving for the future. The result was increased investment in the stock market and predictable business expansion.

E. The 1986 tax act reduced tax rates, reduced the rates of return necessary to attract investment, made tax shelters less important, put investment decisions on a more businesslike basis, and thereupon increased the motive to expand production. Investor attitudes, that had been influenced by government incentives, took second place to return-on-investment (ROI) computations. Meaningful, comparatively low-risk returns became the primary incentive. The number of economically feasible projects increased exponentially without tax-shelter competition and with lower tax rates. A return of 16 percent netted only 4.8 percent when taxes were 70 percent, but a 4.8 percent return can be produced with a project that pays only 8 percent, when tax rates are 40 percent. And the numbers of projects that pay 8 percent are far more numerous and are less risky.

F. Deregulation, a movement begun in the '70s, continued in the '80s. But deregulation not only increased competition and reduced pricing, it also decreased wages and added to the available labor supply. The airline, trucking, and telephone industries were deregulated, and the government took a laissez-faire approach to union problems that allowed business reorganization on more efficient ground. While Congress took these steps, the news media focused attention on unfair businesses and consumerism. The real targets were employees with guaranteed and often restrictive job classifications. Political power used by big business and labor in previous years forestalled actions that could have occurred with less serious consequences. Actions that were good for free enterprise, the consumer, and the future of the world resulted in lost living standards for the private workers who benefited from regulation. Deregulation and tax reform wasn't solely in the interest of the consumer; rather, it created the worker and fiscal surpluses needed for government expansion without noticeable tax rate increases.

In the airlines, passenger rates were left to free-market mechanism, and foreign competition was encouraged. The telephone companies were broken up in a prelude to the coming free market. The steelworkers saw only illusory limits on foreign competition. Trucking rates were no longer controlled, and some efforts were made to increase capacity limits on the highways. Even the mighty railroads, which felt the pressure of truck hauling, saw rule changes and the abandonment of archaic rate schedules. All the changes acted to reduce the need for and strength of the unions.

G. Investors who wasted investments in the Congress-sanctioned tax shelters turned to the stock market, where businesses whose stock prices were devastated by the lack of investor interest were eager to obtain needed capital for expansion and reorganization. New issues allowed for business investments that would foster more efficient facilities and satisfy consumer demands. Investments became less complicated and more productive to the general advantage of the population. Most tax shelters had been eliminated and replaced with investments whose returns came from real consumption, not tax savings. The stock market downs were forgotten, as prices soared.

As the only game in town, the market purveyors joined ranks with those who could no longer hawk tax shelters. Mutual funds outnumbered stocks, as money from pension funds flowed into the equity market at heretofore inconceivable amounts. The infusion of cash to business was needed and long absent. In the 1970s, most companies were forced to borrow to obtain needed cash. Borrowing meant businesses with imaginative ideas had to justify use to conservative bankers and/or sacrifice the balance sheet, which management and stock market disapproved. The equity infusions enhanced investments in research and efficiency. An exorbitant growth of overhead was reversed, with computers that once cost $100,000 showing up on every desk. Investment accomplished the tasks essential to high productivity.

H. Before the 1980s, unions had priced themselves out of the market. But protectionism could no longer save member jobs or high pay. The consumer noticed the increased cost brought on by union contracts, more than the increased cost of government. The politicians weren't going to sacrifice their pork-barrel spending used to buy votes, even for one of their largest contributors. The disproportionate high income and restrictive union rules came under attack. Industry and the unions began to fight to save their businesses from foreign and domestic competition. Wage concessions were more likely than increases, and work rules were changed to allow for increases in productivity. Union workers felt the growth of government, as millions saw their standard of living erode. Unions were the last to feel the pinch, but government pundits realized their numbers were greater than the unions. Unions were a sacrifice to preserve government power and growth. The dream of a four-day workweek evaporated.

I. The end of the Cold War in the late '80s allowed for some reduced military funding. Despite the fear of threats from small countries that might develop nuclear war capabilities, the military budget was cut significantly in the early '90s.

J. As higher inflation begat higher inflation, lower inflation begat lower inflation. As interest rates declined, the rates of return that were acceptable to investors were lower, and more investments occurred. The margin an investor needed over the cost of money also declined with lower rates. The more investments made, the more the consumer benefited. In addition, as rates declined, productive investments that were shelved when investor returns were too low became acceptable. To the investor or to business, investments that return 18 percent less 15 percent money cost will pay the same return as one that returns 7 percent less 4 percent money cost. With added investments, production expanded as was needed to control prices.

K. Next to electricity the computer, fax machine, and cellular phone were the most significant cost-saving devices ever invented. And as their costs declined, their efficiency and capability increased. Entire layers of corporate bureaucrats became unnecessary, and small businesses became more efficient. Even the need for office space was reduced, as work time now included fly time and drive time. Chided as a rich man's toy, cellular phones became popular to help small businesses overcome added costs imposed by government. Cellular phones thus expanded work time and reduced wasted time; ironically, only the rich could afford not to have one. The fax machine reduced travel back and forth and allowed documents to be passed during or preceding phone conversations, reducing face-to-face meetings. The personal computer brought the computer age to the lowest level of business, eliminating secretarial, accounting, and related positions. The availability of these tools supplemented for the workers lost to welfare, unemployment, the expansion of welfare zones which had left potential workers far from jobs. They also allowed for the expansion of the work force needed to perform the numerous regulatory tasks imposed by government. Sales people, executives, and office workers found themselves able to double or triple their productivity.

L. The general business atmosphere was improved as business efforts turned from tax-advantaged investment to profitable ventures, whose returns had to be justified on their own behalf when economy shifting tax shelters were deleted. Providing business with lower taxes, not shelters, and eliminating wasted resources by finagling the tax code saved time and simplified decision making. After the traffic controllers were replaced, the signal from government was clear: it would no longer be an active participant in labor disputes. The signal meant business would be allowed to put its house in order. The layoffs and redefinitions of job descriptions that ensued saw labor force reductions of 20–30 percent at many companies. However, unemployment numbers fell as workers thus released were quickly absorbed by the needs of enterprise and government. The concern of the media—that unemployment would grow—left the media dismayed, but deficit spending, not free enterprise, was given the credit for business expansion.

M. Integration provided needed labor, but immigrants, both legal and illegal, also added to the labor pool. Many were opposed to hiring immigrants, but the demand for willing workers was greater. For most businesses, when survival is in doubt, finding workers is more important than prejudice or boundaries.

N. The overproductive real estate industry had eliminated the need to construct most of the necessary '80s office buildings. Many single-family subdivision lots and a good surplus of residential rental buildings were also carried over. The overproduction of the '70s was an advantage to the '80s, as resources normally spent on construction could be allotted to other needs. Government, however, failed to notice the surplus, as it continued to build new structures or replaced buildings that were supposedly "not worth saving."

O. The oil cartel pricing had encouraged everyone with a drill rig to poke holes in the ground to look for oil. The Russians needed hard cash to satisfy internal problems and increased current oil production to the detriment of their future supplies. Where once an oil shortage loomed, buyers and sellers took drastic measures to be sure the market did not collapse because of a surplus. Prices that once reached thirty dollars per barrel fell to as low as twelve dollars, with a significant deflating affect.

P. One other factor needs to be given its own light: There was pent-up desire for the innovation that came from mankind's imagination and desire to change that which is around us. Entrepreneurs with desire to apply their ideas bought up weak, failing, and inefficient businesses and reorganized them into quintessential examples of business success. Many started from scratch, with companies that provided ideas and efficiencies to an idea-starved market. Individuals invented, researched, and applied concepts to make what they made better, cheaper, or more available. An invigorated workforce enjoyed the result of seeing their ideas successfully applied.

Not all factors are as obvious as those listed above. Some changes were in businesses, in which cost changes are specific to the industry. There were also less subtle changes, as when businesses simply become smaller. Manipulating business size can keep a business outside of state or federal rules or allow them to avoid payroll costs and workers compensation. The forces of free enterprise will divide a business into the most cost-effective size as work groups are broken up, and jobs are subcontracted to avoid payroll costs. Reports of business formations, rather than representing a vibrant economy, may merely be a symptom of the inability of businesses to pay the cost of maintaining traditional employees. Workers compensation, which is intended to protect the worker from income loss when injured and the employer from debilitating lawsuits, is, for many, not affordable. As workers go without and small business people exempt themselves from participation in worker laws, the true intention of these laws becomes meaningless.

As government has grown and saddled workers with debilitating payroll costs and taxes, many who had made an honest effort to follow these laws, sought refuge in the underground economy. Some take from the welfare system and free enterprise, thereby shifting an even greater government burden to those who play by all the rules. Either intentionally, through competitive bidding, or by happenstance, consumers, business, and government support the underground workforce. Payroll costs can be twice what an employee's net pay, and the cost of regular employees can mean the inability to compete. Costs in the underground may be half or less than above ground. Taking the risk for business or the consumer may be a matter of survival.

If welfare populations and government employment continue to increase, producers will give up a greater amount of the production of the nation to nonproducers. Logic dictates that government beneficiaries will vote to continue and to increase their benefits. When aging baby boomers attempt to liquidate their wealth for retirement, inflation in a labor-starved market may leave them with losses, not gains. Because the Federal Reserve perceives economic growth as inflationary, its actions to control inflation, if too stringent, will compound inflation. High interest rates are also likely to limit businesses that wish to grow and improve their products while the consumer who pays credit card rates of 18 percent and more will feel little effect of the Federal Reserve actions. If labor shortages exacerbate inflation, and businesses suffer, the truly rich could end up controlling an increasing amount of capital assets as failed businesses are consolidated.

Growth figures for the '80s do not reflect a true picture of the efficiencies that occurred. Productivity enhancements were hidden by the still incredible government growth. But the '80s and '90s represent a unique period, when the availability of production advances proliferated. The expectation that such growth can continue, coupled with the erroneous belief that business growth fuels inflation, could lead to miscalculations of the economy's ability to absorb government growth in the future. Rather than efficient labor management, Congress pursues a policy based on tax incentives and righteous tax collection. At the same time, the Federal Reserve restricts economic expansion by pursuing a hostile interest-rate policy.

Most importantly for the U.S. economy, the quality of goods and services improved in this period, and continues to improve today, the business sector has never operated better. As it has improved efficiency and cut costs with greater access to computers, business has created even better and less costly products. But this efficiency has been soaked up by government, rather than passed to the consumer as higher living standards.

The economy is approaching a critical state for the United States and for the world economy. Solutions to government expansionism are important. On the weight of sheer numbers, it would appear that deflation is possible. But whereas the factors that might cause inflation are sure, factors that suggest deflation are iffy. Indeed, government no longer seems to need reasons to establish programs, as it simply looks for reasons to spend.

What did the '90s look like using Jimmy the Greek's method?

Factors causing inflation

'90 tax act

'92 tax act

Restrictions of lumber harvest

Continued government growth

Restrictive Federal Reserve policy equating growth with inflation

Strengthened environmental laws

Emphasis on law degrees

Dollar devaluation

Limited small business financing

COLA adjustments for government employees, social programs, etc

New OSHA enforcement

Demand for health care

Fewer pent-up opportunities for investment and growth

Competition with welfare for workers

Factors creating deflation

Continued trade deficit

Continued vacancy in commercial buildings

Continued business atmosphere that places consumers over individual jobs

High stock market investment

High immigration

Reduced military expenditures

Potential for reduction in labor reducing social programs

Continued high potential for innovation

Weak oil prices

Limited tax-shelter investments

Change in the political atmosphere

High demand for dollars in Third World countries

Potential of government to become efficient

High stock prices attract investment and reduce spending

As private workers reduce in numbers, incomes become limited

And for the new millennium, what has happened, what does it look like?

Factors causing inflation

Anticipated Federal tax decrease

Continued high federal spending

911 attack on the U.S.

State and local tax and spending increases

Continued increases in tax revenue

Increasing strength of government employee unions

Factors creating deflation

Tax reduction act of 2003

Flexibility of the free labor market to reduce wages in the private sector

Possible reduction in military spending

Innovation

Business failure and contraction in labor demand

Global recession

Increasing government employee wages and benefits
Weakness of the dollar
High oil prices
Real estate price increases due to low interest rates and easy financing
War in Iraqi
Increase in global involvement
Reduced investment in the private sector
Possible restrictions on employee voting rights
Fear of global warming
Significant increase in private and public spending to reduce carbon emissions
Potentially greater involvement by government in private sector labor relations
Potentially greater involvement by government In private sector businesses
Potential Federal support for states and local governments whose spending is already out of control
Difficulty for a declining private sector labor
force to keep up with the increasing
burden of public sector demands for labor
Failure to properly asses the impact of government on the economy.
Increasing ratio of needed private sector growth in efficiency to offset public sector growth
Potential demands placed on the economy to reduce carbon emissions ala global warming
Emphasis on stimulating consumer spending rather than encouraging investment with lower corporate tax rates
Limitations on the usage of fossil fuels

United States recession

Historically low interest rates
Strength of the dollar
Weak oil prices
Oversupply of housing
Drop in real estate prices
Fear of government spending increases
Decline in the War in Iraqi

The key factors for the new millennium is the increasing ratio of needed private sector growth in efficiency to offset public sector growth in demands and the potential for recession, the cost of imports and the flexibility of free market labor to absorb costs by adjusting employee costs. The ratio quite simply reflects all the government demands placed on the private sector so we can reflect back on it as to the whole of the impact of government. As to recession and the flexibility of the free market labor supply, we certainly wouldn't expect labor costs to inflate in the face of a recession. As private sector businesses struggle to survive, they are likely to either leave wages as their are, cut wages, cut employees, go out of business or close stores and factories, eliminate investments, or cut benefits. Ergo, private sector wages are likely to decline and employees fearful of losing their jobs will accept those declines willingly. That leaves imports which is the fly in this ointment. The dollar has been declining in value but a global recession will encourage exports in order to sustain output in the exporting country. If exporting countries become protectionist or the dollar declines it could have an overwhelming impact on the U.S. economy. One other very important factor is the failure of economists to properly asses the impact of government on the economy. The economist's assessment indicates that taxes in the U.S. are much lower as a percent of gross domestic product than in European countries and they are likely to encourage government growth while putting all blame for economic problems on the private sector. Quite simply, if you don't know what the problem is you aren't likely to fix it.

In the world of economics, allocations of labor and efficiencies created by innovation are still concepts applied to business pricing or are studied as breakthroughs in economic theory. Labor efficiency appears to be a mystery in our economic concepts. To be fair, simple economic explanations are encouraged by a media that doesn't like or understand a complexity they find difficult to report in thirty seconds.

Below is a list of trouble signs that could indicate the inability of labor to maintain productivity.

The areas to watch for signs of trouble include:

- Rising gold prices could signal a lower demand for dollars in the face of a continuing trade deficit.
- Labor unrest is indicative of the failure of private workers to maintain living standards.
- Low unemployment rates. A market that continues to demand labor, a market that no longer releases ample supplies into the workforce through efficiency, is reaching an end, where government growth is outpacing efficiency.
- Volatile interest rates, which reflect a market concern for inflation.
- Devaluation of the dollar or other signals that the dollar is losing its luster could signal a slowing currency demand in foreign countries or an increase in the acceptability of other currencies.
- The trade deficit may drop, as the dollar becomes less attractive. The labor needed to make up for such an occurrence could stifle the market.
- A high discount rate reduces acceptable investments at a time when expansion is needed. Failure to drop the rate could also signal to businesses that as the Fed anticipates inflation, raising prices is acceptable.
- Inflation, once it starts, is difficult to stop. Like a ball rolling down hill, it builds on itself.

- If the response of government in a market that has a declining unemployment rate is to demand more employee benefits, rather than release labor into the market, the result will be inflation.
- Growing ranks of welfare recipients. As inflation in welfare rises well above hourly wages, its attraction will swell the ranks.

The areas to watch for signs that problems will be overcome:

- Reduced reliance on welfare.
- Less restrictive labor laws.
- Legal reforms.
- Incentives to government agencies for efficiency.
- Government's actions to eliminate unnecessary bureaucracies
- Realistic environment laws.
- Quicker response of government to business requests and actions.
- Stronger dollar in the face of a declining trade deficit and improved exporting.
- Lower interest rates.
- Lower corporation tax rates.
- Lower unemployment in the face of reduced unemployment payments or restrictions on taking temporary jobs.
- A positive labor market.
- Government's reflection on the private sector market to value employee wages.
- Government acting more like the private sector in its business practices.

CHAPTER 13

RISK, ECONOMIC FORCES, AND THE WORKER

The United States market seems filled to capacity with our hearts' desires. Money makes almost anything possible. In the market are lots of cars, big houses, luxury vacations, and grocery stores with thousands of choices. Large stores have hundreds of thousands of choices! People believe in money. Money is the dominant force in a market whose only characteristics are demand and supply. If we have money, we can demand, and supply is forthcoming. We are so enthralled with money that the structure of the economy is obscured.

If we studied Communist countries, where money has less meaning, perhaps, our economic structure would be evident. Let's look at the USSR, where a car once cost twenty years of earnings and took three years to obtain. Nothing was plentiful, not even shoes. Government bureaucrats decided what to make, and punishment was the basic form of motivation for factory workers—but jobs were guaranteed and employment was not a risk. Demand was strong but had little meaning in the marketplace. It is hard to imagine that supply-side forces functioned. Decisions were controlled by the politburo, where intentionally disinterested parties decided what was important to the consumer. Money had little power. Bribery was possible, but foreign currencies were preferred. Equality existed; everyone had an equal opportunity to bribe, making equality meaningless or expensive. Money had little to do with economic growth. Incentives? The market was whipped by the stick, not led by the carrot. Bureaucratic influence was a force, and in Mother Russia, citizens could be punished for being critical. In the U.S., bureaucracies are considered more a problem than a force. However, Russian politicians were much like ours; leaders—pictured as professional, disinterested parties, unprejudiced by the experience of business—they were supposed to be fair. Politicians and the dominant media in the U.S. should consider that the USSR was a politician's wonderland.

The USSR had all the forces, demand, supply, incentives, and other natural forces like minerals, oil deposits, and arable land. Most important, the Communist government was motivated to improve the lives of the people. Of course, forces have no meaning unless they act upon something. In science, when we think of forces, we think of them acting on a mass. Without mass, forces are meaningless. In economics, the scientific equivalent of mass is labor. Interestingly, labor, like mass, has the power to act on its own. There is no intentional purpose in the force inherent in mass, but labor can be a force for its own benefit. We can surmise from this that since labor can act on its own, outside forces act for or against the benefit that labor wishes for itself. We also know that when labor acts on its own, there is an element of risk. Risk means no guarantee of reward. The USSR had ample supplies of labor and, in fact, had all that it took to be bountiful. All components were there. Surprisingly, only one major difference existed between the U.S. and the USSR. In the United States, labor could act on its own, be a force, and take risks. But the Communists believed that if labor acted on its own, one worker might take advantage of another worker to form a higher class. Plainly put, Communists feared that if people were at risk, someone might get rich.

In science, when forces act on a mass, scientists describe a medium in which they act. Economies, too, have mediums, called a system. In the USSR, the system was Communism; for the U.S., the medium is free enterprise. Mediums have influences over forces as they act, and for economics, the systems have rules. To interpret these rules, as in science, there is also an organization. An organization defines, administers, and modifies the rules that control forces. In economics, this is government. Government creates forces and controls the medium but is neither. Even a dictator could choose between free enterprise and communism. The components of society are then government, medium, force, and mass, all of which can be intermingled to form economies. We should note that socialism is not a medium or a government; it is a force under government. Socialism operates within both the medium and government but describes mostly allocations of labor and distributions of production. Socialism does not expressly describe how assets are accumulated, so therefore, it is not a system. Below is a list of our economic components: governments, mediums, forces, and mass.

- Governments—Organization
  - Democracy
  - Fascism
  - Republic
  - Kingdoms
  - Dictatorship
- Mediums—Systems
  - Free enterprise
  - Communism
  - Feudalism
  - Mercantilism
- Forces
  - Government forces
    - Government of peace
    - Government of war
    - Actions of government affecting trade
    - Monetary strength
    - Socialism
    - Law
    - Taxes
    - Mandates for performance in enterprise
  - Consumer forces
    - Buyer preferences
    - Consumer demands
  - Supply forces (risk)

- Incentive (creation of wealth, income, punishment, etc.)
- Imagination, innovation, and efficiency
- Product changes, additions, and deletions

Natural forces

- Changes in nature
- Changes in population size (i.e., birth rates)
- Availability of natural resources
- Labor

Mass

- Labor

The USSR supposedly had a democratic structure, but it operated like a dictatorship. Labor was abundant, as most industries had an oversupply. But the USSR failed. It was described as the evil empire, yet its goals varied only slightly from socialist goals in the United States. Communism is the people's system; it wants a fair society and ideally cares for its citizens, their health, advancement, and protection. And, to be fair, Communists want government to make decisions. Government would be fair, and government would eliminate risk. And workers wouldn't be allowed to put another worker at risk, which was considered as taking advantage of fellow workers. For true Communists eliminating risk was very important. Communist administrators, who were ordained by its system, decreed ultimately that workers had no right to work for even their own benefit; they should all work for the government instead. Thus, the right to place even oneself at risk was abolished. The elimination of risk made life fair in the USSR, but fairness meant that everyone except the politicians that administered the system had to stand in line to make purchases. In the U.S., socialists also believe that to be fair, government should make the decisions. Socialists are so endeared to government that some call it a "village." But fairness is hard to administer. What is fair for the tall is not for the short, nor the fat for the thin, nor the worker for the loafer, nor the rich for the poor. To resolve this dilemma, fair administrations simply take away the rights, freedoms, and choice for all but themselves, so there is less to be fair about.

Risk is the component of capitalism that distinguishes it from other systems.

Free enterprise is so fragile that if the right to take risks was relinquished, free enterprise would be much like communism. When government assumes the risk and makes the decisions, people no longer need to have importance or need to function as individuals. People become expendable obligations, not providers. When risk is taken away, so, too, is the motivation and the value of self.

Risk is a principal embodied in all freedoms.

There is a multitude of ways to motivate people to work, to think, and to imagine. If the field is narrowed to major categories, we get punishment, reward, and benevolence. Punishment is a negative incentive and is likely to produce little more than the administrator's demands. Rewards, by definition, require risk-taking and may involve taking advantage of others, but the rewards benefit everyone; otherwise, the risk-taker is a failure. Although rewards are great motivators, the benevolent can work just as hard and just as long and, of course, don't mind giving it all up to someone deserving. If it were a benevolent community, everyone would have to be benevolent, thus necessitating re-education and possibly punishment to enforce a mind-set in those not so inclined. Benevolence would also require a deserving recipient, but then that would allow the undeserving to take advantage of the benevolent? So, how do we know who is and who isn't deserving? Without risk and reward, workers in Communist countries lacked motivation. They were not all inclined to be benevolent, and even if they wanted to take risks, they weren't allowed to. Conversely, community that allow risk-taking have been shown to produce gains for everyone.

When government or organizations, like unions, are omnipotent forces, the power is often used to eliminate risk. In the U.S., guaranteed jobs and income are what government employees have and the unions want. Security is a wonderful idea, but would we stand in line for it? In an irony of circumstances, our democratic government eliminates risk for some but has forced many that are at risk into the welfare line. How many in the USSR sacrificed their living standards to a fair system? How many people from satellite nations took the risk and died while trying to leave the benevolent utopia? If people didn't take risks, how much would we have? It isn't money in this system of greed and self-interest that fills the stores. Russia had plenty of money, but only politicians could direct their self-interests, and they never found a risk-free way to make goods plentiful. The businesses we buy from fill the stores, and they and their employees take risks. Businesses, in their own self-interest, improve our living standards, or the market will cause them to fail. If one holds a position of risk, who takes advantage of whom? Does the purchaser who has the power of choice take a risk when selecting a product, or does the vendor take a risk in displaying the product? Is the fear of risk a concern that, without a fair government, no one would be benevolent to those who don't deserve fairness? Or do politicians to get elected use fear? Are greedy people who work more decadent than those who could work but don't? Is greed an exclusive characteristic of those who have jobs? Do those who live in a risk free utopia's sacrifice their way of living for a guaranteed job they are told will produce happiness?

The guarantee of a job requires that production be limited to that which the job would produce, thus limiting the consumer's choice.

For purposes good or not, politicians traditionally propose to eliminate risk in the name of fairness. Government's first claim to production and its superior credit rating allow politicians to manipulate the market basket and to redistribute its contents using fairness and the elimination of risk as its argument. In contrast to business, government doesn't have to earn its superior credit ratings and is never perceived as being at risk.

When politicians reallocate resources with the intent of eliminating risk, it is a distraction from the democratic actions of the consumer. Doesn't the worker risk loss of the democratic process in the market place for the no risk utopia where government makes the decisions? As an example of what reallocation does, imagine a sphere filled with all the things the economy has to offer. At any moment of time, the sphere is not capable of expanding because all the labor to produce is allocated. Then a law is passed mandating new government controls. Government either assesses the community for the money needed to accomplish the mandate or simply demands that free enterprise perform the task (regulation). Money is used to redirect labor from some other responsibility, and because the law must be complied with, labor is paid whatever is needed to accomplish the task. The sphere must now allow for an additional production. Production, however, is dependent upon labor, and reducing the productive workforce reduces production. But the power of government dictates that labor must perform the new duties. Because the sphere is not expandable at a single point in time, workers are fixed in numbers. People will have to lower consumption to allow room. If there were no such thing as credit or savings, people would simply decide which goods or services to forgo so as to allow the mandate. In reality, people will try to maintain their spending patterns by using saving, credit cards, or borrowing money. But no matter how much money consumers add, money cannot change the number of workers producing goods for our sphere. Something must be given up; total consumption will decline, and consumers and businesses will be in disorder until adjustments have been made.

Eliminating risk acts to contract the workforce.
Risk acts to expand the workforce.

Politicians' reallocation of resources in the private sector interrupts the democratic process for consumers' allocation of productive labor in the marketplace.

A forced reallocation of resources creates chaos in the market for labor and consumer goods.

Risk takers, by nature, discover cheaper and easier ways to produce and transfer goods and services, making products more plentiful. Because of risk takers, when politicians put demands on the market, these demands can be met more easily. When government reallocates resources, risk takers act to offset government reallocations. The result is that the number of new products is limited and new products that do appear are intended to make the market or the production of market products more efficient. If government reallocations reduce the number in society who are at risk and/or redistributes to them a greater share from the sphere, the possibility declines that those remaining at risk in the population can overcome the reallocations. As the portion of the population not at risk grows, the task of providing for them becomes more difficult.

The above example is hypothetical only in the sense that other options can occur. The new insert into the sphere may take the place of an existing allocation that is no longer necessary or is made up through efficiencies in the economy, such as increased miles per gallon. Adding responsibilities for the worker will always mean a change in growth and may require sacrifice. We can infer that government reallocations change our lives by dictating how labor will be distributed, and through such decisions, government affects individual consumption.

The following are an example of some of the ways government reallocates labor:

Laws and rules

Construction codes

Street sizes

Labeling

Highway speed laws

Methods of taxation

Welfare

School cost

Social Security changes

War

Government regulation

Environmental regulation

Fire codes

Drug and patent approvals

Spending and revenue changes

Rules for tax deductions

Armament changes

Higher government wages

Government cost-of-living adjustments

Whether the money to fund reallocations comes from taxes, fees, or borrowing (deficits) or is direct from business or individuals who are told to comply, it makes no difference. Taking money per se is not a reallocation of resources although the manner of taking can cause reallocations. The expenditure alters the use of labor. Reallocations that redistribute the market basket and labor usage change our spending patterns and impact our way of life. When the Clean Air Act was passed, workers were given new duties. Our way of life changed drastically. Politicians claimed that business paid the costs, or that new jobs were created. But businesses survived by passing costs, along with the profit on those costs, to consumers.

In an economy where labor is fixed and not expanded by innovation and efficiency, it would be obvious that reallocations cause reduced living standards, as labor available to production would decline. By increasing the number not at risk with government jobs or federal assistance, the government pushes workers at risk downward toward welfare, and many workers at risk will eventually find welfare economically preferable. The greater the number of reallocations that occur, the more those at risk downshift to a lower economic level, get discouraged, and join welfare ranks as burdens on the community. A worker transferring from jobs to welfare casts off risk, but the economy shrinks accordingly. Actions thus taken to eliminate risk will not only conflict with natural selections, but the actions also will reduce production and change the environment in which we live.

Pure mathematical law dictates that reducing risk reduces production. Risk reduction doesn't just reduce motivation. Reducing risk turns workers into obligations instead of producers. Fewer workers translates into lower production, and the only ones left to pay the cost are those at risk. Anyone trapped in welfare is potentially productive. Simply because people are on welfare doesn't mean that their ability to sustain or raise their own standards doesn't exist. Elimination of risk will put people on the welfare roles, as the trillions spent to solve the problem are the reason the problem grows larger. It is like a farmer, who pumps the flooded field from one end while the water rushes in from the other. The act of eliminating risk draws the flood.

Economic stimulation has been maligned by some economists, but it is well accepted by politicians, if not for the benefit of the workforce, then for benefit of campaign contributors. On the other hand, both politicians and economists generally agree on the necessity of redistribution (i.e., the elimination of risk). An alternative or companion economic theory, supply-side economics, is defined to suggest that stimulating production is the way to create jobs. The news media calls it "trickle down" or the derogatory "voodoo economics"; in either case, they involve government's manipulation of the economy. Interference in the natural selections of the market isn't considered when politicians and economists believe they are adding to, not detracting from economic growth. Their actions, however, infringe upon the right to accept risk, to be rewarded, and the one aspect that differentiates capitalism from less free systems.

Although free enterprise defines itself through the right of workers to solve problems, supply-side and demand-side economic theories fail to elaborate on the importance of labor. Specifically, economists do not consider that freedom is a consequence of free enterprise, and risk is a consequence of freedom. The Declaration of Independence reiterated the right to pursue happiness. Those who wrote this document selected words as carefully as words have ever been chosen. The right of "pursuit" is not a flippant selection of words or the acknowledgment that happiness was a possibility. It embraces the whole manner by which we flourish. We may abhor (and the media will surely castigate) the chance contemplated in placing ourselves *at risk*, but our alternative can only be the slavery of Communism or fairness that places our rights on the desk of a bureaucrat whose experience may have been gained at the previous night's office party. The writers of the Declaration of Independence denounced the government that placed itself above the people. Conversely, today's politicians, the media, and the economists applaud a government that believes the people are incapable of making decisions. This position is no different than that of any totalitarian empire. Fairness dictates that all should be at risk, or none should be at risk. Logic dictates that kindness for those deserving of help will be more likely to find it from those more capable of giving.

An economy at risk doesn't eliminate the opportunity for the benevolence.

Government sees money more as the mass that drives the economy, rather than a force that molds it. Money steered by government obstructs labor from its own path to production and interferes with the force of labor that better serves itself and the economy. Both *supply-side* and *demand-side* rationale have valid applications. Each defines a method to deploy labor, but when labor is factored as a limited supply, actions to be taken are altogether different. To a Communist, labor is unlimited and at risk, but to a capitalist, labor is limited, bears the risk, and realizes the reward. The more complex our society becomes, the more limited and productive will be the labor. In contrast to fair systems, the consumer's selections and preferences determine the activities and production of free societies.

Political actions will change when capitalist ideologues realize that labor is finite.

Economies that constantly endeavor to eliminate risk for the population are separating that population into two groups. Whereas one group is not at risk, the group that is at risk bears the burden of decisions made by the whole of the population. Democratic traditions dictate that the above situation is not "fair."

When benevolent ideologues reach the ultimate goal of eliminating risk for all, the economy will fail.

In the socialist sense, people are obligations and have no value.

Unfortunately, economists don't seem to have defined how the limitations on labor affect production. Also unfortunate, a free exchange of ideas is thwarted by experts in the news media, who use derogatory terms to sell the news and thus have a lot to do with how economists are translated. To the media, workers are dispensable, money-motivated androids, whose function is to collect paychecks, spend money, and be educated by what the media is selling. Name-throwing is a part of politics, and free-enterprise newspapers that throw names sell newspapers. The media, however, that supposedly "only reports the news" but then takes sides on economic viewpoints is attempting to mold social norms. Those who present their views rather than report the news are setting themselves up as experts on how to improve our lives. We therefore have *media economics*, rather than true economic interpretations. This, of course, augments other stances taken by the holy ones of the media that comprises *media science, media justice,* and *media fairness.* One-sided interpretations of the causes for which we live should not be used to control the minds of the citizens. Slanting economic beliefs implies that the media is intuitive enough to judge proper opinion on all subjects. Taking sides, as the media has, abrogates the freedom to choose that comes from the right of people to hear all sides *fairly presented.* This right was decided at the signing of the Declaration of Independence. All who signed had the right to dissolve the committee by refusing to sign. Each made his own decision, and so to should citizens have that right to make decisions with media interpretation that are not biased or slanted. There is a trust that mankind, given the freedom to make decisions, can come to a just resolution. The media was granted the unrestricted right to report the news; nowhere is the media given the right to make our decisions or to govern us by its beliefs.

To a politician, demand-side economics is merely an excuse to spend money, a contrivance, all too easy to justify to the voters. The average politician and the man on the street both believe that when the government spends money in their town, it's good for the economy; it creates jobs. This is not always true, but regardless, the results can be negative. Food stamps may increase temporarily the money in circulation, but productive labor declines, along with productivity, because not only is money going to pockets that must not contribute if they are to receive food stamps, the product they would produce is lost. A community will not gain by having fewer in it contributing to its workings. Work benefits a community, not money; production is the consequence of labor. All the money in the USSR could not fill their stores. Eliminating risk eliminates opportunity and productivity. One worker now produces for at least five in the U.S., and the loss of a worker reduces production by a like proportion. The gap left by each worker that is lost to government dictates leaves an infinitesimal decline in living standards for a community. As this productivity is lost, so too is the community's productivity.

The gap left by a worker at the bottom eventually comes off the top.

The complexity of our society serves to reduce the impact of calamitous occurrences, such as bank failures, shortages, or foreign competition. Complexity is an advantage over evolving societies. Individual economic centers, however, must still offer the labor to support and enliven their own economies. When welfare requirements limit household income, even the minimum wage at the local Food Lion may defer welfare recipients from holding jobs. "For want of a nail," more than a shoe is lost. Without filling unskilled positions, stores are disabled. With the absence of willing and available labor, markets fail, and then communities fail. Rather than one truck bringing the supplies to the community for a thousand people, those in the community must drive, taxi, or bus to available shopping. Considering the cost to move thousands, all with their own timing, and the transportation over the cost to move one truck, the waste is considerable. The loss of a small amount of "work-produced dollars" created in the community leads to the failure of businesses, as welfare dollars go outside the community to find needed staples. Workers provide services for the community, not capitalists and not money. When only the replacement of lost wages and not lost productivity is considered as the return from welfare dollars, workers lose importance in the eyes of government and economists. Welfare fills the cup, but it won't dig the well. The empty and abandoned welfare communities that filled our cities was evidence of the importance of all workers.

The dollar brought into a community that turned over three times offers no comparison to the producer who multiplies by five his own consumption. Politicians don't think twice about keeping an unneeded military base open or building a new courthouse, when other facilities are available. A local community may temporarily benefit from an influx of cash from unneeded construction or the maintenance of nonessential facilities. Communities, however, are better off with the benefits of a new park, the gift of land to encourage new businesses, or the release of citizens to fulfill their own needs. It is befuddling to understand how politicians can publicly degrade businessmen who work and benefit a community, while encouraging "wheel-turning" employees, who work like hell—or not at all—to do something that is unnecessary. Politicians resolving risk are paying people to spend money. A politician will "stimulate" a community through a connected contributor and then act to absorb any benefits of the spending with further stimulus.

Results orientated stimulation leaves a true and efficient community benefit with employment that increases the productivity of the community.

Stimulus that must be followed by stimulus needed to continue the benefit is a burden not a benefit.

When the stimulus is a burden, welfare is the only substitute.

When a city or state wraps its future in welfare, "wheel turning," "job creation," and inefficient allocations of its labor resources, that political entity will soon suffer high taxes and high inflation and become an attraction for those seeking welfare and fraud. People on welfare are right to think how foolish it is to work for nominal gains. When transportation, baby-sitting, crime prevention, clothing, and the other expenses of having a job are considered, taking less than welfare is the more damaging option. Despite the importance of unskilled workers, those who advocate welfare degrade this level of work. Humiliating entry-level workers is admitting that welfare is too generous. Government will always be frustrated in its effort to provide for the poor, as the very process of reallocating labor pushes workers closer to the threshold. Once on welfare, one needn't risk a worse way of life, but a better one is not a risk to be taken, either. When the response to earning is a loss of benefits, welfare recipients refuse jobs. The lack of workers in small inner-city communities to perform basic work skills leaves unskilled tasks for skilled labor, reduces productivity while raising cost, and effectively drives away jobs.

Communism was an attempt to eliminate all of life's risk. It is a system that would guarantee equality and economic security. The communist ideology demands that in exchange for a life without risk, that citizens' possessions and rights be transferred to government. Although freedoms, including free speech, were guaranteed by most Communist constitutions, their politicians limited these rights. Freedom conflicted with the desires of the state, and even lifelong indoctrination couldn't train everyone to think like a bureaucrat.

A government with a million who make all of society's decisions is no less oppressive then government with only one who makes all of society's decisions.

Ironically we are, perhaps, less well off with a simple dictator who makes the decisions, as millions take more time to decide.

Risk is the freedom that affords humankind the right to think as it wishes and do as it thinks.

One cannot risk without possible failure, or fail and have security guaranteed. If even one individual has greater advantage, there can never be equality. However, the hope for inequality is what drives the masses to serve each other in a free-enterprise system. Without this hope, humankind is equal only at a level of subsistence.

Government spending should provide benefits without replacing risk. Even guaranteeing comparatively but temporarily high wages on a government-funded job is harmful, as too often, overpaid workers refuse ordinary wages when the high government pay has ended. When workers are given a false sense of standards, more than high wages are wasted. Workers can lose everything they have when they can't find a replacement for what was an artificially high rate of pay on a government created job. Private enterprise and market compensation guarantee the greatest production and the most work. Workers and what they do have meaning and should not be conduits through which politicians pass government funds in lieu of campaign bribery. Government jobs that once provided useful functions should not become a waste of humankind. Too often, the positive factors have been realized and done, and what was once beneficial becomes home to "wheel-turners" who attempt to justify their existence by being cogs in someone else's wheel.

Until economic thinking factors in the need for risk and the efficient allocations of labor, government will represent a wasteland for the growth we could see in our living standards. As government has fortified its beneficiaries with pay increases and cost-of-living adjustments, those outside bear the cross. When economic efficiency offsets reallocation, there is no fairness when the ones who are efficient merely break even, and the ones who turn a wheel pull ahead. The advantage of free enterprise is thus impaired by the moronic misuse of the public trust. A government-determined and populace-encouraged craving to stimulate the economy and eliminate risk transfers labor from useful endeavors to make-work projects. Our resources are thus squandered, while our families suffer. When labor is reallocated from productive means, production will be reduced by a formulated amount.

Government waste begets welfare, not wages.

At any point in time, a certain amount of labor is needed to produce a given amount of production. Assuming that efficiency does not improve, the addition of a worker will produce a return comparable to the average for the entire workforce. Therefore, in order for production to increase, labor must also increase. The basic formula to determine production per worker is as follows:

a production
---- ---------- = production per worker
b workforce y

Correspondingly:

workforce	x	production per worker	=	total production	=	consumption
b	x	y	=	a	=	d

Consumption equates to total production, because total consumption is dependent upon production. The dollar does not fit in this formula.

Therefore, if the workforce grows, representing b1 and b1 > b then a1, the new production, is greater than a (a1 > a).

new workforce	x	production per worker	=	new production
b1	x	y	=	a1

The new production will be higher.

Those who advocate reducing risk by stimulating employment would not agree with this formula. They believe spending increases employment, but it only indirectly increases production. For those advocating economic stimulation, the presumption is that there is always an overabundance of workers or workers whose incomes are too low. This presumption has not taken into account that methods used to augment demand simultaneously place demands on the labor supply, which has, over time, reduced the proportion of population that produces. Without sufficient technological advances to compensate for this reallocation of labor, inflation will follow and living standards will only decline.

If the government stimuli is taken into consideration, the new formula would look like this:

(workforce	-	Government) workforce	×	production per worker	=	total production
(b	-	g)	×	y	=	a2

Obviously, a2 will be less than a.

Fluctuations in the labor force do not signal the need for government stimulus. The factors affecting unemployment are diverse and likely to affect communities differently. Eliminating the risk of holding a job is only a substitute for productive endeavors. At full employment, this formula is obvious. Unfortunately full employment often means high tax revenues and increased government spending which translates into an increase in demands on the workforce.

Risk is the foundation of humankind's progress, empowerment, and potential for improvement. Eliminating risk diminishes motivation, desire, and the ability to be productive. An economy that eliminates risk survives by force.

Usages for labor are unlimited; labor is not.

Although labor is limited, its uses are unlimited because the possibilities for consumption and innovation are infinite. Efficiencies that change the production per worker increase consumption. Adjusting total dollars to production maintains consumption and eliminates price inflation better than any other arbitrary proviso.

Standard-of-living changes are unbalanced and not felt equally by the population. Government determines who has first claim on consumption, and the balance of the population is left with the residuum. In a free and working economy, normal distribution of production would be as follows:

$$\frac{\text{Total Production}}{\text{Total Population}} = \text{Average Living Standard}$$

Because government allocations are obligatory, the formula reads as follows:

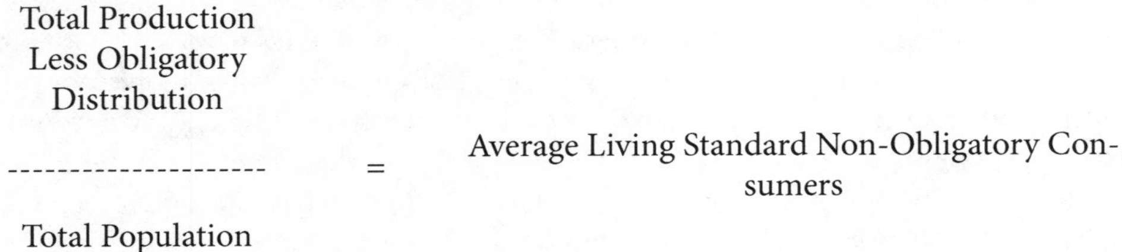

The truly rich aren't likely to share in any loss of consumption.

Wealth cannot be consumed.

Wealth is the perceived value of assets, plus the value of the production of income. It is not consumable and cannot be transformed from wealth to consumption. It can be transferred, but if it is subject to confiscation without just compensation or cause, it has no value. Wealth sold is wealth bought. Wealth taxed is income taxed. Wealth is not depleted by tax, only changed in value by the variances of law, economic principles, or economic conditions. The cost of government increases wealth without adding to the product. The socialists' desire to distribute wealth results in the stagnation and reduction of living standards for private workers, as wealth cannot be confiscated and distributed by government without losing value.

Government entities have a first call on economic growth and are an obligation of the private sector.

Cost of living (COLA) and living standard adjustments (LSA) for government-controlled pension, welfare, government, and pseudo-government classes give these groups a first priority on productivity increases and a priority claim on existing productivity.

Government growth causes inflation.

The transfer of labor from production to government work and welfare leaves fewer in production to meet current demands and necessary growth. Inflation is avoided only by technological advances and by reductions in the compensation (i.e., consumption) of private workers.

Major business cycles in a Complex economy will be caused by government expansionism.

Cycles don't impact Complex societies the way they impact Transitional economies. The economy's complexity resulting from the diversity in job types and a wide distribution of employment means that disturbances in the economy will affect individual markets or business groups but not the entire economy. This is unlike a Transitional economy, wherein business innovation or overexpansion can impact the entire economy. In a Complex economy, the affects of government expansionism can have a significant impact when concentrated on a small group, but the entire economy may show little effect. Government's continuous expansion can eventually result in the inability of the private workforce to compensate, such that inflation and recession would result, affecting the entire economy.

Reallocation results in higher interest rates.

> Reallocations reduce the proportion of the workforce available to provide goods and services within the context of existing technology. Shortages occur that cause inflation and consequently trigger monetary control.

Excessive government-labor requisitions reduce production.

> As fewer workers are available to meet demands, so production is likewise reduced. Both reductions in quality and quantity can occur.

Government-labor requisitions can only be a benefit if there is a necessary product or service that is produced at a cost to compare with the free market. Politicians who depict spending as good economic stimulus have no awareness of the siphoning of labor that results from the redistribution of the money that impacts labor allocations. Labor that is spent on a useless project reduces the community productivity and consequently its living standard. This result occurs because the influx of money for a make-work project siphons labor from useful purposes. Money should be used to guide the economy to lasting and useful endeavors.

AS MUCH AS ONE MIGHT WORK TO SATISFY SELF, ANOTHER MUST BE SERVED. AND FOR THE ONE TO BE, YET ANOTHER WILL SERVE THE ONE.

CHAPTER 14

GOVERNMENT AND THE FREE-ENTERPRISE SYSTEM

Aristotle's definition of politics was "the science which is concerned with the common good." Aristotle would likely have been an attorney today, as his definition leaves a great deal to debate. Because the economy has so much to do with the common good, Aristotle appears to suggest that the economy is government's responsibility. It is, in fact, very common for government and the system to be viewed as a single function. The "system works" or the "system doesn't work," depending upon one's perspective. On the other side, Aristotle may not have been taking sides, or he more likely was a capitalist. In his time, there was little government interference with daily life.

Free enterprise is seen as an imperfect aspect of a system and that government exists to modify and manipulate enterprise in order to preserve the common good. For many, free enterprise has to do with benefiting a few, and it has little to do with the common good. As citizens looked to government to resolve economic problems, government had the last word on how the economy should function, and the study of economics has become a mechanism whose explanations are manipulated to justify political decisions. This is dogma to which we must take issue, if freedom is to survive.

Aristotle obviously envisioned government selecting the rules under which the population functioned. Before the founding of the United States, governments may have functioned as paternalisms, but that was not the predisposition of our founding fathers. Nor was it the disposition of citizens who had already determined that their own common good was best served by the freedom to choose. The republic was established to protect, serve, and support freedom and thus, free enterprise and, accordingly, that would serve the common good.

Free enterprise or the republic did not come before freedom; both were preceded by the ability of mankind, in a distinct community, to choose. Free enterprise and the republic were thus born of freedom. In the democratization of the economy, the people who came to this continent sampled or were familiar with all systems of government and of enterprise. Free enterprise was the selected economic choice as a result of a democratic process that was heard not in the chambers of government but in the repositories of their homes and industries. Free men and women selected their own fates when they chose their daily stores and their mortal appointments. Government could have been a democracy, a republic, a commonwealth, or a monarchy, and as long as free enterprise was preserved, humankind would be free. Our founders selected a republic, perhaps because a democracy allowed for too many decisions, a commonwealth allowed for too little attachment, and a monarchy allowed for too few governors. A republic was much like free enterprise, which would allow the several states to function and to fail in an evolutionary process, without consequence to the entire nation. And like free enterprise, a republic offers competition between the states, with those that are successful serving as examples to the others. It is not so important in the discussion of free enterprise and the republic as to which takes precedence over the other, nor is it important whether federal, state, or local rights should prevail. What is important to the discussion is that the role and the efficacy of government and free enterprise are clear. Free enterprise cannot survive when freedom, free choice, and the economy are functions of the power of government. We must consequently understand how free enterprise serves the common good and why it represents the democratic process, which is what we believe government, ideally, would be.

For each of us, satisfying our daily wants and needs satisfies an individual goal, not a common goal. But in the greater picture, we earn by satisfying others' wants and needs' and from our earnings we choose our own. We thus fulfill the common good, one for another. And as we choose, we use our democratic powers to decide which choices there will be. Democracy is embodied in the free-enterprise system that controls our economy; it is not embodied in our government. If our government were to be a democracy, good government could only be determined by free citizens whose decisions were made with knowledge of the facts, with a free opportunity to debate, and with a vote cast without coercion, compromise, or exchange. Free enterprise manifests these qualities in the market place and is the only functioning democracy that does allow these principles.

Thus far, where free enterprise has functioned, improvements in living standards have followed. Were it not for free enterprise, it is doubtful the world could feed itself. Free enterprise has sustained our government by providing weapons in war and phenomenal commerce in peace. Government spending, laws, regulations, and the question of their need and implementation are the most critical problems facing us. Below, government is compared to free enterprise, so as to understand the problems:

FREE ENTERPRISE	GOVERNMENT
A. Divides decision-making power	Concentrates decisions and power
B. Rewards achievement	Passes laws to punish achievement
C. Rewards profit	Punishes profit
D. Penalizes unnecessary expenditures	Rewards expenditures with additional funding
E. Rewards workers	Taxes workers
F. Rewards working	Rewards not working
G. Production and pricing are determined by a democratic process	Production and pricing are determined by elected bodies and unelected bureaucrats
H. Efficient production is geared to benefit the consumer	Adding employees is more important than efficiency
I. Provides for the entire community but has the appearance of benefiting a few	Satisfies the demands of select groups on the pretext that the community is benefited
J. Encourages new ideas that are voted on by consumers	Creates laws and regulations for the courts to interpret

K. The flow of money is determined by a pricing structure that adjusts demand to supply and increases the supply of money and labor where demand is greatest	The flow of money is determined by influence, intended to stimulate demand or sway votes, and shift labor and money away from market-determined demands
L. Failure or loss of income is the reward for inefficiency, wrong decisions, and incompetence	Lack of sufficient funding is the reason for failure
M. Failure is a successful learning experience	Failure is not acknowledged
N. Encourages problem solving be corrected after the next election, does not recognize problems within government	Creates problems for capitalism to
O. Has a deflationary effect on pricing and production cost	Has an inflationary effect on and is intended to inflate pricing and production cost
P. Takes advantage of opportunity	Closes loop holes
Q. Free enterprise is blamed for the failures of government	Government is commended for the successes of free enterprise

The above comparison is as humorous as it is pathetic. In general, government and free enterprise display an exact opposite intent and purpose. The government that rewards spending with more spending rewards this same act in free enterprise with a government investigation. The very governing system that is responsible for the freedom of mankind and thus the preeminence of free enterprise has become its primary detractor and fails to use its principles in the organization of its own affairs.

Politicians, with the encouragement of the economists, have attempted to manipulate the economy for the presumed benefit of the citizens. Governance by a select few, even though selected by the many, does not change the lessons to be learned from the experiences of the failed Communist governments. Communists, even with the support of their citizens, failed in all attempts to provide, with consistency, the simplest of daily needs. The USSR failed even to clear from view the ravages of a war that occurred fifty years earlier. Japan and West Germany, without the restrictions on their labor force that both encourage today, cleared the ashes and provide goods and services not only for their own but for people throughout the world.

Not forgetting how the Communist governments initiated massacres and deprivations upon their own peoples, the Communist intent was to improve the people's living standards. The Communist goal was quite noble. Today in the U.S., it is the same benevolent, charitable, compassionate, and philanthropic design that reduces freedoms and assails free enterprise. And as with the Communists, government contradicts itself by punishing and controlling the people in order to pursue its goal to help them. The critics of free enterprise see those who provide for the community as taking from it.

And they see the failed government manipulation of the economy as continued evidence of the need to control free enterprise.

The meddling of government in the free-enterprise system has produced negative effects that endure to delay progress. Laws intended to produce activity and provide encouragement to the economy end up producing an oversupply and an eventual business crisis. Temporary personal assistance has become permanent subsistence. Agencies established to protect the consumer hinder progress. Government tries to repair fluctuations in the market that free enterprise corrects on its own. When politicians feel impelled to manipulate the economy, it is done with the force of a Goliath, not the artistry of a piano tuner.

When not trying to stimulate the economy, government has enacted unnecessary laws and regulations in the name of consumer protection. But government walks a line between consumer protectionism and the destruction of the democratic process, without scrutinizing its own footprint. The cost to protect the consumer may far exceed the value of protection in dollars, as well as in lives. The business of protection has become a legal right to pillage the public trust, lavishly benefiting few and costing consumers trillions.

Our always-active politicians and government regulators constantly change ground rules, discouraging workers from serving the public and altering business plans; often, there is a mercifully quick destruction of jobs and businesses. Many of the changes made by government are too subtle to be noticed immediately and extend their detrimental effects over time. In free enterprise, adaptation is called innovation, and business people compliment themselves on how they manage to maintain or limit costs. Outside the system, this is looked at as "defeating the system," but given options that are legal, wise business people take the option that will keep them in business. As in nature, free enterprise encourages evolution by a process of natural selection. Too often, the system is worse off or subject to corruption when costly, inefficient laws are ignored, and the legitimate intent of a law is defeated. Often, too, an encumbered business dies a slow death.

Higher taxes or regulation may encourage one business, while stifling another. The consequences to businesses vary, but government is typically not interested in knowing about negative effects. Government favoritism granted in Congress to local communities or industries is not always wise. Decisions should be based on sound economic reasoning, with purpose, intent, and benefit to society. Government spending is an "A - B = C" proposition—with A being the government project, B the economic loss, and C the result; C should be a positive. Government often has knee-jerk reactions based on political benefits or media hype, as it wanders aimlessly, attempting to solve problems. Government has no formula, no understanding of concepts, and no devise to measure how its actions affect the economy as a whole or businesses and their employees individually. The Federal Reserve changes interest rates in reaction to the economy, as if economic fluctuations are mystically created by waves, mood changes, meaningless indicators, or production changes, when a now-Complex economy would smooth any cycles, if not for government intervention.

Government often acts in ways that seem beneficial to satisfy a poorly enlightened media that demands results. When the economy is ailing, tax laws get passed to encourage real estate construction, home ownership, and the like. Because construction is seen as a leading indicator that foretells the end of a recession, government has used it to jump-start the economy. Producing more apartments or office space than is needed may foster economic activity, but it also places those who are dependent upon construction for their living on a roller-coaster ride from plenty to poor. The wild ride given the construction industry by government affects the families of its many workers. Working wives often sustain these families or risk forfeiture of their homes when the roller coaster heads down. Far too often, construction families spend their lives paying back taxes, government penalties, or year-end insurance assessments because government rules, regulations, and taxes again altered the cost of competition. Many construction workers are the young, whose view of the economy is distorted by this constant government interference.

Many laws are passed purely to repay campaign support from business association bureaucrats, who in the interest of their own job preservation, can tout a law as a victory for association members. As a victory for themselves alone, bureaucrats perpetuate the roller-coaster ride for which government will again allocate unneeded resources. Those impacted by government often see their fortunes rise, only to fall. If not for government interference, production and incomes would grow in an orderly manner in ways that are important to the community and its citizens. Better health care would be the result of a society with a surplus ability to solve its own problems, as well as access to the government-wasted capital.

State controlled workers compensation laws, passed to protect the worker, are often disregarded or circumvented by the workers themselves as they attempt to maintain their living standards. Insurance rates for trades in some states have risen to over 50 percent, which is higher than all payroll taxes combined. Nearly mandatory legal representation for the injured has formed an army of ambulance chasers, who promise large returns in exchange for their representation against a system they describe as unfair. Many workers have spent months proving their injury to the courts, so that attorneys, who benefit by the length of a case, can increase their fees. In the end, the people who are supposed to be protected lose wages, dignity, and occupations. In many cases, the money is never seen, spent quickly by the recipients, or used poorly. And often, the recipient ceases to contribute to society, because work means the loss of benefits. A look at payroll costs over the past forty years finds unemployment taxes have quadrupled as both rate and amount of payroll subject to taxes has increased. Workers compensation in some areas has grown by 10,000 percent. Fraud and excessive settlements are encouraged because insurance companies, with rates "approved" by government, are granted increases to allow profits on increased costs, this encouraging these costs. The higher the cost of claims, the higher the premium and the more the insurance company earns. To a politician, this manipulation is quite fair and logical. The result, however, are charges too costly for businesses; the resultant breakup of business forms into smaller units, the proliferation of a cash trade, and the end of benefits for the workers the law intended to protect.

Fairness is whatever raises taxes, and unequal treatment is described as closing loopholes. So, while politicians demand health insurance, owner employees who are allowed to deduct the cost of employee health coverage from business income, are denied a deduction for their own family's health care. When costs are deductible for employees and not owners, "fairness" for an employer is eliminating employees, their health coverage, or both. Fair government has also allowed general liability insurance costs to increase tenfold in the last forty years to punish businesses for extrapolated wrongdoings.

Government manifests its incompetence in many ways. When farming subsidies created a constant oversupply of food in the 1970s, government projections of food shortages to come in the '80s triggered a land boom that pushed the cost of farmland so high that crop prices wouldn't cover the loan and the interest to buy it, not to mention the seed and fertilizer. Anticipating shortages, farmers added fertilizer, tore up fences to plow the right-of-ways, and looked for more productive seed. The results were foreclosure, bank failures, and the largest farm subsidies in our history. Recently, a bureaucrat of the '90s ignored the impact this travesty had on human life and commented, with pride, how the government-aroused fear had helped to increase farm production. It is all too obvious that when government solves problems, the lives saved are counted; the lives lost are not.

For decades now, the oil industry has gained the favor of our tax laws, and today it is the only surviving tax shelter in which any individual can participate. This shelter encouraged the search for oil, but for most small investors, only losses are produced. The oil business is so well tuned that shelters sold during the "go, go" years of the '70s were sold out in the bad years. Investors were left with ashes; the well informed with the profits—a "buy high, sell low" scenario for the unwary seeking shelter from taxes. A government that is concerned with adding resources would do better to encourage the buying of foreign oil. Perhaps domestic efforts should be used to develop alternate fuels and fuel efficiency, while U.S. oil reserves are maintained for the future generations.

In line with the policy to punish rather than reward, politicians, bureaucrats, and the media believe that telling people how bad off they are will help achieve goals and demonstrate the importance of government. In a recent campaign, much was said about the jobs created in the service sector. One side boasted of the number of jobs created, while the other side degraded them as low-pay, service-sector employment. Most people take pride in their work, especially those at the entry level. A media that conveys jobs as unimportant degrades the individual and the community and reduces productivity. Rather than acting as champions of humankind, the media's negative campaigns are self-fulfilling prophesies of the need for government expansion. Where is the greater hope for those in need of maintaining a livelihood and self-esteem? Is the hope in welfare or in the media-defined unimportant job? On welfare, there will always be a shoulder to cry on, while working people usually have positive attitudes that discourage complaints. The biggest fear the unskilled will ever overcome is the rejection that is certain when finding that first job. For the individual to be told that the job is unimportant makes fear, rejection, and belittlement an incredible mountain to climb. All jobs, just like people, are important.

A great example of the way government intervention hurts the job market and economy is the government involvement in the steel industry. In the '70s, tax credits were enacted to help industry improve capacity and efficiency. Government, however, with its constant intervention in steel labor talks, restricted foreign trade and encouraged union agreements that discouraged investment. Government restricted the trade and the purchase of foreign steel to allow for more steel labor concessions, including work restrictions, six-month vacations, triple time, and pay hikes. Labor practices were so restrictive as to cause strikes if efficiency were suggested. Concessions seemed great in the short run, but other metals and plastics became competitive. Steel production was not replaced by the Japanese, who are so often blamed, but by small industries within the United States. Eventually, the big steel industries suffered plant closings, bankruptcies, and layoffs. The consumer paid for the concessions, but the workers lost jobs, benefits, and even pensions. Protecting the steel industry allowed foreign countries to intrude into the consumer sales of our other products that used steel, while discouraging our expansion into foreign markets.

The Japanese, too, exemplify government interference. Japan protects an archaic mercantile system that has a lofty price. The restrictions on trade may have been beneficial in fostering industries, but without competition, trade restrictions are costly to Japanese citizens. As a country with tremendous export successes in the world, Japan has the most expensive food and shelter, which, of course, are the basics of individual living standards. Encouraging free trade actually discourages imports by bolstering competitiveness and ingenuity. Developed countries that advocate free trade can only enhance their own living standard. Pumping from the bottom to the top can't raise the water in the pond.

Actions that would be effective often will conflict with politically correct ideas. The result is that politicians, to improve their media appeal and justify their jobs, approve useless spending and regulation. Too often, government laws breed little more than nonplussed bureaucracies and costly regulations from the entrails of media-generated fear.

The most onerous restrictions on free enterprise have been on the ability to patent and license drugs and medical devises. The pharmaceutical industry has been encumbered with high costs and burdensome paperwork. Devices have been discouraged that could make treatment easier, make medical equipment more efficient, and provide less costly health benefits. Patents benefit society and should be encouraged, not pigeonholed. To the contrary, government staff has attempted to force patent-right holders to sell patents to anyone. In one instance, our State Department, after being informed by a foreign patent seeker of an infringement, ordered the patent seeker to distribute the patent to everyone who wanted it. With the possibility of misuse, potential for lawsuits and the liability risks of U.S. distribution, foreign retaliation has increased. It is possible that foreigners may not seek patents in the U.S., so as not to give a U.S. business the opportunity to compete in production. Likewise, minor improvements to older medical devices that must be used as originally approved are too costly to obtain in relation to monetary benefit. A device that aids healing or diagnosis might be in service for years, without the minor improvements we are accustomed to in other products. Competition is discouraged; discomforts may not be corrected; new devices are inhibited by cost and difficulty in obtaining patents; devices with limited yet important use may never be produced; and alternative uses of harmless drugs are banned because the government delays approval, for bureaucratic and political reasons.

As government law, regulation, and control on production has compounded, government salaries and pensions have been adjusted for inflation, longevity, reduction of work days, and performance bonuses, for which nearly all government employees qualify. The reasons are always clear: "government employees deserve the same consideration as nongovernment employees." It sounds equitable and correct. There is one question: do all private workers receive the same consideration? The price of goods must consider all costs and allow profitability before wage increases, and that means that all business costs must be made up before private wages will increase. If the cost of government growth is greater than the efficiency of enterprise, inflation will exceed the increases in private-sector wages. There is no assurance that the private worker will ever see the inflation increases received by government beneficiaries. If prices are increased, sales decline, and workers are laid off. Living-standard indicators are government produced and don't show mutations in the distribution of consumption. As averages, the indicators wouldn't show the shifting of consumption away from private workers. To *fairly* distribute the cost of government growth, shouldn't government-recipient incomes reflect the same added government costs as nongovernment workers?

The idea that money provides our sustenance and that fair tax assessments can pay for excessive government and encourage investment fails to recognize that goods spring from labor, not the printing presses. Because economic reasoning endorses government expansionism, inflation adjustments for government workers are seen as normal business practice, not as a strain on the private worker. The result is serious when innovation and efficiency fail to match government growth. Spending power that shifts away from the private worker puts stress on families as well. When welfare payments rise to meet the inflation-adjusted declines in wages of the private workers, workers will welcome welfare. The result could be a fall in production, high inflation, and an increasing cost of welfare.

Government employees should be freed to practice efficiency. Government, government-controlled, and pseudo-government entities now follow job practices that disregard the rules of efficiency if it is in the interest of job preservation. Bureaucratic practices often allow those in one job position an automatic succession to the next. We are reminded of the Peter Principle, that "in a hierarchy, every employee tends to rise to his level of incompetence." In government, employees can go beyond their level of incompetence. The sacrosanct job security that politicians grant a government employee cultivates incompetence and inefficiency, while placing the responsibility on the backs of private-sector workers. Fortunately, government has finally gotten into the age of computers; unfortunately, extra people were hired to use them.

In the '70s, the country that invented the robot had fewer robots than the Japanese. In recent years, restrictions on free enterprise have been removed through deregulation, free trade, and a hands-off policy between the unions and business. But the producing population has not benefited because cost savings have been passed to special-interest groups or because other restrictions placed on the economy have caused significant increases in government-related employment. Because business must first accomplish the tasks that government has legally required, expansion of production, new products, innovation, efficiency, and a better life are secondary considerations.

Free enterprise finds its own solutions. Government should carry out its charge of preserving free enterprise and emulate, rather than oppose, its behavior. High inflation and a slowdown in the growth of living standards in this century began not coincidentally with the Great Society legislation of the 1960s, which was to improve lives. Thousands of laws have been passed to make things better, but very little has been accomplished. Laws and regulation may take years to show up as a cost to society, but when they do, the wealthy or businesses aren't the ones who pay. Costs get passed to the workers, because businesses must profit before employees get wage increases—or the businesses will fail. Similarly, raising taxes on the rich only provokes higher profit requirements; otherwise, investment won't be justified. As the Federal Reserve keeps interest rates high to discourage inflation, investments that might produce greater efficiencies are also discouraged. The high rates only assure that the private worker will adjust slowly to a lower standard. So, government growth causes inflation; inflation is fought with high interest rates; high interest rates result in increased returns on financial instruments, such as CDs; investments are discouraged because borrowing costs too much and because returns on safe investments like CDs make risky investments too risky; and inflation grows larger and has a bigger effect on wages because investments are discouraged.

Bigger government equals lower wages, not poorer rich.

Of all the economic systems, free enterprise is the only one that caters to the freedom of individual choice. All others manifest the need for a higher authority, where even benevolence requires government action. Socialists and Communists attempt a redistribution of resources but lack the individual participation that comes with the motive for profit and wealth. Without the creation of wealth, there is nothing additional to redistribute. Amazingly, some economists believe that creating wealth is accomplished by luck. Lucky people don't work three thousand or four thousand hours a year. If luck and money is the key, Communists have horrible luck. Government must restrict its change, encourage innovation, promote efficiency, and manage its own team.

Politicians should see to the preservation of freedom, safeguarding of the country's assets, funding of good causes, establishment and maintenance of a strong, reliable monetary system, encouragement of scientific research, assistance for the aged and indigent, and most of all, preservation of the system of free enterprise—and then they should go home.

The characteristics of free enterprise are profit, wealth, money, and labor, which should be viewed as follows:

Profit is the result of satisfying needs and wants at a price that is affordable and agreeable; wealth is the value of that satisfaction and is created by those who satisfy or sustain needs and wants; money facilitates the exchange of goods and services; and labor is the device that fulfills demands.

Complex systems do not respond well to government tinkering. Changes in tax codes, spending to stimulate, stop-and-go funding, and redistribution all initiate a reaction that affects the private sector in ways not intended; it ultimately alters peoples' lives. Complex economic systems are like the ecology, wherein the destruction of a life form can disrupt or destroy an entire system. The government tendency to make constant changes disrupts the natural formation of jobs and economic growth. Government lacks the ability to respond to microeconomic needs. Government responds with spending structures that invariably are too expansive, are in the wrong place, are disruptive of employment needs, and are inefficient and dysfunctional.

The current view of free enterprise must change. Mankind is not free without free enterprise, and free enterprise cannot exist without wealth and profit. As Thomas Jefferson said in his first inaugural address, March 4, 1801: "A wise and frugal government, which shall restrain men from injuring one another, which shall leave them otherwise free to regulate their own pursuits of industry and improvement … this is the sum of good government."

CHAPTER 15

WELFARE AND ITS EFFECT ON SOCIETY

The impression is that to feed the children or support the poor, we can tax the rich. That is why, of course, that whenever politicians need money, they talk about taxing the rich. The demands of government are already ten times what the rich earn, so in reality, this isn't going to happen. Many politicians see themselves as modern-day Robin Hoods. But though the rich may have substantial incomes, they are few in numbers. The real cost to society is what the rich consume, which if taken, wouldn't provide much for those on welfare. Because the truly rich aren't likely to reduce their consumption, any additional taxes will likely come by reducing their investments, which will only result in higher returns for them. Who, then, pays for welfare? Those on welfare get a share of production without working, so isn't it the workers' production they are getting? Should everybody work who is able to do so? Does welfare stimulate or harm the economy? If all those who could receive more money on welfare were to take government assistance, would our economy still function?

Welfare is a reward paid for not working, which will usually translate into lost production. The involvement and realities of math in economics is a force of nature and an undeniable fact. Whenever someone refuses to find productive employment, the individual's—and thus, society's—production declines. Small-business people who are unable to expand for lack of workers are painfully aware of employment problems imposed by welfare. Small businesses can't go beyond their communities when workers refuse work or when employers are unable to match wages that large companies can afford. But for small businesses, when work performed by the boss is taken over by an unskilled worker, productivity increases at the top. All work that has to be done must be done. If the unskilled are being paid not to do the unskilled labor, then someone more skilled will perform the task. And time spent by the skilled to perform these functions is lost higher-level productivity, not bottom-level productivity. When such instances are multiplied by the millions on welfare, we can corroborate the impact that welfare has on the domestic product of the United States.

As per the production formula:

Production per worker	×	Workforce	=	Total production
y	×	b	=	a

When welfare is an input to the formula, then it is expressed:

y x (b - workers on welfare) = total production

y x (b - q) = a3

No matter how much innovation, invention, efficiency, or hard work, a (total production without welfare) will always be greater than a3 (total production with welfare). Production is a function of the total who produce. This mathematical formula demonstrates an undeniable fact: that welfare reduces a society's production. The affluent, well-meaning proponents of welfare would find it difficult to imagine stores filled with more produce. Could the affluent imagine higher paychecks for private workers or the services the welfare recipient didn't perform? It takes imagination to see what isn't there in a society that seems to have endless amounts of everything.

As welfare is increased through cost-of-living adjustments (COLAs), it encroaches more and more on the lower ranks of workers. One of welfare's failure to solve the problems of the poor is simply that it keeps defining more poor and fewer productive workers. COLAs make sure the poor stay poor, while workers must produce more just to stay even. In other words, the producers are producing more and keeping less, whereby the welfare recipients are getting more and working less. The worker on the way down is meeting the welfare recipient on the way up.

From the analogy of free enterprise to an ecological system, we deduce that even the smallest animal or plant is important. We can symbolize the importance of a worker by following what the loss of a worker might cause, using the prose about the "lack of a nail." Today, it could be written as follows: For want of a sweeper, a factory is dirty. For want of a clean factory, production is lost. For want of production, a customer is lost. For want of a customer, a factory is lost. For want of a factory, a business is lost. For want of a business, the work is lost. For want of workers, the community is lost. Substitutes for workers lost to welfare can be made, and some employee losses can be sustained by a business. Lost workers, however, at even the bottom of the chain will damage a business at the top. If the boss sweeps the floor, other duties will be sacrificed. No job is unimportant, a fact politicians and bureaucrats who lack business experience may fail to comprehend. Government can tax and pay whatever it takes to get its floors swept. In business, the solution for losing low-paid employees may be to substitute, to move, or to go broke. Just as in an ecological system, low-paid employees are part of the chain.

Although welfare is looked upon as a temporary substitute for lost income, it is permanent once a community loses the economic base—the unskilled form. Communities need workers to perform the tasks that support skilled labor, while learning the work the skilled workers perform. Welfare recipient begets welfare recipient—like a disease, welfare grows when skilled jobs lacking unskilled support get farther away.

No great city was ever built by the economic stimulus provided by welfare. Welfare communities beget more poverty, not jobs.

Economists once perceived welfare as a simple transfer of spending that has little effect on the consumption of others. Some consider the cost in dollars a problem, but the cost in production isn't considered. Yet welfare reduces or eliminates the incentives for work. By law, people who accept welfare and then work or accept money have committed a fraud. The poor are blamed for not working, but government sets the rules, and free people use, misuse, and manipulate them as they feel necessary to sustain their lives. Government is manipulating the laws of math by which production and our lives are determined.

A welfare recipient must agree to and understand the following:

a. The recipient must agree not to work or he or she will lose welfare payments.

b. Should the recipient not keep the agreement, he or she is breaking the law.

If we were compelled by the needs of our families to sign this agreement, what would we do? The "government solution" is always punishment, not reward.

When earnings are reported, welfare is often reduced to the extent that working is not practical. The benefit gained from work may not supplant welfare plus the cost of a job. The cost of a job encompasses the price of getting to work, hiring a baby-sitter, eating meals out, paying auto insurance, buying work clothes, etc. Jobs can be costly in an age when an auto and insurance cost as much as a home. This is the "welfare trap." People are paid not to work. It is no different than the farm subsidies that pay farmers not to farm, except that for farmers, the whole farm usually isn't out of production. If we are paying farmers not to farm because we have too much food, are we also paying welfare recipients not to work because we have too many goods and services?

This quest to help the poor was not intended to become the trap that well-meaning members of the community still seem to perceive it isn't. People at this low base are now spoken of as the unfortunate, the unlucky, or the disadvantaged. Deductive logic supplies the reasons why recipients would not exchange government income for a job that pays less and costs more. Those who have not been in the workforce lack simple work regimentation and are not likely to find positions with more than entry-level compensation. With payroll taxes, work clothing, and so on, accepting employment can be an act of stupidity. Welfare proponents may not believe the poor can reason, but they are poor, not brainless.

We must also not forget the problems people have when seeking a job. The fear that Grandma would have in putting her nest egg in a high-risk capital fund is no different for the young and the poor seeking jobs. Most people look for a job, not by desire but of necessity, as only necessity overcomes the fear of failure in the workplace. The need to contribute to the community and the desire to compound one's achievements is a learned aspect of the work ethic. Minor skills, like showing up at the right place, so apparent to older workers, are apt to be unimportant to new employees. Skills are built like the Chinese built their wall, one skill at a time, with each seemingly insignificant.

Low-paid jobs are where we learn our basic skills. How many of us remember doing something stupid that first work day? Those incredibly "unbrilliant" things, like looking for a left-handed monkey wrench or getting water from a drinking fountain all over our face. Many job entrants don't understand the importance of coming to work on time or even of coming to work, of being responsible for jobs without being told each day, of having clean hands, or simply of finding a job. Most people got their jobs because of a friend, associate, neighbor, relative, teacher, or someone they just met on the street. Welfare can not only pay better than a potential worker's first job; welfare communities don't have the network to provide jobs.

The jobs of those handing out welfare are dependant upon the assumption that the poor are victims of free enterprise, not of government. From the 1970s to the 1990s, local, state, and federal welfare expanded. And as welfare created welfare, it brought into being more government employees. During recessions, government found new reasons and new needs to expand welfare, thereby creating more bureaucracy and more government jobs. Thus, as the welfare population grows, so, too, do its proponents, recipients, and administrators, who all want more funding. Private workers are becoming less of a factor in the voting booths and, consequently, in determining their share of consumption. Welfare restricts the labor force with progressively higher payments, and the difference between welfare and average income is narrowing.

While the private workers who produce our goods and services have been kept busy expanding production, they have become a minority that is unwittingly enslaved to the government to which they look for solutions. In spite of the tremendous restructuring that has augmented production and should advance living standards, the private worker has sacrificed life standards. A revolutionized industry still manages only to stay even, as welfare and other government programs take a greater share. Those on welfare also sacrifice, as it becomes increasingly difficult to free them from the entangled government-designed web.

There is a cycle to this; it starts with welfare payments that reduce the labor force, which reduces productivity, which causes inflation, which increases welfare, which necessitates higher taxes, which restricts investment, which causes inflation, which pushes up interest rates, which cause a recession, which forces more people on welfare, and that constricts the labor force. We end where we began, but while government is adding to the incomes of the welfare recipients to make up for inflation, the private worker is getting less or working harder to maintain an income. Workers, not the rich, are getting less in order to support these government programs, and while inflationary adjustments may seem a fair concession, private workers are not always so blessed. Regional fluctuations in the economy may not make this cycle as apparent as when recessions affected the entire country, but they occur nonetheless. Instead of the whole country being affected at one time, the welfare wave moves from area to area or industry to industry.

Most of us are familiar with the canon that a dollar input into a community turns over several times. By theory, this stimulates an economy. We should then assume that welfare stimulates depressed economies, but what does it do to businesses that need workers. Remember the farmer who gets paid not to farm? How does government compute what the farmer gets? Farmers don't get paid for seed, gas, fertilizer, outside services, or repairs not made, nor do the businesses who would have received these payments. Government subsidizes only farmers, not hardware stores, feed stores, and gas stations. The community suffers for all the money the farmer didn't spend. Welfare recipients, likewise, only spend money that is the replacement for a wage. Gone is the product they would have provided that would have supported other businesses.

Currently, about 40 percent of the population of the U.S. has jobs. At least half work for, on behalf of, or as the result of government and its laws. The balance, perhaps less than 20 percent of the population, produces the goods and services for themselves and the other 80 percent. This means each private worker produces for five. In dollar terms, private workers produce five dollars of goods and services for every dollar they receive for themselves, assuming an even apportionment. Conversely, when workers are paid not to work, the five dollars of goods and services they would have produced is lost.

The problem in a free, capitalist working environment is not usually having too many workers, it's not having enough.

To visualize this situation, let's suppose we were on an island where only 20 percent of the population worked, while the others consumed but did not work, or they governed and did not produce. One day, 20 percent of the workers were paid to stop working, and a 20 percent tax was enacted to pay the ones not working. Government used its authority to tax and chose who could spend. It should be obvious to everyone, except politicians, that when workers are lost to a community, the economy shrinks. Production would shrink by 20 percent, and everybody would need to reduce consumption by 20 percent. If producers paid most of the tax, they would lose more than their 20 percent share of production, because they lose production and pay tax, while the consumption of some could actually increase. We may not notice our difficulty because in a free society, producers are constantly seeking ways to increase production with fewer workers. To break even in this case, our producers would have to work and produce 20 percent more, just to pay the tax and stay even. Producers might realize heavier demands, but producing more with fewer workers is a difficult task. Producers would almost assuredly be working more to sustain production and meet demands but without increasing their own consumption.

If the amount of money on the island didn't change, and production fell 20 percent, prices would inflate by 25 percent to match the production with the money supply. If the island had foreign trade, the people on it might maintain their living standard by importing. But they would need a currency that foreigners wanted, and assuming they had a zero trade balance before, they would now have a trade deficit.

Let's suppose goods were imported to make up the lost production. Employment for the remaining workers would likely shift to services in lieu of goods production, because services aren't imported as easily as goods. Something else might happen. If those we paid not to work had been in lower-paying jobs, such as washing dishes, stocking, and cleaning, those for whom they worked might not be able to operate their businesses. Unskilled tasks must still be done, because no one eats off dirty plates in dirty restaurants with dirty windows. The economy would suffer even further. Even though these lost workers were unskilled workers, their work is important. Consumers may now have to leave the island just to find clean restaurants. If the owner performed these duties, we could say that the work performed at the bottom came off the top. Obviously, there are no unimportant jobs; the floors still need to be swept and if they are not, sales will suffer.

At first, replacements might be found at higher wages. Woefully, the rules of economics, like those of nature cannot be avoided. If the cost to business is too high in comparison to the competition or the ability of customers to pay, sales will decline. When workers are paid not to work, prices in a community increase to attract needed help. When prices are too high to be supported by the community, businesses lose sales and eventually move or are abandoned. In areas where the income earners are principally on the low end, a lot of businesses might close, as customers purchase goods outside the community. As businesses fail, consumers go to other islands to spend. Those financially able would move to where they could get the service that they want. Island housing that can't be sold then becomes low-income rentals, attracting other low-income earners, and the decline in dollars and productivity continues. It continues until the island is devastated by the impact of welfare. And welfare-recipient communities with cheap rentals and a comparable social structure attract welfare recipients, who eventually form a welfare community whose residents are unable to work without breaking the law on an island too dangerous to provide employment.

Paying welfare recipients under the table solves a problem and creates a criminal.

The economic contribution in a community determined by how many times the welfare dollar circulates doesn't exist when goods are shipped in from outside. A dollar of earnings has the same effect as welfare; plus, for each dollar paid, five dollars of goods and services are produced. The welfare dollar is a transfer from one person's pocket to another's, with the condition that the recipient not be productive. The result is lost productivity and core economic activity needed to support a community.

Islands are no different than small communities or the poorest part of town. The influx of cash into a community is touted as a solution to the serious problem of a personal recession. The concept is of demand-side economics. When welfare replaces productive jobs, communities become a blighted example of the need for welfare, rather than an example of a community destroyed by welfare. Because of welfare, depressed communities remain depressed and grow worse. Once active businesses are abandoned, the streets are strewn with waste, and windows are boarded up.

To understand the importance of all economic levels in society, we can simply go shopping in our local communities. The shops are not staffed by high-paid executives; rather, they employ lower-scale workers or the owner and his family. Sons and daughters of affluent families can work, but welfare recipients can lose family welfare if the children earn an income. As the workers at the bottom are attracted to welfare, businesses fail. When enough fail, the community fails, and total productivity falls. Should we wonder why failed families are so often associated with these communities? Without welfare, people find jobs and take their income home to spend. If those on welfare worked, the added production would raise living standards for themselves and others as well. Moving a person from welfare to work would be like a patient in a shorthanded hospital getting out of bed and helping the staff. The effect is one less patient to care for and an added staff member to help the many patients.

Throughout most of the twentieth century, unemployment did not vary significantly. The level was a point determined by factors in a society that are barriers to employment. Welfare is a barrier to employment.

We have often thought of work as climbing the ladder of success. Such ladders are only found in bureaucracies, where having had one position justifies accession to the next. Businesses are better described as pyramids. In a pyramid, each stone supports the next level; none is less important, and those at the top who appear to occupy an entire level are likely the point on which the next level rests. In business, the least skilled are on the bottom and remain there, unless they push or are pushed higher. Different skills may occupy the same levels. Entrants are selected but can force their way onto, into, or through the pyramid, and they can also build their own. Entrants can enter at any level if they have the skills or the education so as to increase productivity and maintain competitiveness, but many enter at the bottom. As with the construction of the pyramids, growth is dependant upon the availability of material (labor), not on the availability of positions. The potential for expansion is infinite. Skills on each level may differ, but all skills support the top and, therefore, each other. If skills are lost or not attracted as needed, the duties must be taken up by others to support the pyramid. Eliminating a skill requires innovation, efficiency, or the import of replacements to fill the gap. Innovation and efficiency occur much like evolution in nature, but in business systems, they occur more quickly. Barriers placed in the way of entry can hinder growth of the pyramid. Forces act on the pyramid at all levels to add to it or tear at its structure. When damaged, it must be repaired, or the pyramid will crumble.

The function of a community is likewise analogous to a pyramid. When welfare was enacted, welfare became a force and a barrier, like a pollutant that interrupts the natural balance. The disruption caused by welfare affected the flow of new entrants to the pyramid, as well as existing workers. So that the pyramid continued to support itself, adaptations had to be made. Those in the level above had to perform lower-level jobs, innovation and efficiency had to be expedited, and/or new entrants had to be pulled into the affected level. If adaptations were not made, businesses dependant upon the missing workers disappeared or were moved, jobs were exported, components were imported, and businesses dependant upon failed businesses were lost. The result was that communities failed or became handicapped. Businesses or communities are representative of pyramids supporting other pyramids, and again support starts at the bottom.

In the early 1980s, a recession interrupted the growth of the complex multi-pyramid economic system that represents the economy of the U.S. Welfare and government growth occurring in the prior decade was having an effect on pyramid stability. Innovation and efficiency had occurred slowly, but after the recession, the process was expedited, and barriers to entry created by nongovernment forces were torn down. Innovation, such as the fax machine, the car phone, and the personal computer, became popular very rapidly.[12] These technologies had been around for years, so their increase in use

12 In the '70s Exxon had written off several hundred million dollars on a machine similar to the fax; the car phone was available

came as the need to innovate reached a crisis. They expanded work time, took the place of lower-level job responsibilities, and allowed higher-level workers to shift downward to lower-level skills without loss of production.

When job skill positions at the lower levels are not filled, the level above must drop into lower position, or skills must be assumed in some fashion by the above levels. Industries may crumble and new pyramids may be created from the rubble, as any disruption in nature or in our structure causes change that can't be predicted. It is not happenstance that in the years since the early '80s, advances in technology have been the kinds that allow upper-level employees to perform lower-level tasks. These technologies and the added demands of government have given rise to complaints by workers that they are working harder for the same money, doing the same job at less pay, or having to perform lower-skill functions, despite higher-level positions. All these instances occur, because unless lower skill levels support the upper skill positions, the pyramid will fail.

The disruption in the natural balance of the system and the job market is the reason for the many social problems that have occurred among welfare recipients. High school dropouts or new entrants are drawn into the job market by the availability of work and the shortage of money in distressed homes, then discouraged as the comparability of welfare payments becomes obvious. Jobs in a community are lost during government-created cycles or when the effects of welfare destroy the community. Jobs are pushed farther away from communities as the welfare cancer grows. Communities and businesses weakened by welfare also make advancement and promotions difficult or futile. Parental complaints about job problems are overheard by children, discouraging young job hopefuls and fostering abhorrence for the capitalist system. Not only are jobs limited in large welfare communities, but entrants are discouraged from low-paying jobs by parents or friends who have "learned the ropes" in accessing welfare. People who are discouraged may satisfy the human zeal to achieve by getting involved in illegal activities. The influx of illegal immigrants no doubt has been compounded by the problems caused by welfare. Illegal immigrants are willing to work at less than welfare income and are attracted by employers in desperate need to support their business. Self-esteem is surely lost, and idle hands are indeed the devil's workshop. We often note with humor the temporary population boom that occurs nine months after a blackout. And we have complained of the proliferation of children born to those on welfare. What if our lives were always blacked out? As welfare has its effects on a community, the heterogeneous social makeup that was once necessary to support the local economic structure is destroyed. Left are islands of economic equals, welfare recipients isolated from a true community. As people recycle to a lower level and find it difficult to rise above welfare, they may be prone to give up, ending homeless—but free and independent—on the streets.

There is no doubt that government's benevolence has caused an upheaval in human life, causing a detrimental effect on society's economic and social stability. Also obvious is why welfare begets the need for more welfare. Welfare is a program that justifies itself by generating new entrants, thus demonstrating its own need. Perhaps welfare can never be eliminated, but as someone on the ship is less likely to drown, working welfare recipients are far more likely to get better-paying jobs.

Laws should not be passed that make work illegal.

The loss of production is more serious than that once caused by discrimination. But as great as the loss may be, there is an incredible potential for gains in product and service from welfare recipients and program employees. The loss in productivity, if restored, would likely be such that the incentive not to be on welfare would reduce its ranks to only those unable to work. Advances in living standards

through radio telephone in the early '70s; and computer technology that had held back the PC suddenly penetrated the market and proliferated.

could make everyone's dream come true. On the other hand, should changes not be made, we may have fostered a permanently disabled welfare society—a group fed by government and taught nothing about choice and work.

Having a job should never be a crime. The popularity of using money to spur the economy is perceived more as the foundation of free enterprise than work itself. But money is not intended as a replacement for labor, nor can the economist make it so. Those on welfare must find work a reward, not a punishment. Earning a minimum-wage job should not be against the law. Politicians should stress the importance of all levels of work, not preach the unimportance of unskilled labor. Politicians preaching that money cures the ills of the poor may get elected, but they won't solve problems.

The welfare system has attempted for years to reintroduce the poor back into higher economic levels by building them homes or apartments in middle-class communities. The attempt to reintegrate the poor into higher levels is a pathetic response to a problem caused by the social system itself. It is pathetic because as always, government does not acknowledge its own mistakes, and it's pathetic because without understanding the cause, government deals only with the symptoms. The pain that is felt is not just by the poor but by workers whose jobs are disturbed and destroyed as their pyramids crumble.

Welfare does the following:

1. Takes workers out of small businesses
2. Reduces productivity
3. Immobilizes recipients
4. Demoralizes individuals
5. Competes with worker wages
6. Traps individuals in a maze of income complexities
7. Keeps people from learning work activity through experience
8. Destroys the natural balance of an economic community
9. Destroys a community's economic structure
10. Discourages respect for the free-enterprise system (capitalism)
11. Encourages other crimes by an acceptance of welfare crime or threats of exposure
12. Encourages crime through the increase of idle time
13. Encourages population expansion in families less able to afford the children

CHAPTER 16

FREE ENTERPRISE AND THE BIG APPLE

Whether or not we favor socialism, the high taxes and regulation that mandate ever more control of our lives and our businesses has drawn us closer to the reality of socialism. In the United States the Socialists, who have passed these laws, aren't called Socialists, nor do they claim to be, but if it walks like a duck and quacks like a duck, it's a duck. These laws are not only expensive today, they will have an even greater impact on future generations. Unfortunately, it doesn't seem that the "we aren't Socialists" Socialists are concerned with cost; to them, the U.S. economy is like a *big apple*—an apple owned by the rich who plunder the poor, and what the Socialist want is cash, to be taken from whomever and handed out. To the Socialist life is apparently about buying things, not building things. Everything we want can be bought; all we need do is slice up the apple. They are the benevolent souls. They are the Robin Hoods, who see the king's forest filled with deer, the storage filled with grain, and all for the taking—taking from the rich, that is, and giving to practically anyone. After all, the "always willing to give someone else's money away" benevolent ones take cash to the storehouse, and everything they want is always there. And, we aren't talking about natures bounty from the forest, we are talking about goods and services.

Curiously, Socialist's claim that the rich are takers, but Socialists would have to be takers if their goal is to distribute wealth. So, who are the providers and why are socialists so much more chaste than the rich? Greed after all is a human characteristic, not limited to political, religious, social, ethnic or, certainly, not ones social or financial background. I've never seen a billionaire on a tractor, but most have some sort of responsibility, on the other hand, most socialists, at least the politicians, haven't had that much experience. Since tax revenues are already several times what the rich earn, is taking from the rich really working? Who is the wealth being taken from? Capitalists, at least, are more interested in building and producing than are Socialists.

Socialists are not concerned that once picked, apples stop growing, and so, too, does the tree, if not tended. To a Socialist, an economy needs only to get bigger when the population grows. And for this reason, growing populations are problems to Socialists, as they ponder how new citizens are to be supported. After all, it's only fair to share someone else's apple, not theirs, because their share is already too small. It's such a worry, so much pressure. How will they build a bigger storehouse when they don't know or care how the old one got there? Surely the rich put it there to take advantage of the masses. Socialists loathe thinking that someone rich, exclusive of their deserving friends, would get richer by building a new warehouse. They console themselves with the knowledge that taxes can be raised only to take back a "fair" share. Or better yet, they can "put" in a warehouse—but maybe not; after all, how do you "put" in a warehouse?

Except to say that the rich own everything, Socialists seldom explain how wealth originated; it was just there. Modern Socialists don't define wealth as farms, factories, eighteen-wheelers, or adding machines. Wealth is stocks, bonds, cash, expensive paintings, and gold, all of which were created by money, not labor. Socialists aren't interested in expanding the economy because without the rich earning more than their share, enough of everything already exists. If only everything could be fair, because Socialists just want to be fair. Socialist judge plant capacities by the existence of unemployed, and because there are always unemployed, they always perceive an excess of capacity. Unemployment isn't seen as transitional, a decision of the unemployed, or a product of state welfare. To a Socialist, cash builds communities, not work. Jobs are what there are never enough of. Free enterprise is inefficient, and the work of a day need serve no purpose. And as work is not relevant to Socialists, neither are individuals. Only the state is important. Socialism need not define a system of creation, only one of distribution and control. But for socialism to work, for wealth to be distributed, Socialists need a system to plunder.

It is ironic that in the United States, which was founded by the poor, the cast-offs, and the repressed, that people would want a system in which government would be all powerful. Kings and queens, dictators, conquerors, the Third Reich, and Communist repression are no different from an elected government that demands, then divides the fruits of all labor. As a country founded on revolution and resolved in change, we seem so intent on revolution and change that we now revolt against our own principles. Do we manifest guilt for success, and fear each other so strongly that we should again form a system of punishment, not of rewards? The controversy *is* of reward or punishment, of carrot or stick, of prize or penalty, of choice or to have choices made for us. Is it fair to take from one and give to another? If each of us only labored in our own house and traded with no others, would it be fair for others to take from our house? When we trade what we made with our labor for gold, does it then make it fair to be taken? Is the question really one of fairness? What fairness has ever been fair? Isn't fair just another way to redefine inequitable?

Communist and Socialist societies use punishment as incentives because rewards, by definition, cannot be divided equally and thus are unfair.

The failure of communism and socialism is the impossibility of defining rewards in the context of a system that seeks to define equality without reference to contribution.

Socialism requires humankind to think alike. When reward is not an element of society, then indoctrination and manipulation are a necessity to form the Socialist's or Communist's views. Citizens of a socialist state, therefore, must be pacifists, and unable to challenge government. However, no law can make everyone benevolent. Communists and Socialists believe that government will have to coerce workers until "enough" exists, and that some people have to be coerced to be "good citizens."[13] Coerce is defined as "to force to act or think in a given manner; to compel by pressure or threat." If we were forced to work, would we be compelled to be nice? *Nice*—a frivolous topic in a serious writing. Yet our attitudes reflect our happiness, and consequently, attitudes can reflect upon the system that provides our living. In the abundant marketplace of today, does selling more result from being nice or nasty? If our livelihood were dependent upon being nice, would we be nasty? After living in a benevolent wonderland devoid of greed, Russians have been known for poor customer relations and nastiness. Perhaps a system that turns evil intent into good endeavors would be better than one that is rife with nastiness. If greed manifests corruption, will corruption not flourish in an empire of malice?

Socialists seek equality through taking, not through the pursuit of opportunity.

13 World Book, Fields Educational Corporation, 1976. "Socialism," pp. 456–458.

Greed is a characteristic of one who takes without compensation. What government gives back isn't likely to be equal to the tax.

In the last eighty years, at least 90 percent of the world population lived with Communism, socialism, dictatorship, monarchies, and every form of repressive economic system and government authority that mankind has imagined. Not tried under one government but hundreds; not one chance to succeed but a thousand chances. In every instance, without a free economic system, totalitarian governments failed to make economic advances or to provide for their citizens' daily needs. Most totalitarian failures are environmental wastelands. Only the United States, with less than 5 percent of the world's population, has flourished, provided massive amounts of economic aid to other nations, and taken the steps to preserve its environment. Yet to the Socialist, the success of free enterprise in the U.S. is not a reason to celebrate or to hold as an example to the world. Success in the U.S. is a reason to feel shame, because we are above the plane of the average world citizen; we are not fair. United States citizens are not fair because people are free to choose; socialism can only be fair when government makes the choice. If one individual chooses better than another, it would not be fair. The world has begun to pass choice and opportunity to its citizens so they may be like us, but U.S. politicians are shackling opportunity with punishment to be more like they once were. Socialism is not an experiment; it has been tried, and it has failed. There is no right way for government to share (distribute) humankind's produce.

Good intention and fairness are parents to failure and confusion.

Pure socialism bears little distinction from communism. They both foretell of a democratic system in which government is to make the decisions and solve the problems for all individuals, male and female, monkey and man. In a controlled economy, even if democratic, individuals who solve problems are selected or voted. Therefore, as with politics in the U.S., decisions made by government are not democratic; only the election is democratic, except that freedoms have been forfeited for the "security" to which the state has the rights. Lest we forget, governments are of men, not of gods. Selfishness and greed by government employees is a greater evil than selfishness and greed in enterprise. And whether successful, unsuccessful, or not even involved in solving a problem, elected officials can be exalted, moved aside, admonished, or ridiculed. Success in government isn't determined by a democratic process wherein profit or loss depicts success. Success in our socialist system is determined by an advertising agency and the politicians' own remarks—the truth is not always present. The concept of profit and loss is ridiculed by self-proclaimed humanists, but considering that no successful alternative exists, profit and loss is the world's best indicator. When politicians fail, they blame the system for a shortage of funds and then ask for more money. They will be right; it was the system and the people within it who chose politicians. In free enterprise, we prove our competence in making decisions and solving problems with success. One who is elected has proven neither the success nor the competence to make better decisions, solve problems, or even to be fair. Perhaps to be fair, we should ask which system gave us the wealth, whose wealth it is, and if it's fair to take the wealth.

Let's imagine a system in which not one but thousands try to solve problems—a system in which millions are solving problems that government doesn't know exists. People, by free choice, look for solutions with no guarantee of gain. And through free choice, not by vote, people solve problems. Often, answers are developed before we have the question. The Post-it, for example, was the result of glue that wouldn't stick. People, who aren't even looking, notice needs they think can be satisfied. Does it matter that people help people for financial gain, not self-gratification? People with AIDS won't care if someone gets rich when a cure is found. Should people not be encouraged to search for cures for whatever reason best suits them? When either wealth or self-satisfaction is compensation to a creator, what great difference exists between buying personal satisfaction and feeling it? Why should we resent people who earn wealth for finding solutions? Selfless acts are selfless because money exists, not in spite of it.

Free enterprise defines and develops solutions for an imperfect society by a natural evolution of thought.

Solutions are directly related to the number in a free and willing workforce who are available to solve problems.

Let's envision the storehouse for free enterprise as an elastic sphere, in which is all the produce of the economy. This sphere is ever expanding and ever growing. It contains our food, housing, TVs, roads, fun, electricity, clean air, welfare, churches, research, eagles, and all the things that people want. People choose how much of each they wish to have, which new things will be a part of the sphere, and the type of work each will do. Everyone can go to the sphere but to take something out, we must put back. Whether executive or garbage man, housewife or shoeshine boy, researcher or investor, each has something to contribute. It is not an economy made of dollars but of people; each is important to the others. If enough people like what one produces, the producer is rewarded. People are motivated to produce by being rewarded with choices. As people become more efficient and inventive, the sphere expands. If people are less productive, the sphere shrinks.

To show how we depend on each other, let's assume there is no money, and we barter for our goods. The farmers this year have an abundance of apples, twice that of last year. Everyone eats more apples. Do the farmers benefit? Maybe yes, maybe no. Without others making more clothes or growing more oranges, for what extra goods could the farmers trade? Like the farmer, each of us depends on the others' increased production to improve our own lives. Our own living standards are thus limited by what others do. Adam Smith's invisible hand was another way of saying that when people compete in the market, they increase the production for each other. Even a Socialist should understand that a farmer doesn't grow apples for his own consumption. It is important that all of us are motivated by whatever suits us, to improve ourselves, our work, and to benefit all others.

The free-enterprise system manifests the creation of wealth for and by an unlimited number of people, whether goods are built at home and kept or traded for another's goods. Free enterprise defines the system in which all are free to create that which each desires and to trade or keep that which each creates.

The aspiration in a free-enterprise system is to acquire assets through creation.
The goal is freedom of individual choice.
The result of freedom is a better life for all.

Free enterprise embodies certain postulates:

1. Money is a tool used to facilitate the exchange of one kind of labor for another.

2. Free enterprise cannot exist without free man, nor can free man exist without free enterprise.
3. Free enterprise nurtures the greatest number of questions.
4. Competition begets the greatest number of solutions.
5. Free enterprise identifies and responds to the infinite needs and desires of the population.
6. Profits are the result of satisfying needs.
7. The greatest profits come from satisfying the greatest need.
8. Laws, rules, and mandates are inflationary.
9. In a free market, the differing types of goods and services increase exponentially with the diversity of occupations.
10. Wealth is created but only exists in a system that ensures the rights of ownership.

Success rests on the ability to provide something beneficial to someone else. Innovation benefits both the entrepreneur and the consumer by providing something that is necessary, less costly, better quality, new, different, or simply enjoyable. Free enterprise allows individuals to choose and to make demands based on unique desires.

Wealth and compensation is the reward for improving someone else's life.

Expanded production translates into wealth, and wealth is recompense for expanding consumption.

In a free system, wealth is enhanced by the cost of government's plunder..

Wealth reflects the cost of production, which cost includes the cost of government.

The gain to wealth from big government is probably the reason so many of the rich support big government. These rich may be unwitting benefactors of a wealth, but unwitting or not, they benefit. Wealth is enhanced by the added cost and inefficiency of government. Having been rewarded thus, they believe generosity is good for the poor. Whether the rich know or sense that government enhances their wealth, or whether they simply don't realize it, doesn't matter, what needs to be understood is that the cost of government is conveyed to the citizens and not the rich. In an atmosphere where government is the dominant force, the evolutionary process by which free enterprise adapts to government growth will leave us with a population of rich whose wealth is dependant on or was derived from growth in government. The nonworking rich are often associated with a belief in Socialist economic values. Without at least minor business knowledge and direct customer contact, these wealthy Socialists are not likely to comprehend the difficulties that business people endure when attempting to maintain pricing to their customers. In other words, to Socialists, workers as individuals are of little consequence, compared to the demands of government.

Socialism concentrates government, power, and wealth.
Free enterprise decentralizes government, power, and wealth.

Most of the settlers of the U.S. were poor. Yet even poor, once given the right to choose a system, choose the system that encompassed the greatest individual freedoms and the least government interference. Free enterprise built both the country and its people and gave them strength. The only manual was the Bible, but not all used that. This country was designed nearly from scratch in an evolutionary process wherein the most successful communities provide the most goods, the most jobs, and attracted the most people. It wasn't the writers of the Constitution who chose this system; it was an elixir that filled the soul of the country.

Socialism advocates that government make decisions, but one government employee or a multitude cannot conceive an infinitesimal fraction of the ideas that the whole of mankind conceives in the free atmosphere of self-determination. Government and like bodies should revise thier rules to enhance only freedom and reward. Too often, government offers negative responses to the human impulse to solve problems. If government encouraged competition and rewards for its employees, government employees would perform efficiently and with greater satisfaction. The common rules of enterprise determined by government constantly conflict with free enterprise. Yet each has faults the other can cure. Government has difficulty managing its business and would be better to take guidance from free enterprise. Conversely, a developing enterprise system needs rules to reduce dishonest and unsafe activities. If government were to accept the workings of free enterprise and define its goals in respect to its involvement, then distrust, confusion, and the lack of respect that each hold for the other could be conquered. Governments, the unions, and associations all perform similar tasks and need to define their own goals. They should:

1. Protect and preserve order.
2. Define rules for equal opportunity.
3. Establish rules for competition.
4. Establish rules for safety and contrive standards.
5. Invest for the common good.
6. Spend for the common good.
7. Educate the population and encourage free enterprise.
8. Mediate or be representative in disputes when requested to participate or legally compelled to.
9. Encourage efficient, innovative, and adaptive government with an emphasis on rewards for success, rather than punishment for failure.
10. Maintain a free and honest flow of information.

By defining goals, government and its agencies could take credit for their own achievements. Giving credit where credit is due establishes the course for future improvements.

A capitalist economy operates very well on its own, whereas politicians, with desires for public office, often take credit for a good economy and blame business for bad behaviors that were often responses to a government action. A good example is civil rights, the denial of which acts in opposition to the forces of free enterprise. Politicians wrote the laws, overlooked discrimination, and set election boundaries to satisfy segregationists and to get elected. But a true capitalist won't turn down profits unless laws, ethics, and community expressions necessitate or encourage the action. Prejudice in the workplace came chiefly from special-interest groups that were concerned for jobs and not the capitalists whose interests are best served without the discrimination that puts limits on commerce. Say what you want about the profit motive; it does not discriminate. We may be familiar with President Eisenhower's signing of the first civil rights act in 1957, his sending of the troops to Little Rock, Arkansas, to enforce civil rights, and his appointment of the first black to an executive position in the White House. Long before these efforts, however, industry integrated its workforce when and where possible, while entertainment brought black Americans to the public view.

Personal beliefs don't and should not define a true capitalist, who will look for the best worker, manager, player, or artist that can be found and capitalize on his or her talent. Baseball broke the "color line" when Jackie Robinson, Ernie Banks, and others were drafted to all-white teams. TV gave white audiences the fun of *Amos and Andy*, and the phonograph gave us Fats Domino, the Coasters, and a thousand others. Prejudice did not grow from free enterprise, where the profit motive is the incentive of owners and managers to look for the best person for the job. Preconceived notions and fear in the population allowed prejudice to flourish, along with the politicians who responded to public opinion instead of fighting wrong with right. Discrimination comes from kingdoms ruled by religious zealots who seek to convert everyone to the state religion, from totalitarian systems, such as the USSR and China, where religion is often in opposition to state policies, and pure democracies, wherein a majority can vote to exclude, discriminate, and even execute by group, sect, or color of people. These systems have shown that discrimination can exist whenever power is concentrated or in the hands of a majority, or where laws can be manipulated by the minorities in power. Where freedom exists, capitalism exists, and both contrast with discrimination. Some say the Constitution of the United States should be a flexible document adaptive to the will of the people. Wouldn't such a constitution be subject to the manipulation of a religion, philosophy, or a dictator?

It is doubtless that politicians need to look important and be viewed as crusaders. But "fairness" dictates that free enterprise should be observed with honestly. Enterprise does not guarantee fairness, but competition guaranteed by free enterprise pays the greatest rewards to the most indiscriminate seller or producer. Our effort to legislate the finite rules of equality and behavior only fosters inequality and special privilege.

Guaranteed employment is an aspiration that Socialist politicians "feel" is socialism's highest achievement. Most Socialists believe that it is government's obligation to provide jobs for the workers. Showing up or working is optional. To a Socialist, if we do not work in an eight-hour day, there either was nothing to do or if we had worked, someone else might be out of a job. The concept of productivity is a wonder until Socialists suddenly develop shortages. The developed countries with the highest unemployment are those with guaranteed jobs. It is very likely that workers with guaranteed jobs are also the least satisfied with their lives and employment. Not only is an employer obligated to keep employees, but the employee is compelled to keep the job—a job for which he or she might not be suited, that is far away from home, or that he or she is simply unhappy with. Leaving a job or being fired often turns out to be a great opportunity to build a business, change occupations, or find a more desirable climate. In a situation where jobs are legal rights, neither leaving a job nor hiring employees may be options.

Unemployment is such a great concern to the population that despite the successes of free enterprise, politicians thrive on cries for more jobs and higher wages. And they nurture this fear by reminding us of the Great Depression. Politicians see unemployment as an opportunity to gain or to maintain office, solved, of course, by creating jobs at which productivity is of no consequence.

Nikolai Lenin believed that unemployment would be the downfall of free enterprise. He said, "Capital, created by labor of the worker, oppresses the worker by undermining the small proprietor and creating an army of the unemployed."[14] The Depression confirmed his fear. Karl Marx further expounded, "Capitalist production begets, with the inexorability of a law of nature, its own negation."[15] In the nineteenth-century perspective from which Lenin and Marx viewed the world, the needs of mankind were limited to food and shelter. Increasing productivity would simply leave workers without jobs. Lenin or Marx could not have envisioned the expansion of consumer goods that went along with the expansion of capital. Even today, we have not yet seen an infinitesimal fraction of the products that are in our future. Free enterprise affects its own balance in time. As fewer workers are needed to produce a good or service, price or incomes adjust, and spenders consume other goods. Capital and labor then move to improve, expand, and meet new demands. Stalin probably saw the annihilation of millions as an economic solution to the existence of the unemployed. To the benevolent Socialists of today, needless jobs and welfare are a kinder solution to the same perceived problem. In a simple society, where jobs are limited and money is cumbersome, efficiency may increase unemployment. In a Complex society, even major adjustments in efficiency for large industries are inconsequential to the whole and cause little more than ripples in the unemployment lines. Likewise, spending adjusts quickly to the cornucopia of products, and the only limitation to consumption is workers to produce, not money.

A capitalist's greatest concern is matching worker skills with the position.

It is a natural human tendency to increase productivity, to maintain one's livelihood, and to be efficient. As farmers were displaced by new farming equipment, they used their experience on the farm to devise new instruments of efficiency. So it is that as efficiency displaces a worker, workers use their experience to design even more efficiency. The result is the constant improvement of our living standard.

Still, fear and evil must be overcome—the fear of free enterprise and the evils of big government. We once ended the use of childhood labor and sweatshops; the depleting of our workforce with wasted labors may yet bring them back. Productivity increases that would release labor for expansion of our economy are being absorbed by a neurotic effort to increase government employment, supplement welfare, and add incentives for not working. The result is that the percentage of the population that really contributes to production is declining. Higher production must now be coerced from a lesser percentage of workers. It is doubtless that the many who are guaranteed their living are faring much better than the private workers, who have no guarantees but are burdened with the added responsibilities. For the Socialist that big apple still produces the limitless flow of goods. For the private worker, free enterprise is reducing wages and improving efficiency, so business will stay solvent in the face of growing government burdens. It is no coincidence that at election time, the political focus and the benefactors of government payments are the same.

14 Pocket Book of Quotations, Simon & Schuster, Inc. 1652, pg 26.

15 Karl Marx, Das Kapital, A Gateway Edition-Regnery Gateway, 1996, pg 356

The politicians who create nonproductive political jobs to absorb the unemployed give us a strong indication of their ideology. Karl Marx remarked that: "Periodic commercial crises [recession, depressions] most commonly brought on by overproduction, regularly threaten the existence of bourgeois society. ... To survive, either productive forces must be destroyed en masse to reduce the quantity of products or new markets must be found on which to dump the excess." There is some truth to what Marx said here. The Great Depression was surely the result of too large a percentage of the labor force being committed to an unnecessary expansion of production. We must realize that the economy was not as developed and cannot be compared to the economy of today. The Great Depression represented a Transitional economy.

In a similar situation involving our Complex economy, where government over-stimulated real estate from the 1960s to the 1980s, the crisis was overcome as we moved from a Transitional to a Complex economy. The result was a recession and not a depression. Unemployment that resulted was redistributed and absorbed, as would be expected in a diverse and complex economy. We cannot forget that it was government that created the great real estate crisis. In a Complex society without government interference we can avoid this circumstance. No efficiency that causes layoffs and no productivity expansion that creates an oversupply of goods that comes from the diversity of private enterprises can be of such a great consequence in a Complex community that the entire economy can be impacted. Only when government alters the financial equation and overburdens a major productive sector can the entirety of a Complex economy be disturbed. Socialists think in terms of citizens in the population and not workers and may never accept the importance of labor. Our current autocratic administration is, in the name of unemployment and a presumed unlimited supply of workers, putting a greater and greater burden on fewer and fewer to provide for more and more.

Governmental interference meant to spur the economy usually comes at the time when the economy is advancing on its own. Governmental incentive, therefore, often results in inflation and the beginnings of a cycle. Economic complexity, absent government interference, dispossesses widespread recessions. Government can cause recessions; if, by chance, enough forces did come into play to cause a recession, we should remember how jet-plane pilots pull out of a dive—instead of pulling the stick back to end a dive, the stick is pushed forward, or down. In a Complex society facing inflation or to avoid recession, the labor supply must be augmented rather than forced into unemployment.

The invisible hand represents each individual's effort in micro-management of the economy vs. government's macro-management that is intended to micro-manage.

Adam Smith said, "People have a natural inclination to pursue their own self-interest in commerce and trade—an apparent hindrance to human progress and social order. However, individualism in truth actually leads to order and progress. In order to make money; people produce things that others are willing to buy. When buyers and sellers meet in the marketplace, a pattern of production and voluntary cooperation results, and overall social harmony is enhanced. ... Thus, self-interest, the motivating force in a free market system, unintentionally promotes the common interest, wherein each individual helps others achieve their own ends, as if by an invisible hand."[16] Adam Smith's simplistic terminology, the "invisible hand" is appropriate for a society engrossed in simplifications. But as simplifications can move a wave of thought in one direction, they can be overcome by other verbal simplifications. In the 1980s, those who wished to dignify their own interpretations of economics translated "invisible hand" and "trickle-down economics" into "voodoo economics." The media is more than willing to use these shibboleths to produce illusory intelligent laughter that actually reflects

16 Wealth of Nations, Adam Smith

glaring stupidity. Adam Smith's simplified explanation of the force that free individuals had on the marketplace was thus translated by the media in another oversimplification as "voodoo."

Those who call Adam Smith's economics voodoo believe that spending money on useless jobs and welfare, taken from those who earned it, helps the economy and the people. Goods that benefit and improve living standards do not suddenly appear because the Socialist has money. The real voodoo economics is the belief that paying shoppers to buy things is beneficial to productive workers. Better to let the workers keep the money and do their own shopping than to enslave them to a Socialist dawdler. Socialists who hide behind Keynesian economic theory can't seem to envision jobs being created, when they who earn it also spend it. Productive workers do not benefit from Socialist economics; only politicians and their proponents benefit. Socialists merely take from the productive worker and add to the compensation of others whose value is not likely to equate to their compensation. Although their minds are lost in a cloud of ignorance, their hands are in someone else's pocket. They have forgotten or never heard that Adam Smith also said, "Self interest … wherein each individual helps others achieve their own ends ..." They also fail to recognize that both the king and Robin Hood were thieves; one likable, one not—but still both thieves.

Though both antagonists and advocates attempt to simplify free enterprise, it is not a simple study. It is much like Newton's laws, wherein the forces that act within it are natural forces that act much like nature. As with nature, simple laws beget a thousand formulas. Below are laws that can define a thousand actions:

The free-enterprises system is fueled by three human actions:

a. Voluntary

   The intention to meet or satisfy a demand

b. Involuntary

   The need to satisfy a demand

c. The desire for freedom

Workers work because they want to or need to. Either way, they exercise their freedom to satisfy a demand. Working to satisfy their own demands requires them to satisfy the demands of another. As with the forces of nature, each action requires an equal and opposite reaction. The greatest actions come from the freedom to act. Freedom is the rock on which we anchor, and the anchor that holds us fast is free enterprise.

In a society where monopoly was once a bad word, many look at free enterprise as being too competitive, thus making competition a dirty word. If the power to compete did not exist, the power that remains would create a power structure that is all in one hand. Monopolies only support ineptitude, disorder, and squander.

Free enterprise proceeds in three basic stages:

Agrarian (simple or Rural)	**A stable phase of an economy in which stability is subject to unnatural and natural disturbances**
Developmental (Transitional)	**An unstable phase of an economy**
Complex	**A stable phase of economic development**

The view of free enterprise that one perceives during these stages can be confusing. Although the rules under which free enterprise operate in each stage are much the same, the impact on individuals, communities, and even nature is different. Of special significance is the diversification of individual responsibilities.

In the Agrarian stage (Rural), the economy is focused on basic pursuits, mostly food and shelter. This represents a stable economy in which workers are self sustaining. Agrarian economies are only interrupted by war, disease, and natural disasters. Although product is available, a readily acceptable means of exchange is not and bartering is still a common. Industries such as shipping require the largest amount of capital, and trade is the focus of government.

In the Transitional stage the imbalance between monetary aggregates and the expansion of production in a fragile economic environment sets the stage for economic disruptions As an economy progresses, the capital needed for single commercial endeavors is compounded and as efficiencies are developed, the economy grows—although the economy is unstable because of the focus of skills in a limited number of major industries. Many workers have lost their agrarian skills. As the economy develops monetary aggregates become more readily available, facilitating domestic trade and reducing the necessity of barter. The economy defines new businesses and trades. Projects of greater size are built, requiring great amounts of labor and capital. Foreign trade is still of great importance. The labor force in this evolving stage is plentiful, as workers move from farm to factory. Labor is taken advantage of, and the ample supply causes inequities in compensation, while profitability of investments encourages expansion. Labor begins to evolve as a workforce and a power to be reasoned with to protect itself from the abuses of management and government. The simple needs of the community define limited pursuits that can result in problems when monopolies, shortages, surpluses, or natural catastrophes occur. The economy is most fragile during this stage. Most important, as the jobs become diverse, the number who rely on agrarian pursuits declines.

In the Complex stage, the numbers of job descriptions are compounding. The difference between Transitional and a Complex economy is becoming more obvious as efficiencies, innovations, invention, and excess investment in an economic subdivision have less impact on economic stability. The availability of labor is the only limitation to progress as the specialized skills to do the complex functions required by innovation become more valuable. As occupations become specialized, research is expanded along with production. Skilled labor is more in demand, which limits the abuses of management. But efficiencies are also abundant to balance the forces of employee and employer. The Complex economy requires that employer be free to alter the worker's employment, the employee requires the freedom to seek other employment with out contractual restrictions. Ideally, both can seek their highest and best use/efficiency. The means of exchange expands to facilitate faster and more generous exchanges. The complexity of the economy reduces the opportunities for monopolies or problems from shortages and overages. The diversity spreads the impact of economic imbalances that in a developing economy would have been noticeable disruptions. The possibility of depressions is remote and the possibility of recessions diminishes greatly.

As free enterprise has progressed to this Complex stage, government tied to the past has hindered the advances the worker would make in augmenting living standards. Despite the failures of socialism and communism, free enterprise has as yet been praised for freedom and success. Mankind, still seeking the absolute power, replaces gods with government.

No law has yet been written to make a bureaucrat a demagogue and capable of making godlike decisions.

CHAPTER 17

WHO GAINS AND WHO LOSES?

Since the 1960s, taxes and regulation have added a tremendous load to the tasks of the working population. Millions of workers are earnings their shares of consumption by performing duties that have only an indirect relation to traditional production. These additional duties asked of the private workforce extend the cost and influence of government far beyond direct government spending. Coupled with added responsibilities, purchasing power has been redistributed, as other millions of people are receiving benefits for not working at all. In 1960, only 24.6 percent of government expenditures represented payments to nonproductive citizens; by 1993, the figure rose to over 47 percent, a 91 percent increase that is coupled with a 50 percent increase in government's share of the economy. This reshaping of private and public spending is a burden to private workers, who have the duty to provide for the consumers' demands based on the redistributed purchasing power. The effort by the private worker to meet these demands has been a valiant one, typical of the spirit of a country where valiant efforts are commonplace. However, only the naive should believe these added demands on the private workforce do not affect living standards or that there are not winners and losers. Yet politicians who look for solutions to the problem of declining compensation for productive workers ignore the impact of government. As a result, in the effort to solve a problem, government influence is expanded and the problems intensified.

In a prior chapter we used a formula to demonstrate the effects that welfare had on production. The formula is expanded here to demonstrate how production is affected by other government actions.

The basic formula is as follows:

Production per worker	×	Workforce	=	Total production
y	×	b	=	a

To demonstrate how paying workers not to work affected the computation, an adjustment to the worker total was made as follows:

Production per worker	×	(b - workers on welfare)	=	Total production
y	×	(b - x1)	=	a3

We can now expand the formula to include other responsibilities, resulting in the reallocation of the private labor force:

x1 = additional workers allocated as workers on welfare

x2 = additional workers allocated to environmental causes

x3 = additional workers allocated to the legal system

x4 = additional workers allocated to social work

x5 = additional workers allocated to animal rights

x6 = additional workers allocated to engineering changes

xX = all other additional worker allocations

The formula would now read:

a x (b - {x1 + x2 + x3 + x4 + x5 +x6 + ….. xX}) = ax

From 1960 to 1995, the workforce increased from approximately 70 million to 128 million, an increase of 83 percent, against population growth of about 69 percent. This increase in the percentage of the working population should have foretold a higher living standard. An increase in the percentage of working females and a decrease in the working male population suggests strongly an increase in welfare families, with single mothers and fathers who work outside the system. The duties of the worker are increasingly nonproductivity-related and government-motivated responsibilities. Obviously, and exclusive of production efficiency, fewer productive workers beget a constricting effect in consumable production (a1 > a2 > a3). This effect is not obvious, as efficiency offsets portions of the reallocated labor, and inflation rations the remaining production. Inflation, of course, is the process by which free enterprise distributes production shortages. The 1970s and '80s inflation evidenced this occurrence. In that period, production failed to keep up with demand, as the shifting of labor affected future as well as existing production.

The adjustment to demand effected by inflation is obvious; however, there is another more subtle effect that changes how income is distributed among the population. As the shortages occur and inflation pushes up prices, the portions of the population that are protected from inflation by automatic income adjustments are not impacted. With shortages still existing, those who are not protected must absorb the entire adjustment and reduce their consumption. We can formulate how, ultimately, through the process of inflation, the limited production is allocated. Let's imagine that all the production is placed in a warehouse and then distributed according to a preference. Those who are guaranteed a share are first given theirs; what remains is divided among the remaining.

Total Product	-	Guaranteed Distributions	=	Product Distributable to Unprotected
ax	-	gd	=	a-gd

The question now is who is guaranteed a distribution? If everyone is, the situation would be impossible to resolve. In countries with controlled economies, the solution is to ration distribution. In a free market, price change is the mechanism that brings the problem to a solution, as shortages are distributed based on the willingness of the buyer to pay. People still have the opportunity to choose alternatives, but those without income protection (cost-of-living adjustments—COLAs) will need to adjust to a lower level of consumption. As prices increase, the income of the unprotected will remain static or decline. The effects of production loses are thus shifted to only a portion of consumers, with a resultant magnification of the effects. Below is a list of organizations, groups, and employees whose consumption is generally protected by COLA clauses or other mechanical income shifts:

Direct government protection

A. Government employees
B. Government funded institutions (education, museums, libraries,
C. radio programs, hospitals, etc.)
D. Social Security recipients
E. Welfare recipients
F. Other government-funded or backed pensions that have COLA clauses
G. Government-owned utilities
H. Pseudo-government organizations, both private and government-controlled, such as airport authorities and business associations

Indirect protection (1)

A. Regulated industries whose rates are adjusted for cost and are protected against competition (electric utilities, insurance companies)
B. Businesses that rely on fixed percentages or cost to determine compensation (realtors, insurance companies) (2)
C. Private workers with guaranteed jobs and COLA clauses (3)
D. Government contracts with COLA and/or wage protections
E. The truly rich
F. Business (4)

(1) Anyone in the private workforce who relies on government funding or regulation is at risk. Deregulation of airlines, trucking, and telephone are examples of workers who once had protection.

(2) Businesses that rely on fixed percentages for incomes are only partially protected because other factors can interrupt their income stream. Sales may decline while factors such as interest-rate–induced recessions can result in a total loss of income.

(3) Without job guarantees, layoffs void any temporary protection of a COLA, while job guarantees often foretell unstable businesses.

(4) The protection afforded to business is not one that occurs without serious consequence. Industries may be forced to reorganize, downsize, or change employee compensation in order to survive. Many may go out of business due to the contractions or changes in spending patterns. When spending patterns are reestablished, the size, cost, and pricing structure of the business will be on a level that considers any new costs, plus a profit. The names of the owners may change, but most industries will survive.

The formula for the net effect of added government costs to the portion of the population not covered by COLA is quite simple and as follows:

C = Percentage increase in business cost before adjustment for efficiency

P = Percentage of population not covered by COLAs

PU = Percent of prior consumption by unprotected consumers

CL = Percentage of consumption lost to unprotected

R = Rate of return to business needed to sustain its equilibrium

$$\frac{C \times 1.R}{P} \times \frac{P}{PU} \times 100 = CL1$$

For example, a 5 percent increase in the cost to consumers, with 60 percent of the population unprotected, who had been consuming 50 percent of the total product, would result in a 10 percent loss of consumption to the unprotected. There are other factors affecting this calculation, such as the increase in profits to business when cost rise, and fortunately, the decrease in cost to business due to efficiency.

E = Rate of increase in efficiency to the economy

The formula would then read:

$$\frac{C \times 1.R - E \times 1.R}{P} \times \frac{P}{PU} \times 100 = CL1$$

It is not as important to follow the formula as it is to understand that added costs not offset by efficiency are borne by the portion of the population that is not protected by COLAs (This might also include the category of workers and groups whose incomes are enhanced by contract). And business will eventually restructure itself to profit by the added costs. Because some things like houses can simply be made smaller, not all businesses will add profits, and some product sales will fall to align with the consumers' inflation-adjusted earnings. There are a multitude of factors that will cause variances in the impact to consumers and businesses, as a miscellany of costs impact differently on a variety of consumers. For example, unprotected consumers who have not accumulated and paid off assets may suffer a greater loss. These adjustments do not occur over short periods of time; they can take years, while the effects are compounded by year after year of changes. Recessions can also occur at times when there are sudden adjustments to our living standards. In any case, the adjustments caused by growth in government are continuous occurrences.

Most of the following text will deal with the change and effect of government growth. This process affects the truly rich in a different manner, so they will take some of the focus. There are concerns by some economists that changes in worker's incomes are not distributed evenly, but it has not resulted in accepted explanations.

Some of the change is evidenced by the shift in reported earnings for higher income groups. There are two basic reasons for this occurrence. First, the reporting of executive incomes is distorted. Government figures do not take into consideration whether the income of executives is in the form of actual salaries or stock options. Options have a value, but when exercised, options merely represent a dilution of the stockholders' interests, which is a market value adjustment. Stock options are often refunded in the open market, but options are not compensation paid out of business coffers.

Second, the value of stock has been exaggerated by the change in the cost of a business, relative to comparative volumes of production. In other words, value is based on profits, profits are based on cost, and there are standard margins in each industry that are usually necessary to sustain asset growth, research, replacements, and credit worthiness. Thus, the value of a business isn't going to change because the business pays expenses that are 30 percent government-related and 70 percent labor, or 70 percent government-related and 30 percent labor. Therefore, as the profits of business increase with the addition of government cost, the compensation of its managers can likewise be expected to increase. This is likely to occur, even though lower-level workers are feeling the effects of the advancing cost of government. Successful managers who have managed to survive the government juggernaut of changes can expect higher skill-based earnings. Therefore, we shouldn't blame the rich. Rather, it is big government that can be blamed for making the rich comparatively[17]_richer.

This is not the only distortion that occurs in the private sector. In moves to maintain employee compensation in the face of the growth in government, lower levels of private workers are also seeing more of their compensation in the form of stock options, with some of this savings passed to the customer. To the extent that it benefits the corporation, the numbers are incredible, if looked at in terms of wealth. A saving in compensation of a dollar after taxes, valued at, say, fifteen times earnings, would be valued at fifteen dollars by the stock market. This exaggerates reported employee compensation, and since government-benefited earners are paid in cash, the shift of consumption is further hidden when compared with employees receiving noncash payments. Unfortunately, the value of employee stock accumulation will represent little overall, if production is not augmented to match the potential purchasing power released upon the sale of this stock in the future.

---

17 The term "comparatively rich" is used to suggest that the rich aren't necessarily getting richer, but in comparison to the majority in the private sector, whose wages are declining, they are getting richer. Also, I suspect that each time government sets up a new regulation that a new high-profit center is established. This means that not only is it a cost to be borne by labor, the owners and managers of a new businesses type will earn above-average incomes and profits, especially during the initial stages.

Because government is the problem, we need to examine government changes and effects. In 1992, the official federal, state, and local employment was 18.7 percent. Total government expenditures, the purchase of goods and services (not including transfer payments, such as Social Security) as a percent of currently computed GDP, was 18.2 percent in 1993. This includes everything that government buys, from battleships to table lamps. This figure is a misrepresentation of facts, because it does not include costs the private sector pays for regulation or costs that have been transferred to the private sector that were once borne by government. Any number thus derived from the use of GDP as a base is distorted. If we subtract government expenditures from GDP and use a *consumption based* GDP, taxes are nearer 50 percent of our purchases. The influence of government in all levels of commerce is massive when we consider governmental mandates (regulation, etc.) that require reallocations of the workforce to jobs that have little to do with historical productive work functions and the expansion of government-manipulated costs in industries such as law and insurance.[18] Whether preparing tax returns or preserving wild life, government impacts our living standards. It is incomprehensible why the economic community and Congress afford so little concern for the adjustment in the lives of the working people caused by government.

It is important to enumerate the government numbers to place its cost in proper perspective. There is no known data that would describe the actual share of the workforce that owe their jobs to government mandates; therefore, we will estimate that number. First, we derive a number in the workforce that provides goods and services to government. We will assume that when government purchases goods or services, the expenditure translates into compensation. If the taxes government raises equal 34 percent of PCE, we will assume 34 percent of the workforce was utilized. To the official numbers, we estimate a number that provide goods and services by performing tasks dictated by government, regulated industries, environmental compliance, social compliance, business reporting, and consumer disclosure. To allow for the private workers who rely on government compliance, regulation, etc., we again must fall to concoction. Let's say that two of six work directly to provide for government. Because the expenditures for private compliance is seriously more expensive and time consuming than the review process of government, it would not be unrealistic to say that 25 percent, or one of four, who remains owes his or her livelihood indirectly to the government. This estimate places total employment at about 50/50, government and private sector. This should include our litigiousness but may not cover the many tasks that have been transferred or created in the private sector that we now take for granted, such as paved roads in our subdivisions that were once government costs, or possibly pseudo-government operations, such as toll-road authorities, trade associations, and lobbyists.

With an approximate total of 120 million employed, 50 percent, or 60 million, would then provide for a population of 260 million. Each nongovernment-related private worker thus produces the food, shelter, transportation, joy, and happiness for 4.3 people. Despite the figure being a concoction, it is obvious that it is a number that has grown considerably in the eighty years since government represented less than 10 percent of gross domestic product and caused little indirect employment. As the percentage of the population that provides for us declines, the difficulty in improving efficiency to keep up will become harder and harder. Where efficiency doesn't make up for government growth, the private worker will be forced to accept less in compensation. Indeed in the 1980s and early '90s, businesses laid off millions in order to maintain profits. Workers were absorbed back into the workforce quickly but many were forced to accept less pay. If government was also striving to be efficient, it should have had similar layoffs. However, a major difference between government and private employment is the guaranteed status of compensation and jobs and the market forces that will release inefficient workers

18 Individual insurance coverage and business coverage are increased to compensate for payouts. If a jury hands out a billion-dollar award, insurance costs will be impacted by a much larger figure to compensate for profits, overhead, administration, and other possible awards from other businesses. A billion-dollar award could be magnified to, say, a $10 billion premium increase by the insurance companies, if the litigation is based on new regulation or is unique with the possibility of being repeated.

back into the workforce. Where private employee compensation can decrease, government employees are afforded inflation increases that effectively alter the distribution of consumption in their favor.

To look at this from a different perspective, let's assume the market basket of goods and services and the share that everyone gets is fixed at a point in time. The ever-changing condition of the market implies that this never occurs, but to describe how forces affect our living standard, we will assume it is fixed. To describe this point in time, we use a line on which everyone rests. The line represents our current living standards. Unless forces act upon this position, no one's living standard will change. We then put all those supported by government on one side and all the rest on the other. The forces acting on the market basket that would move the line can be summarized as follows:

1. Government and legal change and interpretation
2. Product changes, additions, and deletions
3. Innovation and efficiency
4. Changes caused by nature
5. Changes in population
6. War or actions of other countries

Most forces acting on living standards would fall into one of these categories. In a normal economy, the most critical are government, innovation, and efficiency. Product changes are important, but products are added and deleted each year, and net additions likely have more to do with the consumers' available spending.

The line below, then, represents everyone's standard of living (SOL). Not everyone has the same SOL; the line represents an average, like the one government occasionally calculates. The circle in the middle represents a point at which all those to the left are government-supported, and all those to the right are employees in the private sector not supported by government.

LINE OF EQUILIBRIUM

Government supported ----------------------0---------------------- Private sector

Now let us assume that government passes laws that place new demands on the labor force. An example might be a requirement to put scrubbers on all smokestacks or a law to provide additional welfare. People who once did other things would work on scrubbers, and those who could receive as much on welfare as they would working would opt not to work and take welfare. Some on welfare appear to have a lower living standard based on the money they receive, but they no longer need a car, baby-sitters, or work clothing; neither do they purchase these things in their communities anymore.

The market basket has changed. Fewer goods and services would be produced because fewer workers produce. Reaching in, we find that labor has shifted away from producing the items previously included in the basket. If all workers were willing to give up part of their living standard to match the reduced production, then all would share a reduced living standard. The line would go down but remain parallel to the previously described line. In this case, the circle representing the government-supported vs. private sector nongovernment-supported would shift to the right because of the added welfare recipients created by inflation.

In real life, not everyone makes an equal adjustment to changes in the market basket. In order to provide for the addition of government-sponsored consumers, while making up for the reduced production of goods and services, the market basket will have to be reapportioned. However, the change won't be equally distributed. Most taxes are not based on incomes, nor levied equally. Those whose living standard is affected will not reduce spending, while the rich, who may pay higher taxes, may not change real consumption at all. Some private sector workers, such as engineers who design solutions, may be able to demand higher incomes. Some communities that are on government's list to receive contract money may increase spending as funding is shifted away from other communities. In other communities, businesses might lose their share of sales into the market basket. Those on welfare might take jobs off the books to augment their incomes and actually add to productivity. Most government-sponsored recipients will get increases to offset any increased cost of living, so as to maintain their share of the market basket. Some businesses will benefit from the added costs mandated by government. For example, the costs to produce electricity will increase, and so will profits and dividends to stockholders, while consumers must sacrifice spending on other goods and services to pay utilities. If there is a new tax, even those who don't think they are paying the new tax will can lose earnings as an *unseen tax on wages*. Some would reduced spending, some would find ways to maintain spending by using savings or working additional jobs, and others, who benefited by the government changes, would attempt to increase their spending. Of course, if everyone got inflation adjustments, the problem would never be resolved. In other words, the situation gets complicated. A change in government spending may seem like a good idea at the time, but the next day, we or our neighbors will lose jobs and/or be forced to take less pay, not knowing a change perpetrated by government caused a reaction that indirectly impacted our jobs, our businesses, our lives. The big problem is that politicians and bureaucrats don't know that they are the cause either.

There will always be offsets from those who work harder (longer hours), who innovate, or who become more efficient. Others, however, might not have that opportunity and efficiency may be forced on us by the need to produce more so we can maintain our living standard. As the free-enterprise portion of the economy works to maintain production and our living standards, the demand for goods might increase because the new laws stimulate the economy of those who do benefit, the anticipated effects of demand-side economics. That new demand is more likely to cause inflation, and instead of efficiency giving workers higher incomes through lower costs, prices will stay the same or rise in relation to wages. With these variances, it is not hard to imagine that living standards for all the people do not change in a lockstep manner or that the reported percentage of poor people in the country never seems to change. If standards have moved up, it is an average movement and won't be reflected in every household. When change occurs, the line that represents equilibrium may be above or below the old line, but it does not remain parallel to the old line; as shown below, it will now slant. To get the proper slant, we would need to determine everyone's percentage increase or decrease, and chart the new values. The makeup of the slanted line would be mixed. Some private-sector employees will have wage and inflation guarantees, as do government employees, but unlike government employees, they will doubtless be subjected to wage loss at some point in time.

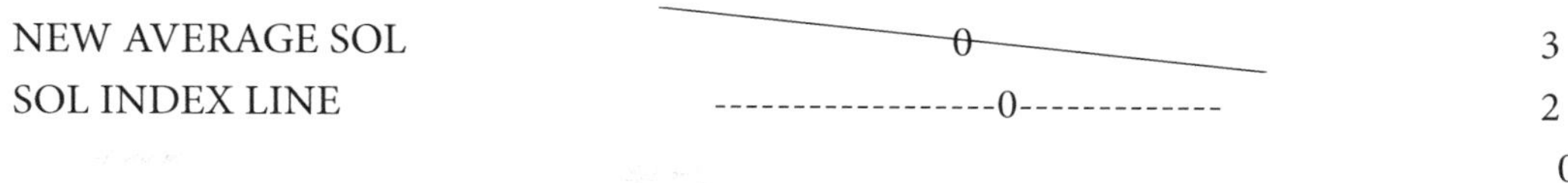

Most of those who are above the old SOL line will be beneficiaries of the new government spending or law. Some, who are not subsidized directly by the government and happen to be in the right place at the right time, will benefit from added demand for their goods and services. All those below the old SOL line would need to adjust their living standards or their lives. The placement of government-supported recipients on the line would be mixed. In the demonstration, the average living standard goes up, but it is more likely to go down. For many, an increase in living standard may be only temporary. Government spending that caused incomes to rise in a community stimulated by government spending can decline when projects are completed. The hue and cry for additional government spending then becomes a constant, and the strength that a politician has in Congress will play a big part as to whether such spending will be forthcoming. A possible government-induced economic cycling would appear to be a business cycle that is ostensibly a natural occurrence of capitalism.

A lower standard of living comes very hard to most people, and many will attempt to increase earnings to compensate by working harder. Failing that, they will use credit cards, bank loans, savings, and other means to maintain their lifestyle. Still others will find that a modern computer-based economy is making credit expansion difficult for those with less-than-impeccable credit records. Unless credit can be expanded to fill the gaps, there may not be alternatives to adjustment. Those without secondary resources are the ones who will be forced below the old SOL. (They are the ones for whom "SOL" will have a double meaning.) People who do push their living standards back toward the original line will bend or curve the line up. Those who used debt but could not make repayments will eventually fall even farther behind. Many will reduce their living standards, some seeking cheaper accommodations, some eliminating vacations, and many losing credit-worthiness. The hunt for cheaper goods and cheaper places to shop will intensify encouraging imports from low cost producers and having a further impact on domestic jobs and incomes. Home values will decline in relation to inflation as the number who can afford any particular size and quality will be fewer in number.

When people make the effort to compensate, a temporary boost in the economy is likely to occur. Demand-side economics will look as if it is working, but increasing the workers' hours, relying on credit, or digging into savings and even the union's COLA agreement are only temporary solutions. Sooner or later, unless efficiency catches up with economy, living standards will decline for most in the private sector.

Money in our demonstrations was not the final determinant of production and our resultant living standards; the availability of productive labor was/is the determining factor. Those who think that goods and services are created by money, rather than by workers, have the idea that government can tax the rich to pay its costs. However, at any point in time, the market basket is fixed, and if the rich refuse to reduce their living standard despite higher taxes, money will simply bid up the values of consumer goods and reduce investments as the rich defer investment money to maintain their purchase goods and services. Even if the rich reduce spending, there would be very little effect on the economy because there are so few rich, as compared to the rest of us.

The truly rich are more likely to reduce investments than consumer spending when their government obligations increase. When investments are reduced, investment returns will increase to attract and compensate for the shortage of capital and the additional costs of the government obligations.

Those with the most constant monetary supply get what they want. In other words, the rich aren't as apt to change, and it will be someone else who will have to pay more for less. The rich are much more likely to reduce investments or savings, with the result that money needed to expand production and meet new demands won't be there. If we assume the rich own the means of production, then they will actually benefit as prices are bid up to not only balance demand against supply but to add value to their existing assets, now made more expensive to replace.

Taxing the truly rich really doesn't mean they will pay for anything, including the tax.

The rich may write the checks to pay higher taxes, but the money will likely come from higher returns on their investments.

Having looked at some of the ways people are affected, the next step is to examine where and when they are affected and to reexamine some of the reasons why government is increasing spending. In a society of several thousand cities, towns, and counties, it is impossible to spread new government programs so that the positive and negative effects of a program on any one community are equal. Therefore:

The distribution of government spending will never be the same as the source nor is the expenditure likely to target the need.

Higher-income communities may suffer a fall in revenue and have no benefits. Lower-income communities may be required to make mandated expenditures without government subsidies. Because every community is different and the distribution, spending, and taxing is different, the effects upon the rich and poor in each community will be as varied as snowflakes.

In any particular community the possibilities for the impact of government spending to produce positive results will be less than the possibilities that government spending will create negative results.

To examine the timing for the negative impact of government spending, we first must examine the reason for the spending. The belief that new spending is good for the economy is translated by politicians as adding jobs or income for the poor. This concept does not consider the varied effects that the process of "tax and spend" has on individuals within society or of the hangover once spending ends. If the bureaucracy assumes that government spending provides a boost to the economy, obviously, additional manpower to perform the tasks will be required. If government spending augments welfare, potential workers are required not to work. Either way, less manpower is available to expand market-driven production. Can we get more from less? Apparently, the politicians think so. If we look at the unemployment line, we see thousands of job seekers, but if we select a particular job description, we may find not even one in the line who will match the skills required. Unemployment resulting from the inherent job diversity of a Complex society gives a confusing signal to politicians. The result is that politicians ultimately add to the unemployment problem by distorting the economy with constant changes in laws and the allocation of funds for varied projects intended to stimulate spending. These changes worsen employment searches for workers, who fail to match the job skills demanded in the workplace, or whose skills become useless when the political atmosphere or resultant spending changes or completes itself.

Inflation actuates interest-rate increases that bring about recessions. If the unemployment lines weren't empty before the economy inflated, why didn't businesses add workers to increase production? More sales, after all, beget more profits. The assumption is that bad economies are the result of a failure to spend, but for the last four decades, recessions have followed inflation, followed by higher interest rates and a forced "soft/hard landing." Simple logic guides us to infer that inflation is the result of not enough production to match dollars; ergo, not enough workers. The complex nature of the workforce makes a worker pool important to sustaining the economy. Likewise, it is important that less-skilled functions be performed by the less skilled, so that each individual can provide the highest level of service. Welfare reduces the pool of labor that supports skilled labor.

It is the job of government to find ways of releasing workers into the labor pool.

If government stimulated the economy to increase demand, did it work? If the economy inflated, was the money not there to add facilities to increase production, or was the manpower not there? Government efforts to increase production by reducing the labor force have more to do with inflation than production. Keynes may have believed that if we buried bottles of money for people to dig up that it would be good for the economy, but even Keynes believed this was only a last resort. Despite the obvious government growth in spending and regulation over the last several years, capitalism gets blamed for inflation, while government is commended for encouraging demand. The logic used by our politicians defies sensibility. If, however, labor is actually a limited commodity the explanation to this puzzle is at hand.

A Complex economy does not need stimulation.

If an economy adjusting to growth is allowed to do so naturally, without adding government demands for labor, then the damage to affected consumers can be minimized as they adjust and as enterprise becomes more innovative and efficient. If the government demands on the workforce grow so much that innovation, longer hours, and efficiency don't offset the demands for labor, then inflation will create a response from the Federal Reserve that will bring about the recession, which is the cause for an ever greater number of workers to be forced into lower living standard.

In a Complex economy, recessions impact occupations (a business category) or geographic areas, rather than an entire country. The exception is when growth in government exceeds the rate of efficiencies in the economy for long enough that a serious and sudden redistribution of consumption must occur.

In the final analysis, as an economy falls into recession or when the impact of government reduces production, the effect falls on those whose incomes are not guaranteed. These workers are forced to a lower living standard when there are fewer hours or they are forced to accept lower wages. This, of course, means that still fewer goods and services are available to consume, not merely that real income has declined. And while those who are guaranteed their incomes receive the same amount of goods and services, those that are not protected receive a reduced share. This distinction is important; it brings into focus the change in demand for labor that occurs when government grows. During recessions, we find it difficult to grasp that the cause of a recession was a contraction in the productive labor supply that created goods and services. Such thinking seems logical only when one follows the chain of events:

Step 1. Government placed demands on the labor pool, reducing the available productive labor and increasing demands for goods and services.

Step 2. Demand increased beyond supply because labor was not available to produce, and inflation occurred. New production was not justified by the higher prices because the cost of new facilities went up.

Step 3. The Federal Reserve increases interest rates to slow inflation in the economy, causing layoffs in interest-sensitive areas.

Step 4. If inflation continued, in order to force consumers to adjust their living standards, the Federal Reserve raised rates until a recession occurred.

It is important to understand that the stimulus that isn't productive and intended to increase living standards can and will cause an overall downward adjustment in living standards, unless innovation and efficiencies overcome the cost to the productive labor pool.

If stimulus is provided during a recession, as Keynes suggested, the added demand might help portions of the economy. Attempting to apportion the stimulus, however, so as to distribute it to the areas in need is impossible. Timing, as well, is difficult. Stimulus added when the economy slows and terminated when growth in the economy ensues would, in the politicians' mind, leave those who received the work without jobs. Therefore, the only "fair" stimulus is to increase welfare. This, however, is government expansion that once granted is never recanted. And stimulus impairs the reformation of the workforce that would enhance production. Rather than the economy's being stimulated, the next economic boom is restrained by the availability of manpower, and the stage is set for the next round of inflation. For government to provide a proper stimulus, politicians would have to anticipate recessions in order to plan for them, and therefore would need to know what caused them. Unfortunately, it isn't reasonable to think that politicians will admit that government expansionism causes recessions.

To demonstrate the effects that government growth and the resultant allocations of labor have on a potential increase in living standards, the following chart demonstrates the possible changes in the ratio of nongovernment to government workers. At varying ratios, starting with a high nongovernment-to-government ratio, the decrease in producers as a percent is calculated. Then the increase in productivity needed to maintain living standards is calculated.

TABLE OF PRODUCTIVITY CHANGE NECESSITATED BY CHANGES IN THE RATIO OF GOVERNMENT WORKERS TO PRIVATE WORKERS			
			NEEDED
WORKER	% GOVT.	PRODUCTION	% PROD.
RATIO	INCREASE	DECLINE %	INCREASE
19/1			
18/2	100.00%	5.20%	5.50%
17/3	50.00%	5.50%	5.80%
16/4	33.30%	5.80%	6.25%
15/5	25.00%	6.25%	6.67%
14/6	20.00%	6.67%	7.10%
13/7	16.70%	7.10%	7.60%
12/8	14.30%	7.60%	8.33%
11/9	12.50%	8.33%	9.09%
10/10	11.10%	9.09%	10.00%
9/11	10.00%	10.00%	11.00%
8/12	9.10%	11.00%	12.50%
7/13	8.30%	12.50%	14.29%
6/14	7.70%	14.29%	16.67%
5/15	7.20%	16.67%	20.00%
4/16	6.70%	20.00%	25.00%

As demonstrated visually above, the difficulty in maintaining living standards progresses with the size of government in relation to productive workers, even though the percentage increase in government declines. Where a 50 percent increase in government at a 17–3 ratio required only a 5.8 percent productivity advance, a 10 percent increase at a lower ratio required an 11 percent increase. Numbers are nondiscriminatory and do not differentiate between direct or indirect government labor. Because indirect government-necessitated labor cannot be assimilated, information is not available to match this schedule with representative years. There is no doubt that the ratios have changed, and the workforce available to the producing portion of the economy has declined. It also becomes obvious why government tax and regulation increases in the 1970s resulted in such high inflation. The disruptions to the economy during that period were greater and occurred over a relatively brief time frame, which didn't allow much time for the efficiencies to offset government control. Much of the growth during that period was transferred to the free-market sector in the form of laws requiring environmental cleanup and utility plant modifications. Payments to the poor and retirement payments were also increased at a rate designed to exceed inflation. If that the ratio changed from say 15–5 to about 12–8, a 25 percent increase in productivity would be needed, just to stay even.

As the working ratio has changed, so, too, has the ratio of the population that provides goods and services. The chart below displays how a change in the population production rate necessitates an increase in productivity. The cumulative increases reflected would seem almost implausible, but in the beginning stages of economy development, going into the Transitional stage from farm to factory, there would have been tremendous increases in productivity. As with the working ratio, a change in the ratio of the population that provides goods and services changes similarly. Maintaining living standards becomes increasing difficult, especially when the ratio of the population that works declines below 50–50. For example, a drop of only 1 percent when the ratio is 20–80 requires a 5 percent increase in efficiency.

TABLE OF PRODUCTIVITY CHANGE NECESSITATED BY CHANGES IN THE RATIO OF PRODUCING POPULATION TO NONPRODUCING POPULATION				
PRODUCING TO NONPRODUCING POPULATION	DECLINE IN PRODUCING POPULATION	NEEDED % TO MAINTAIN SOL	CUMULATIVE INCREASE	CUMULATIVE ASSUMING 5% SOL GROWTH
90/10				
80/20	11.1%	12.5%	12.5%	18.1%
70/30	12.5%	14.3%	28.6%	41.9%
60/40	14.2%	16.7%	50.0%	73.5%
50/50	16.7%	20.0%	80.0%	118.9%
40/60	20.0%	25.0%	125.0%	187.3%
30/70	25.0%	33.3%	200.0%	302.0%
20/80	33.3%	50.0%	350.0%	533.8%
10/90	50.0%	100.0%	800.0%	1229.4%

Certainly, the trend over the last hundred years has been to reduce the total productive working population. When work was mostly farming, we can assume that tasks handled by the entire family included many performed by private enterprise today, such as canning. The trend in the last thirty-five years reversed, as women entered the workforce to supplement family income, thereby adding to the population work participation rate. In fact, the population work participation rate has gone up from about 59 percent to over 66 percent. Conversely, because welfare competes with jobs, we should expect the percentage of the population that provides for us to decline. What has hidden the impact of welfare is the increase of women in the workforce. If we look at the figures closely, we find that employment among the available female population increased between 1960 and 1993, by 52 percent, from 37.7 to 57.9 percent. Male employment has actually declined 9 percent, from 83.3 to 75.2 percent. These are results we would expect if whole families dropped out of the workforce to access welfare, and fathers worked off the books to ensure welfare payments, while other families became two-earner families to sustain living standards. It is not a surprise that much of the decline in male participation, from 83.3 to 77.9, occurred between 1960 through 1975, when welfare was enhanced by implementation of the Great Society.

The addition of women in the workforce will also not reflect a true one-on-one addition to productivity. The work of nonworking mothers in society is not considered in gross domestic product, but additional purchases by working mothers of goods and services for family and themselves is considered. In other words, nonworking mothers contribute to the economy by preparing food at home, maintaining the house, washing clothes, etc. When they begin buying meals outside the home, hiring housekeepers, or sending laundry out, their addition in productivity must be netted against the new goods and services they require as workers. Many families take this fact into consideration when decisions such as this are being made, but government does not. One can be quickly apprised of the contribution of a nonworking spouse by simply suggesting to such a spouse that she doesn't work. A wise husband will always answer yes to any questionnaire that asks whether the spouse works.

They also serve who stay at home.

The male worker participation rates of the period from 1960 to 1993 have been exacerbated, as welfare increases that attract labor were coupled with the following:

A. Efficiency deficiencies to offset reallocations of labor held back income growth for the private worker and raised the value of inflation-adjusted welfare.

B. Concerns for integration put emphasis on hiring minorities but degraded the benefits of job training at minimum wage. Males could have been repelled by minimum-wage job entry that would have eventually lifted them into higher-valued jobs.

C. The demands to equalize female and male employment opportunities emphasized female hiring and education.

D. The growth in payroll expenses discouraged traditional male quests for small-business ownership and expansion.

E. Welfare augmentation has a devastating effect on communities when welfare payments discourage work activity. As businesses close for lack of workers, jobs move farther away from welfare communities.

F. It is very likely that "working under the table" has become commonplace.

We should not be surprised that as women were drawn away from families and into the workforce, and males found the economic environment ever more difficult, that divorce rates escalated. Families facing financial predicaments are more prone to lose the marital bliss that binds them together. It is especially frustrating for a society that was brought up to believe that good jobs were there and that they simply needed to be pursued. While parents in mature job positions with homes that are paid for or partially paid for were realizing inflation-enhanced gains in living standards, new entrants struggled and home purchases became more difficult while apartment rates inclined. The insight that many parents might provide would have no application in the new economic environment. Having moved from a time when jobs that could support a household were abundant to an age when jobs were plentiful but remuneration was not; this would have been difficult for parents to understand. These circumstances offer some explanation as to why the average male lives at home for more years than did his father.

Perhaps if helping the truly poor and improving the environment were the only changes occurring, free enterprise might keep up. But payments not to work, providing useless pork-barrel jobs, unrealistic attempts to redistribute wealth, and the serious effects of cost-of-living adjustments, place too large a burden on the private unprotected worker. A government intent on fairness failed to distribute the added government costs equally, as politicians legislated more equality for some than others. The wealth of a nation cannot be spent; wealth may change in value but unless we destroy it, "it" is always there. The only way politicians and their economists have to raise incomes is to eliminate the competition for an industry or occupation, but then only that industry or occupation would be affected. In other words, politicians can only pass laws that guarantee jobs, COLAs, and income enhancements that don't relate to job performance and which decrease overall economic efficiency. Many politicians believe employees outside government should have guarantees, and they have passed laws to slow layoffs or guarantee benefits. Fortunately, most politicians have given little more than lip service to nongovernmental job guarantees. Fortunate, not because the private worker is not given protection but because the consequences would be inflation that only augments government incomes and places a greater strain on the private worker.

The best job guarantee is a healthy. uninhibited economy.

Having found redistribution impossible, politicians have turned to welfare and pensions to appease their personal egos and appetites for distributing the taxpayer dollars. The attempt to average incomes in the interest of fairness destroys typical incentives for work, and rather than affecting the rich, the cost falls on workers whose harvest is divided in such a way that they retain only what is left by those with guaranteed positions. The result is a bureaucracy that justifies inefficiency in the belief that undeserved paychecks provide work for other members in the community. Many of the goals for clean air, integration, animal protection, etc., were accomplished as a result of laws enacted that mandated private actions and government waste. Unfortunately, the system duplicated efforts in both private and public employment, and the punishments prescribed in the extraordinary legal settlements are yet another load for the private worker.

For business and the rich, legislated failures become a business cost on which an income must be earned. Wealth, thus determined by capitalizing income, increases because of government spending and in spite of high tax collections from the rich. Politicians therefore sustain and consolidate the wealth and income of the rich through their desire to distribute that very wealth.

To demonstrate how redistribution affects the distribution of consumption, the following charts illustrate what happens to the standard of living (SOL) if free enterprise fails to keep up with government growth or how the gain might be divided. Changes represented in these charts can occur over several years or, for the unprotected private worker, in the sudden transformation of his own depression.

Let's assume that the private worker fails annually to achieve the efficiency to maintain the standard of living (SOL), first by 10 percent and then 20 percent. What then would be the decline in SOL over twenty-five years?

Whereas the capitalist system is intended to improve the lives of the population, growth in wasted government spending can significantly reduce our living standards. In the below example a 3/1000 shortage in annual efficiency growth, when government spending increases by an inflation adjusted rate of 3 percent annually, reduces our living standards by 8 percent over twenty-five years. When the shortfall is a mere 6/1000, the shortfall is over 16 percent.

NEEDED EFFICIENCY	ACTUAL EFFICIENCY	STANDARD OF LIVING	STANDARD OF LIVING
INCREASE	INCREASE	LOSS PER YEAR	LOSS AFTER 25 YEARS
	10% SHORT		
1%	0.9%	0.1%	2.53%
2%	1.8%	0.2%	5.12%
3%	2.7%	0.3%	7.78%
4%	3.6%	0.4%	10.50%
5%	4.5%	0.5%	13.28%
6%	5.4%	0.6%	16.13%
	20% SHORT		
1%	0.8%	0.2%	5.12%
2%	1.6%	0.4%	10.50%
3%	2.4%	0.6%	16.13%
4%	3.2%	0.8%	22.04%
5%	4.0%	1.0%	28.24%
6%	4.8%	1.2%	34.75%

In the next chart, we assume that 50 percent of the population is guaranteed its living standard and that when the private worker fails to maintain efficiency, inflation results, which triggers income increases for only the protected population. How much would the living standard decline for the unprotected population over twenty-five years? With only 50 percent of the population absorbing the cost, the above figures double and minor shortfalls become significant.

NEEDED EFFICIENCY	ACTUAL EFFICIENCY	LOSS IN STANDARD OF	STANDARD OF LIVING
INCREASE	INCREASE	LIVING PER YEAR	LOSS AFTER 25 YEARS
	10% SHORT		
1%	0.9%	0.1%	5.06%
2%	1.8%	0.2%	10.24%
3%	2.7%	0.3%	15.55%
4%	3.6%	0.4%	20.99%
5%	4.5%	0.5%	26.56%
6%	5.4%	0.6%	32.26%
	20% SHORT		
1%	0.8%	0.2%	10.24%
2%	1.6%	0.4%	20.99%
3%	2.4%	0.6%	32.26%
4%	3.2%	0.8%	44.09%
5%	4.0%	1.0%	56.49%
6%	4.8%	1.2%	69.49%

This second dramatization displays significant declines in the living standards with only nominal shortfalls in efficiency. One-tenth of one percentage point in a situation where 50 percent of the population shares the shortfall over twenty-five years seems a negligible 5 percent. Because many private workers are protected by inflation adjustments, the entire shortage in efficiency could impact significantly less than 50 percent of the population. In that instance, one-tenth of a percentage point over twenty-five years could translate into severe consequences for small percentages of affected unprotected workers.

In our real world, we have different circumstances that may be much more serious:

A. In the last twenty-five years, government has grown by 3.5 percent annually.

B. The share of workers performing traditional work duties may have declined by over 2 percent, annually.

C. An aging government-employee population receives pay raises that include inflation, longevity of service, and enhancements.

D. An aging baby-boomer population is looking forward to retirement when the ratio of working to nonworking population will change significantly.

E. The advance in productivity in the period since the early '80s has involved a nearly complete reorganization of U.S. industry. This followed a period of high inflation, union labor restrictions, and pent-up efficiencies. It is not as likely that another period of adaptation can follow.

F. The acceptance of the U.S. dollar in the world economy during a period of evolving democracy and capitalism could continue, or it may not. At nearly full employment, it is dubious that U.S. manufacturing does not have the manpower to supplement the shortage in goods and services the foreign trade deficit represents.

If the above strains on the economy result in a deficiency of efficiency of even half a percent annually, the working population would lose one-fourth to nearly one-half of its living standard over 25 years. Such an occurrence might be preceded by inflation and/or serious economic disturbances. In reality, even minor or no inflation can hide the downward pressure on wages as the millions of businesses adjust to higher government costs and taxes. The capitalist system will make what adjustments are needed to sustain itself. Some manufacturers selling to the manufactures of consumer goods are required by contract to reduce the price of products each year. More consequential would be that the political arena would condemn capitalism for the difficulties forged by a government that failed to understand its own system of enterprise.

Even if free enterprise were to keep up, the gap between wages paid in the private sector and those paid by government would widen due to the guaranteed COLA provisions and wage scaling that pushes wages up without reference to productivity increases. In private enterprise, new entrants are being hired at wage scales that are less than those of their predecessors. In the airline industry, for example, unions negotiated lower rates for new entrants and kept old members at higher rates. New workforce entrants in all industries will be settling for less to compensate for efficiency deficits. As welfare payments rise to compensate for inflation, levels of payment will meet the wages of a private workforce, whose income is on the way down.

With a multitude of forces acting on the economy, the force with the most significant impact on efficiency will continue to be redistribution. As a basic theory behind socialism and communism, redistributionists focus on existing resources and ignore the process that created those resources. To the Socialists, providing jobs for an expanding population is a problem. For capitalism, population expansions are opportunities. In socialism and communism, systems jobs are, in fact, mandatory, and government is obligated to provide them. Stimulating the economy is the politicians answer to this problem.

Despite living in the free-enterprise capital of the world, our politicians see their economies through the eyes of Socialists. When not speaking of themselves, politicians speak about more food (chicken in every pot), health, and housing. Politicians are talking of the only human necessities a Socialist deems important.

Socialists define their intention as redistributing wealth and incomes, not creating production. But it is necessary for another system to have been in place to form that wealth.

The hypocrisy of the Socialist's ideology is that socialism can only exist in a parasitic relationship with a successful system, yet socialism does not define any other system as beneficial.

The advocacy of a fair distribution leads to central planning and the ultimate control of the economy by government. Since free enterprise cannot flourish in a controlled economy, it is doomed by the advent of Socialism. Failure of free enterprise would lead to a system that doesn't form wealth because without incentives, central planning lacks any control of the economy. Without a system to build, society would decay, leading to anarchy or totalitarianism.

If government ceases to grow, then conversely, the labor available to free enterprise would grow and with it the unprotected workers' incomes. If government functions were reduced, eliminated, or made efficient, government would reduce the demand on the labor supply. The effort needed by the balance of the community to support government would decline, and living standards could grow. Because government is the greatest cause of inflation, inflation could be eliminated. Without inflation, living-standard growth could be an enticement for those on welfare to join productive forces.

In the purest form of free enterprise, the individual decides how to allocate spending and therefore, has power over the system. Individual choice is the basic difference between free enterprise and all other systems. The monarchies that have been abandoned are not much different than Communist systems; even a monarch has a ruling court, made up of preordained representatives. The economy is controlled with a few making decisions for the many. Only capitalism caters to the freedom of individual choice and to life by the rule of one's own thoughts.

It seems as if many long for a benevolent king to rule, perhaps because there has as yet been an acceptable explanation for the individual's struggle in the face of astonishing inventions and government interventions. But benevolent kings are found only in fairy tales and the explanations so far are political rhetoric, philosophical babbling, socialist elitism, and capitalist arrogance. No true mathematically based and scientifically provable path to economic growth and a higher standard of living has as yet been employed. The explanations against government spending have not as yet been sufficient to convince either politicians or the general public. The solutions exist to the problems that face us. Government, no matter how kind, cannot give us more than we already have without taking something away from someone else. Government cannot give; government can only take. Humankind's progress occurred only when independence gave us the right to live freely, to do as we wish each day, and to benefit or suffer the consequences. Governments of all kinds have attempted to provide for humankind for over three thousand years, while free humankind has provided its own needs for little over three hundred years. What government accomplished in the three thousand years could be explained in a science class in one afternoon. To explain the accomplishments of free humankind would take a thousand lives a thousand years. We should each day be reminded to "dance with the one that brought us."

CHAPTER 18

THE NEWS MEDIA—AN IMPORTANT AND NECESSARY PART OF FREE ENTERPRISE

The existence of the voluminous media dialog that is now available to the public suggests that it is appropriate to question the means used to mold opinion regarding the governance of this United States of America. We live in a world where the intricacies of medicine, science, and physics have taken us into a stratum not imagined in the 1960s. Yet the decisions that are made today are often derived from the personal opinions we find in tabloids and provided by individuals who have not a modicum of the knowledge in the businesses on which they are commenting. Instead of the knowledge of the elite of our social order being disbursed to inspire our judgment, we form our opinions from media science, media justice, media politics, and media medicine and are subject to media economic management of our country. Is it the people who decide or the media who decide what the people should decide? Democracy is the governance by *all* the people to determine and define their own limits for individual actions. The rules would need to be written by free people whose opinions are formed with 100 percent of the facts and a free opportunity to debate.

Free enterprise functions as a true democracy wherein self-interest is a requirement rather than a limitation. Self-interest, after all, even when philanthropic, is the gratification of self. Through this democratic process, all members manifest their desires in their actions and spending. This decision-making power imbues individuals with the capacity to correct and change the system to their own liking. Should individual actions cause injustice or harm, or should the system fail to correct itself, the media has the province to find and advise the populace of any problems. Elected representatives, who must interpret the will and the needs of the people, are likewise dependent upon the media for information and confirmation.

The media and politicians often speak of the wisdom of the people and how we can rely on that wisdom and judgment. However, at times it appears that society's judgment fails. Having pondered this, and at first being cynical of the effectiveness of this democratic process, it becomes clear that the population functions no differently than a computer. As with computers, whether the responses are syllogistic, factual, or pertinent is dependent on the properties of the derivative material. In other words, if we put garbage in, we get garbage out.

The forum for free enterprise and its government is the media; without the media, freedom cannot exist. To paraphrase what Thomas Jefferson said, I would prefer a free press and no government to a government and no free press. Horace Greeley wrote, "Then hail to the press! Chosen guardian of freedom! Strong sword-arm of justice! Bright sunbeam of truth." In order to make decisions, the people and politicians must have information that is unbiased, truthful, and representative of relevant, logical, and substantiated views. Our knowledge is the result of our background, our education, a good dose of common sense, and most important, the respected, dominant media. But who judges the media? Too often this forum fosters knowledge from information that is only a half-truth or not truth at all, and half a truth is no different than a whole lie. It has become acceptable to present facts in any manner to support contrived views. The colloquial directive is, "If you cannot dazzle them with brilliance, baffle them with BS." It is the media is charged to separate facts from fiction, but too often, the media takes a position intended baffle us so as to authenticate their doctrine, not to inform us of the facts.

Individuals from a major media source once used explosives to fabricate an explosion that was supposed to have happened spontaneously when a particular make of truck was hit in the side by another vehicle. Rather than a resounding denunciation, the fabrication was given only minor attention by the majority of the "competing" media, and no criminal charges were ever brought. This was a fraud perpetrated on the viewers with the intention to deceive and for the express purpose of monetary gain and public acclaim. The media avoided the consequences of its dereliction by virtue of its importance to the community. Politicians and businesses rely on the media to promote their causes. Thus, the fear of retaliation is a shield, as each media capitalist protects the other's backside. The event and the response of the alternate media is an example of current biased presentations. In its failure to clean its own house, the media is corrupting our minds, our system, and the guardian of free enterprise, the media itself.

Media owners and employees have the same self-interest and profit motive that free enterprise encourages, but they have an obligation. The media has a unique covenant with the citizens to provide information in such a manner that its view can be justifiable, well defined, and truthful. The media is to report injustices in the market system and to act as a watchdog of the political process. It has never been totally unbiased, but we have always relied on its fairness and the competition inside its ranks. Today, many within the media have assumed an omnipotent mentality. They have decided that people are not capable of making correct decisions and are imposing their own agenda. There is even a term to explain it; they call it "lying for justice." Protected by the Constitution, the media uses its power and has little responsibility for the damage to human existence. The media should not start a riot and then have media pundits declare that they are not responsible for the cities burning.

Rather than an obvious breach of confidence, the media generally promotes doctrine by presenting half-truths. The people in the media act as though everyone has an axe to grind, and the media merely levels the stone. But they judge who is to grind, and who is not. They claim to be simply reporting the news. But the media presents their views to influence people and justify distortions as "necessary" to deal with a corrupt society. Thus, they condone their and society's corruption, while misusing a special position of trust.

Unfortunately, belief in a corrupt society is a self-fulfilling prophesy. If corruption is accepted as normal, corruption will be common. If we act unethically, we will gather those around us who, like us, are fraudulent and deceitful or naive and oblivious to events. The end is a distorted view of reality. As with incestuous breeding, the offspring of ideas may be distorted and moronic. The overzealous bias usually displayed by the media has encouraged the same half-truths in politically correct candidates. Being judged politically correct by the media entitles public figures to placement on a pedestal, despite standards that are not as high as others who are not so consecrated or ordained. As the holy ones, these candidates have no obligation for honest campaigning. Only the meaning of the day is a concern, only that which sounded good when it was said.

The media's attitude toward integrity was probably best exhibited by a New York writer in early 1996. A journalist defending the faults of an important politician commented that the politician had lied, but he explained that all politicians lie. With the bacon, he explained, we are going to get some grease. The journalist characterized the politician and the current moral inclination of certain in the media. Greasy politicians have thus become acceptable through what can only be described as greasy journalism. Rather than plucking out the bad apple, the whole barrel of apples is allowed to rot. Were Lincoln, Roosevelt, and Kennedy likewise bacon?

The news media, with a conscious desire to influence the population, is encouraging the breakdown of integrity, honesty, and morality in politicians and the citizenry. The dominant media influences our votes by seeking and publishing points of view that are contradictory to better evidence, that come from undisclosed or prejudiced sources, that are intended to corrupt existing beliefs, that are given at appropriate times to influence the election or cover up a deceit, and that are published without question as "what has been reported" or "has been said." Honest candidates with good integrity are forced to play on uneven ground, while politically correct, media-advocated campaigners are supported for their perceived good intention. The media legitimizes the con artists, as democracy is deserted for special-interests groups who are observed as having unquestioned honesty and integrity, neither of which they may have. If integrity is not important, it will not prevail, and lying for justice will become acceptable honesty. The media has become a semblance of the spoof created by Gilda Radner, who in a Saturday Night Live spoof would espouse an altogether ridicules position and when corrected would simply say never mind.

Elected representatives have made statements that were described after election as meaningless and "only campaign rhetoric." The media has accepted this explanation as just politics and exonerated politicians of the fault for the falsehood they've used to get elected. The implication is that a candidate's promises before the election are unrelated to the office after. Yet in an incident when another president broke a single promise to the people of the United States by allowing a tax increase, the media hounded the president for the decision from then until defeat in the next election. The media made no mention of a "reported" deceitful promise made by the leader of the politically correct Congress to reduce spending in exchange for passage of the same tax increase. The media and the politically correct party apparently believe that deceit is necessitated to assure their definition of justice. It would follow that if deceit is a tool of justice, justice can only be deceitful. The media today seems more in sync with what Sir Henry Wotton said in the seventeenth century: "An ambassador is a man of virtue sent to lie abroad for his country; a news writer is a man without virtue who lies at home for himself."

The news media needs to at least hold itself accountable for opinions expressed and any presentation of half-truths. Biased political reporting may someday be a factor in the downfall or disabling of a functional two-party system. As a reminder that history, indeed, repeats itself, Dr. John Arbuthnot, over 250 years ago, said: "All political parties die at last of swallowing their own lies."[19] A media intent on deceit is a powerful force in influencing the voting population. Common sense and an economy that cannot perpetuate the Ponzi scheme with which it now functions may eventually result in collapse of the politically correct party or the reverse, an enabling of that party to summon totalitarianism from the ashes of the destruction it created. Unfortunately, even if Congress comes under the tutelage of a more enlightened Congress before corrections are made, the party newly in control could get blamed for a fall. As with ancient civilizations, the messenger carrying truthful but unhappy news might be the one destroyed. The media will be responsible for the abrogation of the good achieved by a two-party system, unless whole truths are exposed.

The printing press and paper are responsible for the proliferation of freedom and formation of the United States. *Common Sense*, written by Thomas Paine, informed our early countrymen of the commonality of their interests and the benefits of freedom. It and other writings advocating the independence of the United States were responsible for the formation of our country. The news media as the watchdog of freedom perpetuates its existence. We are reminded of the power of the media by observing totalitarian societies, wherein they recognize the danger a free press represents. Despite

19 Dr. John Arbuthnot (quoted in *Garnett, Life of Emerson*). *The Pocket Book of Quotations*

the freedom it has brought us and the freedom it helps to preserve, the old adage warns us to believe nothing of what we read and only half of what we see. Still, people are basically trustful. The question that arises is whether the news media is now deserving of this trust. News people display a concern for their autonomy and act as if business represents a special interest that would cause them to sacrifice their independence. They ridicule business and profits, but because we can't feed our families with the gratitude of our friends and neighbors, profits and salaries have proved a necessity.

The media exists, as do all businesses in a system of free enterprise; it has self-interest and profits by selling advertisements to pay often high-salary troubadours. Similarly, wage earners profit by being profitable for their business. Simply put, people who control the media reflect their beliefs in the news they report and can report in the interest of personal gain. In supposed contrast, public radio boasts its lack of advertising and its independence, but it spends enormous amounts of time asking for donations. These donations needed to fund salaries are from contributors who also have a self-interest. Lack of a profit motive in public radio allows it to program anything chosen by its operators, whether profitable or not. But who are the operators? Do they who operate public programs not have their own interest and, therefore, their own agenda? If Congress provided the funding for these public programs, isn't control effectively placed in the hands of the party in power? Government control of the media has always been considered as placing restrictions on freedom. Under totalitarian government, the reason why and by whom the media is controlled is obvious. It should be obvious that everyone does, indeed, have an agenda or an axe to grind. The free press and those in it have the same motives as everyone else, with income and job preservation at the top of the list.

At a time that deception in advertising and labeling is under attack, the media has failed to perceive its own agenda and to control its own deception. Competition in the media once meant getting the correct facts—a sacred oath from those whom we learned to trust. Political positions and the lack of independence by media agents have undone the purification that competition brings. This view, though cynical, gives insight to the concept of self-interest and the importance of competition to make quality a self-interest. The view focuses on the importance the whole truth bears to those who truly wish to be independent. The reality is that to be truly independent, one must be independent of oneself.

The greatest influence in the system of free enterprise will always be free enterprise itself, as free enterprise allows only those who are profitable to survive. Despite our own idealistic emotions toward the media, like all other businesses, it is a profit-motivated economic segment that attempts to inform and excite us for economic gain. Influencing and controlling attitudes of the populace help the media and its operators to sustain their livelihood. The ability to seek the truth, as the media is intended to do, can thus be as tyrannical as a corrupted government would have them.

Over the history of our country, the media has sided with one faction or the other: bull or bear, labor or management, war or peace, righteous or corrupt. In recent years, the dominant media has sided with factions described as liberals, who are sometimes referred to as socialists. Conservatism, by definition, implies that the status quo is to be accepted. But the status quo cannot easily be accepted in an age when workers are hoping new answers will resolve their economic difficulties. Conservatism, by its very name, seems boring, and it is excitement, not truth, that sells newspapers and TV time. What sells newspapers and media time is rape, murder, injustice, mistreatment of the poor, the handicapped, the indigent, the old, and don't forget the evil businessman.[20] It is the strange, not the truth, in the *Enquirer* that makes that publication so profitable.

In the first 150 years of U.S. history, there was excitement to report in New World exploration, new machines, new achievements, and Old World wars. This changed with the advent of TV, wherein the horror of war could be visualized in a way never before seen. As new achievements became common, war became real, devastating, horrid, and more then just the soldiers' bad memories. When

20 Gender intended.

wars ended, the media brought us other pain—the pain of prejudice, animal mistreatment, bad air, bad earth, and reports of bad foods. Good has come from this, as the populace has been outraged by what it sees. The rivers no longer burn, wild animals are safeguarded, the air is becoming clear, and the words "all men are created equal" mean all people should be treated equal.

But the media are in constant need of new frontiers to report. In the endeavor to sell space and excite the readers and the viewers, the whole truth was not sufficient. Abstract attitudes representing even miniscule positions have become front-page reading. The media profits by the half of the truth that sells the best. The media haven't always been devious, but today's market seems ruled by cynics who are willing to report fabrications and half-truths through stooges who are incapable of understanding what they report. Lying for justice is the same as "the means justifies the end," never minding if the end is justified. Noble views are tainted with the need for survival. As in any trade, keeping one's job is important to support one's way of life. Capitalism rewards those who do the best job of selling, whether the truth be sold or not.

The difficulty in finding stories that excite people is reflected in the tedious attention given to crusades of little importance or in asking politically incorrect politicians the same boring questions over and over. The media look for a story and if one is not available, they create one and stick with it until the next one comes along. Like a good quarter horse, the media assemble the herd while constantly culling individual members for the glue factory, proclaiming it only reports the news. Too often, the opinions advocated mean nothing to the media. Like the old joke about the accountant who got the job when asked what two plus two equaled, and he replied, "What do you want it to be?" Like kids in a school debate, they argue their position to win an award. The U.S. economy, however, is not school. Disagreement on basic principles is no excuse to forget logic and reason. That one source of truism, the media, is failing in its responsibility to present views on a fair and equitable basis, and retractions are still reported on the last page. Members of the media create a crisis to earn their daily bread, acting as the court jester, hawking ridiculous positions, and when critiqued, retorting with, "Who me? I just report the news." The media hides their beliefs in supposedly objective reporting and justify themselves only when necessary.

Too often, reporters ask questions to correspond with a story already written, a perspective already taken, an opinion already made. TV uses its limited time to present cases and encourages the bedeviling of a single individual or topic. TV must arouse its audience in thirty seconds or fewer, so presenting one side of the story is timely and profitable. The competitive forces of free enterprise only maintain the side that keeps viewers interested. The media, therefore, create, use, and encourage clichés such as "grid lock," "voodoo economics," and "mean-spirited" to attract viewer attention and simplify their jobs. In the thirty seconds afforded to a newsperson on TV, a hackneyed platitude sells better and quicker and requires less intelligence than pursuing explanations and fostering an intellectual debate. The result is to stifle new ideas, logic, and truth, and the resultant solutions that follow.

Media misuses the issues to provide themselves with substance for their mill. It was back in the '60s when black Americans began their final movement for freedom; the black/white bathrooms and most problems of racism are gone. Everyone profits, as all races can now rise to their highest potential. And those who are newest to the economic pyramid are apt to set the high standards we must all then strive to achieve. Free enterprise was not the enemy; rather it assisted this movement in its own interest.

But the media continues to use its power to create racial disturbance and to direct much of its fury at the system formed by freedom by seeking to make even our thoughts into crimes. It is farcical to assume that all race prejudice or hate can be legislated out of existence, or that racism will abate with peer pressure. Have Jews and Muslins put aside emotions after two thousand years? It is miraculous that the U.S., with every race, creed, or orientation in life, has moved this close to melding. Brothers, sisters, mothers, and fathers have exchanged bitter words, offended one another with inappropriate comments. The media demand rules of conduct beyond the concerns of prejudice between races that we can't equal in our families. The media stir the pot, keep it boiling for its own benefit, making sure that it can profit from race when the other news dies down.

Nearly every race, class, religions orientation or ethnic distinction has come to America and been subjected to prejudice. Even Europeans didn't get along. Chinese, Jew, Catholic, Japanese, French, Irish, Arab, and African have all held and been subject to prejudices and hate.

The media should at times report progress to encourage more progress, rather than the hate to encourage more hate. Black Americans should not be afraid of leaving their neighborhoods, nor assume that prejudice reduces the potential for equality in the job market because the media suggests rampant racism. Whites, lacking knowledge of the politically correct--- vocabulary, should not fear communicating with their neighbor of a different color. The media uses intolerance, hate, and offensive tactics on anyone the media decides does not express correct racial views. Where is it written that we should love one another or listen with an open mind only if politically correct? Politically correctness divides the people in no different a way then Amy Vanderbilt's *Complete Book of Etiquette* could be used to distinguish those who wanted to separate themselves as a class. Though her concepts are intended to encourage courtesy and understanding, those who are ignorant of kindness and love use it to define their own inappropriateness and irrational intolerance. Being politically correct is not a substitute for an open and intelligent interpretation of facts. The media ignores the natural, intrinsic human pride manifest in our ethnicity, that same characteristic that impels us to cheer for our school team.

The media bears as much fault for the prejudice as any that practiced it. For one hundred years, between Lincoln and Eisenhower the media said very little about prejudice. Did the profit motive and fear of retaliation from advertisers cause the media to hold back its views on segregation? Does the media fear loss of revenues now? Racism, for the media, has been a profitable venture, and sustaining racism as an issue is a profitable course. Money talks to the media as well.

Perhaps the media people believe they are making up for one hundred years of silence. Making up for one's dereliction of duty by reporting examples of racism, ignoring successful politically incorrect black Americans, and failing to report the successes of integration is as discreditable as the "silent hundred years." Too many of the problems between races have been fomented by self-appointed and media-anointed leaders who overstate the existence of prejudice instead of praising the harmony between the races, religions, and ethnic backgrounds that exists in our incredibly diverse society. The media needs to recognize its leadership role in ferreting out these false leaders. Successful black Americans, such as Michael Jordan, Muhammad Ali, Sammy Davis, Jr., Jesse Jackson, Bill Cosby, and Mike Singletary have encouraged millions of young black American minds to follow these respective trades. What might these young minds do if they saw with equal respect Clarence Thomas, Thomas Sowell, Alan Keyes, and the millions of other successful minds of their race? These minds have been closeted by the media as "not representative of their race" because the media has determined it is not "politically correct" to suggest that black Americans should share their views. This statement in itself displays prejudice. Often, successful minorities are not publicized for fear that if seen as successful, the cynical media kinsmen can no longer carry their banner.

Today, the four richest athletes are black Americans. Their intelligence, hard work, enthusiasm, and belief in themselves would ensure their success in any endeavor. How might any kid respond, knowing that thousands have been successful because of free enterprise, not in spite of it, and because of their own efforts, not those of the government? Why is it that a Supreme Court justice is described as a molester? Yet, a wife-beater and accused-though-acquitted killer is shown as a hero to a throng of his cheering race. If racism is abominable, it must be abominable for all, and the media must be willing to view racism as such. The black skin of these successful Americans can serve as a symbol of achievement for the poor of any skin or origin who wish to emulate the successes of those they believe to be their peers. But as Charles Barkley said, "There can be only so many basketball players." Perhaps some in the media don't believe that black Americans are as able as a Caucasian, perhaps it is the money, or perhaps they feel it is more profitable to display them as victims of capitalism and not as products of there own efforts. When the media slants or refuses to publicize certain black Americans because "they are not representative of their race," the stereotyping can leave everyone with the opinion that black Americans are limited to athletics, politically liberal, hateful of whites, and genetically incapable of free and varied opinions. Stereotyping is no more than a way to group, grade, and predispose people. Stereotyping is just another form of prejudice.

Racism encourages the granting of special privileges to those of one's own race, while creating distrust and hatred by one of the other. Is it any different if the racist is black and not white? Hate, intolerance, and riots are a better bet to upstage Rosanne, the soaps, or the late-night show. Media personnel often have a perverse concern for the preservation of their ratings, their incomes, and profits, while displaying a disregard for everyone else's and trampling individual rights, family ties, respect, and intellect.

Though their motivation may be born of fear, the poor have an enthusiasm, a special fire within them to achieve what others take for granted. They have a desire that comes from hope; a hope that comes from the examples set by their contemporaries. They cannot lose because they have nothing to lose. But the media supports the poor by encouraging excuses, not work; offering discouraging platitudes, not encouragement to overcome adversity; and creating fear, not courage. Where real life rewards with small victories, the reward for the poor is big government and a place to beg. Money does not overcome adversity. Adversity is overcome when each of us makes the decision to do so. Many ungratified poor sit in jails, join gangs, or are leaving their families because the media has shown them how bad things can really be. Perhaps the poor should question media personnel who demand more for themselves, yet look for solutions to poverty with someone else's money. It is as important to know that failure is a part of life, as important as it is to know that success is the result of one extra effort that didn't fail. Success is also a part of life.

There is no doubt that ethical media representatives believe that broadcasting racial injustice is beneficial to the community. But many have closed minds that they believe are open, have limited associations to others of like mind, and may have forgotten the media hero they emulated in their passion to succeed. There are thousands of heroes in as many professions who deserve more attention than one whose rights were supposedly violated by the Los Angeles police. While the media presents a published and disputable half-truth rather than an indisputable whole truth, a miscarriage of justice can leave viewers with a confused view of government justice. The media has justified its profits by commending itself for lawsuits, pork-barrel backing, community-destroying welfare, and meaningless laws.

Media hype presented for its own gain has caused pain when only a minor amount of inquisitiveness would have proved better explanations. In California, the media produced so much concern over the death of a child, resulting from an inoculation that people refused to vaccinate their children, and years later a far greater number died from a preventable disease. A TV program showed a tearful mother whose child had died in a police chase. Immediately, experts talked about alternative means and the terror and error of the police force, making a strong case for eliminating the chase and encouraging drunks, criminals, kids, and speeders to commit more violations that could result in deaths that would not have happened.

The news media's "we only report the news" ideology and their self-proclaimed expert station is similar to the posture taken by government bureaucrats, who manage failed programs and regulations. It was this same shortsighted government that allowed the Yellowstone National Park forest to burn. Never at fault, politicians excuse failure "because there was not enough money" or explain that what happened was right: "Nature burns the forest; shouldn't we also let it burn? Look how beautifully it is growing back." The same argument could be made to the less destructive clearing of timber for harvest, but the media never reports politically incorrect ideas, even if the opposing view is less destructive. Should all the forests be burned to see how beautiful nature could be, it is sure that nature has done it to itself in the last millions of years? Our environmental and social bureaucracy has defined street puddles and dry land as waterfront property and the Environmental Protection Agency spends time creating fear, hoping fear will do the job they themselves should be doing. The cost government expends to review environmental projects is only a fraction of what business spends to assemble the paperwork and to do the work. Where has the media explained both sides of these issues?

The media, in its pursuit of attention, stirs distrust, and to synthesize a common bond has sided with politicians to create an enemy—the rich, white, not politically correct businessman. No matter what his intentions, his beliefs, his honesty, his hard work, his thoughts and ideas, this citizen is second-class. Since the businessman's motivation is profit, which is not unlike the media's, he is described as greedy and self-centered. The media exploits for its own gain this fabricated bad guy daily, and in so doing, encourages welfare, wasted and ludicrous social and environmental programs, litigiousness, distrust of capitalism, and an anti-business atmosphere. The media degrades business people to encourage litigation for an enormous court system that is managed by a cadre of politicians and their supporters that hold like degrees. The media's anti-business temperament is the explanation for a government budget that is nearly half of total consumption, in addition to distorted and wasted expenditures for government-mandated costs. Should our problems in government be surprising when people who cannot balance their own checkbook run our government? Does our media believe the legal profession holds the franchise for loyalty to country? Ironically, the very act of taxing the rich enhances their wealth.

The waste that the media encourages shows that the media either lacks business acumen or it is devious in using waste for its own profit. Because the media is a business, we find it hard to accept that it lacks acumen. As the media abuses the economy, it exploits those who carry its word. The point is that news people are more interested in boasting their accomplishments like new laws, a chemical ban or a tree saved then of the fallibility of the accomplishment. It doesn't seem to matter to them that a decision is incorrect, an innocent individual has suffered damage, working people in the private sector have lost jobs or there has been unwarranted and costly false litigation. Free enterprise is not perfect, but it manifests the means by which perfection can be achieved. No other system identifies and finds solutions to as many problems as does free enterprise. Perhaps free enterprise will find the solution to the problem of the media. But for now the media seems more a fox who guards the henhouse, it has its own agenda.

CHAPTER 19

THE COST OF WAR

The desire for war is inversely proportional to a society's standard of living.

Another way of saying the above is that people who like to sit on the front porch and drink mint juleps don't want bombs dropped in their front yard. A discussion of war may not seem essential or relative, but economics has been a reason for war, and there are those who believe that war is a solution to economic depressions. War represents a cost to a society in the resources for preparation and in the destruction of both capital and humans. Armaments produced, even when war does not exist, consume incredible amounts of labor.

The major difference between the cost of fighting a war and the cost of being prepared for war is that being prepared is a cost to humanity, while fighting a war is a cost *of* humanity.

World War I was to be the war to end all wars, yet no sooner did the bodies cool than the lesson was forgotten. Rather than prepare for and defend against war, conciliation, appeasement and coexistence with an insidious power became the standard for defense and preparation for World War II. The battlefields of Europe were littered with the dead who would have wished the wisdom of preparedness had won over the peacefulness of pacification. World War II and the Korean War taught the importance of preparation and yielded weapons so destructive that they could annihilate whole cities. The threat of annihilation and the preparation to do so tranquilized much of the hunger for war.

Before Korea, most wars were in the defense of honor, separation, the coveting of land, religion, or the hunger for power. The Korean and Vietnam wars were fought over economic systems. These were battles in a Cold War to determine whether government or the individual would have the preeminent right of choice. Giving government the power to make decisions, with the supposed best interest of humankind to be served, is enticing. In fact, the greater part of the earth's population have, for millenniums, chosen government over their own free choice. Yet despite fewer numbers, individual choice won the Cold War and with fewer casualties than in the world's other great wars—and many fewer than if the ultimate weapons had been used.

It is important to understand that it was the successes of the individual and the failure of the government that won the Cold War. This is important because as we know, "Those who cannot remember [understand] the past are condemned to repeat it."[21] Our government did not defeat their government; it was a fight between Communism and capitalism and these systems' ability to improve and sustain living standards for the population—and still to fight a war. The Cold War was a world war in every

21 George Santayana, American philosopher, 1863–1952, Life of Reason, 284.

sense, including the aligning of nations, the battlefields where lives were lost, development and production of horrible weapons, skirmishes and conflicts throughout the planet, spying, deceit, and defectors and double agents. One thing that didn't happen was that the peoples of the major powers did not fight on their own ground. The fight at home was an undisturbed conflict of economic systems. As Communism requires that rights be placed in the hands of government and capitalism requires individual choice, government lost to individualism.

Individualism faced off with government, Communism lost and capitalism won.

The Cold War did not end the battle for freedom of choice—that war rages on fronts throughout the world in the name of liberalism and a socialism that its proponents have as yet been able to explain. In the U.S., politicians cannot openly discuss socialism because they will be rejected by the people. Therefore, a cunning and covert campaign is being conducted to maneuver the people and, one by one, pass laws that wrestle away individual choice. As many in the world once lived under the failed Communist rule forced upon them, free citizens now move closer to giving up their individualism to government and the concepts that have failed the individual for centuries.

The United States of America achieved its destiny to consolidate its boundaries and in doing so, never sought to expand beyond them. Our wars have since been fought with weapons and words, in the interest of these boundaries, of our citizens, and mostly of the people of foreign lands with whom we have a kinship. Our countrymen have never ceased to be proud of their roots and have shown a consistent concern for the welfare of those of their origins. Our own mixed ethnicity is the most likely reason for our involvement in the world today. Believing that our form of government means instant freedom and a better life, we have constantly imposed our will. Most believe it is elected government that wins the wars, as the difference in systems has been obscured. Also obscured is the distinction in the consequence of actions that are made for the people, rather than by the people.

The communist system embodies government and an economic way of life as one, not separate and distinct as with capitalism. In the endeavor to administer its system, Communists controlled, suppressed, and destroyed the rights of individuals, rather than protect them. Communism is the equivalent fairness doctrine, a concept that what is fair to one should be fair to all. Not only difficult to administer, communism requires that the below average be average. Thus, in the effort to administer equality, leaders destroyed those above-average so as to move everyone closer to an equity below the middle. The attempt by the Communists to be fair resulted in millions of deaths, and the only equality was the suffering they created. Fair governance can only be accomplished through punishment and penalty, not reward.

A doctrine that pushes to the center can never reach the outer limits of humankind's imagination.

Surprisingly, the last battleground where the United States fought Communism with the tools of war was in a country with a people that were barely known to our nation. The popularity of this war matched that presence. The official reason for being in Vietnam was the belief that if South Vietnam fell to Communism, others would fall like dominos. Whether this domino theory was correct is disputed, but before the war, many countries in or near Southeast Asia had Communist dissident activity. In the late '60s and '70s, Communist activity was found not only in the Philippines but also in Japan and Indonesia, and there was always a concern for South Korea. The war forced the Communists to concentrate their efforts in Vietnam, which reduced their influence elsewhere. The domino theory was given some credence, as when the war was over, the threat to many counties had passed.

Before historians pass full judgment on this war and on the value of the lives lost in its defeat, a humanistic and economic view of the war is in order. From a humanist point of view, in the four thousand or five thousand years before Vietnam, all-out war was the solution to conflict. The Communists believed in fighting wars to accomplish their objectives, but that traditional war was not possible; weapons had become too destructive. Nuclear bombs could not be dropped for fear of retaliation. In fact, the only thing that likely stood against Communism and world war was the meager population of the United States and its large nuclear threat. Vietnam marked a beginning of an end to total war and began an era when war no longer concerned one's neighbors. After Vietnam, war was left mostly to those directly involved. The borders of a country now had more meaning, and the fight to maintain those borders and peace was a matter for its residents. Accordingly, the world is dividing itself into New World states, distinguished by ethnic and traditional backgrounds. As this partitioning proceeds, the importance of choice and the individual has become a discernible goal. War is not the option it once was, and the prevailing system encourages a belief in oneself.

From an economic sense, Vietnam was less a war than a battle. It was one battle in the war to determine if Communism would control the people of the world. This battle started in a country where most of those living in it had progressed little beyond basic living. Vietnam's people were susceptible to the reasoning from both sides of the controversy. In the period of the late 1950s and early '60s, even the U.S. had barely begun its transformation to the Complex system that is the stable end of capitalism. Many in the world still had vivid memories of the Great Depression. From a Communist viewpoint, it was important to protect the evolving countries of the world from the failures of capitalism. Had the other countries in the Asian hemisphere been subject to Communist terrorism during their Transitional stage, many more might have fallen. The Vietnam War was critical and allowed countries throughout the world the time they otherwise might not have had to develop. If capitalism is to prevail in this delicate and unstable economic stage, a country needs peace.

The cost to the U.S. in Vietnam was great in human and monetary terms, but it was an occurrence that helped lead to the eventual breakup of the USSR. The example set by the U.S. in our effort to defeat the North Vietnamese likely had an effect on attitudes of many people in the USSR toward war. Friend or foe, the U.S. was respected for its military prowess. The humbling of this world leader must have created a feeling of inadequacy for the world power that saw itself equally as strong. When the USSR failed to dominate in Afghanistan, its appetite for world domination floundered. Certain despondency, augmented by the U.S. failure in Vietnam, must have set in for its people and leaders. The belief held by Lenin, that the workers of the world would embrace Communism, bore a burden of death that the citizens of the USSR were not willing to bear.

The winner of the Cold War wasn't declared until after both sides had lost major battles. The Cold War began after World War II, when the people of the U.S. and the USSR endeavored to fulfill the promise that each system made to improve people's lives. Neither system had a prior history that manifested a clear winner. In the middle, other countries, from Agrarian to Complex, only watched with their own fate in the balance. The battles took place both within and outside our borders. Outside, we fought skirmishes and battles with the weapons of war; inside our borders, we battled to finance the war and to prove that our system could support these wars and our consumptions.

Not only did Vietnam drain the resources of the USSR, but there was also the space race, the arms race, support of Cuba and other Russian satellites, Star Wars, conflicts throughout the world, and, of course, the Afghanistan War. But the important battle was the battle of enterprise inside our boundaries, and whereas the capitalist society of the U.S. emerged to the fight both battles, Communism did not. Free enterprise was strained, but Communism was devastated.

The consequence of a higher demand in a free enterprise system is innovation and efficiency, and when necessary, individuals with aspirations to improve themselves will respond with longer hours and harder work. Ideas don't come from government; they come from people, many of whom work to obtain the reward they love most—profit and a greater share of consumption. If shortages occur in a free-enterprise system, prices adjust upward and people with the desire for profit find ways to fill the gap. Through this mechanism, resources are allocated, and shortages are eliminated. The response occurs because profit is a motive, not a sin, and it is automatic.

War is a greater burden to Communism. In a controlled economy, resources must be shifted, not automatically by the system but by administrators in government. Government makes demands to prepare for war, and government must plan to meet those demands—not an invisible hand, but a bureaucrat with a body and possibly no soul. Centralized planners, who have the innate human characteristic to discourage others from taking credit for "their" work, not only make decisions; they stop others from "interfering." Greed is a human characteristic, in politics greed is a desire for power, in a free and private economy greed can translate into productivity and an increase in living standards. In politics greed results in waste, war, crime, and corruption. To plan for war in a Communist country, prices are fixed, and supply is rationed. The problem is solved, so when shortages become critical, consumers suffer and basic facilities deteriorate, as government shifts limited resources to priority functions. Limitations on the minds of humankind cause the real shortages in controlled economies. When the Iron Curtain came down, the Communists' consumer economy was in a shambles.

Those who fought and died in Vietnam may have fought the most important and decisive battle in the history of the U.S. and humankind. Although the battle there was lost, individual choice ultimately won, and the battle at home to maintain living standards was ours. The United States of America was victorious in the Cold War. The U.S. lost in Vietnam, but those who served and lost their lives there were members of a victorious army. Perhaps for a world with a tradition of war, the futility of world domination is gone. Wars do, however, have a habit of never being the last. If we are to enjoy peace and freedom, we must be willing and able to defend peace and freedom whether at home or away. Few wars have been started with an attack on a principled and superior military force.

CHAPTER 20

WHY UNIONS SHOULD BACK BUSINESS IN CONGRESS (WHY UNIONS HAVE THEIR MONEY RIDING ON THE WRONG HORSE)

As baby boomers age, the labor activists among them are becoming more conservative. But now, as in the past, union leadership is attempting to force raises, rather than earn them. The old ways prevail, and labor unions back the political candidates who promise legal constraints to cinch leverage at the negotiating table, rather than solving problems of evolving businesses under attack by government regulation, taxation, and bureaucratic laggardness and largesse. The unions' number one priority during the last several years has been to pass federal laws that would eliminate an employer's use of "scab" labor (non-union) during strikes, a law to effectively shut down a business that does not agree to union demands, and to eliminate secret balloting in employee elections to unionize a business. These laws would give the unions a stranglehold, should they choose to strike, and undoubtedly make U.S. manufacturing the inefficient producers they were not so long ago. In the 70s and 80s domestic competition was enough to cause union workers to lose the very wages and job security they sought. In recent years, only the teachers unions have gotten concessions by promising that better wages would mean better teachers, solve problems in our schools, and raise student averages. No less of a factor was that the teachers unions also threatened to close the schools and having made millions in political contributions, they have ensured their power. In some places public sentiment is turning against teachers, as parents seek the right to choose their child's school and the public funding to pay for it.

The unions are anti-business and want to restrain the very goose that lays their union's golden egg. In this world of communications, when unions extract raises with a strike, the media reports those raises as a rise in consumer prices. The unions are marketing a program that the consumer sees as demanding higher wages, more restrictive rules, guaranteed jobs, longer vacations, more featherbedding, and strikes, in exchange for higher prices, strike delays, highway shootings, and layoffs. In a day when politicians are packaged, not elected, the unions' packages offer few positive returns.

The unions yearn for the days when they controlled political offices. Ironically, their antipathy toward business and devotion to party leads them to the same political candidates that are increasing competition, allowing more lawsuits against business, restricting growth, raising taxes, restricting access to natural resources, and reducing investment and domestic research by diminishing the advantage of patents. In other words, unions are backing politicians who fight job creation and raise business costs, while restricting the individual freedoms union members covet. Simply put, union leaders oppose business candidates. This position clouds the issues, obscures union goals, and hides the common ground on which union and business stand. Unions still carry a deep distrust from a time when businesses blatantly took advantage of the worker, a distrust that is not unfounded. It was not that many years ago when miners, working under dangerous conditions, were paid in script. The script could only be used at the company store, where prices were so inflated that it was impossible to make ends meet, and workers became indebted to the company. Manufactures would reduce wages, rather than increase them, and injured workers received no compensation and little medical attention. Long hours were a standard that left workers tired and susceptible to injury and left little time for families.

Originally, to achieve their demands, the unions fought not only businesses but government as well. It was a government that was not accustomed to having its stature questioned, nor was it accustomed to the conflict for union rights and the rights of the workers. It was also a government that took the side of business, which gave the unions reason to distrust them both. The first worker protections originated in the streets, not in the legislature.

As demands for compensation, safety, and the health of the worker were met, unions sought after and found political power that fostered governmental favors. Protection from foreign competition was seen as beneficial, union shops closed out non-union labor, and mandatory union membership allowed for higher dues, more control, and increased power. Innovations in the workplace were discouraged, as union members walked out or created slowdowns when efficiencies were proposed. Work rules that required a different trade to turn a screw or open a panel slowed work and raised the cost and need for labor. The unions were protecting their jobs with work rules that slowed production, inhibited innovation, and increased unit labor costs. The regulatory laws that had been passed to establish rail, airline, and utility rates, supposedly needed for stability, fairness, and consumer protection, were used to hike labor benefits as costs were passed to the consumer in rate increases. Regulation meant that competition from within could be eliminated. Regulation meant that eight or nine utility workers, each holding a shovel, could watch one dig the hole. In the name of labor, unions were able to wield the same unrighteous power once used by business.

Their actions were not without consequence. The steel industry is a great example of how restrictions lead to problems. In the '50s and '60s, the steel unions demanded and got incredible concessions, like six months' vacation and double, triple, and even quadruple hourly rates. The possibility of the steel mills shutting down appeared as such a threat to the economy that when the unions and management could not come to an agreement, government mediated to settle the strike. The unions got ever-increasing wage settlements, and the steel mills got import controls on foreign competition to keep domestic users committed to domestic steel. The unions and corporations enjoyed a monopoly, as both became complacent. U.S. steel mills made the best steel in the world, were the largest, and were more efficient than European producers (who had even stronger unions). Furthermore, production was limited to a few domestic companies, which the unions and government played one against the other.

The unions and steel mills controlled the market and demanded and got their wishes. They allocated for themselves a higher proportion of the national income. If consumers wanted something made of steel, rich or poor, they subsidized the compensation, benefits, and inefficiencies of the mills. To capture a greater share of the economic pie, the unions took the same advantage that government now demands for itself. Meanwhile, the U.S. was exporting its technology while unable to use it at home. Along with the equipment, a disgruntled management allowed corporate incomes to fall. Workers interested in changing things were discouraged on union and company levels. From the top to the union worker, workers either joined ranks of the complacent or left to find a free workplace.

In the 1960s, the same political manipulation used by the unions was learned by others to promote causes concerning the environment, animal protection, litigation, equal rights, and the anti-war movement. Other businesses sought regulation because they, too, would benefit by having the state fix rates, such as for liability and title insurance, wherein rates are adjusted for losses, expenses, and, of course, those necessary profits that were added to losses and expenses. The union supported these positions in an anti-business atmosphere that gained general support. As the number of causes grew, so did government. The demand to meet this ever-increasing allocation of labor could not be satisfied. Legislatures recognized that business would have to be more efficient so government could get bigger. Right-to-work laws were passed, and regulation and the unions came under attack. Deregulation became the new way to attack business. But it was not business that was being assaulted. The labor movement was getting in the way of demands from special interest groups and of course politicians with Socialist's leanings who wanted so called wealth distribution. High-cost industry could not afford the investments needed to comply with new laws. Thus airlines, highway, and rail transportation saw reductions in regulation that brought in competition and forced work rule and wage adjustments. With the breakup of AT&T, utilities saw the beginning of the deregulation that, it is hoped, would eventually lead to the purchase of electricity by consumers from a supplier of choice.

Unions were left to their own devices to settle disputes, as they became powerlessness to control the onslaught of non-union production. As inflation and the government grew, the high wages and low productivity led to shutdowns, business contractions, takeovers, and the reorganization of nearly every large industry in the United States. Only the most efficient survived, and workers got layoffs, wage freezes, cuts, lost pensions, and a lower standard of living.

The blame was placed on foreign manufacturers, but competition for steel sales came from within. Alternate metals and materials were used, and small U.S. steel mills, not much larger than blacksmith shops, found ways to provide for ever-increasing amounts of first low-grade and then the high-grade steel that large mills had depended upon to ensure profitability. The U.S. was a large exporter of steel, but foreign mills, using U.S. technology that unions had fought to keep out, were producing lower-cost, high-quality steel and selling it in "our" foreign markets. The unions didn't know it, but they were not struggling against business to obtain benefits. The government that unions supported was looking for flesh, and when power is threatened, cannibalism is an essential politicians' tool. Politicians were voting on the side of interests that wielded more power than the unions, whose vote could be bought with "a promise" for legislation that would eliminate the secret ballot that union leadership believes is the salvation of the unions. Unions made demands of the consumer and the economy, in competition with voter causes, and because the unions can't write laws, they are dependent on politicians, whose greatest concern is getting elected and not the union leadership's wishing well.

Unions, then and now, became unpopular because the consumers realized they were paying for the union's demands, and the workers saw how plant shutdowns could result in no more than lost jobs. Still, the unions don't blame big government or their party. But big government is no more than a fickle friend to once-powerful unions. Union membership has declined in the private sector, while unions hold to their anti-business posture and a political doctrine that no longer serves it. To the union, the party is more important than the worker. Prospective members learned from the problems of industries such as the steel mills and have no aspirations to stand in the picket lines while losing wages and jobs. Many workers realize that jobs are dependent upon the strength of the business from which they draw their earnings. Young non-union workers remembered how the car they wanted went up in price when the union workers' got raises. As a result of a tarnished image of greed and a displaced purpose, union membership has declined. Union leadership is finding it difficult to create admiration from those they wish to call brothers. Prospective members see them as backing a government that takes their jobs, raises taxes, hampers rights, hinders productivity, and reduces living standards. The once-powerful unions that used government to achieve their means refuse to stand with their employer against government growth, greed, or waste, and that refuses to aid workers when government laws take jobs, that embraces the same inefficiency in government that cost its members jobs and security, and that listens quietly to the rhetoric of politicians with guaranteed pensions, whose interest is reelection, no matter what price the union may pay.

An economy restricted by the unions is no different than one restricted by government. The only good job protection is a growing business with quality products, effective research, efficient production, innovation to stay ahead of the competition, and an economy, both public and private, built on the same principles. The unions' responsibility is to provide a safe, healthy, equitable, growing, and stable working environment for their members. Stability is not achieved by seeking the highest wage with the least amount of cooperation. Short-term wage concessions, job restrictions, and suppression of the members' imaginations eventually lead to a dysfunctional, noncompetitive business that shrinks, rather than expands. Job stability and higher wages are concessions easier to obtain from a strong profitable business than from one that is weak, inattentive to the market, and distracted by government demands. Profitable businesses are innovative and invest more than they earn. It is investment and willing workers that expand job opportunities and living standards, not hours of wasted work.

When all businesses are combined, they consume more investment every year than they earn in profits. This investment keeps production up with the growing demand. High profits attract investment, and efficiencies that eliminate jobs also create jobs. Thus, by helping their businesses to be more efficient, workers can enhance investment and earn the higher wages they desire. Staying ahead in world competition begets larger factories, as the best way to compete is with an enterprising workforce that adapts to and embraces new ideas. When innovation is constant, and not the inconsistent applications caused by businesses failure and economic upheaval, growth within a business absorbs the displaced workers. In its worst case, factory jobs that are lost to efficiency will give way to other jobs that echo a higher living standard, perhaps at a vacation resort that has become more affordable to the average worker.

If the unions are to grow, they must consider the common good of the community, not just of their members. If wages and benefits are deserving of change in a reshaping economy, workers must demand them. But the cost of labor is passed to the consumer, and the union must balance its demands with the efficiency to offset its costs, while leaving a share for the consumers and the owners. This is what businesses must do, and unions should follow the pattern. Workers or consumers need not benefit at the expense of the other.

Foreign competition helps to maintain our own competitiveness, push employee skills levels to higher plateaus, encourage innovation, and improve living standards. Union leaders should not forget that their members are consumers, too. Raising wages above productivity hinders not only the potential for business to invest but reduces market share and price competition in foreign and domestic markets. If protectionism were a good idea, Cuba would be the richest country in the world. The best way to raise the standards is to create wealth, and wealth is created when jobs are productive.

Perhaps as business learned from the Japanese, so should the unions. Workers in Japan support the party that supports its businesses; they ride the same horse. Union leaders in the United States have rooted their efforts with a fondness to manipulate, a folio of preconceived judgments, and a political position based on a historical allegiance rather than worker interests. When unions fought change, industry deteriorated. Yet unions still fight change at work, while acquiescing to the loss in living standards brought by high taxes and government's inefficient demands on labor. Unions hang on in a political arena that contradicts the interests of their members. The strength of a country, its economy, its businesses, and the wealth and wages of its workers all go hand in hand with a government that has a healthy open mind and honest disposition. Legitimate change is the companion of integrity and a truthful debate. The interest of the union is the interest of all workers, union members or not, but it is time the unions realign their interests with business leaders, because strong private-sector businesses will mean high earnings for the private worker, and when non-union workers see benefits from unions instead of burdens, their ranks will swell.

CHAPTER 21

POLITICS (SO YOU THINK WHO SHOULD RUN THE COUNTRY)

The sheep theory
The White Knight theory
The rhetoric theory
The old-girl (boy) theory

Politicians form a brotherhood that rules vast numbers of organizations, in addition to the government offices with which we associate them. Unions, business associations, governmental associations, the NAACP, AARP, PACs, a thousand other pseudo-political organizations, and their business managers and lobbyists form the rules by which we build our houses or hatch our eggs. Their focus is our daily lives and the division of consumption. The importance of politics is self-evident. There are reasons and theories as to why we elect the politicians that we elect and reasons why they want to get elected. Fortunately, besides a bureaucracy and large extractions from our paychecks, politicians give us a large dose of humor.

The sheep theory

Most people don't think of themselves as sheep that follow the flock, but we are all sheep in some way. Even when we want to be different, we look for someone with whom to be different. Mankind is gregarious, few are not. We believe our candidate to office will be as independent as ourselves, influenced only by reason and negotiation. Some may remember the movie, *Mr. Smith Goes to Washington*, wherein Jimmy Stewart's character stood alone in the U.S. Congress, speaking out for the citizens, hour after hour, day after day, with no help from his peers. Congressman Smith won that day, but today his time on the floor would be limited by the rules in Congress so as not to hold up the process. In fact, today, an individual alone in Congress is not likely to be even a small force. Congress has passed rules to stop individuals from acting alone. And not following the congressional line might cost representatives important committee assignments or funding for pet projects or their campaign contributors. Assignments are important and can be used to negotiate funding for the politician's state, effect rules, or keep members in line with rules previously passed. For failure to follow the party line, politicians can lose legislative support within their party. (There was a time when "the party line" meant the Communist party line.) Seniority rules have been set by our Congress for the good of the House or Senate to encourage the sheep (or wolves) to follow the pack and supposedly to "get laws passed." No one would ever say these actions represented coercion, bribery, or fraud. Nothing illegal; we would just call it politics. Perhaps there is some need for herding the flock. If there were but ten "Mr. Smiths," Congress would never get anything done. Then again, perhaps it would be better that way.

The White Knight theory

Some people like voting for a judgment-maker and problem-solver, the White Knight, who will conquer the evil republic. We don't know the White Knight very well; after all, the White Knight rides in unexpectedly, looks honest, and sounds believable. Voters, who are intelligent enough to reason and solve problems, believe the problems we face today shouldn't be difficult to solve. This is the "there must be someone who ..." kind of individual. Someone *who* what? Who can be a white knight? Father said, "We get too soon old't and too late smaat". But apparently we aren't "smaat" enough to stop electing politicians who make promises they don't keep. Politicians are often voted in, not for their beliefs but for our hopes.

Reasonable people don't believe they would fall for a con artist, but we con ourselves into believing so that we can cast our votes without congregating serious thoughts. Once, at the behest of a business partner, I listened and followed the actions of a con artist, something all people should do once to understand how they function; that is, as long as it doesn't cost money. This one said he had "tons of platinum down in Brazil." When asked where all this platinum came from, he answered that he bought the platinum "a long time ago, when it was cheaper than gold." A common thread with the con artist is to make statements so wild and unbelievable that the "mark" believes them. Platinum has never been cheaper than gold, but my partner, an intelligent man, wanted to believe. We all want to believe. White knights look like they will do the right things in office, and we believe them, despite their wild statements. After all, they don't look like con artists; they sound like white knights.

The rhetoric theory

People make excuses for just about everything. They even plan their excuses with friends, business partners, etc. Because voters make up excuses, politicians are excused for the same fault. The oldest rational is that "you can't trust any of them, so what does it matter?" Perhaps it doesn't matter because we allow it not to matter. Politicians have won elections on campaign rhetoric since time in memoriam. For example, after Jimmy Carter was elected president, a campaign representative was called to task by a reporter for the promises President-elect Carter supposedly made in the few days before the election. The promises conflicted with other comments that had been made. The response received by the reporter was that what was said "was only **campaign rhetoric**." The dictionary defines rhetoric as "the art, of using words, artificial eloquence, language that is showy and elaborate but largely empty of clear ideas or sincere emotion." There is a more common term used mostly in bars and on construction sites, its called BS. The response was never again challenged, and President Carter, like other representatives, aren't usually called to task for rhetoric, except when those in the media use it to advance a political agenda. In the end, however, President Carter lost voter respect, as well as a second run for the presidency.

We have all told white lies, lied for a friend, or lied to protect ourselves. Age and getting caught usually teaches us that self-respect is more important. But because we realize our own faults, perhaps we forgive our politicians too easily. No one should tolerate a lie, and we should not forgive the rhetoric of politicians so easily. Someone who knowingly makes a false statement, even a "well-intentioned" politician, is still lying. Being a politician should not exempt an individual from honesty. Perhaps there has been so much campaign rhetoric that we don't listen, or we just try too hard to believe that people will do what they say they will. Politicians cannot do everything they say, but that is no excuse for doing nothing or not trying. When the media considers rhetoric an acceptable practice for politically correct candidates or typical Washington oratory, an honest man is no competition for a good liar. As long as politicians can use rhetoric to achieve office, con artists will prevail in a contest of honesty. Father also said, "Locks were made to keep honest people honest." Calling candidates to task for their rhetoric won't guarantee that dishonest politicians can be kept from office, but it is the only lock we have to discourage the meaningless "campaign rhetoric" that candidates use to deceive us.

The old-girl (boy) theory

Seniority rule in the Congress of the United States is a controlling force. With seniority, a congressional representative can rule committees, ascend to majority leadership, control strong voting blocks, or control the voting for the entire congress. At election time, seniority means bragging rights. The electorate and campaign contributors are well versed in the advantages of their candidate's seniority on the floor and in committees. Without regard to voting records, many of the electorate, the media, and campaign contributors cast their votes for the people who have been around the longest because of the power they wield for their district. People vote for the incumbent good old girl or boy. As a result, Congress has lost touch with the voters. Once in office, a politician's voting record and stand on issues is not as important as his or her position of power within Congress. The seniority system that rules our federal and many state Congresses takes precedence over constituent representation. For junior representatives, gaining support from "powerful members" of Congress may mean sacrificing issues or campaign promises, but the good intended will find little hope for their causes or they must sacrifice their integrity to leadership "for the good of the party."

Our founding fathers created a Congress, wherein states would have equal representation and were allowed for proportionate representation based on population. The voices of each, in either house, were supposed to be equal. Nothing in the Constitution said politicians with seniority would be more powerful than any other delegate. As the importance of seniority has grown, so, too, has the importance of unanimity in the constant passage of legislation that testifies to the goals of leadership. With the seniority system, our junior representatives are bought with pork-barrel spending or threatened with being ostracized and denied influence and funding. Laws that bespeak only the desires of the president or the congressional leaders often lack the wisdom, advice, and support of individual members, who merely sell their votes for money to be spent in their district or to aid a campaign contributor. The media has supported seniority and not individual members, with a constant reminder of the importance of party "unity." As the numbers "of the people" have grown, the number who act on their behalf has diminished. Unanimity is not always all behind one; often it is one ahead, with all the rest behind.

Seniority rule is the basis of a power structure that is intended to dissuade junior representatives from taking positions contrary to the wishes of party leadership.

Seniority rule discourages entry into politics and encourages the long years in office that it takes to establish power in the "seniority rule" power structure.

Seniority rule abrogates the concept of equal representation.

For nearly a hundred years, there was a diminutive offset to seniority rules. A single individual could stand and talk *ad infinitum* and delay or encourage the passage legislation. There was one other offset that was much more powerful. The two-party system acted like a three-party system. There was a Democrat faction known as the "Southern Democrats," who often acted as a single voting block. Besides protecting their states from integration, Southern Democrats served another function. These Southerners represented a swing vote and a voting block that neither party could rely upon and, thus, Southern Democrats responded in their own pecking order. These Democrats had been of consequence to the process of government, the passage of laws, and quite possibly in restraining the size of the federal bureaucracy. They might possibly have been a vote of reason as they swung their vote to both sides of the aisle, and Southern Democrats were more conservative and not supportive of socialism or Communism, yet they were still Democrats and influenced by their party.

After the presidency of John F. Kennedy, government changed significantly. Two things that he did caused that change:

1. The inclusion of a Southerner (a Democrat) on the ballot, Vice President Lyndon Baines Johnson
2. Furthered the prospects for the end of segregation

As a result of Lyndon Johnson's inclusion on the ticket, an incredible coalition occurred that is almost impossible to comprehend. Two factions, both with conservative leanings and each opposing the other, aligned with liberal Northern Democrats. Southern black Americans had, for years, been suppressed by the white Democrat political party, but Kennedy, a Democrat with strong Republican support, furthered the actions of Congress and the presidency to end segregation and became the political savior who put black voting strength in the Democrats' aisle. This action would have been expected to bring about a political backlash by Southern Democrats against the Democratic Party, but Kennedy was killed before this occurred, and Johnson, a Southerner, became president.

Johnson, the first Southerner in the presidency since Zachary Taylor, convinced Southern Democrats to stand united for this president. With both the black vote and Southern vote squarely on the Democrat's side, President Johnson attempted to cast himself in the perceived Kennedy legacy and signed an incredible amount of social legislation. Johnson's presidency brought about what was called the "Great Society" legislation in the 1960s, which is responsible for much of the budget deficit and waste that occurred since.

In the South, a transition in politics occurred. As desegregation unfolded and as the black vote became important, the conservative white Democrat disappeared from the party candidacy. Most everyone with apparent or prior segregationist bias was routed out by the media and Northerners controlling the party, in favor of liberal Northern-style Democrats, who voted the party line. Over a hundred years of Democratic tradition made it impossible for the conservative Southern Democrats—still believing in the traditions of the Confederacy, yet seriously anti-Republican—to vote Republican when it served their interests. The old Southern Democrats—those conservative and seriously individualistic but still Democrat politicians, who acted like a third party—eventually disappeared as political figures.

In the last thirty years, presidents like Johnson have just done what the people wanted. Now, if we could find those people and talk to them, we could solve the problem of big government. Lincoln is supposed to have said, "The people aren't always right." Today, however, the next best thing to knowing what the people want is telling them what they want to hear. Knowing what people want isn't easy, so one president resorted to a daily poll and then speaking to the results or taking a poll to find out what phrases would best influence the people. Life is not easy for the some party politicians today, as they must be willing to lead near–Christ-like lives, exposed to scrutiny and criticism, with little hope for forgiveness by a media deeply concerned about its own views—that is, unless the politician is a member of the politically correct party, in which case there is much more latitude in his or her moral and ethical standards. It's a good thing for politically correct politicians that news people have a problem with math. If reporters added things up or looked up the word "rhetoric," a lot of politically correct politicians should be in trouble—or maybe not. The basic rule that politicians do follow is to promise to keep their promises next time—that is, of course, if we will just elect them one more time.

There is another group of politicos that also has a great deal of influence—the largest group of politicians was not voted into any office by the general population. They are the lobbyists and bureaucrats who influence our government through businesses and consumer associations. Most of these people spend their lives talking to each other and to leaders in their respective union or society, and they seldom deal with the working population. Their job is to seek legislation and in return, they keep their jobs. Lobbyists are like presidents; they believe they did what their constituents want them to do whenever laws are passed that affect their industry. They can also encourage laws that assure us an oversupply of things we don't need, when tax incentives are passed that distort returns and encourage production. These bureaucrats are the more frightening because we can't vote them out of office. Our seniority system makes the lobbyists' job much easier, because instead of the need to approach several members of Congress, they only need a relationship with members of a committee—or even better, the senior member of the committee.

Association bureaucrats are shrewd and deserve attention. They can tell politicians and businesses what they want to hear, what they told the other, and make both think what they heard was good for everybody. Not only can association bureaucrats talk out of both sides of their mouths, but they also can laugh so we think they're crying. They can get associations to support candidates that the general members don't like, get laws passed that raise the members' taxes, increase competition, and then get the local business leaders to sit around a table patting each other on the back for what happened. Association bureaucrats would never be politicians. They're too smart. To become elected politicians, they would have to run for office, speak in public, and take only one position on a subject. For an association bureaucrat, politics is the art of keeping a job.

There are no courses given that teach anyone how to run a country. The closest we come are business courses. But the country whose business is business ironically nominates and elects people who have never had a real job to run the government. The closest our recent presidents have come to holding a job was an actor. Somehow, the media has convinced us that people who know how to run a business should have nothing to do with government, which explains a lot about government. This indictment of the media stems from the obvious mistrust they display for any candidate who, as they describe, represents business and doesn't have political experience. Years ago, when the elders talked about politics and improving the laws, they thought electing attorneys would be good. After all, attorneys understood the law and would write what could be understood. Today, only attorneys write laws, and nobody understands them. An attorney friend recounted once that not as many lawyers were in our state legislature as believed. "Attorneys only represent about 60 percent," he said. How does that compare to the share of the working population wherein only 1 percent are attorneys. It would be interesting to know what our bathrooms, bedrooms, and kitchens would look like if 60 percent of all congressional representatives were plumbers. Where once a medical degree was the most desirable achievement of young college students, the lines at law schools now extend around the corners and include the cream of our student crop. As with any government-supported group, the maintenance of the legal profession, its employees, and all those legal settlements show up as a cost in our daily bread or shortages in our paychecks.

In an interview with Dan Rather about Ross Perot, Rather suggested that Ross Perot was not qualified to be president because he was not a politician. Dan Rather said that he "wouldn't let a farmer do brain surgery." The thinking only follows that Rather wouldn't allow a brain surgeon or a farmer to be a politician. Even Barry Goldwater implied that a candidate without political experience doesn't have the experience to serve. Goldwater commented that it took him two years to learn the ropes, implying that we need experience to be politicians. And yet politicians, to avoid "conflicts of interest," will attempt to write laws without input from the people and professions that are to be impacted by their decisions.

Using Dan Rather's theory, laws should be written for people, not by them. The politician's lack of experience in the workforce reflects in our legislation. Obviously, we wouldn't let electricians do heart surgery, but should attorneys fix our plumbing, manage wood shops, or dominate our lives? We aren't even to be heard when our jobs are being discussed, as was evidenced during a government-sponsored discussions on national health care. One arrogant radio talk-show host refused to allow a doctor's wife to interject her experience after having disclosed her husband's occupation. He slammed the phone on her with the righteous indignation of a Baptist preacher. Do the media stalwarts fear a biased view, or are they just too lazy or doltish to place their own knowledge at risk? The media acts with the same attitude in regard to all professions except politicians, attorneys, actors, and their own. They will, however, speak to association bureaucrats (industry spokesmen), who, without question, would make biased statements, but who would never embarrass the media. After all, these are politicians, and they can handle the press. Or perhaps the media sees them as unprincipled charlatans and one of their own. Where does a member of the private workforce go to talk about his job? When the media wants an expert opinion, it talks to the man on the street; the less knowledge of a subject, the more qualified.

Having excluded knowledgeable practitioners from political discussions, the formation of well-informed and knowledgeable political opinions is likewise limited. This gives us insight as to why the media loves rhetoric. The media's engrossment lies more in articulate conversationalist than honesty and integrity. Those with the integrity to be honest require knowledge that the media and politicians see as creating bias. It isn't only business leaders who are viewed with prejudice by the media. The same attitude includes anyone who holds a job in the private workforce. The false logic follows that as government is responsible for the economy, it is responsible for all jobs; and government employees are the only ones qualified to enact laws, without bias or prejudice. One must wonder if workers are excluded from government because Socialists within government ranks realize their own greed competes with the workers' desire to keep their job and more of their earnings. After all, the Socialists want a greater share of what someone else is earning. Work experience would mean predisposed opinions in a debate of work. It is logical if as "captive servants of the people," the workforce is disqualified from debate on their labors.

The founding fathers were a cross-section of the population, including attorneys, but few were politicians. They were statesmen, and their interest was in life, justice, humankind's freedom, and the preservation of their own right to choose, along with everyone else's. The brevity and concise statements made in the Declaration of Independence, the Constitution, and the Bill of Rights displayed deep thought, consideration for the position of others, and integrity not seen in the perplexing, voluminous, and often contradictory laws written today. A statesman is supposed to be a person who shows wisdom, skill, and vision, which is not a definition to be used for today's politically correct politicians.

If people from all walks of life could represent their country, whether plumber, union representative, oil man, or housewife, they would bring to society a wealth and diversity of knowledge that only this broad experience can produce. We could rely on the competition between them to maintain a balance between individual greed and good will. The idea that only the legal profession and the jobless can provide equity ignores the right all have to serve their country. It is not a duty; it is a right; it is a privilege that all should have an opportunity to earn. The knowledge of real life doesn't come from spending one day in at a job or talking to those who work every day; it comes from butt-busting, gut-twisting, and brain-draining work. Government is so off the beam that only politicians and con artists can exist within it—or have they become the same? Practical people represent a threat to bureaucratic government.

We want individuals to represent us, not as sheep, but we let the media criticize politicians who stray from the flock. We want a white knight, and we vote for con artist. We allow campaign rhetoric but sue for false advertising. We want Congress on a short string, and then we hand the strings to another bureaucrat. The good-old-boy (girl) system allows members to be threatened for not voting with their party affiliation and supports chicanery and deception when what we want is chivalry and straight-shooting. Congressional representatives who vote on laws while ignoring the beliefs of their constituents are influenced by the necessity of holding committee positions that "benefit" their constituents with questionable financial projects. The country needs politicians who will represent their country without the strings, equal representation, and not the equal who must resign or sell their ideals to those who are the more equal senior members.

The media shriek the need to end gridlock, exposing on how things would be better if the non-politically correct members agreed with those who were. In a country that has fought so many times for the right to disagree, can we demand that our freely elected officials agree with each other? In a time when Congress was composed of two distinct parties and one nondistinct swing vote, reason often prevailed over unanimity. When congressional representatives are equal, reason will lead to equitable agreements and address the concerns of all parties. There is a name for the elimination of gridlock; it's called a dictatorship.

The news media has too much concern with whether the parties are unified and too little concern with integrity. Congressional representatives from hundreds of districts weren't intended to take office to do the president's bidding or that of senior leadership, nor do voters intend that one party or another has been given consensus to pass whatever legislation or spend whatever monies leadership demands to get their laws passed. When the Declaration of Independence was signed, it was done despite an agreement that all must agree or none would sign. Each made his own decision for his own reasons. Each signed, and none had seniority past good argument, common sense, experience, and logic. When the Constitution was written, input came from all the delegates, without seniority, and yet the most profound document ever written was created. Gridlock in a Congress unencumbered with seniority rules is debate. Is the president, if not of the majority party, to stand against the party in Congress, regardless of the country's interest? Is it all just good press? Most of us are concerned with the problems of this country, and the source for our opinions is the media. What the media gives us and how it's presented affects our attitudes. The media should report the news and disclose failure, lies, illegal acts, dishonesty, and iniquitous acts, not biased viewpoints that align with a political party with the supposed best intentions. The media view should not be what sells best, makes them popular, gets them home early, enables them to feel emotionally involved, or supports their economic system. There is one issue on which we should all agree—that we, like Congress, should be allowed to come to our own conclusions with as much information as needed.

Government was instituted by our forefathers with three distinct bodies. The role of this system of checks and balances was not to encourage agreement, but to protect the rights of the country, its citizens, and our way of life. Surely, within these bodies our forefathers intended that representatives would have the same rights of equality they were ordained to protect. We should concern ourselves less with term limitations and more with the freedom of each representative to express a view on the floors of Congress that reflects personal experiences, not vicarious responses. Only if the politician's rights are protected can we guarantee the outcome that two senators and a House, represented by the population of a state, were guaranteed in the Constitution. Seniority defines an inequality that was not intended. Those who believe that term limitation is the solution may find that without seniority rules, experienced congressional representatives would find their own knowledge enriched, as they enrich that of others. Perhaps senior representatives would be less capable of using our taxes to buy votes from junior delegates or to make outrageous demand for their own districts, and we might be less likely to vote for elected officials because they have the power to spend. The importance and strength of our Congress should come from ideas and imagination, the ability to reason, and the common sense we all need. We often marvel at the Declaration of Independence, the Constitution of the United States, and the Bill of Rights. Seniority was not an issue in their preparation. Good people who are allowed to reason on their own will always come to a good a solution.